Winning with Computers

Winning with Computers
Trial Practice in the
Twenty-First Century
PART 2

John C. Tredennick, Jr., Editor and Project Co-ordinator
James A. Eidelman, Co-Editor

Section Editors
Harold L. Burstyn
Simon Chester
Joseph M. Howie, Jr.
Joseph L. Kashi
Arthur Ian Miltz

Judith L. Grubner, Publishing Board Liaison

American Bar Association
Section of Law Practice Management

The Section of Law Practice Management, American Bar Association, offers an educational program for lawyers in practice. Books and other materials are published in furtherance of that program. Authors and editors of publications may express their own legal interpretation and opinions, which are not necessarily those of either the American Bar Association or the Section of Law Practice Management unless adopted pursuant to the By-laws of the Association. The opinions expressed do not reflect in any way a position of the Section or the American Bar Association.

Library of Congress Catalog Card Number 92-74047
ISBN 0-89707-830-6

92 93 94 95 96   5 4 3 2 1

Discounts are available for books ordered in bulk. Special consideration is given to state bars, CLE programs, and other bar-related organizations. Inquire at Publications Planning and Marketing, American Bar Association, 750 N. Lake Shore Drive, Chicago, Illinois 60611.

In Memoriam
Dennis P. Schuler, Esq.

May 14, 1941—October 24, 1991

This volume is dedicated to Dennis P. Schuler, infantry lieutenant, trial lawyer, and pioneer in applying computers to the practice of law.

Years ago, when David W. Hill started Integrated Concepts, Inc., in Rochester, New York, to develop software for lawyers, he went to his attorney to incorporate. Dennis Schuler was that attorney. As a sometime managing partner, Dennis already recognized the impact that computers could have on lawyering. So he did more than just incorporate the new venture—he signed on as vice-president.

Integrated Concepts' first product was a time and billing system. With so many competing products, Hill and Schuler decided to help attorneys in a new area rather than fight their way into one already crowded. They chose document assembly, the automated preparation of a legal document from previously drafted material. Their product was called FlexPractice.

The legal text in FlexPractice was Dennis Schuler's, drawn from a decade and a half of practice. With a system that any lawyer could use right off the shelf, FlexPractice was the first document assembler that did not require a great deal of extra time to draft or enter legal text. It was thus of special interest to solos and small firms.

Until his final illness, Dennis was an evangelist for using computers in a litigation practice, especially in the several sections of the American Bar Association in which he was active. He often told skeptical colleagues that he had more than doubled the size of his own firm, Schuler & Von Dohlen, founded in 1986, with no increase in secretarial staff.

Dennis Schuler is survived by his wife Lynette and three sons. He will be missed.

Contents

Why Read This Book?   xi
Dennis P. Schuler

Foreword   xiii
Deanne Siemer

Acknowledgments   xv
John C. Tredennick, Jr.

Introduction   xvii
John C. Tredennick, Jr.

SECTION 1
USING YOUR COMPUTER: A BRIEF INTRODUCTION   1
John C. Tredennick, Jr.

An Introduction to Computers for Beginners, or Those Who Were Beginners
Not Too Long Ago   3
Arthur Ian Miltz

    Sidebar: Of Bits and Bytes   7

The Macintosh: An Alternative to IBM/DOS   10
Mark H. Hellmann

Winning with Computers—The Macintosh Way   17
Howard Shapray

Microsoft Windows in the Law Office   27
Roger C. Schechter

SECTION 2
USING OUTLINERS AS THINKING TOOLS   33
John C. Tredennick, Jr.

Using Outliners to Organize Ideas   35
Cullen Smith

    Sidebar: PC-Outline: An Inexpensive Shareware Alternative   38
    Joseph L. Kashi

Brainstorming Tools for Trial Lawyers   42
James A. Eidelman

Contents

Digesting Depositions with Idea Processors   47
Marc S. Klein

Managing Cases, Information, and Yourself with GrandView   55
Mark V. B. Partridge

SECTION 3
DOCUMENT ASSEMBLY FOR LITIGATORS   65
James A. Eidelman

Using Computer-Aided Document Assembly in a Litigation Practice   67
Dennis P. Schuler

   Sidebar: Managing Your Form Files   69
   Joseph L. Kashi

An Introduction to the Use of Document Assembly in Litigation   71
Greg H. Schlender

   Sidebar: Understanding Document Assembly Jargon   74
   Charles E. Pear, Jr.

Who Is Using CADA Today—And How They Use It   81
Charles E. Pear, Jr.

A Litigator's Guide to Document Assembly Programs   88
James A. Eidelman

Document Assembly and Financial Software for the Family Lawyer   92
James A. Eidelman

The Electronic Profit Center: Document Assembly for Litigators   96
Charles E. Pear, Jr.

SECTION 4
PRODUCTIVITY TOOLS FOR LITIGATORS   107
Arthur Ian Miltz

Using Office Automation Programs to Organize Your Litigation Practice   109
Joseph L. Kashi

   Sidebar: English Lawyers Communicate Electronically   114
   Harold L. Burstyn

Using Computers in a Criminal Appeal: A Case Study in Team Productivity   117
Neil E. Aresty

Using Computers to Make Brief Writing More Enjoyable (or at Least Less Painful!)   121
Catherine Pennington

Now Lawyers Can Dictate to Their Computers   125
Harold L. Burstyn

Spreadsheets in Litigation   127
Kenneth M. Laff

Valuation of Claims and Settlement Structures   135
Joshua Mitteldorf
Alice W. Ballard

Using Timeslips to Help Manage Your Litigation Practice   145
Carol L. Schlein

Using Computers to Identify Conflicts of Interest   152
Douglas O. McLemore
Kurt L. Schultz

    Sidebar: Computerized Conflict Checking: How Skadden Does It   153
    Leon Cohen

    Sidebar: Computerized Conflict Checking: The Cravath Approach   155
    Daniel E. Sesti
    Gloria Zimmerman

Hypertext and Hypermedia: Turning Data into Useful Information   158
Joost Romeu

SECTION 5
TOWARD THE FUTURE: PROJECT MANAGEMENT,
RISK ANALYSIS, AND EXPERT SYSTEMS   163
    Harold L. Burstyn

Managing Litigation with Project Management Software   165
David P. Cotellesse

Software to Model the Uncertainties in Litigation   175
Morris Raker

    Sidebar: Evaluating Personal Injury Cases   176
    Joseph L. Kashi

Simple Solutions to Litigation Problems Through Expert Systems   184
J. Ronald Sutcliffe

Artificial Intelligence in Action   188
Charles E. Pear, Jr.

Expert Systems: A Replacement for Lawyers?   201
Thomas H. Gonser

    Sidebar: Decision Support   202
    Joseph L. Kashi

APPENDIX
SETTING UP AN AUTOMATED LITIGATION OFFICE:
PRACTICAL CONSIDERATIONS FOR LITIGATORS   205
Joseph L. Kashi

Setting Up an Automated Litigation Office: One Firm's Approach   207
Arthur Ian Miltz

    Sidebar: Software for Your Law Office   216

Contents

Practicing Law with a Macintosh Computer   219
Ronald L. Crittenden

Peripherals: Keyboards, Video Displays, Modems, Printers, and More   229
Arthur Ian Miltz
Joseph L. Kashi

A Network for Your Law Office   238
Joseph L. Kashi

Where to Get Help: Eight Ideas   244
The Editors

Index   247

Why Read This Book?

Dennis P. Schuler

A MULTIPLE-CHOICE TEST

Please place an *X* next to the choice that best describes why you're reading this book:

_____ You recently discovered that the 40-page complaint just handed to you was put together by one of your associates in less than three hours, *without* a secretary— the same document that would have taken you *and* your secretary somewhere between three days and three weeks to complete.

_____ You have decided to abandon your 19th-century approach to the practice of law before beginning the 21st century—not because it's really necessary, but because every few decades or so you feel like a change. And besides, that old Smith Corona you bought when you opened your first office is starting to make funny noises every time your secretary hits the space bar.

_____ You've had a computer on your desk for three years so your clients would think you were keeping up to date. You accidentally turned it on for the first time yesterday while reaching over your desk to pick up the pile of legal journals that fell over. Now that it's running, you've decided you should take it for a test ride, but you don't know how to drive.

_____ You're struggling with a dwindling "bottom line," otherwise known as working more hours, enjoying it less, and taking home less.

If checking any of the above choices caused discomfort, pain, or just a little interest, great! Read on. While this was a multiple-choice test, any answer will do as long as it helps move you toward more efficiency in your practice.

THE BAD NEWS: THE ILLNESS IS SERIOUS

In many respects, the economic challenges facing the legal profession are grave indeed. Otherwise, this staid profession wouldn't even consider moving towards technology. Most lawyers aren't computerizing because they want to. The simple fact is that economic pressures are forcing us to catch up with the rest of the world in using technology to achieve efficiency.

THE GOOD NEWS: THE CURE IS FANTASTIC

While it's easy for someone who is already there to say *you* should be excited about what you are about to undertake, don't feel alone if the prospect of buying and/or learning how to use a computer doesn't turn you on—yet. As you embark on this adventure, keep in mind that you definitely will not be alone. After a few months of effort, you will begin to ask yourself: "Why did I wait so long?" It was a little scary in the beginning but it wasn't so bad. I should have done this years ago. I can do so much more now, and do it better and faster."

NINETEENTH-CENTURY METHODS HAVE CAUGHT UP WITH US

Much of the pressure on us is the result of still using 19th-century methods. While most lawyers secretly recognize that they work inefficiently, they are only now willing to admit it. While still frightened by the unknown, they are at last embracing technological tools as a way to achieve efficiency.

To maintain the integrity of the profession, we must find ways to become more efficient without sacrificing the quality of our services. Otherwise, legal services soon will be priced out of the reach of more and more people. Or, the quality of services will diminish because time and money pressures will result in cutting corners to keep services in line with the client's ability to pay.

As professionals, we have an obligation to make our profession better, to return something to the profession rather than just relying on it to provide us with a living. If we can become more efficient while at the same time improving the quality of our services, and also help others do the same—fantastic!

WHY COMPUTERIZE?

By now you probably know my answer. We must find faster and more cost-efficient ways of delivering better quality services *now*. The profession needs to modernize. The number of new lawyers entering the profession, the economic crunch facing most clients, increased professional advertising, and other societal pressures all add up to one conclusion: If you are not efficient at what you do, you'd better find another profession.

IT IS NOT DIFFICULT— BUT YOU HAVE TO WANT TO DO IT

Learning how to use a computer is not difficult. Granted, in the beginning only computer scientists could operate computers. But the smaller and more powerful computers have gotten, the easier they have become to use. How do you think your children and your secretary make such good use of them? They probably have little formal computer training, but they do have the essential trait: They wanted to learn.

If they can do it, so can you—if you want to. Don't worry about making mistakes in the beginning; just think about how good you're going to feel when you're there. The rewards are incredible.

"FOLLOW ME" WORKS BETTER THAN "MOVE OUT"

Although I have never been shot at, my two years as an infantry officer taught me two perspectives that have proven invaluable on the legal battlefield: "Follow me" and "Stay low and keep moving."

"Move out!" may work fine in the movies, but not with any law partner I've ever met. "Follow me," or leading by example, is scary, but it's almost always more effective in convincing people to move towards anything new, uncertain, or frightening. Besides, lawyers are extremely polite and much prefer the philosophy of "After you, sir." This is especially true when it comes to getting them to move toward anything as intimidating as technology.

Even "Follow me" doesn't always work. Some are so frightened that they won't move forward until the objective is already attained and they finally become worried that they'll be left behind by themselves (for example, when you can prepare a better pleading in an hour without a secretary than your partner can in five days with hours and hours of secretarial time.)

STAY LOW AND KEEP MOVING

If reason doesn't work, you may just have to bite the bullet, buy your own computer and software, and start using it. But, since low, moving targets are much more difficult to hit, you may want to sneak it into your office at night. Sooner or later, when your partners recognize that you have tripled your productivity and stopped working until midnight, they'll get the picture and might even reimburse you for your computer (when they decide they need one of those "newfangled gadgets" to catch up with you).

Foreword

Deanne Siemer

If this book had been available 10 years ago, I could have saved myself hundreds of hours of trial and error. If it had been available five years ago, I would have saved my law firm a considerable chunk of overhead. This compendium of practical advice for lawyers covers all of the basics, points the way to the next logical steps, and takes you there painlessly.

Although I started using personal computers as an integral part of a litigation practice more than 10 years ago, new uses and opportunities still appear frequently. When drafts of this book arrived, I noticed that Messrs. Sutcliffe, Pear, and Gonser had found artificial intelligence algorithms to be useful in some types of litigation problems. (See their articles on pages 184, 188, and 201.) I had never used that kind of application, and their work prompted an experiment that was on the computer screen in my office when a client came in for a meeting. This client, an overworked and usually impatient general counsel, was so interested in the approach and its potential, even though it was clearly just a first effort, that he stayed for three hours working with me. Shortly thereafter, he gave us two more litigation matters to handle.

Most of the computer methods explained in this book will help generate business, directly or indirectly. Computers can help make our lives easier because they save time and reduce a lot of routine work, but lawyers—even those with computers already on their desks—resist exploring new uses because the tradeoff involved in personal convenience sometimes just isn't enough incentive.

One lawyer who works at my firm has had a computer on his desk for two years, primarily as a large technological ornament. At the office Christmas party, some wag anonymously gave him a typing tutor program and a T-shirt with the slogan "Real Men Type Well" displayed prominently on the front. It worked. Once he got over the roadblock presented by the computer keyboard and began browsing sections of the predecessor to this book for ideas, his billable hours went up, a client hooked him into its corporate electronic mail (E-mail) system, and new business followed. Developing new business and increasing the quality of the legal work product are incentives that, once appreciated, make quick converts.

Corporate law departments are under continuing pressure to become more efficient. Many are already computerized to some extent. When a law department adopts a hypertext system for work in which a number of lawyers must participate, as discussed in the article at page 157, the outside clients that can work with this system will likely choose this law firm over any other.

Technology allows law firms with relatively high rates to compete effectively with firms that offer lower rates. For example, a low-rate firm that handles routine correspondence or high-volume pleadings one piece at a time cannot compete on price with a high-rate firm that uses a document assembly program. (For a discussion of this technology, see the articles in Section 3.) Document assembly, the process of having a computer put together what has been written before to create the document needed now, helps lower cost by allowing junior lawyers and nonlawyer personnel enhance the effectiveness of senior lawyers.

Of course, the enormously important element of personal service in lawyering still remains. No one can succeed in our profession, particularly in litigation, without personal contacts with clients and dedication to the task. But even here, computer technology will give an edge to firms that invest wisely. E-mail connections with clients are made possible by good computer systems and are made much easier with sophisticated computer capability in a law firm. (See, for example, the chapters at pages 114 and 117.) A firm that offers clients' in-house lawyers the opportunity to search and browse electronically among the materials the firm makes available for clients will have an advantage over those firms that cannot offer this service. A successful investment in technology is necessary to provide this capability.

Surveying possibilities is what this book is all about. The wealth of material in this book will get a lawyer started or help a lawyer catch up on what has been developing in the computer field as it relates to law practice. It is an efficient way to learn what you need to know without also visiting materials of value only to those in other businesses. Each of the chapters is written by a practicing lawyer or lawyer/consultant with personal experience using the computer systems he or she describes.

The computer industry envisions a world of electronic data, where photographs, videotapes, documents, graphics, music, and information of all kinds will flow to us through computers in our offices, cars, homes, and briefcases. Those who adapt quickly and efficiently as this technology expands will have a personal and professional advantage. This book will get you started or, if you are already well versed, will give you some more great ideas.

The book covers almost 40 subjects, but is organized for easy access. Section 1 provides an introduction to the three most popular operating environments for lawyers: DOS, Windows, and the Macintosh. Section 2 starts with outlining software, the most basic writing tool for the legal profession. Then Section 3 picks up with document assembly, and Section 4 adds productivity tools like E-mail, spreadsheets, time charge software, and hypertext. Section 5 looks at more advanced systems such as project management, risk assessment, expert systems and artificial intelligence, and networking. The Appendix provides some general guidance for those people getting started in automating their law offices. Each section is divided into specifically focused chapter so you can find what you need, and the authors tell you in plain English what works and what doesn't.

The editors have done an excellent job of pulling together all the kinds of information a lawyer needs to expand computer use intelligently. Take advantage of their expertise and the expertise they have collected here to take the next step in automating your office.

Acknowledgments

Like *Winning with Computers, Part One*, this book reflects the efforts and contributions of many talented people who deserve to be acknowledged and thanked here.

First, let me thank my coeditor, Jim Eidelman, who has been using computers in his practice since the beginning. Jim recognized their potential before most of us knew what a spreadsheet was. He has been out on the hustings preaching the gospel of these machines for years and has done more to help other lawyers computerize than anyone I know. Without Jim's insight, impetus, guidance, and good ideas, these books never would have happened.

Once again I want to thank all our section editors who read the first drafts and found the great articles lurking within the pages. Having the varied perspectives of such a distinguished bunch made a big difference in the final product. Their companionship and support made the project all the more enjoyable.

Thanks also to the many authors who contributed to this book. All have busy trial, teaching, and consulting practices, but each took the time to share his or her knowledge about computers. They also were kind enough to put up with my constant editorial carping and all the other dificulties that are part of a multiauthor book.

As always, the staff assistance at the American Bar Association was first-rate. Jane Johnston, Paula Tsurutani and Mark Ingebretsen helped turn this book from a concept and some ASCII text into a winning final product.

I also want to thank my firm, Holland & Hart, which continues to support my efforts to spread the word about computerization. The firm keeps on breaking ground with new technology, and I am pleased at its willingness to share this information with other members of the bar.

Final thanks are due to my wife, Page, my daughter, Sarah, and our new son, Scott. They will all breathe a sigh of relief knowing that the many hours of Daddy working on the "Peedo" are at an end.

John C. Tredennick, Jr.

Introduction

John C. Tredennick, Jr.

I remember it clearly. A Wednesday night, several years ago. I went home with a stack of books and articles, seeking a quiet place to prepare a speech for the following day. I had promised to speak about drug testing in the workplace. Because of a busy trial practice, I planned to bone up on the subject the night before.

I started into the first article and reached for my trusty yellow pad to take notes. At that moment the thought hit me: "What if I put these notes on my wife's computer?" (We had just gotten married and she had purchased it for graduate school.) I hadn't used a computer before, but I had been thinking about it for some time. Was this the time to try something new?

Why not? I carried my books to the basement and turned on the computer. After calling up the word processing program from the opening menu, I began typing away. By scrolling up and down the screen, I found I could insert each new point in its logical place. By the end of the evening, I had a working outline for my speech. Using my old approach, I would have had a yellow pad full of illegible notes and a lot more work to get ready.

The speech went fine, but the important point is that I never went back to the old way of doing things. Not long after that speech, I learned about outlining software. Unlike a word processor, an outlining program automatically numbers or letters the random thoughts I input. It also lets me move thoughts around and it renumbers them as I go. Once I saw how effective the outliner could be, I began using it to prepare everything: depositions, direct and cross-examinations, even opening and closing statements. Before long, I did all of my thinking on an outliner.

What I discovered was a new freedom. Sure, it took some time to get used to the keyboard, and I made my share of dumb mistakes—but so what? For the first time, I could prepare an argument or examination myself, and I didn't have to worry what went where. With a yellow pad, the order of your thoughts is critical. It's difficult to change them around once you begin to write. With a computer, changes are easy, and you can try different variations as you go. I began to see myself as a builder, not just an abstract thinker. I found new satisfaction in seeing my projects take form.

From there, it proved easy to move to other types of programs. I began making my own revisions with the word processor. Soon, I found myself drafting on the computer. Next, I taught myself a simple database program. Soon, I managed my cases with it. I began keeping my calendar on the computer and my time sheets followed closely behind. All of this was great fun, even if there were bumps along the way.

Winning With Computers, Part Two is about the kind of fun that results from such discoveries. It's also about improving productivity and increasing our effectiveness as lawyers. And it's about changing the way we practice law. To a beginner, starting to use computers is like journeying into uncharted territory. *Winning* 2 helps you begin. Once you're under way, you'll find the going isn't bad. In fact, we've hardly begun to realize what these machines can do for our practices.

The book is organized in five sections. Section 1, "Using Your Computer: A Brief Introduction," offers a tour through the working of your PC. If you have never used a PC, start with Arthur Miltz's introductory chapter. It was written especially for beginners and will give you an idea how computers work and what they can offer. Other chapters in this section provide a look at the competing graphical user interfaces offered by the Apple Macintosh and Windows 3.1. Above all, don't be intimidated by the technology. You don't have to know everything about how computers work to benefit from having one.

Section 2 offers a detailed look at outlining software as a tool for managing your ideas and your practice. I've already told you how useful this kind of software has been for my practice. Here is a chance to see how other lawyers use outliners and to learn more about the different outlining programs on the market. It's no surprise that many lawyers call these programs *thought processors*. More than any other type of software, outliners can help clarify your thinking on almost any issue.

In Section 3, we focus on document assembly programs, a powerful type of software that works with your word processor. Document assembly programs are increasingly common in business and estate practices because they automate repetitive tasks. For litigators, they can be powerful allies in the fight to keep up with a heavy caseload. What's more, they can become a separate profit center for the firm. Section 3 shows you how litigators put document assembly techniques to work in their practices.

One of the key reasons to use computers is to improve our productivity as lawyers. In Section 4, "Productivity Tools," you will find articles on office organization programs, spreadsheets, and financial and settlement calculation software. You'll also find articles on timekeeping, E-Mail, and a host of other programs designed to make you more productive. In these increasingly competitive times, litigators need these kinds of productivity tools to serve their clients better. They can help manage the routine organizational tasks that used to fill up your day. As a result, you'll get to spend more time practicing law.

Section 5 focuses on software that we will be using in the future as well as today. Although project management software has been around for years, few lawyers have considered using it. The same is true for expert systems. This section explores how litigators can use these types of software to better evaluate cases and analyze complex legal issues. It focuses on programs that will soon be commonplace in the law office. If you are tempted to skip this section as pie in the sky, think again. These programs will challenge and change how we practice law in the next decade. The first to harness them will gain a tremendous advantage over the competition.

As an Appendix, we offer an introduction to setting up an automated litigation office. While not a comprehensive survey of the subject (that's beyond the scope of this book), these articles identify the major issues and should give you a running start.

PART ONE V. PART TWO

Many of you have read our first book *Winning with Computers. Winning with Computers, Part Two* is the companion to that book and a natural extension of the material you found there. *Winning 1* focused on how trial lawyers can manage their cases with computers. *Winning 2* focuses on how trial lawyers can use computers to manage their practices. You'll find articles on how computers can help organize your thinking, improve productivity, and ultimately, better your bottom line. Taken in tandem, these two books offer a comprehensive look at the role of computers in a litigation practice.

As in the first book, we offer this warning: The opinions in each article are its authors. Read them with care and common sense. Another lawyer's solution to a problem may not work for you. Moreover, there are vastly different opinions on most computer topics—as there are for most legal topics. We have tried to present a balanced treatment, but the market changes continuously and new software is introduced daily. If we have missed software that is as good or better than what we have covered, we apologize.

Several years ago, one of my partners scoffed at the thought that lawyers would ever use computers in their practice. "What would a lawyer do with a computer besides word processing?" he asked skeptically. I wasn't sure how to answer him at the time, but I knew he was wrong.

Today the answer is clear. There are hundreds of ways for a lawyer to use a computer. You'll find many of them discussed in our two books, but that isn't the end of the story. The computer will become an integral part of a trial lawyer's practice in the 21st century, just as the copy machine and dictaphone are today. Rather than fear the change, embrace it. You'll find you can do far more than you ever imagined (and have more fun doing it). After just a few years of using a computer, I can't imagine practicing law without one.

John C. Tredennick, Jr., practices commercial litigation as a partner at Holland & Hart, Denver, Colorado. He is the chair of the Litigation Interest Group of the ABA's Section of Law Practice Management and a member of the Section Council. He also is the editor and project coordinator for Winning with Computers: Trial Practice in the 21st Century *(American Bar Association, 1991) and the coauthor of* How to Prepare For, Take, and Use a Deposition, *(James Publishing, 1990).*

Section 1
Using Your Computer:
A Brief Introduction

John C. Tredennick, Jr.

We open this book with a brief introduction to personal computers, also called microcomputers or PCs. If you have never used a computer, this is a good place to start. While we can't teach you everything there is to know, we can offer some basic information about computers and computer terminology. We also describe the two main operating systems for microcomputers. Overall, you should come away with at least a beginner's knowledge of computers, which you can use to tackle the chapters in later sections.

Arthur Miltz begins the section with an introduction to using computers. His focus is on IBM-compatible computers, which make up about 90 percent of the microcomputer world. Mark Hellmann and Howard Shapray follow with a look at the Macintosh operating system, which employs an easy-to-use *graphical user interface* (GUI). Roger Schechter offers a counterpoint by discussing the DOS-based GUI offered by Windows.

Using a computer is much like driving a car. You don't have to be a mechanic to operate one but it sure helps to know how it works.

An Introduction to Computers for Beginners, or Those Who Were Beginners Not Too Long Ago

Arthur Ian Miltz

If you haven't turned on a computer, or if you think a megabyte is something you take out of a sandwich when you are really hungry, this chapter is for you. Arthur Miltz discusses basic concepts and terms to get you started and help you understand the material in later chapters. If you are beyond the beginner stage, move on to more advanced chapters.

It all started about eight years ago. I was in a firm where the most automated equipment we had was a Mag Card, which was a step above a correcting typewriter. My wife, a medical education project manager, bought an IBM personal computer. I scoffed at her purchase. Why was she wasting several thousand dollars when a Correcting Selectric typewriter could do just as well for a lot less money? Fortunately, she put up with my ignorance, bought a basic word processor called Volkswriter and went to work. After a while I stopped scoffing. One day, many months later (when she was out, of course), I sat down at the keyboard with the manual and the on-screen tutorial and started to learn. Not long after, I was converted.

INTO THE OFFICE

For the next two and a half years I lobbied (with no success) to get word processors for our firm. Then I left that firm to form another. From the beginning, I decided that we should be computerized. By then, I was pretty good at using my wife's word processor, and I had even learned to use a simple database. Beyond that, I still knew nothing. The operating system, any other pro-

grams, and anything inside the "mystical box," were beyond me.

It was only after we had set up our initial equipment and our consultant had departed that I began to learn. At first it was a labor of necessity—no small firm can afford to bring in a consultant every time there's a problem. As time passed, it became a labor of love. There is no question that using computers has made me a more effective lawyer. I hope that this book and its companion, *Winning With Computers, Part One*, can help you learn about them more easily and much sooner than I did.

WHY SHOULD YOU CARE?

Why should you care about computers? What can they help you do better? Note that I said "help you do," not "do for you." Computers are tools. They will help you be more efficient and organized and get a lot more done, but they won't do the work for you. You must do it, using the help they are so good at providing.

What they can help you do better is really what these books are all about. Both are filled with ideas about how you, too, can use computers to be a more effective lawyer. Just to whet your appetite, however, here are a few examples.

HOW YOU CAN USE COMPUTERS IN YOUR WORK

Word Processing and Document Assembly

We lawyers spend much of our time writing. Have you ever grown tired of scrawling changes in the margin of a document and waiting for your secretary to retype it, only to find that he or she couldn't read your handwriting or that the revision didn't turn out as you expected? If so, try it on a computer. Even if you only use your computer for revisions, you will cut out four or five steps from the revision process and improve your product as well.

To your surprise, the power of computers may lead you to do more and more of your own drafting. You can easily update pleadings and other documents, changing just the parts that need changing. Document assembly programs allow you to modify standard forms to suit your current case. All of this can be done quite easily once you get the hang of it.

Calendars and Diaries

You can keep your schedule, and that of your entire office, on a computer. No more scribbled, crossed out diary books. In-firm meetings can be arranged without a single telephone call.

Tracking Conflicts, Deadlines, and Statutes of Limitations

You can use computers to do all of these things quickly, reducing both the need for staff and the risk of human error. With case management software, you can increase the number of files you can handle without becoming overwhelmed.

Time and Billing

You might never have to keep time sheets again, or prepare a bill, or compile case expenses. The right program can keep track of all of that for you and then print out a final bill whenever you need it.

Litigation Support

Would you like comprehensive access to all aspects of your litigation files, so that you can instantly review, search, organize, and excerpt from depositions, documents, and other discov-ery? No more margin notes or stick-on tabs on the transcript or document! No more hours wasted searching for lost documents!

With a computer, you can prepare and instantly update progress schedules for your case or use sophisticated outlining programs to organize a complicated cross-examination or closing. You can house a warehouse-full of important documents on a small computer as well as hundreds of deposition transcripts.

Other Ways

You can keep directories of names, addresses, and phone numbers, and even have the computer dial the phone for you. You can access databases of information and do legal or scientific research by computer from wherever you happen to be. No more running to the library to check what you don't have. You can enter random notes in a special file as thoughts occur to you while you are working on something else. Later you can look at the notes and make decisions. No more searching for lost notes on your yellow pads.

The list could go on forever. These are just a few of the more common examples. As you read through this book, you'll find more and more ideas to choose from.

WHAT IS THIS THING CALLED A COMPUTER?

At the heart of all computers is a high-speed calculator that manipulates electrical impulses generated in response to combinations of the digits 1 and 0. The various combinations of 1s and 0s represent data, which can be numbers, letters, symbols, etc. The computer itself knows nothing of the numbers, letters, or symbols. It only knows combinations of 1s and 0s. It is only through its ability to manipulate these combinations at lightning speed that we have the magic of computers. Imagine being able to process millions and millions of calculations a second!

All the other parts of a computer system are designed to allow you to use the computer to generate and manipulate the words, numbers, etc. that you work with. As such, they fall into two categories: hardware and software. *Hardware* consists of the physical pieces that make up the computer and the things that connect to the computer. *Software* is the name we give to the programs that tell the computer what to do. Let me tell you a little bit about each.

HARDWARE

Hardware includes the case, which houses the central computer mechanism, and everything inside the case, such as the system board (also called the *motherboard)*, the central processing unit (CPU), the power supply, the disk drives, and optional equipment, such as fax boards. Hardware also includes the keyboard, the video display, printers, modems, and scanners, most of which usually sit outside the case and are connected to the system by cables.

The Case

The case is the metal or plastic box that houses all the circuits, chips, and other computing parts inside. The disk drives, power supply, and various other optional things are usually inside it also. In view of what it contains, the case and its contents are sometimes referred to as the *system unit.*

Cases come large and small and they may be placed horizontally or vertically. Decide where you intend to put each piece of equipment before you buy it, and get the measurements to make sure it will fit. I know one large firm that bought many computers without measuring, only to find that they would not fit on the desks unless they were turned to the side, which made access to the disk drives and power switch a real nuisance.

The System Board

You will often hear this referred to as the *motherboard*. The system board contains the central processing unit, the memory chips, many of the other chips, and the plug-in connections for the various other parts of the computer. It is the central switching station of the computer.

The Central Processing Unit (CPU)

The CPU is a powerful microchip that functions as the "brains" of the computer. The basic "thinking" (i.e., data manipulation) is carried out here. To avoid any confusion, keep in mind that various other kinds of chips are also used in all computers. They are all called chips, but with numerous descriptive adjectives to distinguish among them.

CPUs come in various designations, which correspond to power and speed. For IBM-compatible computers the ones you'll hear about most often are the Intel 8088, 80286, 80386SX, 80386DX, 80486SX, and 80486DX chips. They are listed here in ascending order of power, speed of operation, and cost. Intel's newest chip is tentatively called the "P-5."

The original IBM PC's 8088 chips have been around the longest and are the slowest and least expensive. A tremendous number of computers are still using them today. The P-5s are the newest, and generally the fastest and most expensive (until the next generation comes on-line). The others are in between and make up the bulk of the CPU chips being purchased for use in law office microcomputers. Apple's Macintosh uses the Motorola 68000 series of CPU chips, in contrast to the IBM-compatible Intel chips.

Computers are often designated by the CPU chip that runs them. For example, you'll hear people debate the merits of a "486 machine" versus a "386 machine." All this means is that the computer is built around a certain kind of CPU chip and has its individual capabilities and limitations.

RAM

The computer's *random-access memory* or *RAM* is its active work area. This is where the programs and data are located when you are using them. Think of it as your desktop. The larger the desk—that is, the more RAM you have—the more books, papers, and other information you can work with at one time. Once the desktop is covered, or the available RAM is fully used, you must put one item away before you can work with another.

When you turn the computer off, or if you have a power failure, everything in RAM is erased, and the programs and data you were working with must be reloaded from a storage device. Remember, if data isn't stored, it's lost forever. As a result, you should save your data often, and always before turning off your computer. This means sending a copy of the data from RAM to a permanent storage place, typically your hard or floppy disk.

Most of us have forgotten to save our data at one time or another and have lost our work. Having to repeat your efforts can be frustrating. A key rule is to save and save often as you work.

FIGURE 1.1 Absolute and Relative Storage Capacities of Different Floppy Disks

Physical Size	Double Density	High Density	Byte Capacity	Double-Spaced Pages Capacity
$5\frac{1}{4}$ inch	×		362,496 (360 KB)	150
$5\frac{1}{4}$ inch		×	1,213,952 (1.2 MB)	500
$3\frac{1}{2}$ inch	×		730,112 (720 KB)	300
$3\frac{1}{2}$ inch		×	1,457,664 (1.4 MB)	600

The Power Supply

This is just what it sounds like. The power supply plugs into the wall outlet via an external power cord on one end and provides power to the computer components inside the case from connections on the other end. It is located inside the computer case, with the on-off switch accessible from the outside through an opening in the case.

You should know that the power supply must be large enough for your system, and it should be protected from outside interference. Strong surges in the power supplied to your computer can cause lost data or, worse, disable your machine. Fortunately, there are a host of inexpensive surge protectors on the market. Make sure every computer is plugged into one!

The power supply often contains the fan that cools the computer. Heat is the enemy of computers, and can ruin a system over time. Unfortunately, the sound of the fan, when reflected off the wall behind your credenza, may sound like an airplane taking off. Listen to the sound of the particular system you are considering before you buy.

Disks and Disk Drives

Disks are the magnetic devices on which you permanently store your programs and data. Disk drives record information on the disks and play it back to the computer when you want to recall it. You can think of disks as similar to sound or video recording tapes that you can record onto, play back when you want to, and erase and reuse as you wish.

Floppy Disks

A floppy disk is a portable disk that can be used to store information. The early ones in common use for PCs were $5\frac{1}{4}$ inches, measured by the size of the square external case. The disk itself is round, somewhat smaller in diameter and easily bendable (thus the term *floppy*). They come in both low- and high-density storage capacity versions.

More recently, a smaller portable disk about $3\frac{1}{2}$ inches in size was developed. It is housed in rigid plastic so it is no longer bendable. Nonetheless, it is still called a floppy disk because the disk inside the plastic container is still flexible. Although it is smaller than its predecessor, it can hold even more information than the larger ones. It also comes in low- and high-density versions. It has become more and more popular and should be included in any new computer.

Figure 1.1 will show you both the absolute and the relative storage capacities of the different floppy disks in general usage for IBM and compatible systems.

At least one system in your office should be configured for both the $5\frac{1}{4}$- and $3\frac{1}{2}$-inch floppy disks, so that you can use either size.

Hard Disks

Hard disks are usually mounted inside your computer's case and are generally not transportable. They offer two major advantages over floppy disks: speed and increased storage capacity. A computer can access information from a hard disk between 10 and 15 times faster than from a floppy disk. (Once you begin using a computer, this speed will mean a lot to you.) Equally important, a hard disk can hold a substantially greater amount of data than a floppy disk. For example, a hard disk with a 40-megabyte storage capacity has over 28 times more storage space available than the highest capacity floppy disk.

As a practical matter, any computer you buy should have a hard disk. The hard disk can hold all of your programs as well as your data. The alternative is to load all of your programs and data from floppies each time you start the computer. This is a slow, frustrating, and inefficient way to work.

Formatting Your Disks

All disks, whether hard or floppy, must be *formatted* before initial use. Without getting technical, this involves their preparation for data storage, indexing, and retrieval by the operating system. Hard disks are formatted as part of their installation procedure. You can either format your floppy disks yourself or buy them preformatted for an additional cost. Formatting takes about a minute or two per floppy disk.

Other Hardware Components

Several other hardware components make up a typical computer system. Some are essential, such as keyboards, video monitors (or *displays)*, and printers. Others are optional, such as modems, fax boards, and scanners (or *optical character recognition* devices). All of these are called *peripherals* and are discussed in "Peripherals: Keyboards, Video Displays, Modems, Printers, and More," in the appendix to this book.

SOFTWARE

Software tells the computer what to do from the moment you turn it on until you turn it off. It is really the interface between the user and the computer. For our purposes, *software* and *program(s)* are interchangeable terms.

The world of software can be divided into system programs and application programs. System programs control the basic operation of the computer hardware. They are the link between the hardware and all other programs.

Application programs are the ones we use to do the things we use computers for, such as writing briefs, searching depositions, modeling dam-

Of Bits and Bytes

Bits are the individual electronic units computers work with—literally a 0 or a 1.

A *byte* consists of eight bits. It is the basic unit that represents a single character (a letter, number, etc.). Since a byte represents a single character, it is also the basic unit used to measure memory and storage capacity.

A *kilobyte* is 1,000 (actually, for technical reasons 1,024) bytes, and is sometimes referred to as *1K* or *1 KB*.

A *megabyte* is 1 million (actually 1,048,576, for the same technical reasons) bytes, and is often referred to as *1 MB* or *1 meg*.

For all practical purposes, you can think of 1 K as 1,000 characters and 1 MB as 1 million characters. A *gigabyte* is about a billion bytes, and a *terabyte* is about a trillion bytes.

Typically, memory and storage are referred to in terms of how many K or MB are available. For example, while a floppy may only hold 1.4 MB of memory, your hard disk can easily store many times that amount.

ages, etc. To work, application programs must be compatible with the system program used in our computer. Thus, system programs and applications must interrelate. The hardware is controlled by the system software, which facilitates the operation of the application programs.

System Programs

DOS is short for *disk operating system* and usually is meant to refer to a system program developed by Microsoft Corporation. DOS is the system program used by the vast majority of IBM and IBM-compatible personal computers.

Computer companies often market their machines as "IBM-compatible." For practical purposes, an IBM-compatible computer is one that uses DOS and thus can run the tens of thousands of application programs designed for DOS computers. This means that you can take a disk out of one IBM-compatible computer and put it into another and it will work. Be aware that you don't need to buy an IBM-brand computer to get a computer that runs IBM-type programs. Indeed, many IBM *clones* (IBM-compatible computers manufactured by companies other than IBM) are much less expensive then their IBM counterparts and work just as well.

One of the key distinctions between the IBM-compatibles and Apple Macintosh computers is their different operating systems. Macintosh computers do not use DOS. They have their own operating system, which is based on a graphic interface approach. The Macintosh system allows a lawyer or secretary to use a mouse to activate symbols on the screen instead of typing commands.

Programs designed to run on Macintosh computers will not run on an IBM DOS machine. Generally, the reverse is also true—DOS programs don't run on Macintosh computers. However, some Macintosh models and some DOS machines, with special hardware and software, will run both DOS and Macintosh programs. When you are choosing a computer, make sure it is compatible with the other computers you will be using or sharing files with.

Several other operating systems operate on IBM-compatible PCs. UNIX (and its cousin Xenix) are popular and allow multiple users to access the same computer. Although many engineers and programmers love UNIX, its weakness lies in the fact that it can be complicated to run and has fewer legal application programs available than does DOS. In many cases, however, the software for the UNIX operating system can be more powerful than for DOS, even if both are operating on the same machine.

OS/2 is another powerful operating system that allows *multitasking* (running multiple programs simultaneously) and may eventually become a successor to DOS. Microsoft is developing a operating system that it hopes will become a successor to DOS, called Windows NT. While no one can predict the future, it appears quite possible that one of these operating systems may supplant DOS in years to come.

Application Programs

Word processors, databases, spreadsheets, calendars, diaries, and the thousands of other programs that people use to get things done are application programs. They let you do the things that led you to buy a computer in the first place.

Application programs are developed and distributed in four different ways:

1. *Commercial* programs are generally developed for the mass market, and are sold through computer stores, mail-order houses, and specialized vendors and consultants who sell to lawyers.
2. *Custom* software is typically developed just for your firm and programmed by a consultant you have hired.
3. *Public domain* software is developed by public-spirited programmers, who give up their copyright and let anyone use the software free.
4. *Shareware* is a hybrid between commercial and public domain software. Like commercial software, the developer maintains the copyright and intends to make money from the licensing of the software. Like public domain software, it is freely distributed through user groups and public bulletin board systems, with payment to the author being small and on the honor system.

HOW THE COMPUTER SYSTEM WORKS

When you first turn on your computer, the computer looks for instructions on a special chip containing ROM (for *read-only memory*). Instructions contained in ROM tell the computer to begin by looking for and running the DOS (or other operating system) startup programs stored on the computer's disk.

As part of its start-up procedure, the computer's operating system will typically load the time and date into active RAM (on some machines you need an accessory clock chip), load some *device drivers* (i.e., software routines that control certain specialized hardware such as a printer), and load your beginning application, or a menu that lets you select your application. If you do not have the computer set up to present a menu or automatically load your primary application, it may present the *DOS prompt*, a screen message that shows you which disk drive you are using and which directory you are accessing, depending on how it is set up. From the menu, or the command line, you can load an application program for word processing (or any other use) from your disk (or from your network) into the RAM of your computer. You are then ready to start working.

CONCLUSION

Learning how to use a computer is easier than you might think. Like learning to drive, you don't have to learn everything to get started. Have a friend or consultant help you through the process of selecting and setting up your computer and initial programs, and begin. You can learn the rest as you go along. Don't worry about making mistakes. We all did.

Arthur Ian Miltz practices law in Livingston, New Jersey, in the medical malpractice, product liability, and other personal injury areas. A certified civil trial attorney, Mr. Miltz is a member of the New Jersey and New York bars. Mr. Miltz is active in the American Bar Association's Section of Law Practice Management, where he serves as vice chair of the section's Beginning Computer Users Interest Group and Litigation Interest Group. He is also chair of the Computer Applications Committee of the Essex County, New Jersey, Bar Association, chair of the Product Liability Committee of ATLA-New Jersey, and the author of the Discovery *volume of Matthew Bender & Co.'s* Art of Advocacy *series, as well as numerous book chapters and articles.*

The Macintosh: An Alternative to IBM/DOS

Mark H. Hellmann

For all practical purposes, PC operating systems have been divided into two worlds: the text-based DOS (or *disk operating system*) for IBM-compatible computers, and the Apple Macintosh graphic interface system. In this article, Mark Hellmann, a leading high-tech intellectual property litigator, introduces us to the Macintosh computer operating system and shows us how he uses it in his litigation practice.

Like the law itself, computers are tools for manipulating abstractions. When you sit down at your computer, you want to manipulate the raw material of litigation as easily as your own thoughts. But what happens when you turn on your computer? If you work on an IBM-compatible computer, employing a standard DOS-based operating system, you must control your software packages through abstract commands. If, however, you use an Apple Macintosh, you can view and manipulate your material in a more natural way, through the use of an operating system employing a *graphic user interface (GUI)*.

A GUI system, such as that used by the Macintosh (or the Windows 3.1 environment for DOS), closely resembles the way you would work at your desk if you did not use a computer. With a GUI system, you experience the feeling less that you are directing an agent to perform some task and more that you are doing the work yourself. This increased sense of intimacy is the chief difference to the user between GUI and DOS-based operating systems.

THE MACINTOSH OPERATING SYSTEM

I have chosen to focus on the Macintosh as the primary example of a GUI system because it is the oldest and most developed of its kind currently available to lawyers. In addition, a greater choice of legally oriented software is available for the Macintosh than other GUI systems (al-

though the increased popularity of Windows 3.1, OS/2, NeXT, and other GUIs will increase the amount of legal software available for these systems). The Macintosh is also the system I prefer to use in my own practice.

The Macintosh GUI-based operating system employs such things as pull-down menus, graphic images, windows, and picture icons that are manipulated by the use of a mouse or other pointing device. The latter device allows you to accomplish program functions without the need for typed commands. The system depicts file directories and subdirectories as pictures of file folders, and word processing files as pictures of letter pages. There is even a trash can for deleting files. You simply throw them away.

Instead of learning long lists of command codes, the Macintosh user employs a mouse to pull down a menu from several choices located at the top of the screen. All the user need do is highlight the desired action, click the mouse, and the command will be executed. Simple, wouldn't you say?

A typical GUI screen produced by a Macintosh is shown in Figure 1.2.

UNIFORMITY OF COMMANDS

One advantage of the Macintosh operating system is the uniformity of commands for different software applications. Whatever the program, a number of functions will have been stan-

FIGURE 1.2 GUI Screen

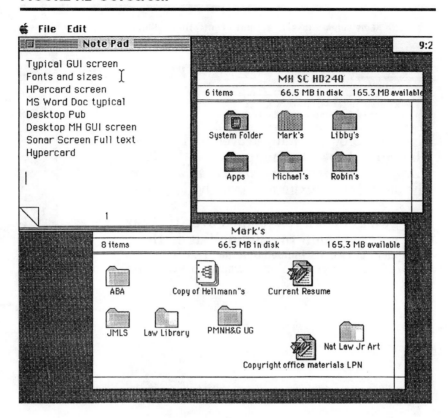

dardized. For example, you open, name, close, and save files consistently on the Macintosh, whether you are using WordPerfect or Microsoft Word. This means that once you learn how to use one program, most of the same techniques will work in any other program. This reduces your learning time for new software in a dramatic way. Even the most casual user can devour new software, learning large parts of any new application in minutes, without consulting a manual.

Thus the Macintosh system is like an automatic transmission; it doesn't change the nature or function of driving, but allows you to get on the road more quickly. Its simplicity enables a lawyer to begin work on the computer right away, without becoming mired in learning *how* to use the computer. In computer literature, this is most often described as "ease of use." Although computers are not yet as easy to use as most household appliances, many people find GUI-based systems less frustrating and easier to learn than DOS-based systems.

You may have heard that the Macintosh is less well suited to lawyers' needs than DOS-based systems. Critics have claimed that the Macintosh is slower and more expensive than IBM-type machines and that fewer software programs are available for the Mac. Several years ago, there may have been some truth to these claims. Today, the newer models have greatly improved in speed and versatility, and excellent software packages are available for nearly everything a lawyer could want to do. The popularity of software such as Windows 3.0, which simulates the function of GUI systems on DOS-based machines, shows that users prefer this way of working.

COMPATIBILITY

The trend in the computer industry is toward a universal operating system to allow software to run compatibly on all systems. If you are concerned about whether a Macintosh will be compatible with your existing equipment, you should know that most of the new Macintoshes come from the factory with an MS-DOS–compatible $3\frac{1}{2}$-inch disk drive already installed. In addition, you can add a DaynaFile drive to your older Macin-

FIGURE 1.3 Type Fonts and Sizes

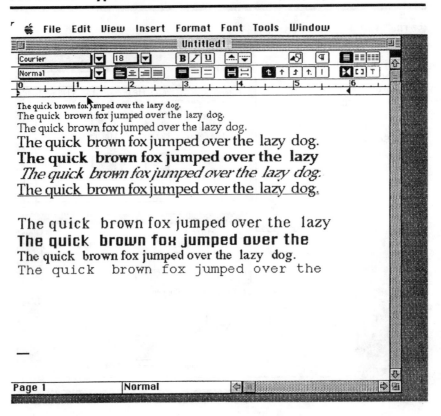

tosh that will make it compatible with MS-DOS machines. All major networking architectures and software are available for the Macintosh. There are also several translation programs available that permit you to transfer files between Macintosh and IBM-type computers, such as Mac-LinkPlus.

WORD PROCESSING

Because of the way it is designed and the software it uses, the Macintosh performs many word processing functions that other systems cannot imitate without requiring complex hardware or extensive training. For example, you can change fonts and type sizes at will. You simply pull down the proper selection from the menu bar, highlight your choice from the many available fonts and sizes, and plug it into your pleading or exhibit to create a distinctive and persuasive look. Figure 1.3 gives an example of what is available.

Moreover, the Macintosh has true *WYSIWYG* (What You See Is What You Get) capability, which shows you on the screen exactly what you will get from the printer. That goes a long way toward giving the casual user complete control over

and comfort with the look and presentation qualities of a document—a feature that can be highly effective for litigators. For example, many courts have local rules limiting the page length of memoranda or briefs. By controlling the type face, font size, and print characters on my screen, I have consistently been able to increase by 20 percent the amount of information I can squeeze onto page-limited documents without sacrificing neatness, legibility, or the good will of the judge. Because I can see exactly how paragraphs are laid out, where pages end, and how emphasis has been added through italics, underlining, or boldface, I can effectively choreograph the presentation of my document.

Refinements to word processing technology have created second- and third-generation products, such as desktop publishing programs. Desktop publishing got its start on the Macintosh, with Aldus PageMaker. The technology has advanced to such a point that the basic features of early desktop publishing programs are now incorporated into today's high-end word processing programs. These features can improve the look of your court documents and exhibits (see Figure 1.4).

FIGURE 1.4 Sample Court Document

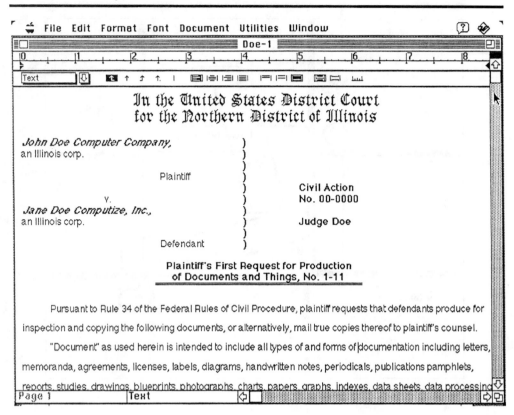

The desktop publishing capability of the Macintosh has opened new avenues for lawyers. For those with limited financial resources, it provides a more efficient way to prepare materials, such as appellate briefs, that formerly had to be sent to printers.

OUTLINING

Lawyers spend a lot of time thinking. Standard on the Macintosh is the cut and paste feature, which enables you to move blocks of text or graphics quickly and easily. This feature, when combined with outlining programs such as MORE or Fair Witness, improves the lawyer's ability to organize his or her thoughts, thereby increasing productivity.

GRAPHICS

Americans live in a visual society. We embrace the visual image, sometimes to our detriment. We can't watch television without dazzling graphics, three-dimensional maps, or multi-image effects. In short, we have become the most sophisticated consumers of visual and graphic images in the world. Marketing professionals, film and audiovisual producers, and media people already know this. Most lawyers don't, or don't want to admit it. We are still slugging it out in trials using presentation devices that were developed 400 years ago.

That is beginning to change, in large part because of the Macintosh's superior graphics capabilities. While there are many general graphics programs available for designers, artists, and other visual professionals, the programs available on the Mac make it possible for individuals like me, who cannot draw a straight line, to create and use crisp, accurate, attractive images. More to the point, many of these programs do not require extensive time, experience, or computer literacy in order to achieve results like those shown in Figure 1.5.

The graphics generated for this chapter were done with a simple charting utility that comes with Microsoft Word 5.0. None of these graphics took more than three minutes to create—really!

For litigators, the possibilities inherent in these tools are exciting. For example, in a simple case, a

13

FIGURE 1.5 Graphic Effects

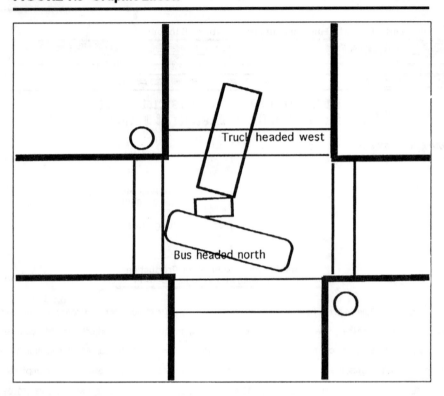

Truck headed west

Bus headed north

lawyer could go to court with the column graph shown in Figure 1.6 and demonstrate that the offending conduct and damages took place in February, April, and June. The impact is immediate. A spreadsheet or classic financial statement, while necessary for evidentiary support, does not have the same effect.

Organization charts, pie charts, line charts, bar charts, and other graphic software programs are available for the Macintosh. It is even possible to create overhead transparencies or slides for use as demonstrative evidence at a trial. Most jurors today can understand presentation graphics but cannot interpret straight financial or statistical information as well. Many programs provide two- and three-dimensional graphics. By using these graphic devices, jurors can comprehend the information in a dramatic way. In addition, the use of graphics with expert-witness testimony at trial can assist in giving your experts clarity and providing them authority. In close cases, this can make the difference in convincing the trier of fact.

HYPERCARD

The HyperCard program is provided free when you buy a Macintosh. HyperCard is a soft-

ware construction set, based on the premise of a stack of 3" by 5" cards. The user has control over the way the cards are called or sorted. The program permits the mixing of graphics with text areas. HyperCard can be used without any background in programming, and it is a straightforward, filing-cabinet–like database program.

Though HyperCard is not the solution for major database applications, it lends itself very well to individual matters and smaller tasks. For example, I've never been happy with the ability of other programs to keep up with the names, addresses, and other particulars of individual witnesses. Now, however, that particular niche in my software toolbox has been filled by Hyper-Card, as shown in Figure 1.7.

Combined with a scanner, HyperCard also becomes an excellent means of cataloging and using graphics or graphic elements in a variety of cases. For example, in a case involving a lot of catalogued parts, HyperCard provides the ability to retrieve, study, and use the graphics of those parts at will.

Borland's Object Vision and Microsoft's Visual Basic for Windows are beginning to provide PC users with the same features and functionality that HyperCard provides for Mac users.

FIGURE 1.6 Column Graph

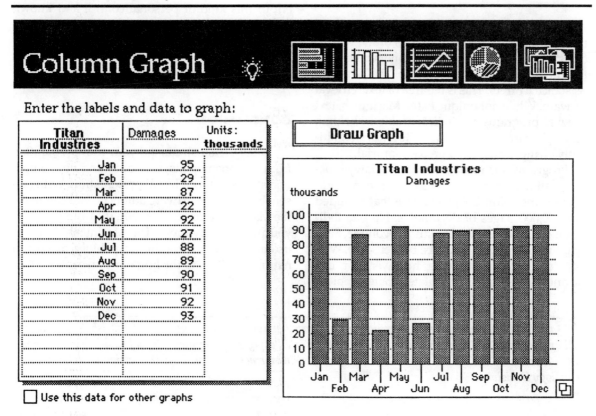

FIGURE 1.7 HyperCard Address File

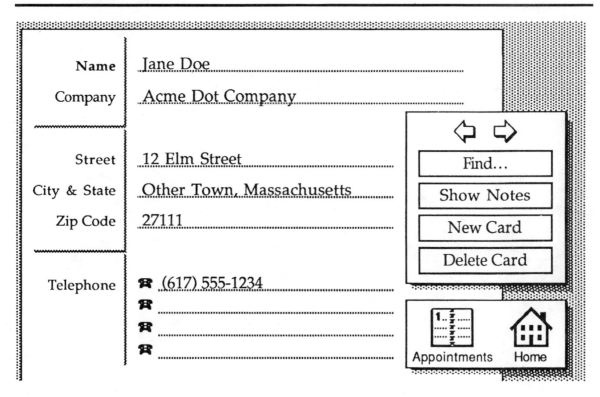

TEXT RETRIEVAL

While the above discussion highlights the unique properties and capabilities of the Macintosh system for lawyers, there is one further area that must be explored, because of the powerful assistance it offers. This is the area of text retrieval software. While not unique to the Macintosh, text retrieval programs are indispensable in helping me to prepare cases. In fact, they have significantly changed the way I prepare for trial.

Programs such as Sonar allow a lawyer access to all the information in a case from an individual standpoint. Imagine a case that included over 100,000 pages of documents. No one individual could deal with that kind of volume. Simply moving it around would be burdensome. With good text retrieval software, however, you can not only access but manipulate whatever piece of information you wish. For the lawyer, the benefit of this kind of personal control and knowledge of the information contained in the case can be priceless.

Windows 3.1 users should not overlook ZyIndex for Windows.

CONCLUSION

The Macintosh can aid your trial preparation from the opening stage of outlining your litigation strategy through trial presentation. With reasonably priced hardware adjuncts, you can make the Macintosh compatible with IBM-type systems you may already have. The Macintosh's ease of use and superior graphics capability make it a natural addition to the litigator's arsenal.

Mark H. Hellmann is an intellectual property partner with the Chicago firm of Pattishall, McAuliffe, Newbury, Hilliard & Geraldson. His practice specializes in all aspects of computer-related law. Mr. Hellmann is a council member of the ABA's Section of Law Practice Management and chair of the section's Computer and Technology Division.

Winning with Computers—
The Macintosh Way

Howard Shapray

Howard Shapray, a top litigator in Vancouver, British Columbia, uses a computer extensively in his busy trial practice. Like most trial lawyers, however, he is not a computer expert and did not have time to learn the different commands required of DOS-based programs. Instead, he turned to the Apple Macintosh, with its highly regarded graphical user interface. He soon discovered that most programs operated in a similar fashion, making them easier to learn. He concluded that Apple may be right in claiming that the most powerful computer may be the one that is the easiest to use. In this chapter, Shapray shows us how he uses several programs for the Macintosh in his practice.

The greatest obstacle to maximizing productivity gains is the workload of busy litigators themselves. Generally they neither have the time nor the will to learn arcane commands for numerous complex and diverse programs, many of which will have been forgotten by the next time that particular function is required. Enter the Macintosh, originally touted as "the computer for the rest of us."

In late 1985, I was retained by a United States mutual fund to sue on what was said to be one of Canada's largest securities fraud cases, a multiparty conspiracy involving a massive stock market manipulation in the securities of 17 companies. My client had been swindled out of $27 million in over 750 transactions at a dozen different brokerage houses. To have any chance of proving the conspiracy, we would have to review and make sense of thousands of securities transactions and put together a complicated case showing bribery, international stock fraud, and market manipulation.

At the time, I was a relative computer novice. I had an Apple Macintosh computer, but I hadn't done much with it. Coincidentally, the forensic accountants we engaged as experts also had Macs that they used for word processing, the odd spreadsheet, and little else. Within a few months, however, we were exploiting the computer in ways we had never before considered.

For those who haven't used a Macintosh, it provided something that no other computer and operating system could provide at the time: a simple, intuitive, *graphical user interface* or *GUI*. During the course of our preparation, I learned to use a dozen or more software products competently. Although they differed in function, they all tended to look and feel the same. I found that once I had mastered the first application, the learning curve to master the second was considerably shorter. The third was easier still. It didn't matter whether it was a database, a spreadsheet, a graphing program, or an outliner. The pull-down menus all looked familiar, and many of the key commands were identical. The more I used one program, the more proficient and productive I became with the others. The consistent interface across Mac software, together with the ability to exchange data between one program and another, provided the productivity advantage that made my extensive reliance on the computer possible.

In my world, productivity is measured by my ability as a crude, "hunt-and-peck" typist to integrate the best of the evidence that has been gathered into a terse, yet compelling, format, be it cross-examination, an opening submission, or a hasty revision of a research memo. The key to this kind of productivity is the integration and synergy that come from multitasking and the ability to enter, retrieve, and swap data from these various programs seamlessly. In the PC world, those converts from DOS to Windows are just beginning to sense the thrill and amazement that Macintosh users first experienced many years ago when Apple introduced a little program called Switcher. This program allowed Macs to run several applications simultaneously and, with a simple click of the mouse or in a single keystroke, to go back and forth between programs and transfer data via the instrumentality of what was metaphorically referred to in the Macintosh operating system as a *clipboard*.

In this article, I want to discuss some of the ways we used the Macintosh to assist in preparing for trial. I will also talk about how I use it in my practice today. I warn you that a review of all of the possibilities is well beyond the scope of this article. What I can do, however, is touch on the basics and a few of my preferences. Every Mac enthusiast will have his or her own personal list of favorites.

BUILDING A TRIAL NOTEBOOK

The savvy Mac litigators I know use outlining software as the backbone of their daily litigation management. Outlining programs are really *idea processors*. They permit you to jot down random thoughts as they occur and to augment, rearrange, and reorganize them in a hierarchical format. As your knowledge base develops, your analysis becomes more profound and your inspirations more focused.

MORE and Fair Witness are the programs of choice for the Macintosh. MORE is based on the concept of headlines and subheadlines. Each headline or subheadline can be a word, a sentence, or a series of paragraphs. The subheadlines are automatically numbered and renumbered as they are augmented and moved around. They provide detail for the topics and ideas expressed in the headlines.

The beauty of an electronic outline is that you can hide subordinate ideas, leaving you with an overview—essentially a table of contents—of your principal ideas. You may then zoom in on any one of those levels to view subordinate ideas and related data.

Fair Witness combines features of an idea processor and a database. It is a true information manager that allows you to collect ideas, group them in logical but unstructured categories, and relate them to other ideas. One nice feature about the program is that it doesn't restrict you to any particular format. You can reorganize material into different views and focus on ideas that relate to the topic you wish to consider.

Fair Witness is a unique, powerful, and feature-laden program, but it requires that you work through the tutorial and carefully read the manual to grasp the concepts of its design. Only then will you be able to exploit its full potential.

Consider the possibilities that these kinds of tools offer you in building a trial notebook. From the moment you take a case, you can start assembling a chronology of your case. Your first heading may contain the details of your engagement. The next may be a list of the issues in the case as they occur to you. Then you might begin building a table of issues, complete with descriptions and authorities.

As you approach the trial, your electronic trial notebook provides a compilation of all of your stray thoughts on the various issues, together with references to cases, articles, other briefs, legal memoranda, etc. Organizing that material into an outline for a closing argument simply means cutting, pasting, and rearranging the "issues" section of your electronic trial notebook into a new outline and adding commentary, analysis, transcript references, extracts, and the like.

Another chapter in your trial notebook may be devoted to the cross-examination of key witnesses. As you mull over the documents, depositions, and your legal research, ideas come to mind. If you scribble these down on the back of a telephone message slip or even a yellow pad, they will likely be lost. With an electronic outline, you simply insert your thought where appropriate and then view it in context of the surrounding related information.

As you ponder the content and order of your cross-examination, random insights spring to mind, perhaps in a most improbable sequence. Don't risk losing those undisciplined flashes; throw them immediately into your outline for the witness's cross-examination. You can preserve them and later reorganize them in any way that you wish—adding, deleting, and highlighting on the fly. (See, for example, Figure 1.8.)

FIGURE 1.8 MORE

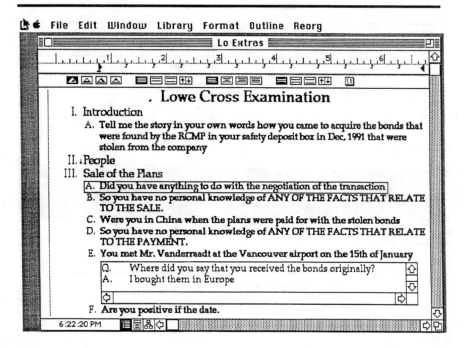

PERSONAL INFORMATION MANAGERS

Personal information managers offer a somewhat different approach to collecting information. Two powerful tools for the Macintosh are ThoughtPattern and Active Memory.

With ThoughtPattern you can save pieces of textual information in a growing information base. As with Fair Witness, these "items" can be linked together with files created in different programs, that is, with word processing documents such as submissions, or outlines, or deposition transcript extracts, or graphics designed to illustrate various pieces of evidence. The possibilities are limitless. You can then categorize them in multiple ways for cross-indexing and later retrieval. You can also enter reminders and to-do items that the program will remind you of, even if it is not running.

Search and retrieval is based in part on the way in which you categorize items. You can retrieve items by building "filters" based on date, priority, etc. Or you can search for text in items that contain user-defined words or phrases. You can also program alarms to remind you of dates, deadlines, and priorities.

The power of personal information managers such as ThoughtPattern and idea processors such as MORE and Fair Witness comes from their ability to handle information that doesn't fit into a single well-defined format. They provide what is called a *free-form* database for random, non-repetitive information.

Figure 1.9 is a ThoughtPattern window illustrating the linking of notes, reminders, and alarms. Links to computer files created by any other Macintosh application can be viewed simply by clicking on the file icon with the mouse.

Active Memory is a somewhat similar program, but it is geared toward multi-users. That means that members of a work group such as a litigation team can *all* provide input to the data file.

MAC DATABASES

The database is the backbone of any serious litigation management. Database software permits the user to store large quantities of information and to extract specific portions of that information through a filter of parameters and criteria imposed by the user, e.g., all documents mentioning a particular person or topic. In simple terms, a database allows you to find information and relate it to other information in a manner that you could not readily accomplish with any manual system. It also enables you to explore relationships between pieces of information by sorting,

FIGURE I.9 ThoughtPattern

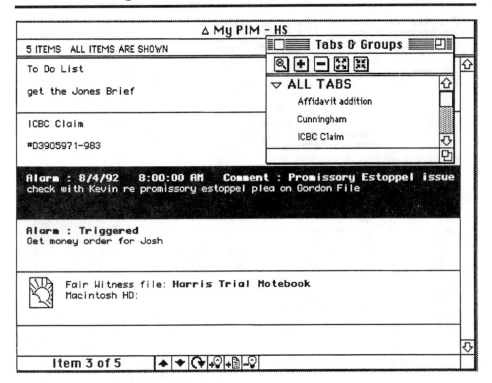

ships between pieces of information by sorting, ordering, and matching data in a manner and at a speed that manual analysis could never rival.

Mastering database software has always been a challenge, requiring specialized consultants to design and program the functionality that the user demanded. However, once the design process was completed, the user was often locked into an inflexible structure before all of the needs of the information retrieval system were recognized.

Certain Macintosh database programs have eliminated the barriers between the lawyer and the data. Mac databases such as FileMaker Pro and Panorama give the relative novice, who is prepared to spend a few hours learning database concepts, access to the power of relatively sophisticated database management techniques.

Consider, for example, the following as only a few of the many uses of a database in the day-to-day management of a busy practice:

- print a fax automatically with all of the pertinent information filled in except the message simply by searching the database for the name of the recipient;
- print multiple labels for a mailing to all counsel involved in a multiparty case sim-

ply by searching for a file number in the same database;
- maintain lists of pleadings, motions, or submissions in multiple actions in a form that can be searched electronically; or
- maintain a firm-wide electronic index for legal memoranda and precedents as well as limitations, conflicts, etc.

You don't have to purchase separate software for each of these tasks. A single generic database such as FileMaker Pro will handle list-type data for most practice needs. Preparing custom output-type reports requires no programming skills whatsoever. Data entry functions are simplified with the use of the mouse to select items from pop-up lists, buttons, and check boxes.

Consider also the productivity gains from a database that permits sorting a montage of facts and documents. This flexibility gives the lawyer an overview of the complex factual mosaic while enabling him or her to sort and view subsets of the integrated data by a variety of search criteria. TrialMaker, a useful and robust FileMaker Pro template, builds in all of this functionality and allows you to customize and reuse it for all of your cases. Designed by a lawyer, TrialMaker provides a tool to compile facts from depositions,

FIGURE 1.10 Data Entry Screen (4th Dimension)

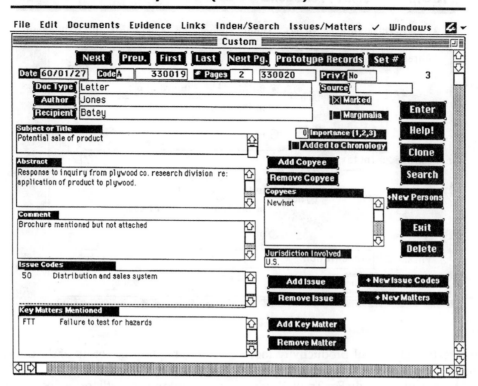

document production, witness interviews, and other sources into an integrated whole. You can then view the data chronologically, by witness, topic, issue, or by any number of other report formats.

Document retrieval is the primary function for a litigation support database. The extent to which counsel will use a database to manage documents in any particular case depends on the number and diversity of the documents. A basic system should provide a unique number for each document, a three-field description comprising the type of document, the author, and the recipient. An Abstract or Comments field is useful in distinguishing a particular document in a hard copy list containing numerous otherwise uninformative descriptions. Alternatively, a Summary field permits the user to search for documents dealing with the same topics.

Mac databases offer the flexible use of graphic tools to simplify the design of custom data entry screens. Figure 1.10 illustrates what a custom-built data entry screen (layout) can look like on a Macintosh running a program called 4th Dimension.

4th Dimension is a complex relational database that requires a reasonably intense commitment on the part of the user to master its variety of flexible design features and programming language. A "4D" (as it is called in Mac circles) database becomes practical when the case requires issue-coding significant volumes of documents.

MACINTOSH TEXT RETRIEVAL

Every litigator can benefit from the use of text retrieval software for the management and indexing of deposition or trial transcripts. Virtually all court reporters will now provide a computer disk copy of the transcript along with the hard copy. There are a variety of Mac software tools available that permit the user to search rapidly through huge volumes of material, extracting passages that contain user-defined key words in context. Some of these packages will automatically create an index of the words in a transcript, complete with page references for all words or all words that appear with a certain frequency within the transcript.

Sonar Professional is presently the best all-around package for the Macintosh since it performs all of these functions at blazing speed. Figure 1.11 provides an illustration of the kind of complex searching that software such as Sonar Professional permits.

FIGURE 1.11 Sonar Professional

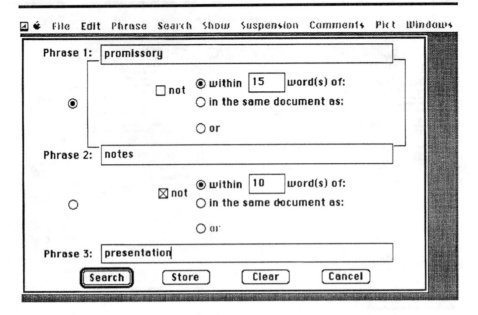

Another extremely useful productivity tool for any litigator who has to tame a mass of deposition or trial transcripts is Ready For Trial!. Ready For Trial! is a sophisticated program that not only offers powerful search capabilities but also permits the lawyer to track exhibits. More significantly, it allows you to annotate and extract the significant portions of transcripts by identifying, flagging, and extracting those "gems" that make your case. It facilitates productive trial preparation by eliminating the need for that inevitable last-minute look for the needle in the haystack.

Another simple package called GOfer permits a less complicated search at a somewhat slower speed. The advantage of GOfer is that it is available at all times as a *desk accessory* to search a document (such as a transcript) from within another program. Once you identify the passages you are seeking, you can cut and paste them into whatever application is currently running. While GOfer doesn't have the power of Sonar Professional or Ready For Trial!, it offers a number of advantages that neither of those programs can provide:

- it is very inexpensive at around $70.00;
- it requires very little memory so it is available to run with other programs on machines where computer memory is restricted; and

- it requires no set-up of the documents that you wish to search, plus it will "read" word processing, outlines, or documents prepared by almost any software program.

A sample GOfer search screen that illustrates the simple manner in which a search query is defined is reproduced in Figure 1.12.

Another screen, as shown in Figure 1.13, permits the user to define the kind of report desired, providing the context of the search "hit," either in hard copy or on disk.

You get significant value for your money with programs such as Sonar, Ready For Trial!, and GOfer. Each is laden with exclusive, well-thought-out features that make them extremely useful allies in the litigation battle.

The Macintosh uses a form of *multitasking*, which means that different programs can run at the same time in various windows, some hidden, some visible. For a litigator, this means that data can be reviewed, revised, and quickly exchanged between programs. I have found this feature useful for cutting and pasting transcript passages into other programs such as a database, an outliner, or a word processor. From the standpoint of effectiveness, inserting the actual passage from the transcript is likely to have far more impact than a mere reference to a page and line number of a volume that a judge may overlook.

FIGURE 1.12 GOfer

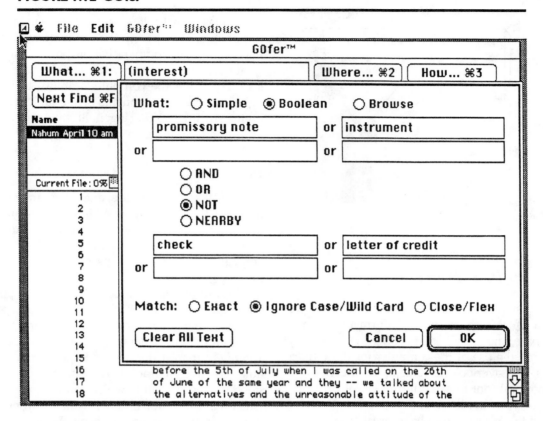

FIGURE 1.13 GOfer

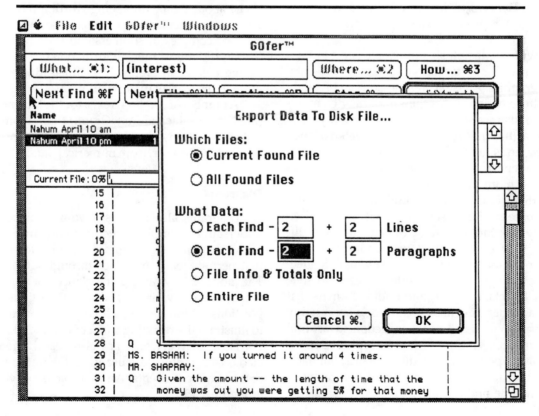

FIGURE 1.14

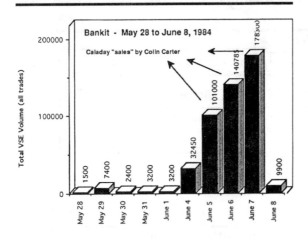

MAKING YOUR POINT

Most people think of using computers for word processing, retrieving information from a database, and "number crunching." However, by limiting the use of the computer for those functions, you overlook its value as an effective and economical tool to assist in the visual presentation of your evidence and submissions. I have found the Macintosh to be of great assistance in making effective, economical presentations. Unlike the DOS world, Macs are built around graphics. Creating professional graphics presentations is a snap.

With a Macintosh, you don't need to be a graphic designer to take advantage of presentation graphics. A visual presentation can highlight key information, focus thinking, draw comparisons, illustrate relationships, and simplify complex factual interrelationships. A well-designed graph tends to put facts in perspective. It allows the reader to focus on a visual image, which leaves a much more permanent and powerful impression than either words or numbers could alone.

Some of the most effective visual aids used in any presentation are text-related and not difficult to use. Mac word processors allow the writer to emphasize parts of a submission effectively through the use of different size and style fonts, bullets, dingbats, and outline formats that grab a reader's attention. These tools are roughly equivalent to using vocal inflection in an oral presentation. A page of text in typical Courier 12 point type without headlines, italics, boldface, and other text tools is the printed equivalent of a monotone oral delivery.

Tables

Tables reveal relationships between categories of data. They permit the summarization of a mass of data for comparative purposes. One can create tables on a typewriter, but they are lifeless. Try using the computer's ability to highlight important components of the table by applying shading, boldfacing, italicization, or other offsetting techniques.

Graphs—The Meaning of Numbers

We all know about lies, damn lies, and statistics. Then there are graphs. While tables of data are useful for a simple presentation of facts and figures, a chart or graph allows you to clarify and emphasize key relationships between facts and figures.

Graphs provide an ideal vehicle to get a point across quickly and emphatically in either an opening or closing submission. Everyone agrees that the brain retains visual images longer and more accurately than it does other kinds of information. Moreover, a graph may be an easily understood reference point to which counsel may refer when summing up. It can permit the triers of fact to see the data as you want them to see it when you are not present to make the point. The cliché about the picture being worth a thousand words is particularly true where the factual issues are complex or cumbersome.

Consider how much information is conveyed by the picture in Figure 1.14, illustrating a key point in the market manipulation case.

A number of programs exist for the Macintosh (the best of which is DeltaGraph) that automatically generate any number of graphs, in the format selected by the user, from numerical data.

Diagrams

Diagrams also can assist your audience to understand a complex structure at a glance. One useful diagram is a corporate organization chart that permits ready reference throughout a case. The judge or jury can see at a glance not only the names of the key players, but also their titles and positions within the overall corporate hierarchy to illustrate the resulting chain of command.

Flow charts, which are also readily generated on a computer, are useful to illustrate a process or chain of events. An example is provided in Figure 1.15.

FIGURE 1.15 Flow Chart

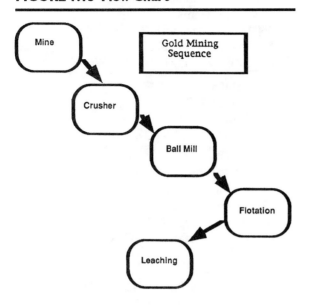

The question may be asked whether presentation graphics are really worth the effort. The answer is twofold. First, with the new generation of software, these graphics are easy to produce. Moreover, studies show that using graphics significantly increases the persuasiveness of presentations. Once you overcome the court's initial reaction to the new presentation technique, you will be perceived as being better prepared, clearer, more interesting, and undoubtedly more concise than your opponent. These subliminal messages may not offer a substitute for a good case, but they may help ensure that a good case does not fail to make the point.

CONCLUSION

I can only scratch the surface of the potential for productivity gains in an article such as this one. The more you use a user-friendly computer like the Macintosh, the more you will realize its potential. If you don't have a Mac but suffer from Mac envy, help is on the way with the continued refinement of Windows and OS/2 for IBM-compatible PCs. Many of the programs mentioned here such as Sonar Professional and FileMaker Pro either have or will shortly have Windows equivalents. MORE has a first cousin in GrandView, which is also produced by Symantec Corporation.

It is not necessary to embrace all of the capa-

bilities of a computer to use it effectively to make significant productivity gains in the area of litigation management. In many cases, simple database systems for document retrieval can provide solutions. More complex relational databases are only necessary for the analysis of voluminous amounts of data. Presentation graphics are certainly not required in every case to get your points across. It is up to you to decide how much computer power you wish to harness in any given situation. However, you must remember that because of its fascinating potential, computing can become addictive. Once started, you soon discover that the only effective limits on your ability to use the power of a computer in litigation management are your awareness of the software's capabilities and your own imagination.

LIST OF SOFTWARE VENDORS

4th Dimension
Acius, Inc.
10351 Bubb Road
Cupertino, CA 95014
(408) 252-4444; fax (408) 252-0831

Active Memory
ASD Software, Inc.
4650 Arrow Highway
Montclair, CA 91763
(714) 624-2594; fax (714) 624-9574

DeltaGraph
DeltaPoint, Inc.
200 Heritage Harbour
Suite G
Monterey, CA 93940
(408) 648-4000

Fair Witness
Chena Software
905 Harrison Street
Allentown, PA 18103
(215) 770-1210

FileMaker Pro
Claris Corporation
5201 Patrick Henry Drive
M/S C-11
Box 58168
Santa Clara, CA 95052-8168
(408) 727-8227; fax (408) 987-7447

GOfer
Microlytics Inc.
Two Tobey Village Office Park
Pittsford, NY 14534
(716) 248-9150

MORE
Symantec Corporation
10201 Torre Avenue
Cupertino, CA 95014
(408) 253-9600

Panorama
ProVUE Development Corporation
15180 Transistor Lane
Huntington Beach, CA 92649
(714) 892-8199

Ready For Trial!
Robbins Analytics, Inc.
245 East Sixth Street
St. Paul, MN 55101-1988
(612) 224-1289; fax (612) 224-2633

Sonar Professional
Virginia Systems
5509 West Bay Court
Midlothian, VA 23112
(804) 739-3200; fax (804) 739-8376

ThoughtPattern
Bananafish Software
730 Central Avenue
San Francisco, CA 94117
(415) 929-8135; fax (415) 929-8146

TrialMaker
Packer Software
12 Roosevelt Avenue
Mystic, CT 06355
(203) 572-8955; fax (203) 572-0765

Howard Shapray is the senior litigation partner at the Vancouver, British Columbia offices of the Canadian law firm of Goodman Freeman Phillips & Vineberg. He has been in practice for 22 years, the last seven of which have been in partnership with his Macintosh. His practice primarily involves complex commercial litigation. He has lectured on computer-assisted litigation support at Canadian Bar Association programs on both the local and national levels.

Microsoft Windows in the Law Office

Roger C. Schechter

In the spring of 1990, Windows version 3.0 took the computer world by storm. To most of us, it represented an alternative to Apple's graphical user interface approach to computing. Although Windows runs under the MS-DOS operating system, many feel that it is an operating system unto itself. Roger Schechter, lawyer and part-time computer programmer, tells us how litigators can use Windows in their litigation practice.

Microsoft Windows is a DOS-based "operating environment" that can transform the way you use your personal computer. Like the Macintosh, Windows offers a graphical user interface. Unlike the Mac, however, it allows you to run DOS-based programs side by side with Windows-based programs—without need for special hardware or software. Among other things, it offers the ability to run more than one application at a time. And when running Windows-based programs, it offers improved ease of operation and the ability to transfer data seamlessly from program to program, all without changing your basic computer hardware.

In this article I will discuss using Windows in your law office, its advantages, and the software and hardware required in order to run it.

ADVANTAGES

Working in Windows offers many advantages over working in the DOS environment, including the following:

- In Windows, you can run more than one program at a time and move between them easily and quickly.
- The DOS command line is replaced with drop-down menus, dialog boxes, and easy-to-recognize icons.

- Windows provides a "clipboard" for copying or moving information from one program to another.
- Information can be automatically exchanged between programs that support a feature of Windows called *DDE* (Dynamic Data Exchange).
- Windows applications are more consistent in operation than DOS applications.

Windows reduces the learning curve users may experience with the DOS operating system by simplifying common tasks, such as file management and printing. It has an on-line tutorial and help functions that let you become productive faster. In short, Windows is a software system that can make your computer easier to use, allowing you to be more productive.

WINDOWS VERSUS NON-WINDOWS PROGRAMS

In the IBM-compatible world, there are two types of programs: Windows and non-Windows. A Windows application is a program that was specifically designed to run under Windows. It will offer a consistent Windows interface, improved memory management, printer fonts, and other Windows utilities. Non-Windows applications are written for DOS. Fortunately most will

FIGURE 1.16 A Windows Screen

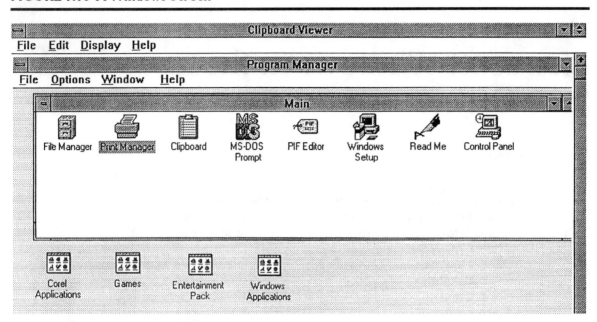

run under Windows as a "non-Windows application." There are advantages to running Windows-specific software, but using Windows will not prevent you from using most of your favorite non-Windows software.

THE WINDOWS INTERFACE

Windows allows you to think of your computer screen as the equivalent of your desktop. You can stack as many objects on the surface of your desktop as your computer will allow. When you start a program, Windows opens a "window" within which the program will run. The size and position of the window depend on what other windows are open. A window can be small or it can fill your entire screen. The active program will be run in the foreground; inactive or other programs will run in the background. (See Figure 1.16.)

Moving between applications is quick and easy. You size and arrange the program windows on your screen, much the way you would work with items on your actual desk. For example, to review a letter and a spreadsheet, you might change the size of their windows, enabling them to fit side by side on the screen "desktop."

Windows is a multitasking system, meaning that all programs open on your desktop run concurrently, but the foreground application— the *active application*—gets the largest share of your computer's processing time. Programs run

more slowly in the background. For example, you might be editing a document in a word processor in the foreground while a communications program retrieves data more slowly in the background.

WINDOWS FEATURES

Applications

The applications programs included in the Windows package are: Write, a word processor; Terminal, a communications program; and Paintbrush, a drawing program. None of these programs should be confused with full-featured applications software available separately, such as WordPerfect, Microsoft Word, Crosstalk, or CorelDRAW, and I would not plan on using either Write or Terminal for the office. In contrast, many law offices have only a limited need for a sophisticated drawing package; for them, Paintbrush is likely to be more than adequate.

The word processing applications available for Windows are worth special mention. Microsoft Windows word processors offer the graphical assistance of *WYSIWYG* (what you see is what you get). In the legal field, three popular Windows-based word processors are Word-Perfect for Windows, Microsoft Word for Windows, and Ami Pro by Lotus. All three allow you to incorporate graphic images and use a variety of type styles and sizes in your docu-

FIGURE 1.17 Windows File Manager

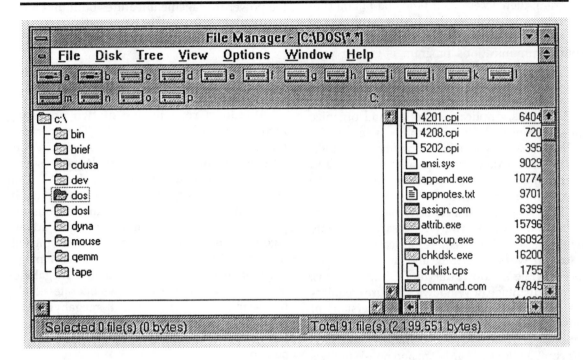

ments. TrueType font technology provides instant access to typefaces in any point size and high-quality WYSIWYG output on any monitor or printer supported by Windows. TrueType allows you to see the actual type styles, type sizes, and graphic images on the screen as you work. Both Word and WordPerfect for Windows are fully compatible with their respective non-Windows versions; files created with one can be used by the other.

Managing and Printing Files

File Manager makes organizing your files and directories easier than using the DOS command line. File Manager presents you with a directory window (see Figure 1.17) that graphically displays the directory structure of the files and directories on your disk. Its organized structure of menu choices makes the task of reviewing directories, copying files, and other routine file maintenance easy.

Windows Print Manager is used to install, configure, and control printers. It works in the background, allowing files to be printed while you continue to work.

Sharing Information Between Applications

Object Linking and Embedding (OLE) allows applications to work together by permitting them to share information. A Windows user can thus create an illustration using the Paint program and embed the graphic in a Write document. If the illustration must be updated, the user can double-click its icon within the Write document, which launches Paint automatically and allows the user to edit the drawing. Because the original graphics file is embedded in the document, there is no need to store or update multiple copies of the image.

Dynamic Data Exchange (DDE) provides a step beyond OLE in that it allows data to be automatically updated between documents. For example, suppose you created a word processing document that included a spreadsheet. If the spreadsheet were subsequently changed, the data in the word processing document would also change. DDE allows groups to work on projects more efficiently. DDE and OLE only work with specially designed Windows applications.

PUTTING WINDOWS TO WORK IN YOUR OFFICE

Windows has two very powerful features that make it worth considering for the law office—multitasking and a user-friendly graphical interface. If you've never tried working in a multitasking computer environment, consider the

29

advantage of being able to check your docket program, then access your time and billing program to make an entry, and finally head back to your word processor, while in the background your communications program is getting your electronic mail from an online service. And Windows's graphical interface makes the PC more accessible. Simple file management—the ability to copy files, duplicate diskettes, and organize directories using DOS commands—is beyond the skills of many who use PCs in the law office. Windows File Manager simplifies those tasks and offers a much easier to understand and use interface for file management.

Weighing against those advantages is the cost of hardware and software necessary to operate Windows. Windows requires at least a 386 processor to work efficiently and at a reasonable speed. While Windows can run DOS applications, taking advantage of Windows's features requires the purchase of the new Windows versions of those programs. There are also persistent compatibility problems between Windows and various combinations of hardware and non-Windows application software. The relative stability of Windows 3.1 in handling non-Windows applications (version 3.0 was worse) and increasingly affordable hardware make a strong argument that may offset those concerns.

WHAT'S NEW WITH WINDOWS 3.1?

For those familiar with Windows 3.0, over 1,000 enhancements have been added to version 3.1. Improvements include increased speed, less susceptibility to crashing, and greater compatibility with non-Windows applications. The improved speed really shows: With Windows 3.0, it took me 32 seconds to move 64 files with the File Manager (a utility program included with Windows). Version 3.1 takes only 3 seconds. Should a problem occur with an application, the Application Reboot feature in version 3.1 now allows a Windows user to press [CTRL-ALT-DEL] and close the offending application without closing Windows. Windows 3.1 users can run more MS-DOS applications concurrently than they could under Windows 3.0.

Users of notebook PCs will appreciate a new feature in Windows 3.1 called Mouse Trails, which makes it easier to find the cursor in an LCD/notebook display. In addition, Windows now supports the Advanced Power Management specification, which allows Windows to support the power management features built into many notebook PCs for longer battery life.

HARDWARE AND SOFTWARE REQUIREMENTS

Windows runs in one of two operating modes: *standard* or *386 enhanced*. The operating mode used depends upon the processor in your personal computer. Although Windows will work in its standard mode on a PC/AT with an 80286 processor, you will find it is limited in speed and in the number of simultaneous applications that can be run. To take full advantage of all that Windows has to offer, you will need an 80386 processor and at least 4 megabytes of memory. Using less than 4 megabytes of memory will make Windows operate slowly. Increasing your memory to 8 megabytes will result in a marked improvement in speed and the number of simultaneous applications that can be run.

A mouse or other pointing device is highly recommended. A significant part of the ease of using Windows is lost by using the keyboard alone. Because it is based on a graphical user interface, Windows is best displayed on a high-resolution color monitor; the preferred video resolution is VGA or better. For the power user, there are a number of video cards on the market that function as Windows accelerators and can boost video performance significantly.

Networking

Windows was designed from the ground up for network use. It includes such features as automatic network reconnection and interfaces tuned for interoperation with all of the leading network operating systems. Windows maintains *persistent network connections*, meaning that information about a remote disk drive or printer is maintained by Windows after a network session is terminated. When the Windows operating system is restarted, it automatically reconnects to the same network connections present when Windows was closed. Windows even prompts the user for passwords if needed.

There are several programs included as "desktop accessories" in the Windows package. These small programs, although limited, can be very useful for the law office. The simpler desktop accessories include

Clock, a clock with digital or analog display;
Calculator, a graphical re-creation of a
desktop calculator;
Cardfile, an electronic Rolodex;
Calendar, a scheduling program; and
Notepad, a simple text editor.

THE FUTURE

Microsoft plans to continue to extend and enhance the Windows operating system. Areas of enhancement will include a more intelligent file system, a more intuitive user interface, and more transparent operation in networked environments. In addition, Microsoft is completing a high-end implementation of Windows that will actually replace, and not just supplement, DOS. This implementation, called Windows NT, is expected to be available in early 1993.

CONCLUSION

Microsoft Windows 3.1 is an excellent product for improving law office productivity. The easy-to-use graphical interface and multitasking capability bring new power to the PC while making the task of using the computer easier.

Roger C. Schechter is a lawyer with Morgan, Melhuish, Monaghan, Arvidson, Abrutyn & Lisowski in Livingston, New Jersey. He is also president of Litigation Technologies, Inc., a firm specializing in customized litigation support and information management software. He is the author of Diarymaster and Diarymaster II docket management systems.

Section 2
Using Outliners as Thinking Tools

John C. Tredennick, Jr.

If you haven't used a computer in your practice, outlining software is a good place to start. We all know about outlines. Teachers made us prepare them in school. We stopped using them the minute we could.

Computers have changed all that. Outlining software offers a powerful thinking tool—not just a way to put off starting that brief. Indeed, the only thing some of us *don't* use outliners for is brief writing.

In this section you'll learn how computer-generated outlines can be used to organize your thoughts, your cases, and, ultimately, your practice. They do this through their automatic numbering ability. Each time you want to add a new thought or piece of information, the computer automatically gives it a new letter or number, depending on where it fits in your outline. As you begin to move things around, the computer renumbers your outline to accommodate the new organization.

Using Outliners to Organize Ideas

Cullen Smith

Cullen Smith, a trial lawyer practicing in Waco, Texas, has been using a simple outlining program for years. In this article, he introduces us to this important type of software and shows how it can help organize your thoughts and your cases.

I have two things to say to anyone reading this chapter. First, if you haven't used a computer to outline, I guarantee that outlining will make you a better lawyer. Second, if I can do it, you can. I can turn on the computer and call up my outlining program and a few other programs even though I don't understand computers. I am a lawyer, not a computer programmer. If I can use a computer outlining program, so can anyone else who has read up to here.

My message thus far: It will help you, and it is easy.

WHAT IS OUTLINING?

We all know how to prepare an outline:

I.
  A.
    1.
      a.

An outline begins with main topics, goes to lesser topics, and ends at the conclusion. I have always liked outlines. I use them to prepare speeches, contracts, briefs, articles, examinations of witnesses, and I don't know what else. If you're like me, you think of the order you want to follow, you leave large spaces on your notepad, because you know you will keep thinking of things to add, you begin writing, and you make arrows to change the order of things. If you have time, you ask your secretary to prepare a draft, hoping she can read and understand your scratches, or, if she cannot, that you can.

That's not the outlining I am talking about. A software outlining program gives me the clear, orderly outline I always tried for when I did it the old way. But, as you will see, there is a big difference.

THE MENTAL PROCESS IN USING AN OUTLINING PROGRAM

With almost every project that contains anything unusual or involved, or that requires planning, I start with my outliner. For one thing, I start more quickly because I do my thinking as I go along instead of thinking it out before I begin. If I must think something through before I get started, I may wait a long time until I become inspired.

With my outliner, I just go to my computer, create a new file, and begin entering whatever comes to mind about the project. It may be important or unimportant. It may be closely related to the prior entry or have no relation at all. It may make sense or it may not. None of this matters. After all, no one is going to see this work product; it's just between your mind, your fingers, and your computer.

Sometimes you make many entries in a minute; other times you just sit there wondering why nothing occurs to you. Then, unexpectedly, a thought surfaces and you start up again. You just keep entering what comes to mind. It's fun, and it's simple. Your entries are usually brief and not complete sentences; they are merely thoughts for you to amplify later.

Some of them will obviously be subtopics of other topics. You can enter them that way or wait until later—it doesn't matter. Do whatever you feel like doing at the time, but keep going. Brainstorm. Spend as little time as possible thinking about form, spelling, or anything else. Just get your thoughts recorded.

One day not long ago, I learned I was scheduled for a meeting the next morning to present some thoughts or ideas about a project. I knew the topic generally and the people who would attend, but for some reason I could not decide how to handle the meeting or exactly what we should cover. I would think about it, but I would draw a blank. That night, after several fretful hours, I got out of bed, went to my notebook computer, turned it on, started up my outlining program, opened a new file under the meeting's topic, and began entering things as they came to mind. Anything at first—I just had to put down something. (If nothing else, I might have begun by typing INTRODUCTION or WELCOME.) One entry made me think of another, and in about 30 minutes I knew exactly what I thought the meeting should cover, item by item. Back to bed for a good sleep.

Like most lawyers I know, without my outliner I would still have made the meeting, I would have presided, had something to say, and it would have concluded satisfactorily. But the truth is that the meeting would not have been handled as well or been as successful. And I would not have had as much sleep.

An outlining program will help you do what lawyers are supposed to do for a living—*think*. It lets you think in a free and unstructured way, in no particular order. It lets you enter thoughts into the computer you might otherwise forget. There is no more reminding yourself to remember something when you reach some point later in your outline or paper, only to find you have forgotten it when you get there.

As your outline becomes larger and your thoughts slow down, you can look back over your work and see that some entries relate to each other. Some are subtopics or minor topics of larger ones. You can organize them by moving the entries around. As you decide the order of your major subjects and minor subcategories, you will continue to think of new entries and ways to expand others. You may eliminate some of your entries because they duplicate others, or you may decide they are not important.

Depending on the time you have, the impor-

tance of the project, or your mental attitude at the time, you may not finish your outline at the first sitting. If the project is an extended one, you probably will continue to make changes and additions as long as you work on it.

It is not unusual for me to feel I have my outline as I want it, start printing it, think of something I must add or change, print the outline with those changes, and go through the process again. There must be something about believing you are finished that causes your mind to think of something else. While that can result in a harmful "one question too many" during a trial, I have found it helpful with outlining. Only a computerized outline allows you the freedom to change your mind easily and neatly.

Thus, with an outliner, you easily move topics around, create major topics, subtopics under subtopics, put the top at the bottom, try it one way and then another, move single lines or many lines.

By way of demonstration, imagine that you are going to take a deposition of an expert witness. (I know—you probably have a form or outline you already work from—but stay with me.) What do you ask?

- Expert's name
- Qualifications
- When employed
- By whom
- Investigation
- Written reports
- Fee arrangement
- Prior testimony
- Articles written
- Recognized authorities
- Photographs

Once you have your topics, you can rearrange this list in any order you like. You can make one a subtopic of the other, and, as you think about it, modify it and add other items. By the time you've finished, you have a complete list of all the questions you want to cover—or, at least, all of the topics. You will be amazed as you watch it grow.

To give another example, let's say I wanted to do some planning for next year. I call up my outlining program, create a new file, which I call NEXTYEAR, and begin to think as I stare at the screen.

A. Attend more bar association meetings
B. Clean up my office
C. Establish a good legal retrieval system
D. Take a spring vacation with family

E. Get control of my docket
F. Get certified in Civil Trial Practice by the state specialization board
G. Lose weight
H. Do a better job of delegating my work to associates and legal assistants
I. Spend more time with my family
J. Screen cases better
K. Get more exercise
L. Develop a plan for visiting my clients at their offices and plants
M. Learn to use an outlining program

We could go on and on, but you get the idea. When you look at this list, it's obvious that these thoughts can be broken down into two areas: my practice and my personal life. So I easily create two major topics and move the entries under the proper category.

A. Law practice
  1. Clean up my office
  2. Attend more bar association meetings
  3. Get control of my docket
     a. Screen cases better
     b. Do a better job of delegating my work to
        associates
        legal assistants
  4. Get certified in Civil Trial Practice by the state specialization board
  5. Develop a plan for visiting my clients at their offices and plants
  6. Learn to use an outlining program
  7. Establish a good legal retrieval system
B. Personal
  1. Spend more time with my family
     a. Take a spring vacation with family
  2. Lose weight
     a. Get more exercise

USING AN OUTLINER IN LITIGATION

Your use of an outlining program for litigation is limited only by your ingenuity. It can help you think and get organized, make lists of things to do, prioritize your list or plans, divide tasks or items into categories, and keep a running calendar of important events for a case. Granted, all of these tasks could also be performed by other programs and databases. By experimenting, you can determine which software works best for you in which situation. The following are some of the ways we use outliners in our trial practice. They may stimulate you to think of your own uses.

DETERMINING WHETHER TO TAKE THE CASE—LISTING THE MERITS AND WEAKNESSES

Start listing them as they occur to you, not in any order. You could begin with what you know about the case without dividing the good from the bad. Just keep listing things you know, you need to know, or you just wonder about. When you are fairly far along, you may divide your list into several areas, such as the strong points, the weak points, the unknown, and the legal issues. You then move each entry to one of those divisions. You will probably find that some entries are actually subpoints of others, and then you arrange them accordingly. Or you may start with three main topics (strengths, weaknesses, and unknowns), and, as you think about the case, move back and forth between these topics.

Before you know it, you have a clear picture of whether the case is for you or what you need to help you decide. With most outliners, you can view the outline on the screen or save and print the outline. As you study, you update the outline. Should you decide to take the case, this outline will serve as a starting point in your preparation.

OUTLINING THE ELEMENTS OF THE CASE AND PREPARING PLEADINGS

If you start with an outline, you often get a clearer picture of the best order for pleading your case and the counts or different causes of action.

Budgeting the Case

As every defense lawyer knows, it is now fairly common for companies to ask their lawyers to provide them, shortly after a case is referred, with a budget, evaluation, and plan for defending the case. While most of us do not welcome this task, two things are evident: (1) It is a good idea, and (2) Outlining will make it much easier.

Preparing for and Taking Depositions

Rather than writing down notes on what you want to cover—with all the arrows, marginal comments you may not be able to read, and an order you do not want to follow—sit at your computer with your outlining program and let your mind roam, entering topics as you think of them. No order or assurance that you

PC-Outline: An Inexpensive Shareware Alternative

Joe Kashi

If you are thinking about an outlining program to help organize your practice or help you prepare cases, consider PC-Outline, a simple, memory-resident program that has been around for years. PC-Outline is a favorite of lawyers. As it is shareware, you can try it free.

PC-Outline can be memory resident as a pop-up program, so you can use it with other programs like WordPerfect or Agenda. Even though there are more sophisticated outlining programs like GrandView (by the same author) and MaxThink, PC-Outline remains popular because it is fast and easy to use. One advantage of PC-Outline is that it runs with reasonable speed on older PCs.

You can download PC-Outline from almost any bulletin board. Since PC-Outline is shareware, you may copy and distribute it freely for private, noncommercial use. If you use it, you should register your copy by sending $89.95 plus $7.50 shipping to Brown Bag Software, File No. 41719, P. O. Box 60000, San Francisco, CA 94160-1719. For your registration fee, you get a complete typeset manual, a copy of the most recent version, automatic notice of updates, and toll-free technical support for one year. If you can't find it elsewhere, for $10 Brown Bag Software will send you a diskette with PC-Outline on it. If you register within 30 days of receipt, you may deduct the $10. Brown Bag Software also offers a site license for multiple copies; phone them at (800) 523-0764.

actually want to cover a topic is necessary. As you think and enter, what you want to cover begins to fall into divisions, and you almost automatically create major and minor topics and subtopics. You continue to add and eliminate until you're satisfied. As you go along, or toward the end, you can rearrange your outline in the order you want to develop testimony in the deposition. As explained later, you can also create outlines for use as forms for different depositions (i.e., plaintiff, defendant, witness, product liability, deceptive trade practices).

Negotiating Settlements

The outliner helps you get a better handle on your case. Then, if you make a presentation, use the outliner to organize its sequence. Naturally, the outline that helps you decide on your approach to settlement is not normally the outline you use for the presentation. In some cases, the presentation outline could be the table of contents.

Working on the Pretrial Order

Assume that you need to prepare a proposed order for a court where you have not prepared one before or the case is sufficiently different that your proposed order cannot be completed with quick dictation. It often helps to take the court's requirements as the beginning of an outline:

A. Summary of pleading and contentions of each party
B. Stipulated facts
C. Witnesses for each party and summary of their testimony
D. Other court requirements

You then fill in your part of the order. You could do this in outline form, or in final form for presentation to the other side and eventually to the court.

Determining the Order of Trial

You have your witnesses, your trial briefs, your exhibits, and you must now decide how to put on your case. Whether you use an outliner or not, you are really outlining your trial—in your mind, on a notepad, or through dictation. I suggest a computer outlining program because it allows your outline to be as brief or as detailed as you want, to list the witnesses and arrange them in the best order, or outline under each witness's name what areas you want to cover. You can rearrange that information as well.

Remember, nothing is fixed until the evidence is presented. When you have your first order of trial, you save that outline on your computer. You can return to the outline as many times as you wish: update this, change that; move a witness; think of something and add it.

Preparing for a Legal Argument

What are the facts, the legal issues, the cases, the other authorities, the rules? What do you want to cover first or last? Make your outline as detailed as you desire. Move points around until you like the order. Use your outline to prepare your presentation.

Questioning the Witness on Either Direct or Cross-Examination

What do you want to cover? Enter everything on your outline. Don't worry about the order at first. Just get things down and then start rearranging.

There are a host of other uses for outliners which need no explanation, such as preparing to select the jury or argue the case; preparing a motion for a new trial; determining points on appeal; evaluating damages (for your pleadings, trial, argument or settlement evaluation and negotiations); drafting interrogatories; and outlining necessary investigation.

CREATING A RUNNING CALENDAR OF EVENTS

Sometimes you'd like to have a record of when events occurred. You may have litigation software that keeps these dates. You probably keep daily time or service sheets from which you can reconstruct events. You may enter into a database the dates of instruments, depositions, meetings, and other events. Each program serves its purpose. However, outlining can be an ideal way to record important events as they occur.

The following is a brief description of how to record such events in your outliner: Open a file in your program. When you start a calendar outline you probably already have one or more dates to enter. For example, you may enter the date you were contacted, or the date of the accident, or the first inquiry from a big company to buy your client's little company.

I suggest you enter dates followed by a brief explanation of the event. This explanation can be part of the date entry (i.e., same level) or a subtopic of the date. Using a subtopic for the explanation will probably be better if it will be lengthy or if several events may take place on the same date. You'll be surprised how often you or your client will want to know when a particular event took place. With your outline, you can promptly find the answer. (Searching for a text string helps you find a key word quickly.)

PLANNING

If your outliner has helped you plan your case, you will probably include a list of what you need to do: research, file suit, and take written and oral depositions. You could add a major category at the end of the outline for completed tasks. When you take a deposition, move it from the needed list to the completed list. This will give you a quick view of what you have done and what needs to be done.

For example, our law firm took part in a complicated sale of a company through merger that required prior approval by one state and several federal agencies. Each had different requirements and time limits. There were many other requirements. I first tried project management software, but either I didn't understand it or couldn't make it work for different (and always changing) tasks. In contrast, my outliner proved to be the best way to keep up with where we were; and it was a pleasure to move items one by one and agency by agency to the "Complete" list. (I suggest you add the date when each task is completed.) Also, you can periodically update your client by mailing a printed copy.

USING FORMS ON YOUR OUTLINE PROGRAM

Many lawyers have a form or *shell* they use in a particular stage of litigation: a deposition outline for different kinds of cases or witnesses, a pretrial order for certain courts and cases, or a trial notebook. These forms are ideal for implementing on an outlining program, particularly where you expect to make some changes. Use them to begin your outlining process. For example, if you have a deposition outline to start your depositions, enter that outline in your software program. You may or may not want to make changes as you go along. Give the outline a file name and save it. This outline contains no names or facts. The next time you take a deposition that requires an outline, call up the computer outline, make a copy, give it a new name, and use it to complete the outline for your specific case.

SOME REAL-LIFE EXAMPLES

It might help to give examples of my recent outlining. Our law firm had to put together and later close a transaction for an out-of-state client. Our outliner let us focus on the outstanding issues, what was done and what needed to be done. We prepared a list of what the buyer and seller needed before the transaction could close. Under each heading, we listed that party's assignments: prepare this document or that, give this opinion or that, get corporate resolutions approved and adopted, complete exhibits, and so on.

Each party got a copy of the assignment list, and responsibilities were discussed and confirmed. The list helped to eliminate some of those "I thought you were going to do that" problems. We then prepared an outline for the closing with a list of preclosing activities: things to be done, people to be present, requirements on closing day, and postclosing matters. It helped us, and I believe our client received it well.

More recently, in analyzing a case referred to us, I used outlining to explore and develop answers to questions regarding the issues, the choices to be made on the best forum, who were to be named as adverse parties, the approach, and the first discovery. I saved the information after each session and modified it as I thought of new things, obtained more information, and moved the case toward final resolution. I find that outlining really helps me get a feel for a file and allows me to bring others up to speed on the case as well. I believe it will help you, too.

In representing a client with environmental concerns, an outlining program can be used almost daily: to develop agendas for many meetings with the client, insurance companies, adverse parties and their lawyers, experts, governmental agencies, and members of the press; to record events and dates; to outline The Plan; to outline topics to be covered with witnesses; and on and on.

DESIRABLE FEATURES

There are a number of good software programs on the market. Many are dedicated to outlining functions while others come bundled as part of a word processing package. One can get into heated arguments over which kind of program is best.

For litigation support, I prefer programs designed primarily for outlining. Some of the more popular programs include: GrandView and MORE from Symantec Corp.; MaxThink, from MaxThink, Inc.; PC-Outline, from Brown Bag Software; and StreamLine from TechnoLogics, Inc. Both WordPerfect and Microsoft Word have outlining features. So do SideKick and PC Tools Deluxe. (For addresses of the software manufacturers mentioned, see Jim Eidelman's article later in this section, "Brainstorming Tools for Trial Lawyers.")

I use MaxThink. I find it easy to work with, and it has made me a better lawyer. Of course, the program you choose does not matter as long as it meets your needs. Make sure it has most of these features:

1. Easy to understand
2. Good help screens
3. The ability to collapse topics under major headings
4. The ability to expand minor topics with ease
5. The ability to move topics up and down and from one level to another
6. A spell checker and a thesaurus (for me, at least)
7. The ability to delete entries with ease
8. An easy-to-use file index to locate and erase files. By *files* I mean outlines
9. The ability to copy files
10. The ability to change the outlining format easily—that is, from standard to military to simple. Also, the ability to change headings and margins without referring to a manual
11. It is simple enough that you don't need to use the program every day to remember how it works. (This may not sound important to you. And if you are a computer whiz, it will not be, but for me this is really important.)
12. Software support

The software company should also provide periodic updates and some type of phone support for when you get stumped or frustrated, as you unfortunately will from time to time if you use your computer as much as you should.

Support from the software producer can make the difference in deciding whether or not to buy a particular program. I am not sure how you find this out in advance, although reading and asking questions will help. I am regularly amazed at the amount of wonderful help from some companies. It's one of the unique features of the industry. I have called for and received help many times (or had someone in this office who really understands computers call for me).

With MaxThink, you get help from the person who developed the program, Neil Larson, by calling the number in his manual, without charge or annual fee. And he calls you back. Other companies can be just as helpful, but I have found that not all companies are alike in providing support.

HYPERTEXT

An interesting feature of the newer versions of MaxThink is the ability to jump from within one file to another. This concept is called "hypertext." Other outlining programs may have the same feature. An innovative lawyer can think of numerous uses for this option. For example, you could establish a master file for depositions or witness examination. This file would act as a table of contents or index for specific witness outlines, such as medical witness—direct, medical witness—cross, fact eyewitness—direct, fact eyewitness—cross, weather expert, or other experts involved with your practice. As additional outlines are developed, they could be listed on the master file and added as individual files. Another possibility would be to use this feature to maintain a list of potential expert witnesses by

areas of expertise. You could then quickly and easily move from field to field and expert to expert. The file for each expert would contain a résumé and other valuable information.

At least for me, this is not an easy concept to grasp. But I have worked with it enough to believe it can really assist a lawyer with information retrieval.

USING A MEMORY-RESIDENT OUTLINER

One issue you should consider is whether you want your outlining program to be memory resident. A memory-resident program, also called a *TSR* program, can be loaded into your computer's memory when you turn it on and can be called up on a moment's notice, even while you are working with another program. GrandView, PC-Outline and READY! can be memory-resident. This feature can be very helpful because moving in and out of a non–memory-resident program is a pain, and you may not use the program as a result.

CONCLUSION

At this point, you realize I have a high opinion of the benefits the average lawyer can derive from an outlining program. I have occasionally found it difficult to get lawyers within our firm to use outliners. They seem to have a mental block about getting started. However, once they try it, an outlining program often becomes their constant companion.

You will have the same experience. It will help you think, plan, organize, get a jump on the opposition, impress your client, and make you a better lawyer. And it really is easy to learn and to use.

Cullen Smith is a member of Naman, Howell, Smith & Lee, P.C., with offices in Waco, Austin, and Temple, Texas. He has served as chair of the American Bar Association Economics of Law Practice Committee (now the Section of Law Practice Management), as chair of the ABA's General Practice Section, and as president of the State Bar of Texas.

Joseph L. Kashi (sidebar) is a sole practitioner living in Soldotna, Alaska. He received his B.S. and M.S. degrees from MIT in 1973 and his J.D. from Georgetown University Law Center in 1976. His practice consists primarily of contract and personal injury litigation.

Brainstorming Tools for Trial Lawyers*

James A. Eidelman

Outline processors can serve litigators as powerful tools for organizing facts, ideas, details, and random thoughts, allowing litigators to be more creative and brainstorm at the keyboard. In this chapter, Jim Eidelman shows how trial lawyers can put this powerful software tool to use as he surveys the leading products on the market.

Most attorneys already think in outline format. Some of us create an outline in our minds, pick up the dictating machine, and dictate a draft serially, from start to finish, inserting headings and section numbers in appropriate places. Others find organizing a major document too difficult to do in their heads. So they write the document out on legal pads, permitting them to insert, delete, draw arrows, cut, paste, and move easily from one part of the document to another.

An outline processor (also called an *idea processor* or *outliner*) is a specialized, highly interactive kind of word processing program designed to simplify the task of creating text at the keyboard. An outline processor works as well for organizing and reorganizing random ideas and facts as it does for methodically drafting a brief.

HOW "OUTLINE PROCESSING" DIFFERS FROM WORD PROCESSING

Most word processors help a writer with the basics of using an outline. For example, with WordPerfect 5.1 a lawyer can:

- Create an outline on the screen, with indented headings.
- Type text under each heading.

* An earlier version of this article appeared in *From Yellow Pads to Computers: Transforming Your Law Practice with a Computer*, 2nd ed. (Chicago: American Bar Association, 1991).

- Have the computer automatically number the headings in an outline format.

An "outline processor" can do these things, and more. An outline processor can perform the following functions that a word processor cannot do:

- View or hide (expand and collapse) points under a heading to any level of detail.
- Zoom into and out of text under a heading.
- Move whole sections of an outline, with associated subheadings and text, when the user simply moves the top-level heading.

In effect, the lawyer has a table of contents of the document on the screen. At the push of a button, the lawyer can look at just the chapter or article headings, the section headings, or subsection headings, expanding and collapsing headings to any level of detail. By pressing the zoom key, the lawyer can edit the text on any point, then return to the outline view.

THINKING WITH AN OUTLINE PROCESSOR

Most lawyers find that once they have begun to use an outline processor, it becomes an essential tool, and working without one is frustrating. As Jerry Pournelle, science fiction writer and computer commentator, stated, "If you are not using [an outline processor], you are working too hard." Stated another way by lawyer Leon

Gary, "Several years ago, I discovered ThinkTank and GrandView. My life as a lawyer has not been the same since." Noted trial lawyer Gerry Spence uses MORE, an outliner for the Apple Macintosh, to organize each of his cases and prepare for trial.

I have found that using an outline processor has had a dramatic effect on my creative process. Writer's block disappears; the document grows naturally from general headings to general headings with subsections. Finally, the sections, which are small and manageable, are easy to fill in and reorganize. Afterthoughts are simple to incorporate, and further editing of later drafts is easier. Although I have used a wide variety of standard word processing programs in the past, I have given up most of them for outline processors. The more I use outline processors, the more I appreciate them and depend upon them.

APPLICATIONS

The ways in which a trial lawyer can use an idea processor are limited only by his or her imagination.

- Drafting briefs and other lengthy documents.
- Taking notes during depositions.
- Organizing and creating opening statements, presentation and cross-examination of witnesses, and closing arguments.
- Organizing research notes and evidence.
- Managing complex cases or groups of cases.
- Creating to-do lists and general notes.

INTEGRATION WITH OTHER FEATURES

Once you get used to the idea, the outline processor seems completely natural—the only way to organize ideas. The combination of the hierarchical organization and the ability to view only what you want, whether general or specific, becomes compelling.

It is not surprising, then, that the concept is growing, so that it is being included in a wide variety of products, including standard word processing programs (Microsoft Word, Ami Pro), integrated programs (Framework, Symphony), personal information managers (GrandView), automated document drafting programs (Scriv-

ener, FlexPractice), memory-resident utility/notepad programs (PC-Outline), and project management software (TimeLine, MS Project)—even in operating systems.

The idea is catching on and spreading, and outline features will become standard in almost every word processing program in the future.

LEADING PRODUCTS FOR WRITING WITH AN OUTLINE PROCESSOR

GrandView and MORE

The first outline processor was ThinkTank by Living Videotext, since acquired by Symantec Corporation. Symantec's next product was READY!, a memory-resident outline processor/utility program, with built-in rolodex and telephone dialer. Like other TSR ("terminate and stay resident") programs, you can pop it up at the push of a button.

Symantec has since continued its tradition of innovation. MORE is a state-of-the-art idea processor for the Apple Macintosh. It offers incredible control of how organized information appears, with options for organizational charts, standard documents, and presentation graphics.

GrandView is Symantec's latest program for the PC. It replaces ThinkTank as a full-featured word processor/outline processor, with the added ability to organize and sort lists of things to do, telephone numbers, and other information. Although it organizes information differently, GrandView competes with Lotus Agenda as a leading high-end personal information manager (PIM) for the PC. GrandView is as useful for organizing the hundreds of miscellaneous details in a major litigation as it is in drafting a brief. Many of the best litigators I know carry an Apple Macintosh PowerBook with MORE or an IBM-compatible notebook PC with GrandView.

Framework

Framework is one of my favorite programs and the program I have used most often for several years. Framework is an integrated, multifunction program whose backbone is an outline processor. Presented in a Macintosh-like environment, with pull-down menus and pop-up windows, any outline can contain a word processing document, another outline, a spreadsheet, a limited database, a graph, or a telecommunications session. It is a wonderful package that does almost everything you need. Unfortunately, neither the program nor its publisher were successful, and after Borland's purchase of Ashton-Tate, it appears that Framework, an idea before its time, will not be enhanced and will soon be too far out of the mainstream.

Word Processors with Outlining

Microsoft Word is the most complete word processing program for law offices, and the first one to offer a complete outline processor integrated with a comprehensive word processor. It offers footnotes, indices, laser printer support that is close to desktop publishing, and wonderful document assembly/merge features for assembling standard wills, contracts, and pleadings. The program also supports style sheets, which allow you to easily specify the font and printing style of headings at various levels. Since Word's headings are not as rigid, it is much easier to move text from a heading to the body of text and back than with a dedicated outliner.

Word for Windows, running under Microsoft Windows, and Word for the Mac make outline processing extremely easy. They can also read and write WordPerfect files. Lotus Ami Pro, another Windows-based word processor, implemented outlining in a way that is very similar to Word, and future versions of WordPerfect are expected to follow suit.

WordPerfect 5.1 has added the ability to move sections of an outline but not to collapse, expand, or zoom headings and text. The ABA Law Practice Management Section's WordPerfect Interest Group has been urging WordPerfect Corporation to incorporate these idea processing features into its products, and we hope that future versions of WordPerfect's otherwise wonderful program will do so.

While the results won't be as dynamic as with using GrandView or MORE, using the integrated outlining features in word processing packages makes it easier to work with secretaries and others in the firm who can't take the time to learn another program.

Others

Other programs to help you organize your thoughts are MaxThink, which goes far beyond a simple outline processor, and Lotus Symphony

Outliner Add-In. Acta is an excellent outliner for the Apple Macintosh.

OTHER USES OF IDEA PROCESSING

Project Management

Modern project management software offers outline-processing features or allows you to enter and organize all of the component parts of a task, such as the course of a litigation or the steps of a complex acquisition. You then link the steps together, assign resources (people and cash), and print out various reports, including PERT (program evaluation and review technique) charts. Symantec incorporates an outline-processing structure into its leading project management software, TimeLine, as does Microsoft's new Project for Windows and OS/2. Symantec has also released a simplified version of its project management software called On Target.

Idea Generators

Outline processors help you organize your information and ideas, and in the process they make it easier to be creative. However, they do not go as far as some specialized programs that help you generate new ideas. In theory, using these programs is like hiring a consultant who knows all the right questions to ask to help you come up with goals and with fresh ideas targeted to reach those goals.

The Idea Generator was designed by Gerard I. Nierenberg, author of *The Art of Creative Thinking*, which comes with the software. The program is interactive; it leads you through the creative process of describing your situation, listing your goals, describing the people involved and their goals, and coming up with fresh and creative ideas. It also includes a "notepad" for noting inspirations and some examples of metaphors. The program can assist you in looking at a problem from five points of view: optimist, pessimist, realist, dreamer, or parent. Idea Generator Plus is more structured than other programs, but can be quite helpful in approaching a problem creatively.

Idea Fisher is the most robust software tool for brainstorming. It includes a wide variety of tools, including an idea bank, an idea thesaurus, and a series of questions to help with problem solving. While not designed specifically for lawyers, the software can help them keep the creative process going.

Another favorite tool for lawyers is Max-Think, which is sort of a cross between an outliner and a creative-idea generator. In addition to the outlining functions, it includes a variety of other tools, such as "bin-sort" to sort random ideas and hypertext linking features to support the lawyer in the planning and problem-solving process. MaxThink, Inc. also offers other excellent tools for working with non-hierarchically organized knowledge, including TransText, for creating hypertext links between depositions and other text, and Houdini, for generalizing and abstracting from large amounts of information.

Negotiation Software

There are two excellent software tools available to help you organize your objectives and strategies in preparation for negotiations. While these can be tedious to use as you organize, the process is excellent, as there is no substitute for adequate preparation. The two products do not compete, but rather complement each other. The Art of Negotiating presents a series of questions and makes a recommendation as to how the negotiation should be approached. It includes Gerard Nierenberg's book, *The Compleat Negotiator*. Negotiator Pro, on the other hand, is a much broader, more flexible expert system. It helps you plan your approach in a more open way, putting on line the tactics and information one could only find in 50 separate books on negotiation.

Lawyers are hired to think creatively and solve problems. Using software to help you organize complex information and enhance your creativity will help you achieve better results and feel more in control.

PRODUCTS MENTIONED

Many of these programs are available from commercial software dealers at discounted prices. The addresses of the manufacturers are listed here for your convenience in the event you cannot find a particular program through a dealer.

Outline Processors

ThinkTank *(IBM PC and compatibles, Apple II, Apple Macintosh)*
MORE *(IBM PC and compatibles, Apple II, Apple Macintosh)*

GrandView *(IBM PC and compatibles, Apple II, Apple Macintosh)*
READY! *(IBM PC and compatibles)*

Symantec Corp.
10201 Torre Ave.
Cupertino, CA 95014
(800) 441-7234 or (408) 253-9600

Framework *(IBM PC and compatibles)*
Borland International
P.O. Box 660001
Scotts Valley, CA 95066
(800) 331-0877

Ami Pro *(IBM PC and compatibles—Windows and OS/2)*
Symphony Text Outliner Option *(IBM PC and compatibles)*
Lotus Manuscript *(IBM PC and compatibles)*
Lotus Development Corp.
161 First St.
Cambridge, MA 02142
(800) 343-5414

PC-Outline *(IBM PC and compatibles)*
Brown Bag Software
2155 S. Bascom Ave., Suite 105
Campbell, CA 95008
(800) 523-0764

StreamLine *(IBM PC and compatibles)*
TechnoLogics, Inc.
2 Sheridan Ln.
Littleton, MA 01460
(508) 486-8500

Fact Cruncher *(IBM PC and compatibles)*
Infostructures
P.O. Box 32617
Tucson, AZ 85751
Microsoft Word *(IBM PC and compatibles, Apple Macintosh)*

Microsoft Corp.
16011 N.E. 36th Way
Redmond, WA 97017
(800) 426-9400

Acta *(Apple Macintosh)*
Symmetry Corp.
761 E. University Dr.
Mesa, AZ 85203
(800) 624-2485

Idea Generators

Idea Generator *(IBM PC and compatibles)*
Experience in Software, Inc.
2000 Hearst, Suite 202
Berkeley, CA 94709-2176
(510) 644-0694

MaxThink *(IBM PC and compatibles, Apple
   Macintosh)*
Houdini *(IBM PC and compatibles, Apple
   Macintosh)*
TransText *(IBM PC and compatibles, Apple
   Macintosh)*
MaxThink, Inc.
2425-B Channing Way #592
Berkeley, CA 94707
(510) 540-5508

Negotiation Software

Art of Negotiation *(IBM PC and compatibles)*
Experience in Software, Inc.
2000 Hearst, Suite 202
Berkeley, CA 94709-2176
(510) 644-0694

Negotiator Pro *(IBM PC and compatibles,
   Apple Macintosh)*
Beacon Expert Systems, Inc.
35 Gardner Rd.
Brookline, MA 02146
(800) 448-3308, (617) 738-9300

Project Management

TimeLine *(IBM PC and compatibles)*
Symantec Corp. (see above)

Microsoft Project *(Windows & OS/2. IBM PC
   and compatibles)*
Microsoft Corp. (see above)

James A. Eidelman is an Ann Arbor, Michigan, lawyer and director of practice systems consulting with Automation Partners, Inc. He is a council member of the ABA's Section of Law Practice Management, chair of the Practice Systems Interest Group, and a popular speaker and author on computer applications for lawyers.

Digesting Depositions with Idea Processors

Marc S. Klein

> Marc S. Klein uses GrandView, a leading outlining program, to create deposition digests. In the past, most of us used word processors to accomplish this task. Klein offers another, possibly better way.

Litigation frequently generates volumes of deposition testimony. To cope with this enormous amount of information, lawyers have historically relied on deposition digests prepared by paralegals. In theory, these digests provide us with concise summaries of the testimony and enable us to rapidly locate key testimony within the transcripts. In reality, digests are often no better than the transcripts themselves.

This article addresses some of the limitations of traditional deposition digests prepared by paralegals. It then suggests that, as an alternative, lawyers may prepare their own deposition digests with outlining software, also known as *idea processors*. Deposition digests prepared by lawyers with an idea processor can be far superior to those prepared by paralegals. In addition, when you prepare your own deposition digests with an idea processor, you may acquire powerful new insights about your cases.

TRADITIONAL DEPOSITION DIGESTS

The preparation of a traditional deposition digest entails two distinct operations. First, the paralegal condenses the testimony. This task is relatively straightforward. The paralegal simply eliminates irrelevant or unnecessary testimony; paraphrases or quotes relevant testimony; and abbreviates terms.

Once the paralegal has condensed the testimony, he or she must arrange this information in accordance with some organizational principle. The most common is the sequential digest, which presents the summarized testimony in the order

matters were raised in the deposition. In other words, it simply provides a page-by-page summary of what each witness has said.

The utility of the sequential summary is limited because it does not provide us with any index to the testimony. To find a particular line of testimony (for example, when and where the parties signed the contract), you must read through the digest. Moreover, you may need to read the entire digest to make sure that you have seen all references to a particular issue.

One alternative to the sequential digest is the topical digest, which presents a condensed version of deposition testimony arranged by subject matter, rather than simply in the order it arose in the deposition. To prepare a topical digest, a paralegal will typically label sheets of paper with topic or subtopic headings and summarize the testimony on those discrete sheets of paper as he or she proceeds through the transcript. With the deposition testimony digested in this fashion, you can review all of the statements made by the same witness on a particular topic or compare what several witnesses have said about the same subject.

Unfortunately, a topical digest can be time-consuming to prepare. For each entry, the paralegal must stop and think, "How do I categorize this testimony?" As the work progresses and the topics (and subtopics) multiply, the work slows down. It can also be tedious and cumbersome. The paralegal must either write the entries on each sheet in longhand, type them (moving sheets in and out of the typewriter with every new subject), or constantly jump from screen to screen in the word processor.

47

Working directly with an idea processor, lawyers can create their own deposition summaries. These summaries will have all of the advantages of a topical digest. Moreover, lawyers will produce superior digests and broaden their understanding of the case.

INTRODUCTION TO IDEA PROCESSORS

In some ways, idea processors resemble word processing and database programs; however, idea processors work by structuring information in outline form. For purposes of this discussion, I will focus on GrandView 2.0, the premier idea processor now on the market. There are several other good idea processors (including MORE, MaxThink, READY, and PC-Outline). These idea processors share common operating premises and capabilities.

In GrandView, like most other leading idea processors, files consist of two primary elements: documents and headlines. A document in the idea processor is nothing more than free-form text; it may be as short as one word but is often a paragraph or more. A headline in the idea processor is like a newspaper headline; it is designed to signal the reader about the subject matter of the document that follows. Thus, headlines in an idea processor reflect the central idea of the information in the documents subordinate to them.

USING AN IDEA PROCESSOR TO DIGEST DEPOSITIONS

Three steps are involved in digesting a deposition with an idea processor: you must summarize the testimony, label it, and contextualize it. Each of these steps will enhance your understanding of the case.

When you summarize testimony with an idea processor, you are required to comprehend the testimony and articulate its meaning. By doing this personally, rather than delegating the task, you will acquire a far greater understanding of the testimony and its impact in the case.

When you compose a headline, you label the idea—the summarized testimony—reflected in your document. The labeling process is valuable because it requires you to think about the idea you are labeling, to stop and ask, "What are these words about? What is the main idea here? Why am I noting this testimony? What shall I call this chunk of testimony?" The very process of label-

ing these units of information will reveal many insights.

Finally, after summarizing and labeling the ideas, you must place them in context. They must be slotted within the grand scheme of the outline. This process itself often will reveal connections between points in the case—relationships between lines of testimony—that you might never have otherwise observed.

Thus, digesting a deposition with an idea processor is not simply a means to an end. The process is not simply mechanical, it is also intellectual and will not only produce a superior deposition digest but powerful new insights as well.

THE ADVANTAGES OF AN IDEA PROCESSOR

An idea processor like GrandView enables you to perform the following tasks while digesting a deposition transcript:

Structure the Information

Depositions often proceed in a disorganized or random fashion. Indeed, good deposition technique calls for a certain degree of randomness to keep the witness off guard. In digesting a deposition transcript with an idea processor, you can take the ideas that arrive in random order and process them into a logical structure.

The first headline in an outline is termed the *summit* or *home* headline and reflects the central idea of the entire outline. With a deposition digest, for example, the summit headline might be "Deposition of Ralph Smith." The summit headline should have subordinate headlines which, in turn, may have subordinate headlines. (See Figure 2.1.)

A well-constructed outline not only indexes the information in the digest, it also provides an intellectual framework for the balance of the case. With this framework in hand, you can more easily prepare for other depositions, draft briefs, and prepare for trial.

Cope with Spontaneous Information and Ideas

The idea processor enables you to cope with unexpected information and ideas immediately, as and when they emerge.

Testimony concerning one issue is often found amidst testimony concerning another.

FIGURE 2.1

With idea processors, information that arrives in random order is placed into a logical, hierarchical structure. In this illustration, the summit headline, shown as I, captures the main idea of the entire document (a digest of the Deposition of Ralph Smith). Below it are five subordinate headlines that serve as the main categories for the information in the deposition. The plus signs to the left of the headlines indicate that they have at least one subordinate headline of their own hidden from view.

```
┌C:\GV\SMITH_DP════════════════════════════════INS═══════6k═══1┐
| + I. DEPOSITION OF RALPH SMITH                                |
| +    A. Background                                            |
| +    B. Contract Negotiation & Execution                      |
| +    C. Construction Process                                  |
| +    D. Closing Date                                          |
| +    E. Miscellaneous                                         |
|                                                               |
|                                                               |
|                                                               |
|                                                               |
|                                                               |
|                                                               |
|                                                               |
|                                                               |
|                                                               |
|                                                               |
|                                                               |
|                                                               |
|                                                               |
|                                                               |
|                                                               |
|                                                      ═1.17"═  |
└───────────────────────────────────────────────────────────────┘
     Press F10 for Menus; Ctrl-Return to Create a New Headline; F1 for Help     279k
```

With an idea processor, you can quickly create a headline, summarize the testimony concerning the new issue in a document attached to the headline, and return to the larger topic addressed by the deponent. (You need not decide immediately where the discrete point fits within the broader scheme of things. It can be moved quite easily later.)

In a deposition, you may ask a builder whether the purchasers authorized the builder to place the fireplace someplace other than where shown on the architect's plans. The builder could simply answer yes or no. But he might say, "Yes, and by the way, they told me to move it the same day they told me to add a skylight to the master bedroom" (another feature not shown on the plans). In digesting this answer, you would want to note the builder's answer with respect to the fireplace under the fireplace subject heading. But you might also want to record the information volunteered about the skylight. With the idea processor, you could create that note immediately and move it to an appropriate place in the outline later.

While engaged in summarizing testimony, you can also note ideas about trial issues or matters for further consideration (perhaps collecting these ideas at a separate place in the outline). While digesting with an outline processor, for example, I may suddenly think of information needed from other witnesses on a related point. I will usually note it under a subsection of the final section of the outline. (See Figure 2.2.)

After I have prepared a digest, I separately print out the miscellaneous headline (and all information subordinate to that headline) and keep the printout with my to-do list.

Focus on the Details

Another important feature of the idea processor is its ability to collapse and expand headlines and documents at will. (See Figure 2.3.)

This feature of the idea processor gives it a major advantage over outlines prepared with word processors. GrandView permits you to focus on one discrete point at a time.

FIGURE 2.2

Idea processors enable you to focus on and complete a discrete item and then step back to review the entire work. In this frame, you enter a miscellaneous note (four levels deep in the outline) about information you need to obtain later in the case. After you have completed the entry, you collapse the outline and hide this note while working on other points.

```
┌C:\GV\EXAMPLE═══════════════════════════════════════════INS═══════6k══1┐
|+ I. DEPOSITION OF RALPH SMITH                                          |
|+    A. Background                                                      |
|-    B. Contract Negotiation & Execution                                |
|+    C. Construction Process                                            |
|+    D. Closing Date                                                    |
|+    E. Miscellaneous                                                   |
|+       1. Information to Obtain from Other Witnesses                    |
|-          a) Electrician                                               |
|-          b) Plumber                                                   |
|                                                                        |
|                Ask plumber whether builder informed him of buyers' need for |
|             special sink.                                              |
|                                                                        |
|                                                                        |
|-          c) Mason                                                     |
|-          d) Mortgage Company                                          |
|-       2. Improper Objections for Motion                               |
|-       3. Documents to Review                                          |
|+       4. Legal Issues                                                 |
|-       5. Trial Preparation                                            |
|                                                                        |
|                                                    ═══════════1.17"═══ |
└════════════════════════════════════════════════════════════════════════┘
     Press F10 for Menus; Ctrl-Return to Create a New Headline; F1 for Help   264k
```

Comprehending the Whole

Both the collapsing and hoisting features of GrandView allow you to shift instantly from a discrete point to the big picture. It is often very useful to step back from the small details and view things from an holistic vantage point.

The ability to collapse and expand headlines and documents at will gives the idea processor a major advantage over outlines prepared with most word processors. The idea processor permits you to freely examine any part of your work, to whatever level of depth may be desired, without the clutter of what remains. With paper or documents in a word processor, it's all there and it won't go away. Indeed, to take a "grand view" of what is on paper, you may be required to prepare an outline. (After I have written the first draft of a brief, I frequently outline it just to comprehend what I have attempted to say, to make sure my ideas flow logically, and to ensure that I have actually covered all the bases.)

To get a sense of where a deponent has taken me, I often collapse the entire outline and then expand it by levels. I first review the main head-lines (reflecting the major issues involved in the case). I then expand to the next levels one step at a time to get a sense of the depth of the discussion pertaining to each of the major issues. In this respect, the headlines take on a hypertext quality. To further explore a particular point, you need only position the cursor on the pertinent headline. With one keystroke, further layers of information—subordinate headlines or documents—are revealed.

With GrandView, you are not compelled to forfeit many of the powerful features of today's advanced word processors. For example:

Table of Contents

When an outline is complete, the program automatically generates a table of contents. (See Figure 2.4.)

You may select the level of detail to be reflected in the table of contents. (If the work is many levels deep, it may be desirable to limit the number of levels.) With this table of contents, you will be able to lay hands on any line of testimony very quickly.

FIGURE 2.3

By placing the cursor on a headline and pressing the + key, you expand the outline to reveal subordinate headlines. By pressing [ALT-PLUS], you further expand the outline to reveal documents. By pressing [F5], you can shift into DOCU-MENT VIEW (second frame), where you can truly focus on just the point at hand.

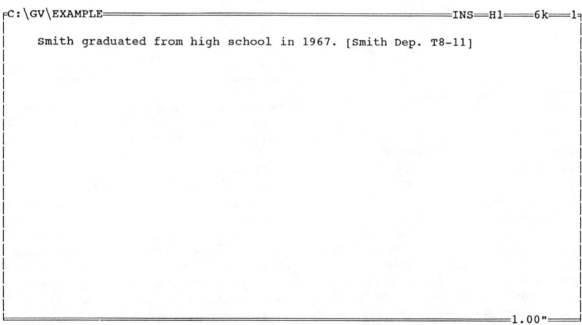

```
┌C:\GV\EXAMPLE═══════════════════════════════════INS═══════5k═══1┐
│+ I. DEPOSITION OF RALPH SMITH                                   │
│+    A. Background                                               │
│-       1. Education                                             │
│                                                                 │
│               Smith graduated from high school in 1967. [Smith Dep. T8-11]
│                                                                 │
│                                                                 │
│-       2. Experience in Building                                │
│-       3. Formation of Smith Builders, Inc.                     │
│-    B. Contract Negotiation & Execution                         │
│+    C. Construction Process                                     │
│+    D. Closing Date                                             │
│+    E. Miscellaneous                                            │
│                                                                 │
│                                                                 │
│                                                                 │
│                                                                 │
│                                                                 │
│                                                                 │
│                                                                 │
│                                                                 │
│                                                                 │
└══════════════════════════════════════════════════1.17"═══┘
      Press F10 for Menus; Ctrl-Return to Create a New Headline; F1 for Help   265k


┌C:\GV\EXAMPLE═══════════════════════════════════INS═H1═══6k═══1┐
│                                                                 │
│   Smith graduated from high school in 1967. [Smith Dep. T8-11]  │
│                                                                 │
│                                                                 │
│                                                                 │
│                                                                 │
│                                                                 │
│                                                                 │
│                                                                 │
│                                                                 │
│                                                                 │
│                                                                 │
│                                                                 │
│                                                                 │
│                                                                 │
│                                                                 │
│                                                                 │
└══════════════════════════════════════════════════1.00"═══┘
      Press F10 for Menus; Ctrl-Return to Create a New Headline; F1 for Help   264k
```

FIGURE 2.4
GrandView generates a table of contents automatically when printing. You may define the number of levels to be shown in the table of contents and, as well, whether the items should be indented in accordance with their levels in the outline.

```
DEPOSITION OF RALPH SMITH ...................................  1
    Background ..............................................  1
        Education ..........................................  1
        Experience in Building .............................  1
        Formation of Smith Builders, Inc. .................  1
    Contract Negotiation & Execution .......................  1
        Date of Negotiation ...............................  1
        Date of Execution .................................  1
        Place of Execution ................................  1
    Construction Process ...................................  1
        Authorized Changes ................................  1
        Unauthorized Changes ..............................  1
        Specific Changes ..................................  1
        Architect & Plans .................................  1
            Agreement on Initial Plans ....................  1
            Smith's Reliance on Plans .....................  1
            Role of Architect in Changes ..................  1
    Closing Date ...........................................  1
        Original Negotiations .............................  1
            Date in Contract ..............................  1
        Agreements to Extend During .......................  1
    Miscellaneous ..........................................  1
        Information to Obtain from Other ..................  1
            Electrician ...................................  1
            Plumber .......................................  1
            Mason .........................................  1
            Mortgage Company ..............................  1
        Improper Objections for Motion ....................  1
        Documents to Review ...............................  1
        Legal Issues ......................................  1
            Waiver of Contract Terms by ...................  1
        Trial Preparation .................................  1
```

Windows

With GrandView, you can load up to nine outlines at one time and switch between them with one keystroke. GrandView allows you to display several outlines at the same time through tiling or overlapping windows. (See Figure 2.5.)

As I digest a deposition, I will often keep open one or two other outlines. (These other outlines may or may not relate to the case at hand. For example, I keep my general to-do outline open to cope with spontaneous thoughts about my other active matters.) In this manner, I can record my ideas on other issues as soon as they come to me.

Find and Replace

GrandView can search headlines and documents for each occurrence of a word or phrase (to a maximum 59-character string.) You can use this feature to locate text in the outline or edit text by automatically replacing words or phrases with others.

Unfortunately, GrandView limits the search to one particular string of words, and does not permit Boolean searches available with full-text programs (like ZyIndex). The FIND feature is useful nonetheless to locate a particular reference in the transcript. In larger cases where I also use a full-text database, I have printed my outlines to an ASCII file and actually loaded the outlines in the database for searching along with the full text of the transcripts.

Spell Checking

GrandView has a powerful spell checker that presents a menu of potentially correct spellings

FIGURE 2.5
With GrandView, you may have up to nine outlines open at one time. They can be placed on the screen through windows of different types. In these two frames, two outlines are shown in vertical and horizontal windows. Note that the active outlines are numbered. To jump from one to the other, you simply enter [ALT-(Number)].

```
┌C:\GV\EXAMPLE══════════════════1┐ ┌C:\GV\TO_DOEX═══════════════════2┐
|+ I. DEPOSITION OF RALPH SMITH   | |+ I. TO DO                       |
|+    A. Background               | |+    A. BUSINESS                 |
|-       1. Education             | |+       1. TOXIC TORT CASES      |
|-       2. Experience in Building| |+          a) Expert Development |
|-       3. Formation of Smith    | |-             1) Read Epidemiology|
|           Builders, Inc.        | |                 Articles        |
|     B. Contract Negotiation &   | |-          b) Bill Maryland Cases|
|        Execution                | |+       2. COMPANY/NEW MATTER (JONES)|
|+    C. Construction Process     | |-          a) Reschedule Deposition|
|-       1. Authorized Changes    | |-          b) Interview President|
|-       2. Unauthorized Changes  | |-          c) Amend Counterclaim |
|-       3. Specific Changes      | |              (Property Retained)|
|+       4. Architect & Plans     | |+       3. BANK/SMITH            |
|-          a) Agreement on Initial| |-          a) Papers to Bank     |
|              Plans              | |+       4. COMPANY/EMPLOYMENT CASE|
|-          b) Smith's Reliance on| |+          a) Preparation for Trial|
|              Plans              | |+             1) Schedule Discovery|
|-          c) Role of Architect in| |-                a] Plaintiff Dep.|
|              Changes            | |                    Continuation |
|+    D. Closing Date             | |-                b] Contact Key Witnes|
|+       1. Original Negotiations | |+             2) Experts         |
└═══════════════════════1.17"═══┘ └═════════════════════════════════┘
```
        Press F10 for Menus; Ctrl-Return to Create a New Headline; F1 for Help   265k

```
┌C:\GV\EXAMPLE════════════════════════════════════INS══════5k══1┐
|+ I. DEPOSITION OF RALPH SMITH                                 |
|+    A. Background                                             |
|-       1. Education                                           |
|-       2. Experience in Building                              |
|-       3. Formation of Smith Builders, Inc.                   |
|-    B. Contract Negotiation & Execution                       |
|+    C. Construction Process                                   |
|-       1. Authorized Changes                                  |
|-       2. Unauthorized Changes                                |
|-       3. Specific Changes                                    |
└══════════════════════════════════════════════════1.17"══════┘
┌C:\GV\TO_DOEX════════════════════════════════════INS═════10k══2┐
|+ I. TO DO                                                     |
|+    A. BUSINESS                                               |
|+       1. TOXIC TORT CASES                                    |
|+          a) Expert Development                               |
|-             1) Read Epidemiology Articles                    |
|-          b) Bill Maryland Cases                              |
|+       2. COMPANY/NEW MATTER (JONES)                          |
|-          a) Reschedule Deposition                            |
|-          b) Interview President                              |
└═══════════════════════════════════════════════════════════════┘
```
        Press F10 for Menus; Ctrl-Return to Create a New Headline; F1 for Help   265k

in descending order of probability. I have found that, 9 times out of 10, the first choice presented by the program is the word that I intended.

Macros

The program has powerful macro capabilities along with a macro editor. In preparing a deposition digest, I designate [ALT-C] as my citation macro. Consequently, after summarizing a line of testimony, I insert the citation with one keystroke (e.g., "Smith Dep., 6/2/89, at ___"). I also have a macro ([ALT-S]) used to insert strategy considerations. By invoking this macro, the program proceeds to a new line, indents for a new paragraph, and inserts (in capital letters) STRATEGY CONSIDERATION. I also have macros to set up a block quote of testimony that I anticipate using for cross-examination at trial or later in a brief.

Importing and Exporting Files

With the import feature, GrandView allows you to incorporate files created with other programs. GrandView permits you to directly import files created with, among others, Q&A Write, WordPerfect, WordStar, ASCII, and some of the other leading idea processors. Moreover, Grand-View recognizes the outline commands of these programs. (I will frequently take someone else's outline created in WordPerfect and import the outline into GrandView.)

GrandView's export feature is even more useful. It permits you to transfer all or any part of an outline to a text file in one of these pro-

grams (or basic ASCII). You can elect to create an outline or simple text file in these programs. (When I write a brief or article now, I typically create my first draft in GrandView. Once I have the basic organization and text in place, I then export my outline to WordPerfect to prepare the final draft.)

Printing

GrandView's printing capabilities are impressive. The program comes with a substantial number of print drivers and hence supports a wide range of printers (including laser printers) and fonts (including italics, bold, compressed, and enlarged type).

CONCLUSION

A good deposition digest should reflect your thinking about the case at hand. It should summarize only testimony that you consider to be relevant and enable you to rapidly locate testimony in the deposition transcript by subject matter. It should be structured in a way that is consistent with your theories of the case.

The most effective way to create a good deposition digest is to use an idea processor. While creating a deposition digest with an idea processor will unquestionably take more of your time, that time will be well spent. It will result in a superior, far more useful digest, and the process itself will both focus and expand your thinking about the case.

Marc S. Klein graduated from Swarthmore College in 1976 and the University of Pennsylvania Law School in 1979. He is a partner with Sills Cummis Zuckerman Radin Tischman Epstein & Gross, P.A., Newark, New Jersey, and litigates claims involving computers and other advanced technology products, pharmaceutical products, and employment. He has written and lectured extensively concerning the lawyer's use of personal computers.

Managing Cases, Information, and Yourself with GrandView

Mark V. B. Partridge

Mark Partridge uses GrandView as a case management tool for his intellectual property litigation practice. In this article, he shows how GrandView's more sophisticated features, such as the ability to display information in different views and to link different outlines, give it the ability to function as a case and practice management tool.

GrandView is a powerful outlining program and my program of choice because it functions the way I do. Indeed, I would probably find it indispensable for its outlining features alone. In the days "before computer," I worked extensively from outlines etched on yellow pads. Now I build and use them faster and more effectively in GrandView. But GrandView offers much more than outlining. Its category and calendar features, together with its ability to sort, find, and gather information, make it a very useful tool for managing cases, notes, and activities.

I rely on GrandView every day in my practice, and find I am better organized and more efficient as a result. GrandView also helps me appear more knowledgeable and attentive to clients and others by providing quick access to information and by facilitating faster preparation of memos, correspondence, and other documents.

Before going further, a caveat: I am not a computer expert or techno-whiz. In fact, I have only been using a computer in my practice for about a year. If I can do it, you probably can, too.

PUTTING GRANDVIEW TO WORK: A TYPICAL DAY

I begin at breakfast (running the program from a notebook computer) by reviewing the TO-DO section of my main outline in outline view and moving the items I hope to handle that day

to the TODAY section. The basic outline is shown below in Figure 2.6.

Pressing [F4] switches GrandView to CALENDAR VIEW. This displays a calendar on the left side of the screen with today's date highlighted. The right-hand side of the screen lists all assignments made to that date. By moving the cursor in the calendar, I can check my schedule and select additional things that require attention that day. At this time I also add notes and additional items under the TODAY headline.

Once in the office, I may begin by discussing pending matters with my associates. Pressing [F3] moves from outline view to CATEGORY VIEW. In a block on the upper left of the screen appears a scrollable list of the categories applicable to the outline. In the upper right is a list of the assignments made to the highlighted category. To review matters with associate MTM, I highlight the assignment category, then scroll to MTM. All headings assigned to MTM are displayed at the bottom of the screen. The display can also include additional categories as shown in Figure 2.7.

I note in the appropriate headline that I discussed a matter with MTM and enter a new headline to indicate the action we agreed upon. The new headline will appear in the same section of the main outline as the headline appearing above it in the CATEGORY VIEW. While discussing assignments with MTM, I can also delete unnecessary entries from the MTM cat-

FIGURE 2.6 Basic Outline

Outline	Client	Matter	Date
+ I. THINGS TO ACCOMPLISH			
+ A. TODAY			
– 1. Arrange depositions in Mercury.	Acme	Mercury	
– 2. Interrogatory answers due in Mercury on 10-10-92.	Acme	Mercury	10-10-92
– 3. Call all witnesses in Electra to confirm appearance at trial.	Bradford	Electra	
– 4. Call Collins about settlement offer.	Bradford	Electra	
– 5. Dispositive motions due 11-02-92 in Electra. Check status of motions with CEP	Bradford	Electra	11-2-92
– 6. Pretrial order due 11-9-92 in Electra.	Bradford	Electra	11-9-92
– 7. Draft settlement agreement in Samson.	Crane	Samson	
– 8. Call MTM about article.	Firm	Associate	
+ B. RELATED FILES			
+ C. PENDING MATTERS			
– 1. ABA committee meeting 10-27-92 noon	ABA	Committee	10-27-92
– 2. Have MTM prepare document requests in Electra	Bradford	Electra	
– 3. Trial begins 11-16-92 in Electra	Bradford	Electra	11-16-92
– 4. Pretrial conference in Samson, 4:15 P.M., 10-15-92	Crane	Samson	10-15-92
– 5. Meeting with John Thompson about Hiring, 10:00 a.m., 10-10-92	Firm	Hiring	10-10-92
– 6. Partner's meeting, 3:30 p.m. 10-11-92	Firm	Partner	10-11-92
+ II. DAILY RECORD			
– A. UNBILLED			
– B. BILLED			
+ III. MISCELLANEOUS			
+ A. INFORMATION			
– 1. Thompson office phone:	Firm	Partner	
– 2. MTM home phone: 312-666-6666	Firm	Associate	
– 3. Acme address: 252 N. Wacker Drive, Suite 2000, Chicago, Il 60606.	Acme	Mercury	

FIGURE 2.7 Assignment Categories in GrandView

———— Categories ————	———— Assignments ————	
Date	CEP	
Priority	*MTM	
Activity		
*Assignment		
Client		
Matter		

	Client	Matter
■ Call MTM about article.	Firm	Associate
■ Arrange depositions in Mercury. Assign to MTM	Acme	Mercury
■ Have MTM prepare document requests in Electra	Bradford	Electra
■ MTM home phone: 312-666-6666	Firm	Associate

FIGURE 2.8 Revisions Made to Assignments

```
 ──────────── Categories ────────────         ──────── Assignments ────────
  Date                                   CEP
  Priority                               *MTM
  Activity
 *Assignment
  Client
  Matter

 ─────────────────────────────────────────────────────────────────────────
  ■  Depositions tenatively set in Mercury for 2-20-92 at our offices.  MTM
     will arrange.
  ■  Arrange depositions in Mercury. Assign to MTM. Discussed with her on
     2-10-1992
  ■  Have MTM prepare document requests in Electra. Discussed with MTM
     2-10-1992
  ■  MTM will prepare document request drafts in Electra for review on 2-17-92
  ■  Call MTM about article. Discussed with MTM 2-10-1992.
  ■  MTM will have article outline 2-24-92


 ─────────────────────────────────────────────────────────────────────────
```

FIGURE 2.9 TODAY Section Revised

Outline	Client	Matter	Date
+ I. THINGS TO ACCOMPLISH			
+ A. TODAY			
− 1. Draft settlement agreement in Samson.	Crane	Samson	
− 2. Do research on preemption issue of Electra brief.	Bradford	Electra	
− 3. Pretrial order due 11-9-92 in Electra.	Bradford	Electra	11-9-92
− 4. Dispositive motions due 11-02-92 in Electra. Check status of motions with CEP.	Bradford	Electra	11-2-92
− 5. Call all witnesses in Electra to confirm appearance at trial. Assign to CEP	Bradford	Electra	
− 6. Call Collins about settlement offer.	Bradford	Electra	
− 7. Interrogatory answers due in Mercury on 10-10-92. Call client to check on status.	Acme	Mercury	10-10-92

egory assignment. Using **[ALT-DELETE]** in CATEGORY VIEW removes the heading from the category assignment without deleting it from the main outline. After another cup of coffee I review the TODAY section of the outline. I press **[F11]** to send completed items to the BILL section and other items discussed with MTM to the PENDING section. Figure 2.8 shows the revisions made to the MTM assignments after our conversation. Figure 2.9 shows the TODAY section revised after my conversation with MTM.

At that point, an important client calls with a new outrage. Its chief competitor is infringing the trade dress of its best-selling product. I make a note of the call under the TODAY section of the outline, then press **[F5]** to switch to document view. This brings me to a blank page that functions as a standard word processor, that is, without GrandView's automatic outlining features. I press a macro to bring up a memo template, then enter my notes about the call. After the call, I can transfer the rough memorandum to my secretary, who puts it in a format suitable for the client. Later I will edit it further and send

FIGURE 2.10 Confirming Memo of Conversation

```
                  M E M O R A N D U M

To:       Edward K. Johnson
From:     Mark V.B. Partridge
Date:     2-10-1992
Re:       Infringement of Delta trade dress by Diana Agroproducts

CC:       File
```

Discussed potential infringement action with Mr. Johnson. Diana has just introduced a directly competitive product using a confusingly similar trade dress. Mr. Johnson wants us to investigate, obtain product samples, and begin preparations for seeking a preliminary injunction.
　　　　We will take the following action:
　　　　　　1. Run computer search for business information on Diana.
　　　　　　2. Send paralegal to local store to obtain the products of Delta, Diana and third parties.
　　　　　　3. Review jurisdictional basis for suing Diana in Chicago.
　　　　　　4. Draft preliminary injunction papers.
　　　　The matter will be assigned to LJP and CVP.

FIGURE 2.11 Revised TODAY and BILL Sections

	Outline	Client	Matter	Date
+	I. THINGS TO ACCOMPLISH			
+	A. TODAY			
–	1. Do research on preemption issue of Electra brief.	Acme	Electra	
–	2. Call from Ed Johnson at Delta about new infringement action against Diana Agroproducts Inc	Delta	Diana	
+	B. RELATED FILES			
+	C. PENDING MATTERS			
+	II. DAILY RECORD			
+	A. UNBILLED			
–	1. Attention to summary judgment in Electra. 2-10-1992	Acme	Electra	2-10-92
–	2. Discussed status of summary judgment motion in Electra with CEP. Draft promised 10-27-92.	Acme	Electra	2-10-92
–	3. Attention to pretrial order in Electra. 2-10-1992	Acme	Electra	2-10-92
–	4. Call client to check on status of Interrogatory answers in Mercury. Done 2-10-1992	Acme	Mercury	2-10-92
–	5. Arrange depositions in Mercury. Assign to MTM. Discussed with her on 2-10-1992	Acme	Mercury	2-10-92
–	6. Call Collins about settlement offer. Discussed settlement of Electra with Collins. He will check with client and get back.	Bradford	Electra	2-10-92
–	7. Call all witnesses in Electra to confirm appearance at trial. Assign to CEP. Discussed with CEP 2-10-1992.	Bradford	Electra	2-10-92
–	8. Draft settlement agreement in Samson. Reviewed, revised and sent to client 2-10-1992.	Crane	Samson	2-10-92
–	9. Call MTM about article. Discussed with MTM 2-10-1992.	Firm	Associate	2-10-92

FIGURE 2.12 Report of a Case Showing Date and Activity Sorted by Date

```
A. BRADFORD v. ELECTRA ELECTRICAL
   SUPPLY CO.

   1. Call Collins about settlement          Call
      offer.  Discussed settlement of
      Electra with Collins.  He will
      check with client and get back.

   2. CEP will call all witnesses in         Call
      Electra.

   3. Do research on preemption issue        Research
      of Electra brief.

   4. Attention to pretrial order in     2-10-92
      Electra. 2-10-1992

   5. Attention to summary judgment in   2-10-92
      Electra. 2-10-1992

   6. Call all witnesses in Electra to  2-10-92  Call, Trial
      confirm appearance at trial.
      Assign to CEP. Discussed with CEP
      2-10-1992.

   7. Have MTM prepare document          2-10-92
      requests in Electra. Discussed
      with MTM 2-10-1992

   8. MTM will prepare document request 2-17-92
      drafts in Electra for review on
      2-17-92

   9. Assigned first draft of Electra   2-20-92  Draft
      pretrial order to CVP. draft
      promised 2-20-92.

  10. Discussed status of summary       10-27-92 Motion, Draft
      judgment motion in Electra with
      CEP.  Draft promised 10-27-92.

  11. Dispositive motions due 11-02-92  11-2-92
      in Electra.

  12. Pretrial order due 11-9-92 in     11-9-92
      Electra.

  13. Trial begins 11-16-92 in Electra  11-16-92 Trial
```

it to our client as a confirming memo of our conversation and proposed action. (See Figure 2.10.) Once completed, the memo can be displayed as part of the main outline or hidden and retrieved with a keystroke.

As the day proceeds, I try to get to the rest of the TO-DO items on the TODAY list, review the mail, making notes in the outline, and deal with phone calls and meetings. My TODAY list is revised along the way, with completed or new items moved to the appropriate place in the main outline. I use a macro to date completed items, change priority to DONE, and send the item to the unbilled section of the outline. By midafternoon,

the TODAY and BILL sections appear as shown in Figure 2.11.

As the day ends, I have a chance to focus specifically on trial preparation in the Electra case. I keep the record of daily activities concerning it and other cases as part of my main outline. Using CATEGORY VIEW, I can focus specifically on past or future events in the case, and can print out a report organized according to category. Figure 2.12 is a report of the case showing date and activity sorted by date. I edit a version of Figure 2.12 to send to the client and to the others on the case so we can make further plans.

After reviewing the dates in the Electra case,

FIGURE 2.13 Time Sheet

I. TIME SHEET - MVBP

   A. February 10, 1992

1. Attention to discovery in the Mercury case; telephone conference with client re interrogatory answers.	Acme	Mercury	1.5
2. Attention to discovery, summary judgment, trial preparation and settlement in the Electra case; telephone conference with Mr. Collins.	Bradford	Electra	4.5
3. Review and revise settlement agreement in Samson; preparation of correspondence.	Crane	Samson	0.5
4. Telephone conference with Mr. Johnson re potential infringement action against Diana Agroproducts.	Delta	Diana	2.0

I turn to the Electra CASE NOTEBOOK outline, which is linked to the main outline where the case name appears in the FILE section, and is quickly called up by moving the cursor to the case name and pressing **[CTRL-GRAY PLUS]** (plus key on numeric keypad). To prepare for upcoming depositions, I switch to CATEGORY VIEW so that I can print lists of all exhibits and of all references in the notebook to the scheduled deponents. I also switch to CALENDAR VIEW to print a chronology of facts and documents. Finally, I complete and print the deposition outline I have been working on for the past few days.

The last activity of the day before leaving the office is preparation of a daily time sheet for billing. In the main outline I move to the BILL section of the main outline, use a macro to change the column display of categories to client, matter, and time, and sort by client and matter. Personal and nonbillable entries are deleted or moved to another section using **[F11]**, depending on whether a record of the matter is useful for future reference. I press **[ALT-J]** to join related headlines into one, then edit the text and switch to the category column to enter times. Another macro lets me format and print the suboutline as a time sheet as shown in Figure 2.13.

The train trip home gives me a chance to review advance sheets and update my REFERENCE FILE. I also begin an outline for a preliminary injunction brief in the Diana matter. **[ALT-F]** lets me search and mark all headings in the REFERENCE FILE that include a reference to preliminary injunction. **[ALT-G]** gathers the marked headings and copies them under one heading, which can then be cut and pasted to a new outline to prepare the brief. I save the new outline in a new CASE NOTEBOOK dedicated to *Delta v. Diana* just as the train reaches my station. Once at home, I press **[ALT-B]**, and GrandView cooks dinner and puts the kids to bed.

THINGS IT DOESN'T DO

Well, GrandView doesn't actually cook dinner or put the kids to bed. But other than that, my typical day is not a fantasy. There are, however, some features not in GrandView that I would like to see in the next update.

GrandView's handling of dates would be much enhanced if it could automatically recognize dates and assign them to the date category when they are entered in a heading. You can set GrandView to do so with the assignment rules, but the process is tedious. A macro can also be created that dates headlines and the date category, but that adds some extra time and keystrokes to the process. I think the problem might be easily solved (from an end-user's point of view) if the assignment rules in GrandView accepted wildcards.

Lawyers are constantly faced with the need to schedule actions or deadlines 15, 30, 60, or 90 days from a given date but not falling on a weekend or legal holiday. GrandView does not provide a method for assigning dates in that fashion, leaving us to count dates for ourselves.

I wish GrandView had a notepad that could pop up over the current outline. I often have random thoughts or information arise while working in an outline but don't have time at that moment to find the right spot for the entry. The problem can be solved by using other programs, such as InfoSelect or Instant Recall, in conjunction with GrandView, but it would be nice to have it all in one program.

Another feature I'd like to see is the ability to calculate totals of figures in a category. When doing billing reports, for example, it would be useful if GrandView could be set to print a sum at the end of a column of time segments.

Given how useful the program as a whole is, the lack of these features is a small matter. GrandView does much that fits my practice, and the more I learn to use it instead of some of the other computer and noncomputer tools available to me, the more organized and efficient I feel.

CREATING YOUR OWN MANAGEMENT SYSTEM IN GRANDVIEW

The organizational strategy I use involves several related GrandView outlines:

- TO-DO list, where I schedule activities, list matters to be accomplished, record daily activities, organize time sheets for billing, and monitor matters delegated to others.
- CASE NOTEBOOKS, where I organize trial preparation, discovery, documents, and settlement negotiations, and assemble the information needed for pretrial orders, summary judgment motions, and final trial preparation.
- RESEARCH FILE, where I keep notes on decisions and articles that may later prove useful in my area of practice.

TO-DO List

The heart of the system is a TO-DO list outline, which combines my calendar, reminders, general information, and a history of all my activities. I could, of course, keep a separate outline for each pending matter, but I find it more useful to have one main outline that covers all cases and activities.

The TO-DO list begins as a simple outline, including the names of pending cases, deadlines, appointments, etc. I also include general information, such as phone numbers and addresses, and an ongoing list of things to do.

The next step is to organize the entries into categories. GrandView lets you build categories of information, assign outline entries, or *headlines*, to appropriate categories, then sort or view headlines by category. You can assign key words in headlines to a particular category by pressing [F2]. GrandView can be set to learn the assignments you make manually and to apply the same assignments to future entries containing the same key word. You can also teach GrandView to recognize that certain key words are associated with particular assignments: the appearance of *Hera* in a headline may always mean the client is *Delta* and the matter is *Diana*, for example. Perhaps most significant is that categories and assignments can be modified or created at any time, and re-applied to the existing outline, as new ideas or needs emerge. You don't have to get it right or think of every possibility the first time. The process is easy. It takes longer to explain than to do.

By default, GrandView has two preset categories: DATE and PRIORITY. The additional categories I find useful for managing cases and my daily schedule are:

- Activity (e.g., meeting, deadline, call, deposition).
- Assignment (names or initials of persons to whom I have delegated certain tasks).
- Client.
- Matter.
- Person (the names of clients, witnesses, opposing counsel, etc.).
- Information (for phone numbers, addresses, birthdays, etc.).
- Time (for appointment times and billing).

Figure 2.14 shows the TO-DO list with assignments to the client, matter, and date categories displayed in columns. GrandView will display up to three columns of categories in an outline, or all

FIGURE 2.14 TO-DO List

Outline	Client	Matter	Date
+ I. Let's Get Organized!			
+ A. Pending Matters			
- 1. Interrogatory answers due in Mercury on 10-10-93	Acme	Mercury	10-10-92
- 2. Pretrial conference in Samson, 4:15 P.M., 10-15-93	Crane	Samson	10-15-92
- 3. Meeting with John Thompson about Hiring, 10:00 a.m., 10-10-92	Firm	Hiring	10-10-92
- 4. Trial begins 11-16-92 in Electra	Bradford	Electra	11-16-92
- 5. Dispositive motions due 11-02-92 in Electra	Bradford	Electra	11-2-92
- 6. Pretrial order due 11-9-92 in Electra	Bradford	Electra	11-9-92
- 7. ABA committee meeting 10-27-92 noon	ABA	Committee	10-27-92
- 8. Acme address: 252 N. Wacker Drive, Suite 2000, Chicago, Il 60606.	Acme	Mercury	
- 9. Thompson office phone: 312-555-5555	Firm	Partner	
- 10. MTM home phone: 312-666-6666	Firm	Associate	
- 11. Arrange depositions in Mercury	Acme	Mercury	

FIGURE 2.15 Outline Headings Sorted by Client and Date

Outline	Client	Matter	Date
+ I. Let's Get Organized!			
+ A. Pending Matters			
- 1. ABA committee meeting 10-27-92 noon	ABA	Committee	10-27-92
- 2. Acme address: 252 N. Wacker Drive, Suite 2000, Chicago, Il 60606.	Acme	Mercury	
- 3. Arrange depositions in Mercury	Acme	Mercury	
- 4. Interrogatory answers due in Mercury on 10-10-93	Acme	Mercury	10-10-92
- 5. Have MTM prepare document requests in Electra	Bradford	Electra	
- 6. Call Collins about settlement offer	Bradford	Electra	
- 7. Call all witnesses in Electra to confirm appearance at trial.	Bradford	Electra	
- 8. Dispositive motions due 11-02-92 in Electra	Bradford	Electra	11-2-92
- 9. Pretrial order due 11-9-92 in Electra	Bradford	Electra	11-9-92
- 10. Trial begins 11-16-92 in Electra	Bradford	Electra	11-16-92
- 11. Draft settlement agreement in	Crane	Samson	

the categories at the bottom of the screen. Menu commands can be used to change the column display of categories, or you may speed up the process with simple macros.

GrandView will automatically sort information on two categories. Once you create categories and assignments, you can, for example, reorganize your list by client and matter, date, or whatever is appropriate to your needs. Figure 2.15 shows the outline headings sorted by client and date.

A simple list makes a satisfactory TO-DO list outline, but it can become unwieldy as the number of entries increases. I prefer to divide my list into five main sections:

- TODAY, for things I want to complete on a given day.

FIGURE 2.16 The Organization of Typical Entries in the Outline

Outline		Client	Matter	Date
+ I. THINGS TO ACCOMPLISH				
+ A. TODAY				
– 1. Call Collins about settlement offer.		Bradford	Electra	
– 2. Draft settlement agreement in Samson.		Crane	Samson	
– B. RELATED FILES				
+ C. PENDING MATTERS				
– 1. ABA committee meeting 10-27-92 noon		ABA	Committee	10-27-92
– 2. Trial begins 11-16-92 in Electra		Bradford	Electra	11-16-92
+ II. DAILY RECORD				
– A. UNBILLED				
– B. BILLED				
+ III. MISCELLANEOUS				
+ A. INFORMATION				
– 1. Thompson office phone: 312-555-5555		Firm	Partner	

- FILES, where I list CASE NOTEBOOKS and other files that are linked to the TO-DO list outline for quick access.
- PENDING MATTERS, for ongoing actions and pending dates.
- DAILY RECORD, where I keep a record of completed matters and daily activities further divided between UNBILLED and BILLED; and finally,
- INFORMATION, where I keep—you guessed it—miscellaneous information.

Each of these headings can be named. Sub-headlines can then be sent to the appropriate category using the **[F11]** key. Figure 2.16 shows how entries can be organized under appropriate headlines within the outline.

Case Notebook

The second key component of the system consists of CASE NOTEBOOK files for specific cases. I keep assignments, deadlines, and daily activities in the main outline. The notebook outlines are used to list facts, legal contentions, documents, exhibits, and witnesses; organize discovery; review deposition transcripts; maintain copies of key pleadings; and draft briefs, among other things. I try to set up the basic outline in a way that will aid trial preparation, particularly for preparing the extensive pretrial orders sought by most of the federal district courts.

Figure 2.17 shows a typical CASE NOTE-BOOK outline. Copies of relevant pleadings and deposition transcripts can be included in the outline as complete documents, excerpts, or summaries, or searched for key words, with excerpts copied or cut to other places in the outline. Pleadings and other documents from outside sources can also be divided into headlines using Grand-View's import features and then categorized as any other headlines. The NOTEBOOK usually includes the same categories as the TO-DO list combined with categories specifically relating to litigation, for example:

- Issue
- Admit/deny
- Bates number
- Exhibit number
- Key words

Organizing cases in a CASE NOTEBOOK outline makes it very easy to compile and sort lists of facts, exhibits, and other information in various ways: by date, by exhibit number, by person, by Bates number, by issue, by whether a fact is admitted or contested, to suggest a few. Similar listing and sorting can be done using database management programs, but GrandView lets you modify, manipulate, and organize your information in ways that are difficult or impossible with traditional database programs.

A very powerful GrandView feature is its

FIGURE 2.17 A Typical CASE NOTEBOOK

```
+  I. CASE NOTEBOOOK
-     A. PARTIES
-     B. COURT AND ATTORNEYS
-     C. WITNESSES
-     D. NOTES
-     E. CHRONOLOGY
-     F. SCHEDULE
-     G. LEGAL RESEARCH
-     H. DEPOSITIONS
-     I. EXHIBITS
-     J. DISCOVERY SUMMARIES
-     K. WITNESS STATEMENTS
-     L. RULINGS
-     M. SETTLEMENT
+ II. RECORD FILE
-     A. COMPLAINT
-     B. ANSWER
-     C. INTERROGATORIES
-     D. REQUESTS FOR ADMISSIONS
```

ability to find individual words or text strings, to mark the hits, and to copy or move all of the hits under one headline with a few quick keystrokes. This is especially useful when working with exhibit digests, deposition excerpts, factual summaries, and the like. For example, if you want to gather all references to Zeus in a new outline for use at a deposition, you could select the FIND feature from the GrandView menus (or press [ALT-F]), enter the name, direct GrandView to MARK ALL, locate the cursor under a new heading devoted to Zeus, and select the GATHER command from the menu (or press [ALT-G]) to cut or copy the headlines containing those references to the new headline.

Another powerful method of finding and organizing relevant information is to view or print the information in CATEGORY VIEW after assigning new category rules to the existing outline. For example, suppose the defendant's method of promoting its product becomes a key issue in a case. You could create rules assigning certain key words (*advertising, advertise, television, radio, promote, promotion, magazines,* etc.) as *promotion* under the issue category. After reapplying the assignment rules to the CASE NOTEBOOK, you could switch to CATEGORY VIEW to see or print all the headings that have the promotion assignment under the issue category.

RESEARCH FILE

The final component of my system of organizing information is a RESEARCH FILE outline, where I enter notes on decisions and articles. The basic outline is extremely simple, with headlines for CASES, ARTICLES, and MISCELLANEOUS. Under those headlines go citations and a brief summary or set of key words. Subheadlines include more detail: quotes, other citations, excerpts from briefs, general notes. The basic categories are:

- Court.
- Year.
- Area (namely, the substantive or procedural area of law involved).
- Key words.

Other categories can be created easily as the need arises. Using GrandView, the information in the RESEARCH FILE can be quickly searched, sorted, viewed by category, or cut and pasted to a new outline.

CONCLUSION

The practice of law is filled with uncertainty. It is impossible to foresee every aspect of a problem when it first arises. A key virtue of Grand-View is its flexibility. The outlines I've described are not only easy to create, but they are also easy to modify and supplement to meet the changing demands of particular problems and cases.

Using computers in your practice can make you better organized, more efficient, and more attentive to your clients' needs. The trick is to find the right tools. GrandView is well suited to the needs and habits of lawyers who rely heavily on outlines and lists to organize information and activities. It offers a combination of flexibility and organizational features not easily matched by most word processing, database, and calendar programs. It may be the right tool for you.

Mark V. B. Partridge is a partner in the Chicago office of Pattishall, McAuliffe, Newbury, Hilliard & Geraldson, a firm specializing in trademark, copyright, and unfair competition litigation. He received his J.D. from Harvard Law School and his B.A. from the University of Nebraska. He is a member of the adjunct faculty of the John Marshall Law School and has been a frequent speaker on trademark law and litigation.

Section 3
Document Assembly for Litigators

James A. Eidelman

Document assembly programs are a powerful type of software that can be used in conjunction with a word processor. Their purpose is to help you assemble pleadings and other kinds of documents. They work in a variety of ways such as allowing you to select from pre-stored clauses or asking you questions to gather the information needed to build your document.

Most of us can imagine how they might be useful to a business or real estate practitioner who must churn out hundreds of repetitive documents each month. Were you aware that they also have a place in a litigation practice?

In this section, we focus on document assembly systems that can be used to automate parts of a litigation practice. We begin with a look at how simple document-assembly systems can be used to advantage in a trial practice. We then turn to some more specialized systems that are of interest to family practitioners. We conclude with a case study showing how one firm profited greatly by establishing a document assembly system to automate its real estate practice. You will discover that the same combination of savings and profits can accrue to litigators who put document assembly systems to work in their practices.

Using Computer-Aided Document Assembly in a Litigation Practice

Dennis P. Schuler

Dennis Schuler was one of the early pioneers in document assembly for lawyers. He forcefully demonstrates in this article how document assembly can be put to profitable use in a litigation practice.

One of the biggest contributors to law office expense and inefficiency is staff-intensive document preparation. In the law, the final product of almost every legal project is some type of document. From summons and complaint to judgment and appeal, we trade in documents. In fact, the largest tangible product of a law office is the variety of documents we create every day. Preparing them remains one of the most tedious, labor-intensive jobs we do.

Long ago, lawyers had to be efficient. When they needed a document they wrote it out and that was it—done! (Or so the older lawyers tell us.) With the typewriter came a transfer of much of the document assembly responsibility to others: We explain our needs to our staff; staff translates author's instructions (i.e., read author's mind); staff assembles and types form-book paragraphs and other author-selected/created passages; staff inserts client/case details; staff continues retyping documents until they reflect author's intentions. Throughout, we review and revise again and again.

Word processing, while an improvement, was still very inefficient. Electronically stored text could be cut and pasted. However, instructions, interpretation, manual keyboarding of client/case details as well as passages from form books and other sources were still required every time we required another document. We still often took days or weeks to finish documents.

THE DILEMMA: HOURLY BILLING VS. VALUE BILLING

Back when lawyers created their own documents, they often charged fixed fees based on the value of services. Profits were geared to productivity, and the practice of law was rewarding and profitable. Computerization brought automated billing and with it a greater emphasis on fees charged by the hour or minute. At first, hourly billing made sense. Soon it became obvious that it limited annual income to the number of hours worked each year. Income was now tied to how many minutes you billed rather than on how efficiently you worked. Hourly billing also focused clients on seemingly high hourly rates rather than value, and caused considerable resistance to legal fees.

Inefficient document creation, combined with hourly billing, substantially limited options for improving income. The two most obvious options, and perhaps the least desirable, were to raise hourly rates, or work more and more hours every year. Obviously, there are limits to each. Put another way, two of the most important factors in determining our income are (1) how efficient we are at producing our firm's main product—documents, and (2) how we bill. If our fees are *only* tied to how much time it takes to do a job, we have no incentive to be more efficient and must raise our rates or work more hours to increase our income. If we raise rates, we risk losing clients. If we work too many hours, we risk a whole lot more.

SOLUTIONS ARE AT HAND

Solution: Find a way to produce documents more efficiently and bill our clients for certain parts of our total services on a value basis. In your retainer agreement, consider including set fees for services over which you have time control and combine these set fees with hourly fees for items over which you have no time control. It works, and clients love it because you are telling them, up front, that you are also concerned about legal costs.

Automated document assembly means author-created documents. Author-created documents mean efficiency. If you are efficient, you can value-bill. If you are not efficient, you would be foolish to value-bill. Going one step further—if you are efficient, you *have to* value-bill. Will you charge your hourly rate of $125 for that 40-page contract you prepared in three hours, which formerly took you and your staff days to prepare? Study the time you and your staff spend transforming legal decisions into the multitude of documents prepared in your office each day, and you'll quickly see where so much of your time and money is wasted.

DOCUMENT PREPARATION: THE OLD WAY

Before automated document assembly, this is what most lawyers had to do to put together documents:

- Gather facts, organize them, and decide which document was needed.
- Perform extensive research to determine necessary document contents.
- Search for needed phrases and paragraph precedents in form books, reference books, statutes, and closed files.
- Continue looking until precedents were found to cover all items to be included.
- Cut, paste, copy, and mark up old documents and forms, add notes and instructions, and try not to forget anything.
- Write and/or dictate portions.
- Give marked-up forms, word processing sections, handwritten notes, dictation tapes, and instructions to secretary to cut, paste, and type draft.
- When draft was returned, mark up and return to secretary for revision, re-mark up, and more revisions, etc.
- Continue this process until the document is in final form.

A BETTER WAY: USING A DOCUMENT ASSEMBLY PROGRAM

With a document assembly program, this is how lawyers now assemble documents:

- Select the document needed from the program menu.
- Select text to be included from the menu of choices.
- Enter the client/case specific details not already included in preceding documents.
- Return last week's phone messages while the program assembles the document.

HOW WE USE DOCUMENT ASSEMBLY

We use FlexPractice, a document assembly program that I helped to create, in our litigation department. Today, almost every litigation document is prepared with FlexPractice, from summons and complaint to responses to demands for discovery to judicial conference closing statement. Depending on the complexity of the case and the document, either a paralegal or secretary prepares the initial document, or the lawyer does it directly. If a paralegal or secretary prepares the document, the handling lawyer reviews it to ensure that the correct decisions were made and all allegations or text that should have been included were included. Then it's ready to go.

If the lawyer prepares the document, most of these steps are eliminated because he or she has already done this as the document was created.

Most litigation documents take from less than one-tenth to one-half of the time they formerly took, both in elapsed time and real time. Secretaries have been freed to do more challenging and rewarding tasks, rather than pounding on keyboards all day. They enjoy their jobs more and are much more productive.

Everyone is more efficient. More cases are

Managing Your Form Files

Joseph L. Kashi

Computers are wonderful tools to help you organize form files. Have you ever tried to find a pleading that you know is similar to the one you are working on now? Finding that document is easy if you have enough hard-disk data storage. Several programs will help you find what you need.

Magellan is a highly rated but inexpensive hard-disk management, text search, and indexing program that will work on both local hard disks and networks. It is very fast and easy to use once you have set up the search patterns. Magellan requires no prior preparation of the form files, aside from periodically using Magellan's own indexing routine, and works with common word processing programs. If you don't find the exact match the first time, select the language most similar to what you are seeking and instruct Magellan to display every file that is similar to the exemplar file. This so-called fuzzy search is a very useful feature and is unique to Magellan. Magellan's major drawback is its limited capabilities, Boolean search, which filter results through AND, OR, and NOT search modifiers like those used by LEXIS and WESTLAW. Magellan's document display features are very convientent.

ZyIndex is another text-indexing and search program that comes in several versions and whose price and capabilities are matched to the user's needs. It is similar to Magellan and has been used by law firms for years.

You might also try the Windows version of ZyIndex, or PC-Index if you like shareware. If you have several thousand stored documents, then good search speed is crucial, and indexed programs like ZyIndex and Magellan will always prove faster in such an environment.

GOfer is a proven alternative to the other programs mentioned here. It's a "pop up" TSR program that offers Boolean searches but does not use indexes. Give some consideration also to WordPerfect's document summary. This may be all that you need for a small form file.

Magellan's low price, fast speed, other useful DOS features, and fuzzy search capability suggest that it is the best choice for small and medium law offices.

---

handled each year, and clients are impressed by our streamlined operation and prompt response time. For example, our firm has been selected to represent an employee benefits program that administers benefits for more than 20,000 local employees—primarily because of the response time and reasonable fees that our document assembly system allows us to provide. Again, automated document assembly is a very powerful marketing tool.

The same methods are used for each area of law we handle. Because of our heavy use of document assembly, set fees (value billing) are much easier to establish, and the clients are delighted. In many cases, set fees for set services (where we control the amount of time necessary to complete the project) are combined with hourly billing for work we cannot control or predict in terms of time and effort.

The effect on me personally has been tremendous. I am much more confident of the quality of work that I have not personally handled that goes out of the office. I know that the author of any document prepared with FlexPractice *had* to consider the correct options before the work went out, and that there is consistency of work product.

NOT THE END

Office efficiency, combined with billing techniques that combine lower legal cost to the client and more profit for you, make for more and happier clients. It can also make for more and happier personal time for you—on a bigger sailboat. A well-designed automated document assembly system saves both time and money because it combines the power of the personal computer with the advantages of form books. Unprofitable areas of law now become profitable, and your staff is returned to performing functions that make better use of their talents, further increasing firm profits.

Of course, we do a lot more with computers in my office than just prepare documents, but that's another topic. With good document assembly programs, we now have a tool to help *lawyers,* rather than the office manager. In other words, lawyers can now do things with computers that lawyers do—faster, better, easier, and more profitably. What a combination!

A good automated document assembly systems is not just a long-term investment that will pay off *someday.* It will start saving money immediately, and you can see the results every time you use it. I can honestly say that without computers in my office, I would not still be practicing law. They have truly brought some of the fun back into my practice.

Dennis P. Schuler practiced law with Schuler & Von Dohlen in Rochester, New York, until he passed away in 1992. He specialized in personal injury and matrimonial litigation. Mr. Schuler developed the FlexPractice Automated Document Assembly System, which is currently marketed by Integrated Concepts, Inc., of Rochester, New York.

Joseph L. Kashi (sidebar) is a sole practitioner living in Soldotna, Alaska. He received his B.S. and M.S. degrees from MIT in 1979 and his J.D. from Georgetown University Law Center in 1976. His practice consists primarily of contract and personal injury litigation.

An Introduction to the Use of Document Assembly in Litigation

Greg H. Schlender

We have come a long way since the cut and paste days of document assembly. Word processors offered the first advances. Now "document assembly engines" have taken the technology many steps further. In this article, Greg Schlender, a practicing lawyer and part-time consultant from Boulder, Colorado, introduces us to document assembly programs and shows how they can help in a litigation practice.

If you've ever had to prepare a new version of a document from one created in the past, you'll probably see the value of document assembly. Whether contracts, pleadings, or settlement agreements, most documents are filled with paragraphs and clauses from previous documents. When it comes to finding, cutting, and pasting old paragraphs, computers are much faster than any of us. Why not take advantage of their capabilities?

In the old days, we used cut-and-paste techniques to draft documents: First, find an old document that matches the present case as closely as possible. Take a pair of scissors and cut out the various sections. Throw out the parts that do not apply. Fill in the holes with handwritten or dictated material. Put the pieces back together with some tape. Have a secretary type it.

Indeed, with one variation, this scenario is not far from current practice in many law firms today. Rather than have a secretary type the entire document from scratch, the old document may be on computer. Under this variation, the word processor provides a glorified pair of scissors, but the basic cut-and-paste technique remains the same.

Today's document assembly programs offer many advantages over the cut-and-paste approach, even if you use a word processor to do your cutting and pasting. In this article, I will first discuss several simple document assembly techniques that can be done on a word processor.

These include the merge feature for repetitive filling in of blanks and using a point-and-shoot macro as a crude method for automating the selection of alternate clauses. I will then offer a look at a more sophisticated document assembly program and show you how it can integrate the tasks of filling in blanks and selecting clauses.

USING MERGE FEATURES TO FILL IN THE BLANKS

Creating pleadings provides a good start for simple document assembly techniques. A multitude of blanks need to be completed in a pleading: the names of the plaintiffs and defendants, the name of the Court, the case number, etc. If several pleadings need to be filed simultaneously, each of these items of information may have to be retyped.

The cut-and-paste approach required the typist to take an old form, manually search for the items that needed to be filled in, delete the old information, then type in the new information. If the item belonged in several different places in a single document, or if it went into several different documents, the process had to be repeated until all of the insertions were made.

One solution, the merge feature, is provided by nearly every word processor. I will use Word-Perfect 5.1 (WP) as an example of this simple document assembly tool. While the specific com-

FIGURE 3.1 A WP Secondary Merge File

```
{FIELD NAMES}Plaintiff~Defendant~Court~Case Number~~
JOHN R. SMITH{END OF FIELD}
MARTHA L. VINES{END OF FIELD}
DISTRICT COURT, BOULDER COUNTY{END OF FIELD}
89CV-1359{END OF FIELD}
{END OF RECORD}
```

FIGURE 3.2 A WP Primary Merge File

```
{FIELD}Court~, STATE OF COLORADO
{FIELD}Case Number~_____
COMPLAINT_____
{FIELD}Plaintiff~,
Plaintiff
vs.
{FIELD}Defendant~
Defendant._____


          Plaintiff, {FIELD}Plaintiff~, etc.
```

FIGURE 3.3 Result of Merge

```
DISTRICT COURT, BOULDER COUNTY, STATE OF COLORADO
89CV-1359_____
COMPLAINT_____
JOHN R. SMITH,
Plaintiff,
vs.
MARTHA L. VINES,
Defendant._____


          Plaintiff, JOHN R. SMITH, etc.
```

mands you may need will vary from one word processor to another, the basic concepts are the same.

To understand merge techniques we should start with a few definitions. A *field* is a particular item of information. A *record* is a set of fields. In order to distinguish between the various fields in a record, the fields must be delimited. WP knows that a field has ended when it sees the code {END OF FIELD}. The end of a record is marked by the code {END OF RECORD}.

Merge features allow one to enter the items of information that go into the blanks *once*. In WP, the variable items of information are en-

tered into a specially formatted file called a *secondary merge file*. The documents, or forms, are set up with *field codes*, where the variable items of information will go. In WP, these specially encoded forms are called *primary merge files*.

After the variable information is typed into the secondary merge file, the primary and secondary files are merged—that is, the items of information contained in the secondary merge file are inserted into the forms where the field codes, or blanks, occur.

In order to distinguish which field is which, the fields in a record must always occur in the same order across all records of that type. For

FIGURE 3.4 Interrogatories for Point and Shoot

```
================================================================
1. What is your name?
================================================================
2. What is your name?
        a. By what other names have you been known
           or called?
        b. Has a change of your name ever been
           approved by a court?
        c. What name do you use for signing legal
           documents?
        d. What name do you use, if any, in
           published telephone directories?
================================================================
3. Where do you now live?
================================================================
4. Where do you now live?
        a. Where are you registered to vote?
        b. Where are your automobiles registered?
================================================================
5. Where do you work?
================================================================
```

example, field 1 might be the court, field 2 the case number, field 3 the name of the decedent, field 4 the name of the personal representative, etc. Once the secondary merge file data is entered, the same secondary merge file can be re-used as often as you like.

Figure 3.1 shows an example of a secondary merge file.

Figure 3.2 shows an example of a primary file. Notice in Figure 3.2 that the field codes in the primary file use names. This makes the form easier to read. This is made possible by the codes at the top of the record in Figure 3.1, where the field names are listed in the order in which the fields appear in the record.

Figure 3.3 shows the result of merging the two together.

USING A POINT-AND-SHOOT MACRO TO SELECT CLAUSES

A second purpose for document assembly is to gain the ability to select from among various standard clauses. For example, in asserting jurisdiction in federal district court, the two most common choices would be diversity of citizenship or the existence of a federal question. Rather than using cut-and-paste techniques, what if you could choose from a menu with those two choices during the process of assembling the complaint? A single keystroke response would insert the proper clause for jurisdiction.

Before exploring more sophisticated document assembly solutions, consider creating a more basic tool for selecting clauses on your word processor. I am talking about a "point-and-shoot" macro. A macro is a feature in most word processors that records a sequence of keystrokes one uses repeatedly. A particular job may require 20 or 30 keystrokes, but invoking a macro to run the entire sequence can reduce that effort to a single keystroke.

The point-and-shoot macro records a sequence of keystrokes for copying the selected portions of a form to the assembled document. It works well with interrogatories, so I will use that system as an example.

First, all the possible questions are listed in a master form. Automatic paragraph numbering is used so that when the unwanted questions are discarded, the remaining questions will properly renumber. Each interrogatory is separated in the master form by a hard page code. The hard page code appears on the screen as a double dashed line. The master form might appear as in Figure 3.4.

Understanding Document Assembly Jargon

Charles E. Pear, Jr.

Lawyers, especially new lawyers, often feel compelled to clothe legal documents in legalistic terminology. Indeed, clients willingly pay their lawyers to wade through documents peppered with *hereinafters, hereinaforesaids,* and similar legalisms. Many have heard the lawyer's version of giving an orange to someone:

> The party of the first part does hereby give, grant, bequeath and set over unto the party of the
> second part and his heirs and devisees, that certain fruit more particularly described as that certain
> orange, together with the skin or other outer surface thereof, the rind thereunto affixed or attached,
> the seeds therein contained. . . .

Unfortunately, document assembly software developers quickly seized on this practice. As a result, some document assemblers are more heavily jargon-laden than the mortgages of yore. This sidebar provides some guidance to the novice.

SHELLS, FORMS, AND SYSTEMS. A document assembly system generally consists of two parts: the shell and the forms.

The *forms* are much like their paper counterpart. They consist of boilerplate clauses and paragraphs formatted for, and often created with, your word processor. They identify which paragraphs and clauses are standard and which are conditional. Sometimes they also state the conditions for including or excluding conditional text. The forms also contain blanks in which to fill in information; but unlike paper forms, each blank has a name. Some people call the forms *scripts* or *templates.* Almost everybody calls the blanks *variables.*

The *shell* is the document assembly engine. Its primary function is to edit your forms according to your instructions. It produces a word processing document that you can revise or print with your word processor (WordPerfect, Word, etc.). Some people use the terms *document assembler, document assembly engine,* or just *engine* to refer to the shell. Note that in most cases, the shell not only builds the completed document, but also contains tools that help you build the forms as well.

Most document assembly shells come with only a few sample forms; you must develop your own forms. In this regard, a shell is like a word processing program. A word processor comes with few, if any, documents. After all, you buy it to process your own documents, not documents supplied by the developer of the word processing software.

By combining your forms with a shell, you create a system for building documents in a hurry. You might refer to your system by a variety of names such as an *application system,* a *practice system,* a *substantive system,* a *document assembly system,* a *document drafting system,* a *CADA (computer-assisted document assembly) system,* or, unfortunately, just a *system.*

DEVELOPER, AUTHOR, AND USER. The *author* is the person who creates the forms. The author decides what text is conditional and when it should appear. The author must also identify and name each blank in the form. Likewise, the author must specify any rules governing how and when to ask questions, the kinds of answers permitted, and how to use those answers in building a document.

The general idea behind document assembly is that the author thinks about all legal issues in advance and then compiles a set of forms to handle each issue. After that is done, anyone else—perhaps another partner, an associate, or a paralegal—can use the shell and the forms to produce a document. Anyone other than the author who uses the shell and the forms to build a document, is a *user* or an *end-user.*

The *developer* is the company that created and markets the shell as a commercial product. As previously noted, the developer usually provides few forms. Several third parties, however, offer libraries of ready-made templates that you can use with your shell to generate specific legal documents. Law book publishers and entrepreneurs supply most of these libraries. Indeed, CCH, BNA, Lawyer's Co-op, Matthew-Bender, and various other legal publishers are testing the market now. These firms are *publishers,* although some people call them *developers* too, even though they did not develop the document assembly shell.

We call the libraries of templates they publish *applications.* Many people use the term *applications* interchangeably with terms like *system, substantive systems, practice systems,* and so on.

PROOFLIST. Some shells save the end-user's answers for later reuse. This way, if the document must be changed, the user need not key in all the answers again. Instead, only the items that change and any related questions must be reanswered. We call this list of answers a *value table* or *response file.*

With some shells, the response file serves another important function. It records each question asked and the end-user's answers. This records the user's answers for future reference. In addition, a supervising lawyer can quickly check a printout of the answers and assumptions of the end-user against the list of questions, thereby speeding the document review process. When used this way, we refer to the list of answers as the *answer checklist, prooflist,* or *audit trail.*

Note that many people use the terms *value table, response file, answer checklist, prooflist,* and *audit trail* interchangeably.

WORKSHEET. Some lawyers refuse to work with a computer directly. Instead, they prefer to fill out a paper checklist of questions pertaining to drafting a particular document. Ordinarily, they give this checklist to an associate, paralegal, or secretary, who then prepares the document based on the way the lawyer completed the checklist.

Some document assemblers can accommodate the work habits of these lawyers. They can print a list of all questions with blanks for the lawyer to fill in. The lawyer gives the completed list to a paralegal or secretary, who feeds the data into the document assembler and builds the document. This paper checklist of questions is a *worksheet.* Often the document assembly engine can generate a worksheet automatically. Worksheets are also referred to as *master information lists,* or *MILs.*

MACROS AND MERGES. Sometimes lawyers and their staff create practice systems using only their word processors. Programs like Word and WordPerfect contain two important features for building homegrown practice systems.

Macros. With macros you can first record a sequence of keystrokes and then play them back at the touch of a single key. It works something like a video recorder. For example, you might record the phrase *American Bar Association* and then assign it to the **[F12]** key. The next time you need to type *American Bar Association,* you would instead press the **[F12]** key. Your word processor would then type it for you.

Each set of keystrokes you save is a *macro.* Generally, you can create a large number of macros. For example, the **[ALT-A]** key may contain one macro, the **[CTRL-A]** may contain another, and so on. Different word processors have different constraints on the number of macros you may create and the keys to which you can assign a macro.

A macro can do more than just record text for future playback. It can also record a series of keystrokes that, for example, open another word processing document and copy its contents to the current document. Or it can search through an entire document for a symbol like LENDER'S NAME and replace it with text such as *Bank of Eastern California.*

By combining these features, you can copy a series of paragraphs into a new document and then search for and replace key words and phrases such as PLAINTIFF'S NAME with text specific to the present case such as *John Doe.*

Most word processors have a macro capacity, and some of them are quite sophisticated. For example, Microsoft's Word for Windows contains a subset of the BASIC programming language.

Merge. The merge feature of a word processor is most often associated with creating mailing lists. For example, you could create a form letter with blanks for the names of the addressee, his or her address, the greeting, and so on. Then you create a second document containing a list of everyone who will receive the letter. Your word processor can generate a separate letter for each addressee, consisting of the form letter with the blanks filled in from the list of recipients. The terms *merge* or *mail merge* refer to this process of filling in the blanks in the form letter with text from the list of recipients.

FIGURE 3.5 Commands for the Macro and What Happens

Recorded Keystrokes	What is Happening
[F2], [Ctrl-Enter], [F2], [Left], [Alt-F4] [Shift-F2], [Ctrl-Enter], [F2] [Ctrl-F4], 1, 2	All of the text between the hard pages before and after the cursor is blocked and copied.
[Shift-F3]	Go to Document Screen #2.
[Enter]	Retrieve the copied text.
[Home], [Home], [Down] [Enter]	Move the cursor to the bottom of Document Screen #2 and place an extra hard return before the position where the next clause will go.
[Shift-F3], [Page Down]	Return to Document Screen #1 and move the cursor to the next clause. If that clause is not wanted, press **[Page Down]**. If the clause is wanted, press **[Alt-P]** again and the process repeats.

The point-and-shoot macro utilizes WP's two document screens. The master form is loaded into document screen number one. Document screen number two starts as an empty screen. The user then presses **[Page Down]** to go to the first clause he wants to select. The macro is then invoked. (If the macro was **[Alt-P]**, one would press the **[Alt]** and **[P]** keys at the same time.) Figure 3.5 shows the commands for the macro and what happens.

With this simple WP macro, 18 keystrokes can be reduced to 1. The result is a simple tool to allow you to select specific interrogatories for inclusion in a master document.

This point-and-shoot macro proves useful because it is so easy to use, both for the person setting up the master form and for the person using the macro to create a document. The person setting up the master form need only separate each clause with a hard page code. The user only has to page through the alternate clauses and invoke the macro for each clause he or she wants to use.

But the point-and-shoot macro also has limitations:

The master form is strictly a linear set of yes/no questions. If there are clauses that are mutually exclusive, one must answer no to one and yes to the other. For example, a case is either in state court or in federal court, but not in both at the same time. In an ideal document assembly system, only one response would be required. The point-and-shoot macro would require two responses.

The point-and-shoot macro does not allow for branching. One cannot have a branch of possible clauses appear or not appear, depending on a single answer. For interrogatories, one might want to choose at the beginning between long and short forms (e.g., items 1 and 2, or 3 and 4, in Figure 3.4), with individual selections then being possible within each. With the point-and-shoot macro, one must always go through all of the possible clauses.

The point-and-shoot macro does not remember answers for reuse later. Selecting a particular clause in the statement of facts for a complaint may require another clause in the prayer for relief. The point-and-shoot macro will require that the decision be made twice.

The point-and-shoot macro does not allow logical operations to be performed on answers (e.g., IF the answer is X, THEN Clause 1, ELSE Clause 2).

Decisions for clause selection in the point-and-shoot macro cannot be tied to answers for filling in blanks (e.g., a blank might be the state of the defendant's residence, with a logical structure performed on that answer to determine what clause is required for personal jurisdiction).

TRUE DOCUMENT ASSEMBLY SOFTWARE

Powerful stand-alone software tools are now available to address the shortcomings of the point-and-shoot macro and merge systems. These document assembly software packages, also known as *document engines,* can add the power of *logic* to the process of filling in the blanks and choosing among alternate clauses. For example:

    i. IF statements permit the selection of alternate clauses and branching to alternate series of questions.

    ii. WHILE statements permit repeating a question until a condition is met.

    iii. LET statements permit setting variables, such as genders and plurals, throughout a document.

    iv. Sections and subsections can be automatically numbered so that their references change automatically depending upon the number of sections and subsections in the final draft.

A well-designed document assembly model can act as your mentor by asking you only the questions that are relevant to your situation. Moreover, it performs the functions of your legal assistant by actually assembling the first draft of the document based upon the answers you give to questions it asks.

The first document engine to be developed was LawProcess, by James Sprowl, for the American Bar Foundation. It is marketed today by West Publishing Company as part of a textbook called *Computer Applications in the Law.* An understanding of how LawProcess works will give you a good overview of how such systems work.

With LawProcess, you start with your form document and embed fill-in-the-blank questions and logic statements (i.e., IF, WHILE, and LET statements) right in the document itself, wherever there is a variable feature. After the model is complete, you run the LawProcess program using the model. The program then asks you the questions you embedded in the model. Based upon your answers, it fills in the blanks, selects the appropriate clauses, renumbers clauses, and writes the final document to a file that most word processors can edit.

Figure 3.6 illustrates an example of a release agreement with LawProcess embedded codes. The coded fields are enclosed in brackets (i.e., << >>.)

In theory, any word processor that permits you to embed IF statements in a document can be used to design document assembly models. WordStar has offered that feature as part of its Mail-Merge package for several years, and Microsoft Word and Samna IV do also. WordPerfect 5.1 also has added a programming language as part of its merge feature. All of these programs incorporate some sophisticated document assembly features, but you will soon tie yourself in knots trying to do complex document assembly programming in a word processor merge language.

As an alternative, there now exist over a dozen document assembly engines that incorporate both basic and sophisticated document assembly features. These include FlexPractice, ExperText, CAPS, Jumpstart, WorkForm, Scrivener, Blankity BLANK, and OverDrive.

CAPS—An Example of a True Document Assembly Engine

For several years, I have used CAPS for sophisticated document assembly projects (CAPSOFT Development Corp., 2155 N. 200 West, Suite 90, Provo, UT 84604, [801] 375-6562). The key to understanding CAPS is the concept of *elements,* which are like building blocks. CAPS offers 15 discrete elements, which can be used, independently or in conjunction, to build a practice system. Each type of element is useful for different functions. For example, a document element can be used to provide an outline for a practice system—either for the overall system or for smaller subparts of the system. A frame element is particularly useful for designing and defining screens for queries and explanatory material that are presented to the user for input. A text element is generally used to store large chunks of boilerplate text for incorporation into the finished document. An essay element is used to request longer text answers to questions asked of the user. A computation element provides the capacity for automatic performance of computational-type functions, ranging from arithmetic/date computations to setting personal pronouns.

CAPS elements may be used as objects. By *objects* I mean that each element can be separately constructed and tested, and then the separate elements can be used and reused in larger systems. For example, consider the phrase from a Release Agreement:

```
I, _____, hereby agree
to indemnify and hold harmless
_____, his/her heirs
and assigns (or, if a corpora-
tion, "its officers, directors,
successors and assigns")...
```

FIGURE 3.6 A Release Agreement with LawProcess Embedded Codes

```
<<IF general release>>
        GENERAL RELEASE
<<ELSE>>
        RELEASE
<<ENDIF>>
        <<Payee>> has made certain claims against <<name(s) of defendants>> for
<<brief description of injuries, contract, or
claim>>.

<<IF one defendant ("Payor")>>
        NOW, THEREFORE, in consideration of the sum of $<<amount>> paid by
<<Payor>>, receipt of which is acknowledged, and for other good and sufficient
consideration, <<Payee>> for <<IF Payee is an individual>> <<himself or herself>>
and <<his or her>> personal representatives, heirs, and assigns, <<ELSE>> itself
and its successors and assigns, <<ENDIF>> releases <<Payor>> and <<IF Payor is an
individual>> <<his or her>> personal representatives, heirs, agents, and assigns
<<ELSE>> its directors, officers, employees, agents, successors, and assigns,
<<ENDIF>> from all claims which <<Payee>> now has, or which <<he or she or it>> or
<<IF Payee is an individual>> <<his or her>> personal representatives, heirs,
<<ELSE>> successors <<ENDIF>> or assigns may have in the future, by reason of
<<brief description of injuries, contract, or claim>> <<IF general release>> or
any other matter or occurrence from the beginning of the world to the date of this
instrument <<ENDIF>>.

<<ELSE if more than one Payor>>
        NOW, THEREFORE, in consideration of the sum of $<<amount #1>> paid by
<<Payor #1>>, $<<amount #2>> paid by <<Payor #2>>, <<etc>>, or a total of <<total
of all amounts>>, receipt of which is acknowledged, and for other good and suffi-
cient consideration, <<Payee>> for <<IF Payee is an individual>> <<himself or
herself>> and <<his or her>> personal representatives, heirs, and assigns,
<<ELSE>> itself and its successors and assigns, <<ENDIF>> releases <<Payor>> and
their <<IF any of Payors are individuals>> personal representatives, heirs,
```

This phrase might be scripted in CAPS using four different types of elements—a document (DO) element, a fill-in (FI) element, a selection (SE) element, and a computation (CO) element—as follows:

1. The DO element would combine several different elements and might look like this:

   ```
   I, FI/INDEMNITOR'S NAME, hereby
   agree to indemnify and hold harmless
   FI/INDEMNITEE'S NAME, CO/
   INDEMNITEE'S PERSONAL PRONOUN...
   ```

2. The FI elements referenced in the DO element, called *Indemnitor's Name* and *Indemnitee's Name* would contain fill-in-the-blank information (i.e., the respective names of the parties to the Release).

3. The CO element referenced in the DO element would look something like this:

   ```
   IF SE/INDEMNITEE IS A CORPORA-
   TION
       "its officers, directors,
       successors and assigns"
       ELSE
           IF SE/INDEMNITEE IS MALE
           "his heirs and assigns"
           ELSE
           "her heirs and assigns"
           END
   END
   ```

   It would compute the correct language for the personal pronoun phrase in the document, based upon the answers to the SE elements.

4. The SE elements (*Indemnitee is a Corporation* and *Indemnitee is Male*) quite obviously constitute nothing more than Boolean On/Off (Yes/No) switches. SE elements give the user choices among alternate clauses.

```
<<ENDIF>> <<IF any of Payors are corporations>> directors, officers, employees,
successors, <<ENDIF>> agents, and assigns, <<ENDIF>> from all claims which
<<Payee>> now has, or which <<he or she or it>> or <<IF Payee is an individual>>
<<his or her>> personal representatives, heirs, <<ELSE>> successors have
<<ENDIF>> or assigns may have in the future, by reason of <<brief description of
injuries, contract, or claim>> <<IF general release>> or any other matter or
occurrence from the beginning of the world to the date of this instrument
<<ENDIF>>.
<<ENDIF>>

<<IF number of defendants is greater than one and number of Payors is less than
number of defendants>>
        <<Payee>> reserves the right to pursue any claim against any person other
that <<names of Payors>> and reserves the right to claim that another person or
persons, and not <<names of Payors>>, are solely liable to <<Payee>>. If any other
person is liable for <<brief description of injuries, contract, or claim>>, the
execution of this release shall be a satisfaction of <<Payee>>'s claim against
that other person to the extent of that other person's pro rata share of the joint
or common liability which has been satisfied by this release.
<<ENDIF>>

<<IF Payee is not an individual (is a corporation)>>
        The undersigned officers of <<Payee>> warrant that they are duly authorized
to execute this release.

        IN WITNESS WHEREOF, <<Payee>> has executed this release this ___ day of
_____, 19___.
<<ELSE>>
        IN WITNESS WHEREOF, <<Payee>> has set <<his or her>> hand and seal this ___
day of _____, 19___.
<<ENDIF>>
```

The most significant aspect of CAPS is this modular, object-oriented methodology for building a document assembly model. Each element can be structured and debugged on a stand-alone basis. After each element is constructed and is running properly, you can put them together any number of ways.

The job of the document assembly author is significantly simplified by the modular approach of CAPS. But the user sees none of this. CAPS allows the author to custom design wholly flexible user interface screens and techniques for gathering the data that is stored in FI and SE elements. Menus can be designed easily to permit data entry in a variety of ways. Information can be typed in from the keyboard either in short phrases or in volumes at a time. It can be entered as *single* choices (e.g., "Choose ONE of the following:") or *multiple* choices (e.g., "Choose SOME OR ALL of the following:"). For the simple release language illustrated earlier, the user might see the data-gathering screen shown in Figure 3.7.

Another significant feature of CAPS is its virtually unlimited capacity for explanation to the user. One of the most important benefits of any document assembly application is the potential for *knowledge leveraging*—the capability for institutionalizing expertise in the system so that it may be used by persons who, without the help of the system, would not have the degree of legal skill and experience to prepare first drafts of complex legal documents. To this end, CAPS provides the author with a hypertext-like system of footnotes, known as resource elements. An author of a CAPS practice system has the option of inserting footnotes at any point throughout the system, or even footnotes within footnotes. If explanation is needed, then the user can call it up. If the user already has sufficient knowledge to

FIGURE 3.7 Data-Gathering Screen ndex

| File | Edit | Settings | Windows | Calc | Help/Examples | PRESENT VALUE SCREEN |

Single Payments:

Date	Amount	Value
7/ 1/85	6,000,000	7,978,572
7/ 1/86	8,000,000	9,553,824
7/ 1/87	10,000,000	10,996,589
7/ 1/88	12,000,000	12,365,454

Periodic Payments:

From	Through	PerYr	Amount	COLA%	Value

Effective Date	True Rate %	Loan Rate %	Yield %
XX	12.0000	12.0602	12.7497
1/ 1/86	9.5000	9.5377	9.9659
1/ 1/87	7.0000	7.0205	7.2508
1/ 1/88	6.0000	6.0150	6.1837

Value computed with
rate table at left:

As of	Interest Computation	Total value
1/ 1/89	COMPOUND	40,894,439.59

Settings: COLA: Ann 360 1950 12perYr

respond to the queries without additional help, he or she can simply proceed to respond to the queries and ignore the explanation.

CAPS is not for beginners. The more features a document assembly engine has, the harder it is to master—because there is so much more to master. Since CAPS is so feature-rich, it should come as no surprise that getting up to speed is not a task for your spare time. It takes real perseverance and practice, practice, practice!

Greg H. Schlender is a shareholder at Chrisman Bynum & Johnson, P.C., Boulder, Colorado, specializing in tax and corporate law. He began using computers in 1981 and has had a computer on his desk for the practice of law since 1984. He has been active in the Law Practice Management Section, having served as director of the Computer Tools User Group, director of the Practice Applications Users Group, chair of the Estate Planning Practice Applications Users Group, and chair of the Electronic Communications Users Group.

Charles E. Pear, Jr., (sidebar) is co-chair of the ABA Section of Law Practice Management's Hypermedia Interest Group. He is presently a visiting professor (law and computers) on the faculty of law at the University of British Columbia.

Who Is Using CADA Today—
And How They Use It

Charles E. Pear, Jr.

Think computer-assisted document assembly is an idea years ahead of its time? Not any more. As Charles Pear shows, firms and corporate law departments across the country and across the world are developing systems for their practices. Here is a chance to check out what your competitors are doing.

Interest in computer-aided document assembly (CADA) as a legal tool has risen significantly in the U.S. and Canada. A year or two ago, very few firms had tried document assembly beyond perhaps a sophisticated macro or two. Now it looks as though most major American and Canadian law firms will begin automating their practice within the next 12 to 18 months.

Many reasons are cited for this: First, the recession has lightened lawyer workloads; excess capacity can be put to good use in preparing these systems. Second, and more importantly, once one firm starts with it, the others feel compelled to do so.

This chapter starts with a look at the likely trends in adoption of CADA. Next, we identify a few of your competitors who are using CADA today, both in the United States and in other common-law countries. Finally, we will look at two Australian firms that were willing to discuss their CADA efforts openly. Their story depicts the level of sophistication that some law firms are bringing to bear in automating their practice, both in the U.S. and abroad.

THE CADA WAVE

The role CADA will play in a firm depends on its size, the nature of its practice, and various other factors. The needs of a general practitioner are quite different from those of a highly specialized boutique firm. The needs of one department in a large firm may differ significantly from those of another department within the same firm. Nonetheless, some useful generalizations may be made. Existing data and case histories suggest that CADA will be integrated into daily law practice in three waves: the pioneering wave, the follow-the-herd wave, and the wait-and-see wave.

Pioneering firms are likely to expand their client base and work volume significantly. In addition, they stand to recover their initial investment and to reap substantial rewards beyond it. (See "The Electronic Profit Center," later in this section, for case studies confirming this point.)

The spectacular success of the pioneering firms has precipitated wider interest in CADA systems. As more firms began developing systems, their competitors started feeling compelled to do likewise. The FUD factor (fear, uncertainty, and doubt) is motivating these firms to adopt CADA as a means of meeting, not rising above, the competition.

These are the "follow-the-herd" firms. They probably will not experience runaway growth like the pioneering firms, so recovery of their entire investment is not as assured. Even so, automation will allow them to maintain their existing client base and charge normal fees for work prepared in a fraction of the time previously required. Excess profit in such transactions will offset to some degree the costs of system development in time; however, price competition will develop and inevitably fees will be reduced.

A third group of firms will take a wait-and-see view of CADA, with potentially disastrous financial consequences. They will adopt CADA only after fee cutting by the follow-the-herd firms makes it impossible to compete without automating. Consequently, these firms may have to absorb the entire cost of system development from funds that otherwise would be distributed to partners as income. They may never recapture the lost revenue, as they will be paying for the system as a means of regaining competitive standing and perhaps rebuilding a depleted client base.

Further, not only will these firms feel a definite pinch in partner revenues, but adverse tax consequences may also ensue as the system development costs will have to be paid currently but amortized over a period of time. As there will be no offsetting boom in firm revenues, less money will be available for distribution to partners.

WHERE ARE WE NOW?

Recent rising interest in CADA suggests that the pioneering period is nearing an end. Firms now considering document assembly for the first time should be aware that the window of opportunity for landslide profits will soon close, if it has not done so already.

In most areas, the second wave—industrywide gearing up—has commenced. Widespread adoption of such systems, or fear thereof, is compelling many firms to join in the fray as a defensive measure—a means of remaining competitive in the delivery of legal services on an increasingly more economical basis.

Note that wide adoption of CADA does not necessarily mean uniform adoption. A firm's entire practice cannot be automated overnight. So, most firms will proceed by identifying key practice areas to automate. Although there is likely to be some overlap among the firms, it will be quite some time before all practice areas are automated. Thus, opportunities for pioneering-style financial results will persist. Visionary (or perhaps lucky) firms will use the rewards of these opportunities to offset the cost of developing and maintaining systems in other areas that are subject to heavier competition.

The recession may be encouraging a somewhat premature onset of the third phase. In some areas, the third phase has already begun. This phase is characterized by price competition for business. Firms that have usable systems can and are undercutting their competitors. The efficiencies of the system permit them to bill for their services at a rate that cannot be matched by competing firms that propose to do the work in the traditional fashion. In some cases, legal documentation that used to take weeks to prepare can now be delivered in a day; more importantly, the firm's bill reflects only a day's fee for such work. Few firms are doing this as yet; those that are will not tell their story publicly for fear of losing their competitive edge. In time, however it will become obvious to their competitors.

One other development may hasten the adoption of CADA systems. Concerns over high legal fees have prompted corporate counsel in various companies to take note of the potential for economies offered by CADA systems. These lawyers view legal services as a cost to be controlled, not a profit center. They were quick to recognize the value of reducing legal expenses in the long run by making a short-term capital investment in CADA. Work formerly done by outside counsel now can be handled in house at a tiny fraction of the former cost.

In contrast, law firms servicing some of these corporations were less than motivated to develop CADA systems. These firms lived by the billable hour. More work meant more billable hours. As workloads increased, the firms responded by hiring more lawyers, who could produce even more billable hours. Little thought was given to developing CADA systems because they entailed a significant capital outlay with no guarantee of cost recovery; worse, a CADA system was, at least from a shortsighted perspective, unable to fill out a time sheet or generate billable hours. The net result was lost business to the law firm in the long run and, with the economic downturn, cash flow declines and attorney layoffs.

Meanwhile, corporate counsel have begun to reap the benefits of automation. Some corporations are building second-generation systems while their law firms try to decide whether and how to build their first. Law firms find themselves unable to compete with in-house counsel—a rather startling development.

Moreover, some corporations have retained law firms to develop CADA systems for the corporation's legal department. The law firm provides to the client the legal expertise and the text of the documents in the form of a completed CADA system. The law firm is also responsible for maintaining and updating the system as the law evolves. In essence, the firm is paid an hourly wage for capturing its expertise to a computer program. The client can then draw on that expertise repeatedly and without further expense other than periodic updating charges. Ironically, had the firm developed the system on its own initiative, perhaps it could have met the client's needs at a price low enough to discourage the client corporation from developing a parallel system while maintaining law firm profitability at reasonable levels.

This is a new area of law practice, and it is likely to expand. (In fact, at least one firm has been created solely for the purpose of designing and building document assembly systems. Smith, Moskatel, Schlender & Smith is a "national law firm" that specializes solely in constructing document assembly systems for other law firms and corporations.) Legal headhunters are now advertising for lawyers with document assembly skills. Demand for lawyers with such skills is rising.

WHO IS USING CADA—YOUR COMPETITORS

The following, which is current as of June 1992, is not meant to be a comprehensive list of CADA users, nor even close.[1] Rather, it should give you an inkling of the many firms and companies that have purchased CADA shells. These firms may be using CADA to gain a competitive advantage over you!

Atlanta

The Coca-Cola Company uses a CADA system for contract drafting and administration. The system uses the ExperText CADA engine. Coca-Cola's own lawyers and MIS staff collaborated with a lawyer from Simlaw Systems, Ltd. to design and develop the forms and database over a period of about six months. Attorneys at the corporate headquarters in Atlanta now use the system extensively. In addition, the company is deploying the system in the corporate counsel's field offices throughout the world.

Long, Aldridge and Norman, a 100-lawyer firm, has developed several iterations of a CADA system for commercial loan documentation. Partner Barbara McIntyre developed these systems and most recently migrated them to the Short-Work CADA engine. She is particularly fond of a feature that allows her to modify her system on the fly. She feels that this makes it both natural and appropriate to charge clients for use and expansion of the system.

Baltimore

The Rouse Company is the largest publicly held developer and owner of shopping centers, office projects, and mixed-use commercial properties in the U.S. The firm developed several CADA systems for commercial leasing to speed the work of its 10 lawyers and 20 legal assistants who draft and review such documents. The lawyers are primarily responsible for reviewing the substantive content and legal logic of the systems and, to a lesser degree, building and maintaining the systems. Three legal assistants are primarily responsible for building and maintaining the systems under the supervision of a lawyer. The firm uses the CAPS shell.

Boston

At *Mintz, Levin, Cohn, Ferris, Glovsky & Popeo,* associate Cliff Jones built CADA applications full time before leaving a year ago to form his own consulting firm with Marc Lauritsen, Harvard law school's director of lawyer practice systems. The Capstone Group, based in Mansfield, Massachusetts, continues to build CADA applications for Mintz, Levin as well as a number of other prestigious East coast firms. Mintz, Levin uses the CAPS shell.

Chicago

Richard H. Weise, Senior Vice President and General Counsel of Motorola Inc., devotes a chapter of his new book, *Representing the Corporate Client: Designs for Quality,*[2] to Motorola's "automatic contract engineering" system. Over a three-year period, the department developed CADA systems for a wide range of documents using the Clause-It shell on Macintosh computers. Each form in the system was developed by a staff attorney who is an expert in the substantive area of law.

Denver

Holme, Roberts & Owen developed a blue-sky system for preparing and tracking state securities filings in all 50 states and 3 territories. In January 1992, CCH Legal Information Systems, a subsidiary of Commerce Clearing House (CCH), licensed the Holme Roberts system and began marketing it under the name Blue Sky

Advantage. A significant number of law firms, primarily large and prestigious firms with national practices, now subscribe to the system at a price of about $10,000 per year. Holme, Roberts receives a royalty from the system and is responsible for maintaining and updating its legal content every two weeks. The firm is realizing an "excellent return" on its CADA investment.

Lawyers Norv Brash and Steve Proett worked full time for the last five and three years respectively in the firm's Legal Systems Division developing computer applications for lawyers. They spent about 80 percent of their time developing CADA systems and the balance on building expert systems, video imaging systems, and other technology systems. Prior to joining the Legal Systems Division, Mr. Brash practiced for five years in the firm's tax department and Mr. Proett practiced securities law for three years in the firm's corporate department. Over a two-year period, Mr. Brash and Mr. Proett spent about a full year each on the blue-sky system. Holme, Roberts also has applications for wills and trusts, oil and gas leasing, real estate title analysis (primarily for oil and gas properties), incorporations, and a diagnostic system that balances and weighs factors as to whether a client should set up an S corporation, a C corporation, a limited partnership, or a general partnership. In July 1992, the two lawyers formed an independent consulting and legal software development firm under the name Jurisystems Corporation in Denver. They will be developing further commercial CADA systems for CCH in addition to providing consulting services for individual law firms. Holme, Roberts uses the CAPS shell.

Detroit

Leroy C. Ritchie, Vice President and General Counsel for Automotive Legal Affairs of Chrysler Corporation, considers CADA a key component for law firms seeking Chrysler's business. In a March 1992, paper,[3] he stated:

> With regard to a firm's institutional knowledge, we need law firms that have a knowledge base of their own—who can call up research work that has been done before and tailor it for our new problem.
>
> We value law firms who have the forms we need, the document assembly capability to take written work that has been done before and assemble parts of it into new formats, and the pro-

cessing and procedures that ensure that work is done efficiently.

> This factor can save us more money than any other single thing we can do.

Houston

Vinson & Elkins, a firm of about 440 lawyers, has developed a number of systems, including over 52 different documents in the personal tax/estates department alone, as well as applications for hospital refinancings and bond-issue refinancings. The firm uses the WorkForm shell.

Los Angeles

Paul, Hastings, Janofsky & Walker has developed CADA applications for audit letters, engagement letters, stock purchase agreements, lease agreements, promissory notes, real estate loan documents, corporate dissolutions, incorporations, and estates and trusts. The firm uses the WorkForm shell.

Minneapolis

In January 1991, *Dorsey and Whitney*, a firm of 350 lawyers, hired lawyer Kingley Martin as their first "expert systems programmer." Mr. Martin spends 100 percent of his time developing document assembly systems for the firm. According to partner Philip F. Bolton, the firm developed an estate planning system first and then a blue-sky system. Next they developed an employee benefits ERISA system and a banking system. Most recently they have been working on a system for municipal bonds and public finance, and on systems for real estate and litigation.

New York

Document assembly is not just a large-firm tool. *Schmulker & St. Clair*, a three-lawyer firm in Brooklyn, uses the FlexPractice shell in their matrimonial, criminal law, and personal injury practice.

On the other hand, big firms are embracing document assembly in a big way. Consider *Davis, Polk & Wardwell*, a firm of about 435 lawyers in New York City. The firm maintains some 600 standard forms on its word processing system. For the last nine months, lawyer Michael Mills and three full-time staff members have been converting these documents into CADA author is responsible for the substantive content of each document in the system.

Milbank, Tweed, Hadley & McCloy is a 450-lawyer firm. Jonathan Blattmachr and Dan Hastings, both partners in the firm, have developed an estate planning application for the firm's trusts and estates department. The firm uses the General Counsel shell.

Omaha

Sherrets Smith & Gardner, a seven-lawyer general practice firm, has developed half a dozen CADA systems under the direction of partner H. Daniel Smith. These include federal pleadings (under the rules of civil procedure), incorporations, partnerships, loan documentation, estate planning, real estate conveyancing, and others. The firm uses the CAPS engine.

Philadelphia

Daniel Evans developed an extensive wills and trusts CADA application while a partner at *Dilworth, Paxson, Kalish & Kaufman*. He believed it to be so productive that he went on to found the company that produces the Scrivener CADA shell.

A *Morgan, Lewis & Bockius* associate spends half of his billable time working on the development of computer applications for lawyers including CADA applications, work product retrieval, and docketing systems. The firm is developing a large number of CADA applications with much of the coding being done by several members of the information systems department. The firm is using the CAPS shell.

Salt Lake City

Callister, Duncan & Nebeker is a firm of about 38 lawyers. During the past two years, the firm has developed applications in the fields of estates and trust documentation and loan documentation, and is currently working on an incorporations package. The firm estimates that it has invested about one man-year of billable legal time in building these applications. One person in the information services department works full time programming and maintaining CADA applications under the supervision of the section heads of the various practice areas of the firm. The firm is using the CAPS shell.

San Francisco

Morrison & Foerster is a 229-lawyer firm. Hampton Coley, Practice Support Analyst, was hired specifically to develop document assembly applications for the firm and spends 100 percent of his time in that capacity. The firm's first application is in their estate planning practice area, where 10 lawyers are using the system. The firm uses the General Counsel shell. Features of particular importance to the firm are database integration with document assembly in a multi-user environment.

BOT Financial Corporation is one of the largest bank-affiliated asset-specific financing companies in the country. Its six lawyers conduct a transaction-oriented practice where speed of document turnaround and accuracy is at a premium. The legal department used a CADA system to consolidate five libraries of parallel documents into one master set of forms, ensuring that all transaction documents include the most current enhancements. Vice President and Senior Counsel Mark Hellman chose the First Draft shell because it allowed him to work with bracketed alternative clauses, much like his manual system, but with the added ability to link these alternatives with logic he specified.

London, England

Linklaters & Paines has developed a Eurobonds offering system; a pension rules system; a share purchase agreement; service agreements for consultants, goods, and services; an offer for sale of securities; and a vendor placing agreement intended for stock transfers. Many other projects are in development. Lawyer Maureen McDonald spends her full time heading a department of four persons responsible for building CADA applications. The firm uses the Work-Form shell.

Vancouver, Canada

Campney, Murphy & Co. decided that partner John McConchie should devote one-half of his billable time to building CADA applications. Mr. McConchie developed several CADA applications in the labor law area, particularly dealing with time-sensitive matters such as injunctions for wild-cat picketing. Mr. McConchie found it difficult to juggle a thriving practice with document assembly development. As a result, last year he billed a full year's worth of regular bill-for wild-cat picketing. Mr. McConchie found it difficult to juggle a thriving practice with document assembly development. As a result, last year he billed a full year's worth of regular billings plus time equal to another half of a billable year on document assembly. Recently Mr. McConchie and thirteen other lawyers from the firm formed a new and highly automated law firm specializing in labor matters under the name Harris & Co. The new firm maintains a working relationship with the Campney firm.

McCarthy Tétrault's Vancouver branch of about 80 lawyers uses CADA systems in numerous areas. Systems Manager Sherry Turner built and maintained the firm's CADA systems until she was promoted to Systems Manager. The firm has implemented five major CADA applications using the WorkForm shell. In addition, the firm's Toronto office is currently finalizing two more applications for use in the corporate law department.

SOPHISTICATED APPROACHES TO CADA: TWO CASE STUDIES FROM AUSTRALIA

Mallesons Stephen Jaques is one of Australia's largest law firms. It has offices in Sydney, Brisbane, Melbourne, and Canberra, as well as in New York, London, Taipei, Singapore, and Hong Kong. The firm has about 150 partners and several hundred employed solicitors (associates). During the past year and a half, litigator Anthony Borgese spent 100 percent of his time developing CADA applications using the WorkForm shell.

The firm has a very sophisticated approach to document assembly. A partner who is an expert in the particular subject matter prepares each standard form, or *precedent*. The expert then forwards the form to the firm's precedent management department. Partner Philip Argy heads this department and devotes about 50 percent of his time to its management in addition to practicing in the banking and finance areas. Two other lawyers devote all of their time preparing standard forms as well. As a result, the firm has a well-developed paper forms system in the areas of banking, finance, real property, and various other areas.

The precedent management department does more than manage the firm's form files. It annotates each form with case law and statutory citations as well as explanations of the practical effects of particular clauses.

The precedent management department has one other interesting member. Dr. Robert Eagleson is a former English professor from the University of Sydney. He now spends his full time reviewing all forms required to be in plain English to ensure that they meet applicable standards. These would include, for example, insurance policies and other documents subject to plain language requirements. They also include forms that the firm drafts for the Australian government. In addition, Dr. Eagleson reviews the firm's other forms to ensure that their meaning is clear and understandable.

After the standard forms are finalized, the precedents department sends them to the firm's document assembly department. There Mr. Borgese and his staff (each of whom has a background, if not a degree, in both computer science and law) encode the firm's forms for use with its document assembly engine.

The partner who served as the subject matter expert in preparing the initial draft of the form is also responsible for drafting periodic updates. When circumstances require that a form be changed, the partner makes the changes and notifies the precedent department, which then performs its functions and passes the revised form to the document assembly department for codification. Mr. Borgese notes that having a domain expert revise the form and then asking the document assembly programmers to program it is very effective and substantially speeds the update process.

Clayton Utz is a large national law firm with perhaps 200 lawyers in its Sydney office alone. For the past four years, senior solicitor Roslyn Newman has devoted 100 percent of her time to developing CADA applications. She works with other lawyers in the firm to identify target applications and see them through to implementation.

Partners who are subject matter experts in each domain prepare standard forms with the assistance of the firm's Precedents Department. Lawyer Jane Stackpool, Director of the firm's Precedents Department, manages the process with the help of her staff of assistants. When she feels a precedent is completed, she sends it to Roslyn Newman and her staff of programmers in the CAD (computer-assisted drafting) Department. The CAD Department converts the paper form to a computerized version, complete with legal its CADA systems in a current and up-to-date state. The firm has developed applications in litigation, banking and finance, corporate, and real property subject areas and is developing new systems daily. The firm uses the WorkForm shell.

CONCLUSION

CADA systems can and will change the face of law practice. Lawyers will be able to produce more in less time while being freed from routine drafting chores. Clients will receive better service and at a lower cost. In time, sophisticated clients will insist on working only with firms whose practice incorporates this modern tool. And CADA will make it economical for lawyers to provide legal services to previously underrepresented groups.

ENDNOTES

1. Informal discussions with various CADA engine developers suggest that the number of lawyers and law firms that have purchased CADA tools now number well into the thousands. They also report that interest in CADA has taken a dramatic upswing during the last 12 months.
2. Prentice Hall, 1992.
3. "What Do Sophisticated Clients Expect You to Be Able to Deliver—and How Can Technology Help?", in *Technology in the Law Practice: The Future is Now* (Chicago: American Bar Association, 1992).

Charles E. Pear, Jr., is co-chair of the ABA Section of Law Practice Management's Hypermedia Interest Group. He is presently a visiting professor (law and computers) on the Faculty of Law at the University of British Columbia.

A Litigator's Guide to Document Assembly Programs

James A. Eidelman

Jim Eidelman has been following the development of document assembly software since software developers first targeted the legal market. In this chapter, he catalogs most of the document assembly systems available for lawyers.

At its best, document assembly is the use of special software to teach the computer to "think like a lawyer" in drafting documents. For example, the computer might present choices or ask the lawyer questions, as in the following example:

```
Is there a claim for loss of consor-
tium? Y/N

Is there a claim for punitive damages?
Y/N

Which of the following did the defen-
dant do?
_____ Drove while intoxicated
_____ Failed to keep a careful lookout
_____ Violated speed laws
_____ Ran a stop sign
_____ Drove recklessly
_____ Followed too closely
```

A lawyer or paralegal can then answer the questions on the screen and have the computer insert the appropriate text into the first draft of a word processing document. The more complex the documents, the more a lawyer can benefit from this type of software.

The primary benefits of using this kind of software are:

1. *Higher volume.* A lawyer can competently handle more cases and, assuming that the lawyer is not charging by the hour, therefore earn more.
2. *Quality assurance.* Computerized checklists and systems help the lawyer to consider all of the options and avoid possible mistakes. Also, once set up right, the computer won't make mistakes.
3. *Faster response* to clients.
4. *Delegation and teaching.* Systems permit more standard work to be done by legal assistants and younger associates. They also educate the paralegals and associates as they draft documents.

Listed below are document assembly software packages and forms for trial lawyers who are using IBM PCs (unless otherwise specified).

DOCUMENT DRAFTING TOOLS

CapSoft (also for some UNIX systems)
CapSoft Development Corporation
226 West 2230 North
Suite 200
Provo, UT 84604
(801) 375-6562

> *Offers the most robust interface to lawyers and paralegals, is very fast, and is well supported in most cities. Steepest learning curve, but getting easier. Good for publishing complex systems.*

Clause-It (Apple Macintosh only)
311 North Second Street
Suite 303
St. Charles, IL 60174
(708) 513-4240

> *The only document assembly system for the Macintosh.*

DOCUDRAFT
Canterbury Legal Systems Division, CMS/Data
30 St. Patrick St.
Suite 200
Toronto, Ontario M5T3A3
Canada
(416) 977-8434

> *Integrates with external database files and WordPerfect. Powerful programming language with user-definable functions.*

ExperText (with Canadian litigation and divorce
  forms)
Simlaw Systems, Ltd.
144 Front Street West
Suite 700
Toronto, Ontario M5J2L7
Canada
(416) 971-8454 or (800) 387-2625

> *Integrated internal database, good speed, and templates.*

FastDraft
Interactive Professional Software
3495 Piedmont Road
11 Piedmont Center
Suite 806
Atlanta, GA 30305
(404) 262-2340

First Draft
First Draft Legal System
P.O. Box 1951
Sausalito, CA 94966
(415) 332-8507

FlexPractice (includes personal injury and
  divorce forms)
Integrated Concepts
2090 Ridge Road West
Rochester, NY 14626
(800) 724-3648

> *Forms were developed with, and previously marketed by, Lawyer's Coop division of Thomson Publishing. Uses runtime version of Framework's programming language to present series of menus and select clauses. Decision tree model, and therefore easier than many others to set up. Excellent templates.*

General Counsel
The Technology Group
36 South Charles Street
Suite 444
Baltimore, MD 21201
(301) 576-2040

Jumpstart
ProBATE Software Publishing Company, Inc.
3527 West 12th Street
Suite B
Greeley, CO 80634
(800) 288-9169 or (303) 352-3445

> *Starter system that uses numbered fields to merge into WordPerfect.*

LawProcess (also known as ABFjr)
West Publishing Co.—Textbook Division
West Telemarketing
610 Opperman Drive
P.O. Box 64526
Eagan, MN 64526
(612) 687-7000/7629 or (800) 328-9352

> *The "student version" (more limited, but very powerful and easy to use) of Jim Sprowl's original ABF document assembly language, developed at the American Bar Foundation. An excellent starter system to learn about document assembly. Disk available with Maggs & Sprowl,* Computer Applications in the Law, *available from West or the ABA.*

Scrivener
Dianoetic Development Company
P.O. Box 230
Flourtown, PA 19031
(215) 233-3892

> *Written in Prolog, the only true artificial intelligence system among the programs listed here, it allows the integration of powerful rules, decision tree for easy template creation, and a built-in programming language. Limited database functions.*

Supra II (with litigation forms)
TSC Computing
ATT: Wilma
P.O. Box 40158
Spokane, WA 99202
(509) 535-7447

WorkForm and WorkTool (also for UNIX, Wang,
  and other minicomputers)
ShortWork
Analytic Legal Programs, Inc.
350 Cambridge Avenue
Palo Alto, CA 94306
(415) 321-3330

CASE MANAGEMENT SYSTEMS WITH INTEGRATED DOCUMENT ASSEMBLY

CCT/CCM Client Case Management System
SAGA N.A.
576 5th Avenue
Suite 1103
New York, NY 10036
(212) 768-3531

Case Master III
Software Technology, Inc.
1621 Cushman Drive
Lincoln, NE 68512
(401) 423-1440

> *Based on the original LegalSoft, this flexible and inexpensive system allows user-definable fields and merges with WordPerfect.*

LawBase
Apogee Computer Systems
6825 East Tennessee
Suite 500
Denver, CO 80224
(303) 320-6378 or (800) 527-6433

> *Built-in programming language that creates documents and updates calendar.*

Personal Injury Case Management System
Shepard's/McGraw-Hill, Inc.
555 Middle Creek Parkway
P.O. Box 35300
Colorado Springs, CO 80935-3530
(719) 488-3000 or (800) 541-3334

Privilege
FutureLaw, Inc.
709 West Huron
Ann Arbor, MI 48103
(313) 668-1947

> *Merges with WordPerfect only.*

WORD PROCESSING MERGE/MACRO UTILITIES

AutoLaw (WordPerfect macros, Auto-Personal Injury)
11545 West Bernardo Court
Suite 202
San Diego, CA 92127
(619) 485-5570

Blankity Blank
Softstream Technologies
2740 Hollywood Boulevard
Hollywood, FL 33020
(305) 920-9292 or (800) 888-9292

Generic Practice System (GPS)
Rick Rodgers
P.O. Box 1119
Buies Creek, NC 27506-1119

> *Send a disk and disk mailer with $1.00 in postage or access through bulletin board: Frolic & Detour BBS for Lawyers, (919) 893-5206.*

OverDrive 2
OverDrive Systems, Inc.
23980 Chagrin Boulevard
Suite 200
Cleveland, OH 44122
(216) 292-3425

BASIC FORM SYSTEMS FOR LITIGATION AVAILABLE ON FLOPPY DISK:

California Personal Injury (California)
Matthew Bender & Company Legal Systems Software
1275 Broadway
Albany, NY 12204
(800) 833-3630

DL Drafting Libraries
Attorney's Computer Network, Inc.
333 East 43rd Street
Suite 803
New York, NY 10017
(212) 661-6114

Handling the Automobile Accident Case: A Systems Approach
The Institute of Continuing Legal Education (Michigan)
c/o Legal Update Company
721 East Huron
Ann Arbor, MI 48104
(313) 769-1500

Lawriter Legal Software (Ohio)
Anderson Publishing Company
2035 Reading Road
Cincinnati, OH 45202
(513) 421-4142

Microcomputer Concepts, Inc.
6424 Central Avenue
St. Petersburg, FL 33707
(813) 381-4010

The Pleading Processor (New York)
Legal Labs, Inc.
5 East 76th Street
New York, NY 10021
(212) 439-6724

James A. Eidelman is an Ann Arbor, Michigan, lawyer and director of practice systems consulting with Automation Partners, Inc. He is a council member of the ABA's Section of Law Practice Management, chair of the Practice Systems Interest Group, and a popular speaker and author on computer applications for lawyers.

Document Assembly and Financial Software for the Family Lawyer

James A. Eidelman

> Family law practitioners must master a number of different substantive fields including business law, tax law, and general litigation. In this article, Jim Eidelman discusses many of the leading document assembly and financial software programs available to help accomplish these tasks.

We are in the midst of a revolution in which the tools family lawyers have traditionally used are being replaced by microcomputer applications. The PC that you use for word processing can automatically draft pleadings and separation agreements and can calculate divorce settlements or run tax analyses. In this chapter, I will discuss some of the better software programs on the market to help perform these tasks.

DOCUMENT ASSEMBLY

One of the most powerful and effective ways to use a computer is in formulating standard documents. Fortunately, many word processing programs now provide sophisticated merge capabilities, with the ability to include different material depending on the particular facts of the case. In addition, many off-the-shelf document assembly programs can merge with widely used word processing software, to create integrated family law practice systems.

Here is a description of some of the better document assembly packages currently available for family practitioners:

General Programs

FlexPractice is a very easy-to-use document assembly engine that works with the Framework integrated software. FlexPractice has several modules, two of which are of note to the family

law practice. The user selects from outlines of documents and is prompted for necessary information that is then inserted into standard documents. The system has an elegant user interface and makes it easy to customize documents. Two editions are available: the Matrimonial Pleadings for New York and the Separation Agreement editions, available from Integrated Concepts, 2090 Ridge Road W., Rochester, NY 14626; (800) 724-3648.

AutoLaw Corp. sells AutoDomestic, a set of templates that use the macro/merge system to assemble divorce documents. It has 39 forms relating to divorce matters, including a property settlement agreement, a petition for dissolution, and general interrogatories, with macros to prompt for specific information and subject choices. The forms are generic and can be modified for any state. Contact AutoLaw Corp., 11545 W. Bernardo Court, Suite 202, San Diego, CA 92127; (619) 543-9044.

Attorney's Computer Network, Inc., offers more than 20 different document assembly programs, with versions of most for all states except Louisiana. The software includes a document-assembly merge system that supports conditional text inclusion and variable merge, provided at no extra charge. Two packages are relevant to divorce lawyers: The Separation Agreements Library is available in versions for every state, while the Divorce Pleadings System is available only for New York.

State-Specific Programs

California

Attorney's Briefcase, Inc., publishes legal texts in a hypertext environment. Since they reside on your hard disk, there are no on-line costs to worry about. Packages such as California Family Law and Children and the Law are organized into topics and subtopics, and are conveniently indexed. A rapid word search function retrieves briefs of cases and the full texts of statutes, regulations, and court rules. Periodic update service is available, as well as inexpensive on-line updating and research services. Contact Attorney's Briefcase, 519 17th Street, 6th Floor, Oakland, CA 94612; (800) 648-2618.

New York

For family lawyers practicing in New York, the Attorney's Computer Network package covers an extensive array of provisions, including support, visitation, property division, taxes, insurance continuation, and more. If a lawyer purchases the complete library of 20 systems, a credit will be given for the individual modules previously purchased. All systems are compatible with WordPerfect, WordStar, MultiMate, and other major wordprocessing packages. Contact Attorney's Computer Network, Inc., 333 E. 43rd St., Suite 803, New York, NY 10017; (212) 661-6114. (The systems are also marketed in New York by Julius Blumberg, and nationally by Excelsior-Legal.)

Texas

There are several systems available for Texas divorces. A sophisticated WordPerfect macro-driven program called Div/Texas is available from The Electric Lawyer. Once the client information is loaded into the master information list, which contains 70 or more fields, the program will generate a wide variety of pleadings and documents. The pleadings are menu-driven, and even allow options, such as inserting into the pleading claims for adultery or cruel treatment as well as no-fault grounds. It will also produce the deed to transfer the family home and transfer documents for vehicles. Contact The Electric Lawyer, Box 276, Lewisville, TX 75067; (214) 221-9830.

Owl Software sells a Texas child-support calculation program and a divorce inventory program. The child support program will produce exhibits for court and will document exceptions to court guidelines in attempting to raise or lower child support. It also generates comparative spreadsheets that show the incremental effects of differing levels of child support. The divorce inventory program, while more accurately a spreadsheet, walks the user through virtually all the data necessary to complete, revise, and recalculate an inventory. Contact Owl Software, 515 North Velasco, Angelton, TX 77515.

Finally, RHR Marketing produces LawText, which is another document-generating program that uses a master information list. Contact RHR Marketing, 3707 North St. Marys, #111, San Antonio, TX 78212; (512) 735-8100.

South Carolina

For South Carolina attorneys, Legal Software Systems offers a package of hundreds of domestic law forms, with merge fields and a client checklist database, and also includes a document assembly program for WordPerfect. Contact Legal Software Systems, 903 Elmwood Drive, Columbia, SC 29201; (803) 765-9945.

Canada

Matlaw is a Canadian-based document assembly system using Simlaw's full-featured ExperText document assembly engine. It merges client information with a comprehensive set of Canadian pleadings and agreements. Contact Simlaw System, Ltd., Suite 700, 144 Front Street W., Toronto, Ontario, Canada M5J 2L7; (416) 971-8454.

FINANCIAL ANALYSIS PROGRAMS

Many lawyers are now using electronic spreadsheet programs like Lotus 1-2-3 and Microsoft Excel to replace their calculators. It is much easier to use an electronic spreadsheet than a calculator to tabulate client assets and expenses. You can also do interest calculations, valuation of pension plans, real estate closing statements and prorations, client costs, and the many other calculations a lawyer must perform.

Spouse and Child Support Obligations

Most states have now adopted guidelines to determine child support obligations based upon the income of the parties, custodial arrangements, other support obligations, and other factors. Twenty states use a variation of the income shares model developed by Robert G. Williams at Policy Studies, Inc., in Denver.

It is no surprise that many states now have computer programs to perform these calculations. For example, the Michigan Friend of the Court has now developed a program that is available to all Michigan lawyers for a give-away price. Many other programs have been developed commercially. For a description of Disso-Master (California Family Law Report), Cash Flow (Michael Kalcheim), DSA (Law Ware), and Supportax (Norton Family Law Systems), see "Tools of the Trade" in the Spring 1988 *Family Advocate* (p. 61).

One vendor offers a program for Colorado lawyers to gather factual information, print financial affidavits, and calculate recommended child support according to court guidelines. Contact Custom Legal Software, 3867 Paseo del Prado, Boulder, CO 80301; (303) 443-2634. Its program also performs after-tax comparisons.

The Support Arrearage Program is a menu-driven program that calculates interest, costs, and lump-sum support payments. It automatically calculates due dates for many types of orders, and does all necessary calculations for a writ of execution. All of these modules are available from Howarth Ltd., 199 S. Monte Vista Ave., Suite 6, San Dimas, CA 91773; (714) 592-7917.

Property and Tax Issues

Howarth Ltd. offers several financial analysis programs that will help you with related property and tax issues. Taxrammer is a menu-driven program designed to calculate tax consequences of spousal and child support. It performs calculations of California guideline figures using federal and state tax tables. It will also show actual net spendable income of both parties. Divi-Up is a simple, single-screen program for property division. It calculates tax consequences for proposed settlements and shows totals for each party.

Research Press offers DivorceTax, a Lotus 1-2-3 spreadsheet that calculates child support, property settlement, tax credits, and some state income taxes. Contact Research Press, Inc., 4500 W. 72nd Terrace, Prairie Village, KS, 66208; (913) 362-9667. DivorceTax software is an inexpensive

program that provides federal income tax estimates and comparisons. Contact DivorceTax Software, Inc., P.O. Box 1047, Pryor, OK 74362; (918) 825-7400.

Shepard's/McGraw-Hill, Inc., offers its Divorce, Alimony, and Child Support Tax Planning and Calculation software. This package contains six questionnaire screens to gather all pertinent information from client interviews. It calculates the financial impact of proposed settlements on either party and offers the most sophisticated tax analysis of any of the packages mentioned. It can prepare client budgets and lets you set up the system for state income taxes and basic state child support guidelines. It can handle Colorado and other simple states, but may require some side calculations for states with more complex guidelines. Contact Shepard's/McGraw-Hill, P.O. Box 1235, Colorado Springs, CO 80901; (800) 522-1050.

California Family Law Report, Inc., offers two programs that can be used in any state. DissoMaster was reviewed in the Spring 1988 *Family Advocate* (p. 61). Propertizer performs marital and separate property settlement calculations, figuring equity and tax impact on either party. Contact CFLR, Inc., P. O. Box 5917, Sausalito, CA 94966; (800) 444-2357.

Adoption

Most software specifically designed for a family law practice relates to divorce. I have found only one package for adoption, and it is specific to Pennsylvania. Developed by Vince Lackner, it uses a Lotus 1-2-3 template to calculate a wide variety of options to determine which facts must be gathered from the clients, which forms are necessary, whose consents need to be obtained, which parties must be served, and other information depending on the facts of the case. Contact Lackner Computer Group, Carnegie Office Park #290, 700 N. Bell Ave., Pittsburgh, PA 15106; (412) 279-2121.

Research Databases

Like other areas of the law, cases relating to family law are beginning to appear in electronic format. A good example is the Minnesota Family Law Database for IBM compatible machines, which is available from Digital Legal Research; (612) 780-3157. It uses a Folio Views Database of all Minnesota cases from North Western Reporter since 1942. CD-ROMs are also being published for a wide variety of areas of practice, including general legal databases that can be of help in matrimonial cases, such as Mathew Bender's California Civil Cases on CD-ROM; (800) 223-1940.

CONCLUSION

In this increasingly competitive legal market, computers will play an integral part in providing prompt, efficient service to clients. By using computers effectively, family law practitioners will be able to spend more time counseling and showing concern for clients, and less time creating and shuffling papers. In the end, practices will be more profitable and clients will appreciate the improved service, so everyone will benefit.

James A. Eidelman is an Ann Arbor, Michigan, lawyer and director of practice systems consulting with Automation Partners, Inc. He is a council member of the ABA's Section of Law Practice Management, chair of the Practice Systems Interest Group, and a popular speaker and author on computer applications for lawyers.

The Electronic Profit Center: Document Assembly for Litigators

Charles E. Pear, Jr.

The importance of computer-aided document assembly systems lies in their power to make us more productive *and* more profitable. Charles Pear, a practitioner and now law professor, shows how document assembly systems can be useful to a litigator and follows with two case studies showing how it can be extremely profitable.

Why is computer-assisted document assembly (CADA) important to lawyers and law firms? Because it can provide a competitive edge in an intensely competitive industry. It also can boost revenues when income is flagging, and it can improve service to clients while reducing errors at the same time. That's fine for partners handling business transactions, but what about a litigator? Well, look around. Your filing cabinets are crammed with mounds of pleadings for your current cases. Moreover, you probably keep mountains of form files full of pleadings, briefs, and agreements from prior cases. Although litigators try cases from time to time, they sell paper for a living—reams of it.

"Yes," you think, "but document assembly is not for me, because every piece of paper I generate is unique, a masterpiece." If so, then why stockpile forms? Like it or not, the reality of modern litigation is preparing pleadings, releases, and other repetitive documents. Instead of hoping they will go away, why not make them an even smaller part of your life and generate some profits as well? Document assembly can help you do this. Your transaction partners have already discovered this. Now it's time for you to explore CADA, too.

In this chapter, I will discuss several ways a litigator might benefit from a CADA system. I will then focus on two case studies showing how CADA can be used to bring in clients and improve profits.

HOW LITIGATORS USE CADA

Computers are very effective at performing tedious chores or eliminating time-consuming, repetitive tasks. Litigation is fraught with procedural tasks bearing exactly those characteristics. Relegating such work to CADA systems allows litigators to focus on more challenging and interesting aspects of litigation such as the tactical, strategic, and legal issues of the case.

Examples of the kinds of matters suitable for automation include:

Repetitive documents such as routine pleadings and correspondence.
Repetitive cases such as personal injury litigation.
Time-sensitive matters such as temporary restraining orders.
Almost any other document where a checklist of requirements would be useful.

Repetitive Documents

Litigators generate heaps of paper, most of which consists of standard pleadings, standard letters, and so on. Many standard documents can be made into paper forms consisting of boilerplate clauses and blanks to fill in. Any document that you can reduce to a paper form is a good candidate for automation.

Here are some examples:

Pleadings

Pleadings that can be produced by CADA systems include: notices of oral depositions; notices of depositions upon written interrogatories to obtain (e.g., medical records in a malpractice case or trading records in a securities case); requests for production of documents; requests for inspection or examination; pattern interrogatories; offers of judgment; routine court orders (The motion for _____ filed by _____, having been heard by the Honorable _____ on _____, 19__, is hereby [granted][denied].); and notices of appeal.

Some standard motions are suitable for automation, such as motions for entry of default. Others are appropriate for partial automation. For instance, a motion for summary judgment routinely includes a memorandum reciting the applicable rules of civil procedure and the principles for granting such relief as set forth in the jurisdiction's leading case on point.

Various jurisdictions compile standard jury instructions in paper form, such as *California's Book of Approved Jury Instructions*. You can automate these forms readily by using CADA systems. Litigators find these especially useful when the issues change during or just before trial.

Settlement agreements, releases, and so on generally spring from a handful of forms in the litigator's form file. You can prepare these more efficiently with a CADA system.

Correspondence

Lawyers use standard engagement or retainer letters as well as letters declining employment and letters noting the completion of the requested legal work. Letters hiring, declining to hire, and dismissing associates and staff are well suited for automation and can serve a preventive function as well. Insurance defense status reports can be generated by using CADA systems that track the progress of a case. Letters informing witnesses and court reporters of deposition or trial scheduling, rescheduling, or resumption can and should be automated.

Class actions involving large numbers of clients become more manageable with CADA systems. Keeping clients informed is easier if you use a CADA system that can prepare a form letter to each client in a database file. Database hooks also let you use CADA to answer interrogatories in class actions.

Finally, most firms already use standard forms for court filing instructions, service instructions, and delivery instructions. You can simplify these further by using CADA systems. For instance, instead of having your secretary type a list of the lawyers who must approve the form of a court's order, let the system automatically generate the list by reading the list of counsel from a database as it generates the order itself.

Repetitive Cases

Many litigators specialize in particular kinds of cases. Their practices not only involve repetitive documents but also have common factual or legal issues and a common sequence of events. Such cases are ideal for automation. Examples include: collections; foreclosure proceedings; mechanics lien claims and enforcement proceedings; worker's compensation cases; auto accident cases; landlord/tenant cases; probate matters; family law matters such as divorce proceedings, adoptions, and name changes; and so on.

Cases like these can benefit from CADA systems that link to or have built-in case management features. Such systems can monitor the progress of the litigation, generate pleadings at appropriate times, and provide reports to clients on the status of the matter at periodic intervals.

Time-Sensitive Matters and Documents

Some matters are sufficiently time sensitive that it makes sense to provide for them in advance. Labor lawyers, for example, often must seek restraining orders on a moment's notice.

While not all such matters are routine, the point here is that since time is critical, the lawyer may have little or no time to prepare the moving papers and supporting memorandum or, conversely, a responsive pleading. CADA permits the lawyer to anticipate and address these needs in advance.

When the time comes, the CADA system can churn out useful pleadings effortlessly and quickly. A quick edit can adapt them to the situation at hand. Although the pleading may not cover all relevant points, it is much better than appearing in court empty-handed. Further, a partial supporting memorandum containing le-

FIGURE 3.8 Volume History Before Document Assembly

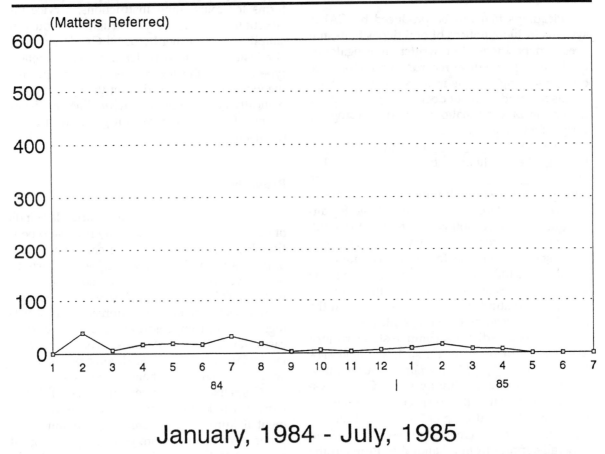

January, 1984 - July, 1985

gal points and authorities can serve as a check-list of threshold issues for reference in oral argument or in chambers.

Documents Where a Checklist of Requirements Would Be Useful

Whenever a checklist is useful for preparing or reviewing a document, you should consider automating that document. When preparing a complaint, for example, some lawyers use a checklist to make sure that they have adequately covered all causes of action. A CADA system can present the same checklist on the computer screen. As you choose relevant causes of action, the system prepares a complaint alleging those causes of action almost instantly. This technique is especially useful in notice pleading jurisdictions such as the federal courts.

Furthermore, CADA systems can prevent the lawyer from overlooking procedural require-ments. For example, F.R.C.P. 9(b) requires that fraud allegations be pleaded with specificity. When you instruct the system to include a fraud count in the complaint, the system can remind you that fraud must be pleaded with specificity and then request a statement of those specifics.

CASE STUDY I: CADA AS A MARKETING TOOL

While stories like the following abound, few reported studies actually document the benefits of CADA. The following case study addresses the impact of CADA in a business practice context but is instructive for litigators as well. Although highly subjective in nature, it illustrates the powerful impact CADA can make on a firm's practice. Names and miscellaneous details have been altered to preserve the privacy of the parties.

Step 1: Using CADA to Bring in New Clients

Lawyers in this U.S. state routinely prepared certain documents called *conveyancing documents* for the sale and financing of residential properties. The process generally involved preparing a deed or assignment of lease or, when acting for a lender, a note and mortgage. Unlike many states, the firms performed no accounting or settlement functions. At the relevant time, the law firms received the princely sum of about $50–100 for each such transaction. Ordinarily, skilled (and well-paid) legal assistants prepared the documents and lawyers reviewed them.

In the 1980s, four of the state's five largest firms (meaning 50–100 lawyers) had well-established conveyancing departments—staffs of legal assistants who did nothing but prepare conveyancing documents. Historically, these firms dominated the market—especially with respect to preparation of mortgage loan documents.

In mid-1985, while I was a partner at a mid-sized law firm, I noticed that our small conveyancing practice had dwindled to nothing. In prior years, the firm had managed to produce a modest amount of conveyancing work—about $10,000 per year—primarily representing small mortgage banking and mortgage brokerage firms. But as Figure 3.8 shows, the firm received no requests for documents in May, June, or July of 1985.

I decided to build a CADA system using an IBM PC that automated the preparation of conveyancing documents. We then hired a clerk-typist to run the system. She had no prior experience drafting conveyance documents. Starting in September 1985, we invited clients and prospective clients to try the firm's new service.

At first, large lending institutions were reluctant even to try us. They had strong ties to the large firms and were hesitant to risk dealing with a new firm with only limited experience. Perhaps out of politeness, however, a lender sent a transaction or two.

We were careful to prepare these early transactions properly and return them promptly. In nearly all cases, we returned the requested documents less than 24 hours after the client requested them. This favorably impressed the lenders and they showed it by sending more requests. Such requests increased to one a week, then several a week, then one a day, then several a day.

Monthly Conveyancing Volume

Although gross conveyance billings for 1985 remained in the typical $10,000 range, the final three months of the year clearly suggested that an increase in volume and income was coming. The volume of requests did increase the following year, as Figure 3.9 shows.

The increased volume translated directly into greater billings for the firm. In 1986 the firm's conveyance practice billed more than $250,000—over 25 times its average annual income for each prior year. Figure 3.10 contrasts the income for that year to that of the prior two years. The bulk of this income came from work for large lenders usually represented by the large firms with well-established conveyancing practices.

Of course, the additional volume of work required expansion of the conveyancing staff, so we hired an additional clerk-typist and installed a second PC. We also asked two members of the word processing department staff to spend part of their time helping to prepare these documents.

What Contributed to the Firm's Success?

The firm succeeded in building its client base by providing high-quality documents coupled with very quick turnaround time. Our CADA system let us return the documents in a day or two. The large well-established firms took three to four days. The clients repeatedly cited this difference in turnaround time as the single most critical factor to them when choosing a law firm.

Of course, turnaround time was only relevant if our legal work was comparable to that of our competitors. However, we had only three lawyers and no legal assistants who knew how to do the work. By leveraging the knowledge of these lawyers via a CADA system, we were able to use untrained clerk-typists and word processors to prepare legal documents of sufficiently high quality to meet the competition.

The system also saved lawyer review time while enhancing accuracy. For example, the name of each borrower appears at least four times on a standard note and mortgage. Lawyers soon realized that if the name was correct the first time it appeared, it would be correct throughout the document. Similarly, if the lender's name was correct, its address, place of formation, and so on also would be correct since

FIGURE 3.9 Growth in Volume After Introducing Document Assembly

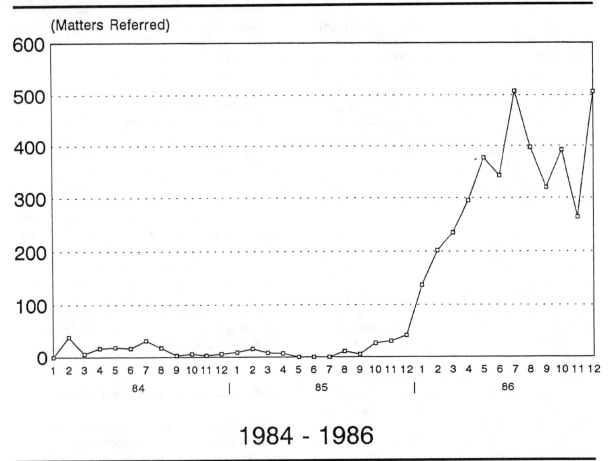

(Matters Referred)

1984 - 1986

the program supplied this information automatically. This streamlining curtailed the chance of errors and reduced lawyer and staff boredom. Informal discussions with clients confirmed that the firm's documents contained fewer errors than those prepared by its competitors.

Step 2: Using CADA to Recapture Lost Clients

In 1987, several of the large firms began to solicit my attention, leading me to move to one of them (Firm B). Firm B had the largest, best, and most experienced conveyancing department in the state.

After joining Firm B, I examined the volume of its work for a client the Bank shared with my former firm. The results were astonishing. Firm B's work for the Bank had declined almost exactly inversely to the growth of my former firm's

work for the Bank. By the middle of 1986, Firm B was no longer preparing conveyance documents for the Bank. (See Figure 3.11.)

Firm B expected me to automate the firm's conveyance practice. When I left my former firm, I left the conveyance practice intact. Believe it or not, I felt that this was the fair thing to do in view of the firm's investment in hardware and staffing. I did not take any of the staff from the firm (except my personal secretaries) nor any clients; Firm B had a strong client base, and I was confident it could be made stronger through CADA.

As a result, I had a unique opportunity to compete against my own document assembly system. Although the following observations were not derived using scientifically exact methods, they are instructive.

After Firm B automated its conveyancing system, its turnaround time matched that of my former firm, which I will call Firm A. Addition-

FIGURE 3.10 Growth in Annual Billings Before and After Document Assembly

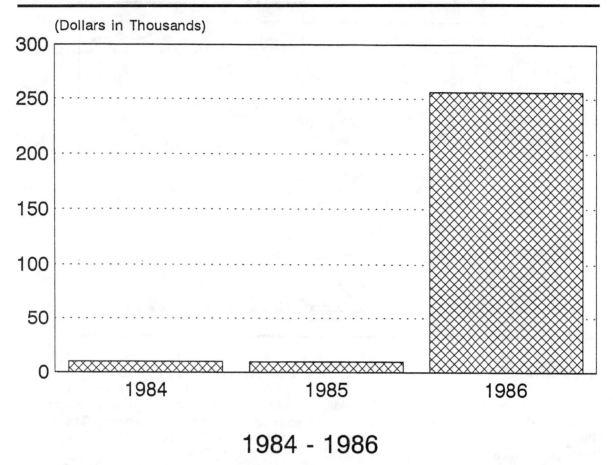

(Dollars in Thousands)

1984 - 1986

ally, Firm B's more experienced staff had fewer problems completing the work as requested. Nevertheless, Firm B had a hard time recovering a share of the Bank's work. In contrast, when Firm A introduced its CADA system, it found it much easier to take the Bank's work away from Firm B.

You could attribute the difficulty Firm B faced in regaining a share of the Bank's work to any number of factors. The most plausible explanation, however, is that Firm A succeeded in attracting clients, including the Bank, because Firm A was able to offer service markedly superior to that offered by competitors. In contrast, when Firm B sought to win back the Bank's work, it could at most offer service comparable to or perhaps somewhat better than that offered by Firm A, but not dramatically better.

Interestingly, before Firm A arrived, a third firm—Firm C—split the Bank's work with Firm B. Now that Firm B has automated, it and Firm

A seem to do the bulk of the Bank's work. Informal discussions with a partner of Firm C (also one of the state's large and well-established firms) suggest that Firm C may have been the ultimate loser; apparently it received little or no conveyancing work from the Bank during that period.

CASE STUDY 2: CADA AS A PROFIT CENTER

This is the story of a large firm (numbering in the hundreds of lawyers) that in 1988 automated a branch of its litigation practice using CADA tools. Until then, the department had used WordPerfect macros to generate the documents used in this practice area. As with Case History 1, the facts have been altered in insignificant ways to hide the identity of the firm, but the essential analysis remains the same.

FIGURE 3.11 Illustration of Decline in Firm B's Monthly Volume for the Bank

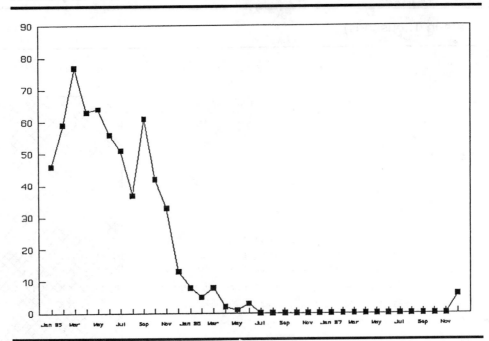

The Motivation

Like many large firms, the forward-thinking vision of its lawyers did not precipitate this firm's decision to automate. Instead, a much more practical consideration came into play. It seemed that most of the department's work came from a single institution, which supplied a steady stream of files. The firm handled all files of that type for that client within the jurisdiction. However, internal and external pressures began to mount on the client to break up the existing exclusive relationship with the firm. As a result, there were rumblings that the client intended to distribute its business among numerous regional firms.

The firm decided to automate to preserve the existing exclusive relationship enjoyed by the firm. In addition, the firm anticipated a rise in the workload in this practice area due to the growing recession and felt that a CADA system would help it market its expertise and technological capabilities to prospective clients.

Pre–Document Assembly Statistics

Before developing the system, a single lawyer handled the practice area with the help of three paralegals and a legal secretary. This crew handled about 150 active files at any one time, with an average turnover of three months per case or about 600 cases per year. The practice had generated about $400,000 in each of the prior three or four years.

Development of the CADA System

The firm then asked Simlaw Systems, Ltd., to help automate this aspect of its practice. Simlaw markets the ExperText document assembly engine.[1] The law firm explained its document assembly requirements. One of the most important design criteria was incorporation of database facilities to record information, generate status reports, search the files, and generally perform case management functions. Simlaw prepared the initial databases and supplied them to the firm. The firm then completed the development using the databases and certain additional tools supplied by Simlaw.

The initial software investment was $10,000. It took about six months to develop a working system. Cumulatively, the firm estimates that it invested about $80,000 of otherwise billable lawyer and staff time in developing the system. The firm permitted lawyers and staff to docket time to the project as if it were billable time. During a three-month implementation period, it successfully transferred all active files onto the CADA system and phased out old files by completing them the traditional way.

Result

The firm reports that its new CADA system permits it to process the files for their existing client far more efficiently. In fact, the firm established a modem link with the client in order to receive file information electronically. It also placed a computer in the client's office, so that the client can dial in to the firm's network. The client uses this to obtain status information and to enter instructions directly into the firm's CADA system. The firm also provides the client with regular detailed reports generated by the CADA system. As a result, the client sends all its business to the firm.

The firm also began to actively market its capabilities by using the system as a technology showcase when giving potential clients a tour of the office. They highlighted the firm's efficiency in managing the practice using the database facilities of the CADA engine.

The marketing effort succeeded in attracting several major new clients. One such client took its business from another firm that did not use the technology. Other new clients who previously distributed their work among several other firms chose to centralize it and give it all to the firm.

As the economy deteriorated, the anticipated rise in the workload materialized. The firm was optimally positioned to take on the increased workload. It was able to inform prospective clients that it had no upward limit on its capacity to handle more files because of the CADA system.

The combination of these factors resulted in an increase in the practice to almost 2,000 active files (a 13-fold increase) and 4,500 files annually (a 7.5-fold increase). The files tended to be of much greater complexity than in the nonrecessionary period; and with increased client demands, the average file now required almost twice the level of documentation as the files handled in 1988. The firm estimates that it now generates 25 to 30 times more documentation than it did in 1988.

Annual Billings: 1988–1991

As Figure 3.12 shows, annual billings rose dramatically—from approximately $500,000 in 1988 to $600,000 in 1989 and to $1,900,000 in 1990. By 1991, annual billings jumped to $3,000,000 plus an additional $700,000 of spinoff work (nearly a tenfold total increase over the preautomation figure). And growth continues with the addition of new clients.

A return-on-investment analysis cannot be made without access to figures such as lawyer and staff salaries, floor space rentals, equipment and furnishing costs, and so on. Even so, the fact that the firm now grosses double its investment in developing the document assembly system (about $100,000) *every month* suggests that an opportunity exists for an excellent return on the investment. (Monthly revenues changed from $33,000 to $250,000, an increase of $217,000.) Of course, the CADA system requires periodic updating and maintenance. These figures were not available, but one lawyer estimated that they might represent another $100,000 investment over the four-year period.

Staffing increases were modest in comparison to increases in volume. The practice is now conducted by 5 full-time lawyers, only one of whom is a partner. There are now 17 paralegals and 3 secretaries. All 25 staff members have access to the CADA system through the firm's local area network.

So while the staffing increased about fivefold, the gross billings increased tenfold. This means that each staff person is about twice as productive as before the CADA system was introduced. This is even more dramatic when one considers that the CADA system only affects a portion of the time spent by each staff person.

Physical tasks such as filing documents, sealing envelopes, and communicating with clients and other parties used to take up to half of the staff time. Now these activities comprise an even greater proportion, because staff members are handling more active files and producing more documents. One paralegal stated that the document assembly system now produces more documents per day than she can physically process in terms of filing and delivering the documents; she has reached an upper limit in terms of what the automated system can do for her. (The only way to expand that limit would be to implement automatic filing and electronic delivery of

FIGURE 3.12 Document Assembly Payoff

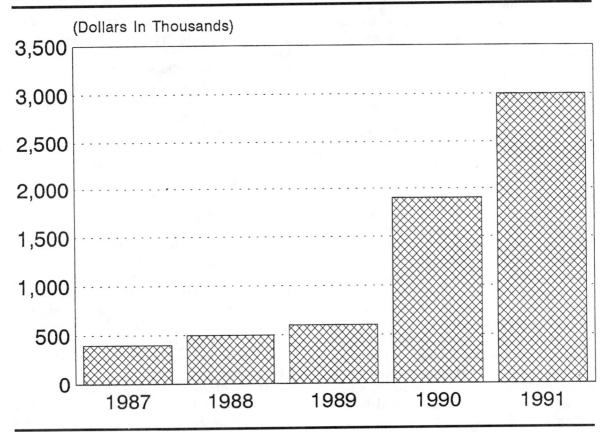

(Dollars In Thousands)

documents.) Whenever an employee's time is maximized, new staff must be hired to fill excess demand.

The average annual billings per lawyer increased from $400,000 for one senior partner to $600,000 per lawyer, most of whom are associates. The ratio of staff per lawyer remained consistent at four to one, but the total cost of lawyers and staff represented a smaller proportion of the amounts billed—meaning the profit margin increased accordingly.

The firm also reports that the CADA system provided other efficiencies as well:

1. The system can generate 40 to 50 demand letters in an hour, including drafting, printing, review, and signing time. Without the system, it would take one or two persons a full day to handle such volume. Each letter involves detailed mathematical calculations.

2. The system now takes only one or two minutes to generate and print complex documents, such as complaints, which used to take at least an hour to draft.

3. The system can prepare groups or packages of documents. Many times, only a single keystroke is needed to select a batch of related documents. Each batch takes a minute or two to assemble and a few minutes to print. More importantly, each batch includes all documents needed for a given legal step, including check requisitions, checklists, reporting letters, envelopes, instructions to process servers, and so on. This batching reduced errors and training time dramatically.

4. The system generates numerous reports in minutes in an unattended manner. In the past, the firm compiled these reports manually from a laborious file-by-file review.

Billing Rates

You might think that clients aware of the greater efficiencies of the law firm would put significant downward pressure on the fees the firm could charge. However, this was not the case. Billing rates remained steady, although client demands for greater reporting and documentation did mean that the firm was preparing more documentation. In sum, the firm delivered a higher level of service for the same fee and with less effort. Billing was based on value rather than hourly rates. Even before automation, the firm tended to have value billing rates slightly below the competition. They were able to maintain this price advantage but did not have to drop prices. The clients were satisfied with greater levels of service and reporting rather than reduced fees.

Subjective Costs/Benefits

Besides the economic costs and benefits, the firm reported certain subjective costs and benefits.

Subjective Costs

The subjective, or nonfinancial, costs included the following:

1. Introduction of the system disrupted the status quo resulting in natural staff resistance to change. The implementation of each phase of the system created a level of stress and tension. The firm spent a significant amount of time selling the system to staff members used to doing things in certain ways. In addition, the firm had to correct problems with the system as soon as they arose so as to maintain staff morale.
2. The staff also had a natural fear of the automation process, including concerns about loss of their own jobs. While this fear eventually dissipated as the practice expanded, it was nevertheless a real factor in introducing the system.
3. Another subjective cost is that the staff faces a system that sets the pace for them rather than the other way around. Some regard this as a loss of control, although management obviously appreciates the

benefit of greater confidence in tasks being completed according to a preset schedule.

Subjective Benefits

The subjective benefits of the system included these:

1. The greater level of automation meant that documents were more accurate than before. The computer performs mathematical and date calculations automatically, reducing the number of such errors.
2. The database facilities of the ExperText product helped the firm address the ever more demanding needs of the clients for reporting and performance. These reports included file activity and status reports. The firm described the improvement in reporting capability as a quantum leap.
3. The database capacity also allowed the firm to identify patterns in the database and participate in strategic decision-making with the client.
4. As clients became accustomed to the firm's reporting service, it became less and less likely that they would move their files to a firm that was not automated. The firm reinforced this lock-in by installing computers on the client's site for electronic retrieval of information and by creating automatic data transfer links via modem between the client and the firm.
5. Employees reported greater satisfaction in being able to produce higher volumes of work.
6. The system permitted the firm to crystallize the expertise of senior lawyers and staff. Notwithstanding inevitable staff turnover and the retirement of a senior partner from the firm, the firm continued to expand its practice and provide a similar level of service. The firm effectively has captured some of the legal and practical expertise as intellectual capital, which remains independent of the personnel in the firm.
7. The firm was able to spin off a portion of the practice to a much lower-cost suburban location.
8. As the CADA system stimulated rapid

growth in the firm, it became necessary to hire and train new personnel. The simplicity of the CADA system made it possible to train new people and integrate them into the firm's operation very quickly.

Further Systems

As a result of the success of this system, the firm has now developed several additional CADA systems. They have attempted to select areas of implementation strategically and have built CADA into their marketing strategy.

In discussing this, I asked one partner whether a lawyer should develop the system or whether someone else (a paralegal or perhaps a programmer) should do so. He responded that the system author must be a lawyer. Although a clerk can develop simple systems, to be most effective and to maximize efficiency and profit potential, the system must embody sophisticated concepts. Usually this requires a lawyer who is attuned to the legal system, who knows where the decision points are, and who understands the legal implications of each. Furthermore, the partner I spoke to felt that it takes a special kind of person who really likes doing this kind of work. Although there are hundreds of lawyers in his firm, not a single one has ever asked him to teach him or her how to do the authoring. Moreover, as the firm has identified new areas of law for CADA development, it has asked him to do the authoring.

Managerial Aspects

The lawyer in charge found that the nature of his practice changed. He characterized it as a change from the *craft* of lawyering to the *business* of lawyering. He spends a great deal of time managing the firm's practice in his area, and yet he finds that the efficiency of automation permits him greater time to deal with the human facets of the cases. This derives from his now having greater control of information crucial to the administration of the practice. This, in turn, permits him to personalize otherwise impersonal aspects of the legal business when dealing with, for example, a defendant's request for an extension of time in hard circumstances.

CONCLUSION

CADA systems can and will change the face of law practice. Clients will receive and expect better service and at a lower cost. In time, sophisticated clients will insist on working only with firms whose practice incorporates this modern tool. This trend has already begun.

Some firms are now positioning themselves to capitalize on this development; others already have done so. In most cases, this entails a substantial investment in money and lawyer time. Some firms will be put off by that cost and will choose instead to continue the old ways. These firms will soon find themselves in an uncompetitive position. The words of that famed jurist, Yogi Berra, seem apt in describing the outlook of these firms: "The future ain't what it used to be."

ENDNOTE

1. Simlaw Systems, Ltd. (in Canada), 144 Front St. West, Suite 700, Toronto, Ont. M5J 2L7, Canada, phone (416) 971-8454, fax (416) 971-8456; or ExperText, Inc. (in the United States), 25 E. Washington, Suite 600, Chicago, IL 60602, phone (312) 444-1030 or (800) 387-2625, fax (312) 444-1033.

Charles E. Pear, Jr. is co-chair of the ABA Section of Law Practice Management's Hypermedia Interest Group. He is presently a visiting professor (law and computers) on the Faculty of Law at the University of British Columbia.

Section 4
Productivity Tools
for Litigators

Arthur Ian Miltz

One of the key reasons we use computers is to improve our productivity. Telephones, dictating equipment, photocopiers, and fax machines all made us more productive as lawyers. We used them (even if we sometimes cursed them), because they offered a better way than before.

Computers represent the next step, and they promise to outdo all of the earlier technology. With a computer, one lawyer can do the work of several and needs less staff to do it. In increasingly competitive times, litigators need every advantage they can muster. Clients expect no less, and they will hire other lawyers if you can't provide it.

This section offers a potpourri of programs that can help you become a better, more productive lawyer. It begins with a look at office organization programs and continues with chapters on spreadsheets, financial and settlement calculation software, timekeeping, E-mail, and a host of other programs designed to make you more productive. These kinds of programs can help you manage the routine organizational tasks that once filled your day. Even better, they will allow you to spend more time practicing law.

Using Office Automation Programs to Organize Your Litigation Practice

Joseph L. Kashi

One of the most useful types of software for lawyers is actually a collection of programs. Although they go by different names, most office organization programs include a calendar, E-mail, note files, and a menuing system with which to integrate other programs. Joe Kashi, a solo practitioner who office-shares with several others, tells us how he uses one such program, Futurus Team, to keep his office organized.

There are many reasons to use office automation programs to keep your office organized. A good one can help the firm keep track of appointments and deadlines, it can help you communicate and check conflicts, and it can provide a means to share files and notes on your cases. Indeed, it may even save you money. Insurance carriers often reduce malpractice premiums for law firms with comprehensive docketing systems and office organization programs. Besides, your staff deserves tools that will let them concentrate on their jobs rather than on the minor communication details inherent to working in an office environment.

In this chapter, I'll discuss how we use one automation program, Futurus Team (formerly Right Hand Man), to keep our small office organized. We've used different versions of Futurus Team for nearly five years. Even the most computerphobic professional has come to appreciate how much more smoothly our office works as a result. In addition, I'll mention several other office automation programs that you might consider. Most offer similar features and can be used for many of the same purposes as Futurus Team.

A good office organization program should have most or all of the following features:

1. Scheduling and tickler files.

2. Database and Rolodex-like cardfile options.
3. Notepad options to record information.
4. Electronic mail (E-mail) and office messaging.
5. Built-in calculators.
6. File management and DOS utility functions.
7. The ability to cut and paste between various programs.
8. Network compatibility.

Although there are several good programs on the market, we chose Futurus Team because it's simple to use, frequently updated, and provides excellent functionality for a small office. Also, it operates in a RAM resident mode—that is, it's always available and can be called up on top of any other program, including Windows. The program only requires between five and six kilobytes of conventional memory because it uses extended or expanded memory efficiently. This efficiency can be important when you use a large program like WordPerfect 5.1 or Agenda on a local area network. Finally, Futurus Team works well with all Novell networks and every DOS-based network that I've tried so far. I'm always on the lookout for that ultimate office organization program, but to date have not found anything superior to Futurus Team's overall usefulness.

FIGURE 4.1 Appointment Calendar

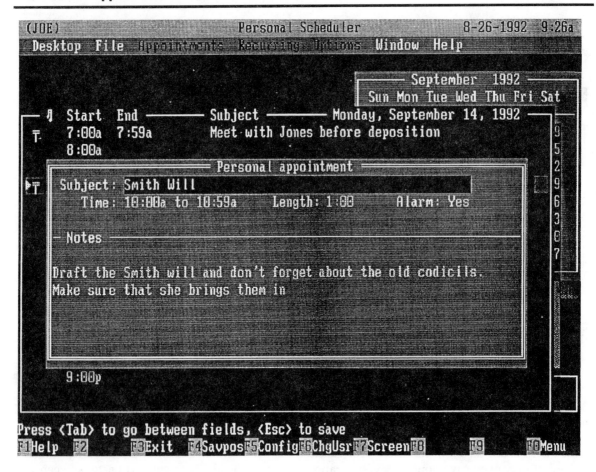

SCHEDULING FUNCTIONS

Individual Calendars

We use each lawyer's individual appointment calendar as the basic organizing tool of the office. Entered on the appointment calendar are:

- All pretrial order deadlines.
- Other deadlines to be calendared.
- Warning notes on motions, etc., set 5 to 10 days in advance.
- Warnings by which dates discovery may be served.

To help calendar trial warnings, we have a pop-up database of civil rule times, such as the number of days within which one must respond to a summary judgment motion. Our support staff uses this database to do the initial calendaring before the mail is even placed on the lawyer's desk. Since I only have 40–50 major open files at any particular time, separately

calendaring each pretrial deadline is not burdensome. Some legal-specific programs, like Abacus, automatically calculate and enter all pretrial dates, but this seems like overkill for most small offices. Doing this manually is not unduly burdensome for the number of cases that a small office ordinarily handles.

Each lawyer doublechecks all calendaring from his or her own terminal. With this system, we have found it easy to schedule not only deadlines but multiple cascading warnings about trial and discovery deadlines.

The lawyer or secretary can insert or check daily appointments. Recurring appointments, such as a Rotary meeting or Bar lunch, are inserted as preset meetings on the appropriate day, week, or month. Warnings for recurring court deadlines can be similarly inserted.

The appointment calendar allows you to search for a particular name, date, or item in an individual lawyer's calendar. This search can help if you remember that you have a deposi-

FIGURE 4.2 To-Do List

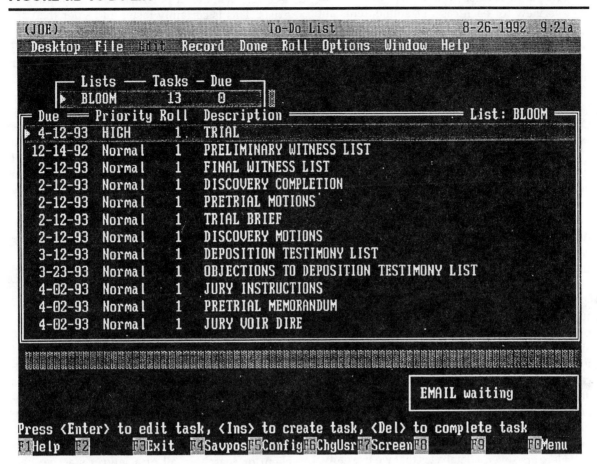

```
(JOE)                          To-Do List              8-26-1992  9:21a
 Desktop  File  Edit  Record  Done  Roll  Options  Window  Help

      ┌─ Lists ── Tasks ─ Due ─┐
      │ ▸ BLOOM      13      0  │
 ┌─ Due ══ Priority Roll ═ Description ═══════════════════ List: BLOOM ═┐
 │▸ 4-12-93  HIGH     1   TRIAL                                         │
 │ 12-14-92  Normal   1   PRELIMINARY WITNESS LIST                      │
 │  2-12-93  Normal   1   FINAL WITNESS LIST                            │
 │  2-12-93  Normal   1   DISCOVERY COMPLETION                          │
 │  2-12-93  Normal   1   PRETRIAL MOTIONS                              │
 │  2-12-93  Normal   1   TRIAL BRIEF                                   │
 │  2-12-93  Normal   1   DISCOVERY MOTIONS                             │
 │  3-12-93  Normal   1   DEPOSITION TESTIMONY LIST                     │
 │  3-23-93  Normal   1   OBJECTIONS TO DEPOSITION TESTIMONY LIST       │
 │  4-02-93  Normal   1   JURY INSTRUCTIONS                             │
 │  4-02-93  Normal   1   PRETRIAL MEMORANDUM                           │
 │  4-02-93  Normal   1   JURY VOIR DIRE                                │
 └──────────────────────────────────────────────────────────────────────┘

                                                   ┌─────────────────────┐
                                                   │  EMAIL waiting       │
                                                   └─────────────────────┘

 Press <Enter> to edit task, <Ins> to create task, <Del> to complete task
 F1Help  F2      F3Exit  F4Savpos F5Config F6ChgUsr F7Screen F8  F9  F10Menu
```

tion in the John Doe case but forget the exact date.

You'll select all calendar functions from either the main or subsidiary menu. In addition to the detailed view, the appointment calendar gives a quick overview by month superimposed upon a summary view of a particular day's activities. (See Figure 4.1.)

Group Scheduler

Futurus Team also has a group scheduler that allows you to make the same appointment for several individual members of a group. The program automatically searches through each calendar for the specified individuals, finds an open time slot of the desired length, and then completes and inserts into each individual's calendar the details of the group appointment. Again, one chooses the functions from a simple menu. In a multimember firm where several lawyers and support staff handle a single litigation project, this function is a great timesaver.

To-Do Lists

Each user can create an unlimited number of to-do lists for daily reminders. A separate to-do list may be kept for each case as a simple case management project planner. The to-do list shown in Figure 4.2 allows several levels of detail. You are automatically reminded of any overdue tasks when you start your computer each day.

Calendaring Deadlines

Our office follows a set procedure for each deadline item. First, we calendar the deadlines of the court's pretrial order for the appropriate lawyer or paralegal. Then we fill in for each case a to-do list, including discovery schedules, depositions, internal dates for preparing work product or completing investigation, or similar functions. Using a separate to-do list for each case eliminates the confusion that occurs when all deadline items are entered onto a single listing.

A separate list also gives a quick and immediate overview for each case. Deadline items and related warnings can also be entered on the daily calendar. Individual litigation to-do lists may be readily created, deleted, viewed, or searched for individual key words across every input list.

DATABASE FUNCTIONS

Futurus Team allows you to create an unlimited number of pop-up databases that may be accessed from inside most other programs. These are flat file databases, meaning that each individual record stands on its own and the data from different sets of records cannot be interrelated to each other. Nonetheless, a flat file is usually more than sufficient for telephone numbers, addresses, and basic case data. And, it's quite fast.

As with the other Futurus Team multiuser functions, an individual may maintain his or her own databases on an individual directory while sharing main databases with the entire office. Our individual databases range from 3-line records for conflict of interest checking to 18-field records for active cases. The record size and number of fields are entirely up to the user. Visitors are amazed at how quickly and easily a simple pop-up database can be created and data found.

Here are several databases that we use daily.

Rolodex-style Files

The database most frequently used officewide is our Rolodex-like database, listing general telephone numbers and information. It includes court reporters, other lawyers, businesses, office supply stores, etc. Futurus Team will automatically dial a telephone number listed in the database by simply highlighting the number and selecting AUTODIAL.

Conflict of Interest Database

We also use a simple database to keep track of conflicts of interest. Our conflict of interest files include only the name of the client and opponents, plus the names of any known principals of a business association and the name of the responsible lawyer. Upon an initial telephone contact from a potential client, a lawyer connected to Futurus Team can pop up the conflict of interest database in the middle of any other program, do a quick search, and immediately

ascertain whether a potential conflict of interest exists. This is certainly faster and safer than accepting a client provisionally, taking appropriate information from the client either by telephone or in person, and then checking with other lawyers at a later time or trusting your good reputation to a clerk.

If you question whether a name is correctly spelled in the database, merely type an asterisk and enough of the name to find a reasonable number of matches. Any resulting partial matches then display as a series of data cards in the search result. For example, if one simply typed *SMALL, you would find not only Mr. Small, but also any item listed as a small claim. The ability to search less than a full name while still finding the necessary data is useful in avoiding a missed conflict of interest or other record because of a possible misspelling.

Witness, Expert, and Client Databases

We also maintain individual databases of witnesses, doctors, and experts, who can be selected by case or by specialty. Client databases contain the basic information on telephone numbers for clients, including alternate numbers, addresses, opposing lawyer, and other data to which we may refer when writing a letter to a client or searching all of a lawyer's active personal injury cases. Since the computer can match only text patterns, a consistent nomenclature when entering data is important. When an individual client has more than one case, a separate active record is maintained for each one. The active case file lists those cases not fully resolved and provides information specific to the individual active case. When the case is closed, the date of closure is listed on the case card. (See Figure 4.3.)

Futurus Team can protect or encode databases using a separate database module. As a result, data can be made accessible only to persons knowing the appropriate password.

Notepads

Case notes are kept in individual case notepads, of which you have an unlimited number. We normally start a new notepad for each case and put in it basic information pertaining to the witnesses, the names of doctors, symptoms or other difficulties, basic investigatory material, and the like. Essentially, the computer notes

FIGURE 4.3 Case Card

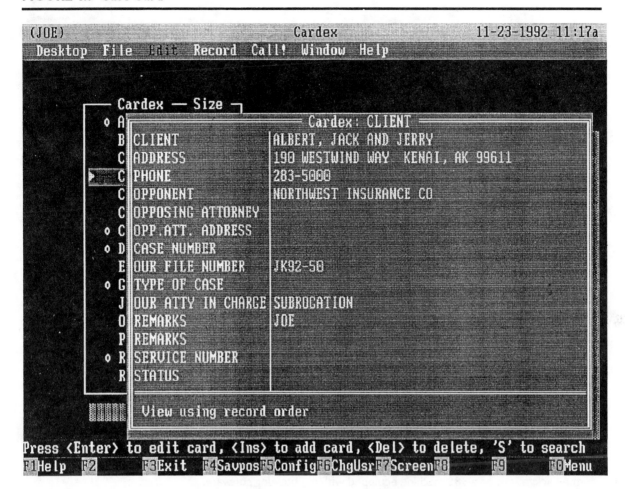

supplement those that would otherwise be kept with pencil and paper. Each notepad may contain about 40,000 characters, or about 20 double-spaced sheets. If the page limitation proves a problem, we create multiple notepads for various witnesses or cases.

One advantage of computerized notes is that the information may be reviewed while you work on a document in your word processor, even if the file is in someone else's office. Likewise, several people can contribute to the notepad and build the data together. This is a handy way to avoid losing notes that you take while interviewing the client or talking on the phone.

Futurus Team also allows you to search for a particular term throughout all notepads then residing in your directory, including any notepads in common use. For example, I frequently fly my twin-engine Cessna to Merrill Field in Anchorage. If I wish to find all the occurrences of the word *Merrill* in every notepad, I

would simply search for the word *Merrill*. The result would be a list showing each notepad where the term was found along with the line in which the word *Merrill* occurs. By pressing the **[ENTER]** key, I could then view every pertinent notepad at the occurrence of the word *Merrill*, which might include unrelated client names or other information.

We also use Futurus Team notepads to keep information useful to the organization of our office. For example, we keep a log of aircraft time for Internal Revenue purposes on Futurus Team. We also keep listings of all dial-up databases to which we subscribe and their access codes. Each case we accept is immediately logged onto a case number notepad with the office file number, client name, and matter. This notepad gives us a running log of all active cases and allows us to doublecheck that no case is inadvertently overlooked. The case number file continues from year to year, with only the yearly identifying numbers changing.

English Lawyers Communicate Electronically*

Harold L. Burstyn

As most American lawyers know, the legal profession in the United Kingdom is divided between solicitors and barristers. Solicitors see clients, draft documents, and handle transactions. They even appear in the lower courts. But when the matter requires appearing in a higher court, solicitors "brief counsel." That is, they turn to barristers. Only a barrister may represent a client in the higher courts. The client meets with the barrister rarely, and then only in the presence of the client's solicitor.

Although solicitors draft most legal documents, they do not prepare pleadings. If a matter goes to court, a barrister drafts the pleading. Since only the barrister may argue before the judge, the barrister is also responsible for briefs and motion papers. However, with only the solicitor in direct communication with the client, the barrister's information is always secondhand. One consequence is that documents in various stages of preparation continually move back and forth between solicitor and barrister.

Because of their divided profession, British lawyers have established a system of electronic document transfer. Prodded by the Society for Computers and Law, the Law Society (to which all solicitors in England and Wales belong) and the Bar Council (the governing body for barristers) have sponsored a slick MS-DOS program interface called LIX, for Legal Information Exchange. Any IBM-compatible with 640 KB RAM, a hard disk, a Hayes-compatible modem, and MS-DOS 3.0 or higher can run LIX.

With LIX, anyone can send a document electronically, in editable form, as easily as sending a fax and much more economically. From the main menu, the sender enters information similar to that on a fax cover sheet. Receipt of a document instantly brings an addressed envelope icon to the screen. The recipient manipulates the icon to read the transmission or to transfer it to another machine on a network or to a diskette. Alternatively, one may send a document to a password-protected mailbox for later collection. Other options on the main menu convert documents received in incompatible formats, as from Microsoft Word to WordPerfect. The program keeps a log of all transactions, and it can run in the background on a 386 machine equipped with multitasking software.

INTRAOFFICE COMMUNICATIONS

Our intraoffice communication has been greatly enhanced by Futurus Team's electronic mail (E-mail). Electronic messaging is available in a fraction of a second as a TSR pop-up function. It is much simpler and more convenient than paper or the intercom. You can forward a message or reply to it just as easily. I believe that convenient, easily accessed electronic mail is a necessity for any law office. More than anything else, E-mail helps you stay organized. At least, you won't lose your messages, reminders, and phone calls.

The E-mail program can be configured so that you get an audio warning whenever a new message arrives or if you have messages that have not been read. The function may be turned off if you want to concentrate. When you choose E-mail, the screen first shows a list of all messages by number, date, time, sender, and sub-ject. Then, by selecting a particular message and hitting the [ENTER] key, you may read it. A message may then be deleted, saved in another named mailbox, exported to a file or notepad, or forwarded to another user.

Futurus Team also has a phone message center that seems to duplicate the E-mail function. Also, it has a two-way interactive CHAT function that lets people type messages back and forth interactively through a split screen. We don't use these functions, since we find that E-mail is more convenient. Our office would be lost without E-mail and the pop-up databases.

OTHER FEATURES

Futurus Team also includes several other useful features:

1. A background communication program

In addition to transferring documents directly from one lawyer to another, LIX can provide an interface to legal and general databases, rather like ABA/net in the United States. LEXIS, Dialog, and the British equivalents of other American databases can be accessed through the same friendly interface. So can the teleconferencing that American lawyers have in ABA/net or on CompuServe. Future plans may include databases of unpublished opinions in particular practice areas.

By establishing a single standard for secure file transfer, the Law Society and Bar Council promoted electronic links among the entire legal profession in the United Kingdom. To that end, the two bodies formed a nonprofit corporation, Legal Information Exchange, Ltd., to distribute the software. The first step was to pair individual barristers and solicitors. Transfer of documents back and forth between the solicitors' firms and the barristers' chambers permitted the bugs to be worked out before the final version was marketed to the two professions beginning in March 1991.

Now the number of LIX installations is more than 100, including one-fourth of the 100 largest firms of solicitors. (Barristers must practice individually, though they group themselves physically in sets of chambers and share clerical staff and equipment.) An existing software house has taken over the marketing of LIX outside of London through its dealer network. Beginning in March 1992, the Official Referee's Court in London is conducting a six-month trial, sponsored by Wang UK, of receiving certain kinds of filings via LIX.

Because LIX is useful to individuals other than lawyers, an independent company is developing and marketing the program outside the legal professions.

The LIX interface has several components. Its engine is ODYSSEY, a communications program not otherwise known in the United States, which contains both MNP5 error correction and a sophisticated programming language. LIX, written in the ODYSSEY language, ties ODYSSEY together with SOFTWARE BRIDGE for file translation, PKZIP and PKUNZIP for compressing and expanding files, and QUERY for preparing messages off-line.

The LIX project was the work primarily of John Mawhood, a solicitor, for the Law Society, and His Honour Judge Sean Overend, at the time a barrister of Grays Inn with chambers in the Inner Temple, for the Bar Council. For further information, communicate with Legal Information Exchange, Ltd., 10 Ranmere St., London SW12 9QQ, England, phone and fax (081) 675-9337.

*An earlier version of this sidebar first appeared in *The National Law Journal,* vol. 13, no. 13, Dec. 5, 1990.

---

that lets you transmit or receive a fax or data file through your modem while working on another matter. A separately sold remote module provides fast two-way (full-duplexed) interaction from a notebook computer on the road.

2. A pop-up calculator.

3. A keyboard macro function that lets you define a series of keystrokes as a single operation to be chosen by a hot key. The macro key function is unusual in that, with proper editing, it can be used to actually run other programs such as hard-disk compression and maintenance programs. As a result, repetitive but time-consuming tasks such as hard-disk maintenance can be automated and accomplished overnight.

4. A transfer window that lets you cut and paste text or numbers between Futurus Team modules and other applications.

5. A DOS command line window, which can be called even when you are working within another DOS program such as WordPerfect or Agenda. You can use it to execute simple DOS commands, such as copying a file, formatting a disk, or viewing the contents of a directory. It cannot be used to run DOS programs that require any substantial memory.

Each function of Futurus Team runs in a separate on-screen window. The functions can be used in conjunction with each other, and several different ones can be called up and superimposed, with the user alternating between each function's window. For example, you may bring up an E-mail message that a client called, search your appointment calendar for wherever that client's appointment shows up, and bring up an index file with the client's work number.

OTHER OFFICE ORGANIZATION SOFTWARE

Here's some other useful office organization software suitable for small to medium offices and usable on Novell and DOS networks. This listing is not intended to be exhaustive:

WordPerfect Office, now in version 4.0, provides a file manager, very capable E-mail, officewide calendars, and multiple notepads. It's extremely popular in legal offices since its keystrokes are consistent with WordPerfect 5.1. Although I found Futurus Team to be faster and more functional, I understand that WordPerfect Office proclaims its forte to be wide-area networking, something that is of greater concern to multiple-location law firms. Training staff already accustomed to WordPerfect should be fairly easy.

Instant Recall, Cronlogic, Tucson, Arizona, has a very nice interface and feature set. A network version is available. Instant Recall is a viable alternative to Agenda if you are only concerned with taking a few notes and organizing your time.

Agenda is the personal information manager of choice in many law offices because of its tremendous versatility as both an organizer and case management/litigation support tool. Add-on products like Partner's Planner, Phase Three Computing, Toronto, Ont., Canada (416) 925-8760, adapt Agenda quite well to managing your day and your law office. Remember, though, that Agenda is not a TSR program and does not have

inherent network support or E-mail. These are significant limitations when you need a quickly accessed office organization tool. Lotus will not be updating Agenda, and instead is focusing its efforts on Lotus Notes, its important "groupware" system.

Microsoft Mail and Scheduler, DaVinci Mail, Higgins, cc:Mail, and Network Scheduler are widely distributed E-mail and office organization products similar to Futurus Team, but with different interfaces. I prefer Futurus Team.

Finally, you might consider a shareware product. There are some surprisingly good ones that will do the job but not as conveniently as a pop-up modular TSR like Futurus Team. I've tried several and can definitely recommend Einstein E-mail, a Novell-specific office organization product that you can download at minimal charge from the Netwire Forum on CompuServe. The requested donation is $249 and the product is definitely worth it. Setup and use are surprisingly easy.

CONCLUSION

Desktop organization programs running on a single computer are convenient. They will do wonders for your personal productivity. However, office automation programs such as Futurus Team, which run on a network and offer officewide communication, can raise the productivity of your entire office to new levels. Everyone contributes to the stored data and the value of the overall product. Coordination and messages flow far more smoothly and surely, and that translates to a better product in less time, a more pleasant, less chaotic office environment, and greater profitability.

Joseph L. Kashi is a sole practitioner living in Soldotna, Alaska. He received his B.S. and M.S. degrees from MIT in 1973 and his J.D. from Georgetown University Law Center in 1976. His practice consists primarily of contract and personal injury litigation.

Harold L. Burstyn (sidebar) is a member of the New York and Florida state bars and a registered patent attorney. He practices with the Morrison Law Firm in Mount Vernon, New York, and consults on legal automation.

Using Computers in a Criminal Appeal: A Case Study in Team Productivity

Neil E. Aresty

Neil Aresty takes a look a how notebook PCs, with sophisticated litigation support and word processing software and telephone modems, tied together a diverse team of legal professionals from across the country. This case involved one of the more notorious criminal appeals in recent times. Although the notebook PCs could not guarantee a reversal of the conviction, they did enable the team to operate more efficiently and effectively.

The message said *"Urgent,* return call ASAP." I returned the call. "Neil, we need you to drop everything and help us with a criminal appeal." "It's big," he continued, "that's right, the one you've been reading about." "You're kidding, *that* case?" "That case!" he answered.

"What are we talking about?" I asked. He started in immediately: "The defense team will be spread across the country. A couple of law firms, one in Boston, two in New York, two law professors, one in Cambridge, the other in L.A., two CPA firms in New York, and a private investigator in Washington, D.C. We need someone to help computerize the case. Can you do it? Forget about doing anything else for the next few months. By the way, what's your billable rate?"

Immediate billable time! "Sure, I'm available, no problem." I was to start the next day.

GEARING UP: GETTING THE TEAM OUTFITTED WITH NOTEBOOK PCS

Our first task was to coordinate the efforts of the team of attorneys, investigators, paralegals, and accountants. The trial had lasted over 43 days. There were approximately 9,000 pages of trial transcript, over 6,000 exhibits marked for identification and another 8,000 documents cataloged as potentially relevant. In addition, we had to review hundreds of pages of pre- and posttrial motions, briefs, and affidavits.

Two members of the team were designated to start reading the entire transcript, and two paralegals were asked to pull each exhibit that was referenced in the testimony so that it could be examined.

One of our first organizational tasks was to standardize the computer systems that the defense team would be using. Almost immediately, we purchased laptop computers with 40-MB hard disks and 2,400-baud modems for each office that did not already have DOS-based personal computers. We also arranged for each office to have an ABA/net E-mail account and basic telecommunications software. Using ABA/net, each team member could communicate electronically with every other member. It also provided an easy gateway to upload and download drafts for review and revision.

The idea was that there would be lots of writing, drafts constantly being circulated, edited, and then recirculated among the team. Rather than use fax, or overnight mail, we would transmit files through the electronic mail facilities of ABA/net, download them onto our respective disks, and then open, edit, and print them with our word processor (WordPerfect). The ABA/net electronic mail tied the defense team together in a wide area network.

FIGURE 4.4 Screen Shot of Transcript Hits from Discovery ZX

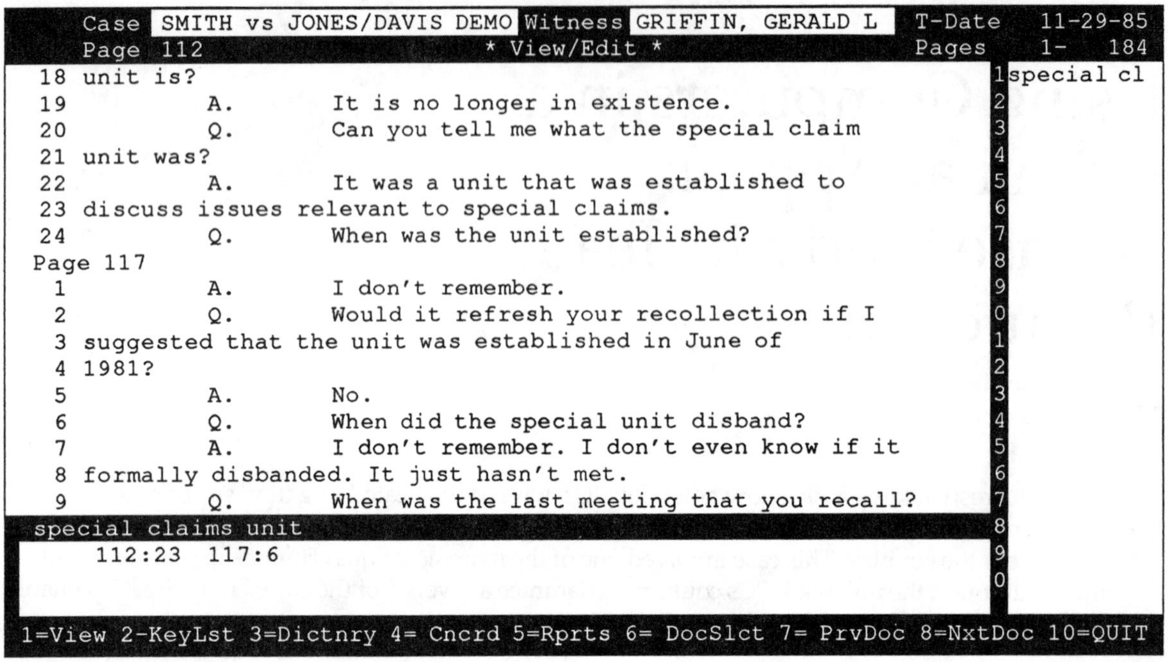

```
┌─────────────────────────────────────────────────────────────────────────┐
│  Case │SMITH vs JONES/DAVIS DEMO│ Witness │GRIFFIN, GERALD L│ T-Date  11-29-85│
│  Page 112                    * View/Edit *              Pages    1-    184│
│   18  unit is?                                                  1│special cl│
│   19        A.       It is no longer in existence.             2│          │
│   20        Q.       Can you tell me what the special claim    3│          │
│   21  unit was?                                                4│          │
│   22        A.       It was a unit that was established to     5│          │
│   23  discuss issues relevant to special claims.              6│          │
│   24        Q.       When was the unit established?           7│          │
│  Page 117                                                      8│          │
│    1        A.       I don't remember.                         9│          │
│    2        Q.       Would it refresh your recollection if I   0│          │
│    3  suggested that the unit was established in June of       1│          │
│    4  1981?                                                    2│          │
│    5        A.       No.                                       3│          │
│    6        Q.       When did the special unit disband?        4│          │
│    7        A.       I don't remember. I don't even know if it 5│          │
│    8  formally disbanded. It just hasn't met.                  6│          │
│    9        Q.       When was the last meeting that you recall?7│          │
│  special claims unit                                           8│          │
│      112:23  117:6                                             9│          │
│                                                                0│          │
│  1=View 2-KeyLst 3=Dictnry 4= Cncrd 5=Rprts 6= DocSlct 7= PrvDoc 8=NxtDoc 10=QUIT│
└─────────────────────────────────────────────────────────────────────────┘
```

FULL-TEXT RETRIEVAL SOFTWARE

The next task was to contact the court reporter on the case and to find out if the trial transcript was available in electronic format. Fortunately, it was. The court reporter still had the entire trial including the pre- and posttrial hearings available in an ASCII file format. They sent us some 40 disks containing all the transcript. We then had these converted into the Discovery ZX text retrieval format and then copied the transcripts and the text retrieval software onto each of the PCs being used by the defense team.

I had never loaded 9,000 pages of trial transcript into a PC, nor had I ever used the transcript management software on such a large case. The 43-day trial or 9,000 pages of transcript only took up about 17 megabytes of disk space! There was plenty of space left for the other applications, documents, exhibits, etc.

The test, however, was to see if it worked and, if so, how it would be received by the team. I typed in a few key words that I had remembered from the trial and, lo and behold, there they were! Two hits; the first at page 112, line 23 and the second at page 117, line 6! (See Figure 4.4.)

Showing lawyers how full text retrieval works on 43 volumes of text loaded into a 7-pound notebook computer is fun. Imagine the look on the faces of the two bleary-eyed attorneys who had just finished reading the entire 9,000 pages! "You mean you can show me every page where exhibit 2002 is discussed in seconds!" Teaching them how to do search and retrieval from that point on was easy.

One of the witnesses in the trial was an older gentleman. He was helping the defense team get a handle on some of the salient facts, and so, he, too, was given a laptop loaded with the transcript. When I delivered the machine to him, he apologized for not understanding anything about computers. He said he was not sure that he could operate it. I suggested that it was easier than he might think, sit down and I would give him a quick lesson.

Sitting in front of the screen with the transcript displayed, he said that he thought his name was mentioned by other witnesses maybe four or five times throughout the trial. We typed in his name and it came up 68 times! That was all the motivation he needed. "How do I see the next hit?" Within 15 minutes he was searching the transcript and using the MARKER function to identify those portions of the text that he felt were relevant.

Within a matter of days, Discovery ZX had become central to the defense team's work. After

FIGURE 4.5   Screen Shot of Embellished Transcript

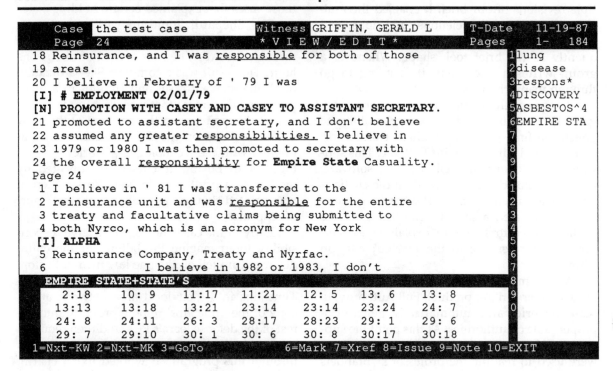

the transcript was read and the issues of law for the appeal were clarified, the transcript retrieval program was used extensively to "embellish" the transcript. Not only was the Discovery ZX program used to retrieve and find text that dealt with the issues of law and fact but the "issue markers" and "note fields" were also used to help digest and sort the various parts of the transcript that dealt with specific issues on the appeal. (See Figure 4.5.)

For example, one of the Constitutional errors alleged dealt with the right to a fair and impartial trial by jury. The transcript was replete with discussion that helped to support the argument that our jury had very likely been influenced by extraneous information that did not come from the witness stand. We were able to electronically mark each and every reference to this issue, including the jury instructions, which were arguably inadequate to cure, and then cut and paste sections of the transcript right into the appellate brief. We also made extensive use of the page and line reports to collect all colloquy relating to other issues.

ABA/net also provided the defense team with gateway access into the LEXIS and DIALOG information systems. As specific issues of research became necessary, the team was able to go on-line and perform computer-assisted research through these massive electronic libraries. With respect to the fair trial issue, we were able to search close to a thousand newspapers, journals, and magazine articles for stories about the instant case. We found over 40 headlines, dated prior to trial, which contained extraordinary prejudicial comments about the defendant. We were also able to find articles containing interviews with some of the jurors, which enabled us to determine that some of their decisions had been influenced by material from outside the courtroom!

FINISHING THE BRIEF

One problem we faced in exchanging drafts over ABA/net was keeping track of revisions. CompareRite by JuriSoft provided one solution. This software allows you to compare different versions of the brief to determine what has been revised. The program shades all words that have been added and displays deleted text with a strikeout, or dash through it. It becomes a simple matter to glance at the revised draft and immediately focus on the revisions themselves.

We found CompareRite extremely helpful

because it allowed us to keep control over multiple revisions of our brief. It enabled the multiple users to track deletions, additions, and movements of text, which occurred quite frequently as the brief took shape. Whenever a group writes a document, it is going to go through many changes.

As the appellate brief came together, we began using a number of other legal utilities to polish the final product. To check citation format, we used CiteRite by JuriSoft, Inc. This software is analogous to spell checking software; CiteRite scanned the brief, read all the citations without the need for manually marking them, and then created a separate file listing all the citations and errors it found, explaining each error with a reference to the *Bluebook* citation manual.

As we moved toward a final product, we used another JuriSoft product, Full Authority, to scan the brief and automatically generate a proper table of authorities. At this point the support staff became real computer converts. They were used to reading the professor's "Brandeis briefs," manually cross-referencing, alphabetizing, verifying citation form, and doing all the other incredibly tedious tasks associated with drafting a table of authorities. What normally should have taken a couple of days only took a couple of minutes!

In order to Shepardize all the cases and statutes cited in the brief, we used a product called SuperCite by SuperLex, Inc. To Shepardize close to 200 cites would have taken four people at least a week, not to mention all the review time of the analysis. SuperCite allowed us to load the table of authorities document that was generated by Full Authority into its program interface.

We were then able to do an "off-line" pre-Shepard analysis of each cite indicating whether we wanted a full Shepard's analysis or a restricted analysis of the cite. That is to say, we could toggle check marks on the screen that would limit the Shepardization of the case to only those cases overruling the case, or only those cases that explained certain holdings, etc.

The Shepardization analysis took two or three log-ons to LEXIS' Shepard's service through the ABA/net, for a total of about one hour. The result was a complete Shepardization of all the relevant cases and statutes in a word processed document that was easy to read.

At this point, even the partners at the New York law firms on the defense team were impressed with the technology. The brief was put together in Boston and telecommunicated by modem to a print shop in New York, where it was printed, bound, and filed with the Court of Appeals.

Early in the case, the administrative responsibility for managing the billing for the entire defense team fell on the one law firm in Boston. We loaded a time and billing program called TimeSlips into their local area network and a copy of the TimeSlips' remote program into the rest of the defense team's PCs, and then required everyone to keep track of their time and expenses through this program. It worked like a charm. Every month the client got a detailed invoice, and the lead attorneys were able to generate reports showing the amount of time spent per type of activity (legal research, drafting, telephone conferencing, etc.) as well as reports showing types and amounts of expenses.

The PC-based technology used on the appeal became the story behind the story. It changed the way the members of the defense team practice law today. Every lawyer now uses a notebook-class PC, types their own work product, takes copies of all transcript on disk, and communicates with each other via E-mail. In fact, the lawyers on the team became the biggest fans of computer technology.

From time to time a member of the team calls to see if there is any new software out there that will just write the whole damn brief from the transcript. Not yet, I tell them, but we're working on it!

Neil E. Aresty is a lawyer practicing in Boston, Massachusetts. He is also a principal in LEGAL COMPUTER SOLUTIONS, Inc., which provides computer consulting to the legal profession. Mr. Aresty is an active member of the ABA's Section of Law Practice Management and a lecturer for the National College of Trial Advocacy of the Association of Trial Lawyers of America.

Using Computers to Make Brief Writing More Enjoyable (or at Least Less Painful!)

Catherine Pennington

Preparing briefs can be one of the least fun aspects of a litigation practice. While there are no short cuts to writing a persuasive legal argument, Catherine Pennington, lawyer and head librarian at a major New York law firm, reviews several programs that help you assemble and improve your final product.

When I taught law, I forbade my legal writing students from using cite verification software to check the citation form of their assignments. I wanted them to learn the *Bluebook* first. Of course this did not stop me from using those products to check them! Cite verification software is one of several terrific software products that can make your life easier, your legal writing more professional, and most importantly, your research more accurate and up to date. Let's take a few moments to explore some of the products available.

CITERITE

CiteRite was the first cite checking software marketed to the legal community. It was developed by Jurisoft, now a division of Mead Data Central of Lexis/Nexis fame. Essentially, CiteRite checks an entire legal document, locates the citations, checks them against the standards of *A Uniform System of Citation* or *Bluebook*, California citation form, or even your own office's customized style and tells you where you went wrong. Alternatively, you can choose to run CiteRite in what Jurisoft calls pop-up or memory-resident mode. For example, I can type a cite, hit a couple of keys, and CiteRite—because it is memory resident—becomes available to me to check the cite while I am typing.

The downside of this capability is that for some word processing packages, most notably WordPerfect 5.1, CiteRite takes too much memory and I cannot run them both at the same time. I find that I seldom use pop-up mode anyway. I would prefer to type the entire document and let CiteRite check it after I have completed it. I work the same way with a spelling or grammar checker. Using any one of these programs while I am writing would interrupt my thinking processes.

Assuming you wanted to check a file, you would start the CiteRite program. After loading, the program will have a line of commands across the top (see Figure 4.6), and you select options from each one, telling the citation format you are using (i.e., *Bluebook*, California, or in-house), what type of document it will be searching, the name of the document, etc. You can also set up some of these variations as options. For example, although the law firm I work for is located in New York, we have an office in Los Angeles. I have set up an option sheet that will check a WordPerfect document against California citation style.

Once CiteRite completes its work, it creates an error file (which you have named). You can then call up the error file, either on the screen or by printing it, using your word processing program, or by pressing **[D]** in the Activity menu. My personal preference would be for CiteRite to work like a spellchecker, suggesting changes as it scans the document and making the changes upon your affirmation. As it is, you have to go back into your original document and make each

FIGURE 4.6 CiteRite II Software Main Menu

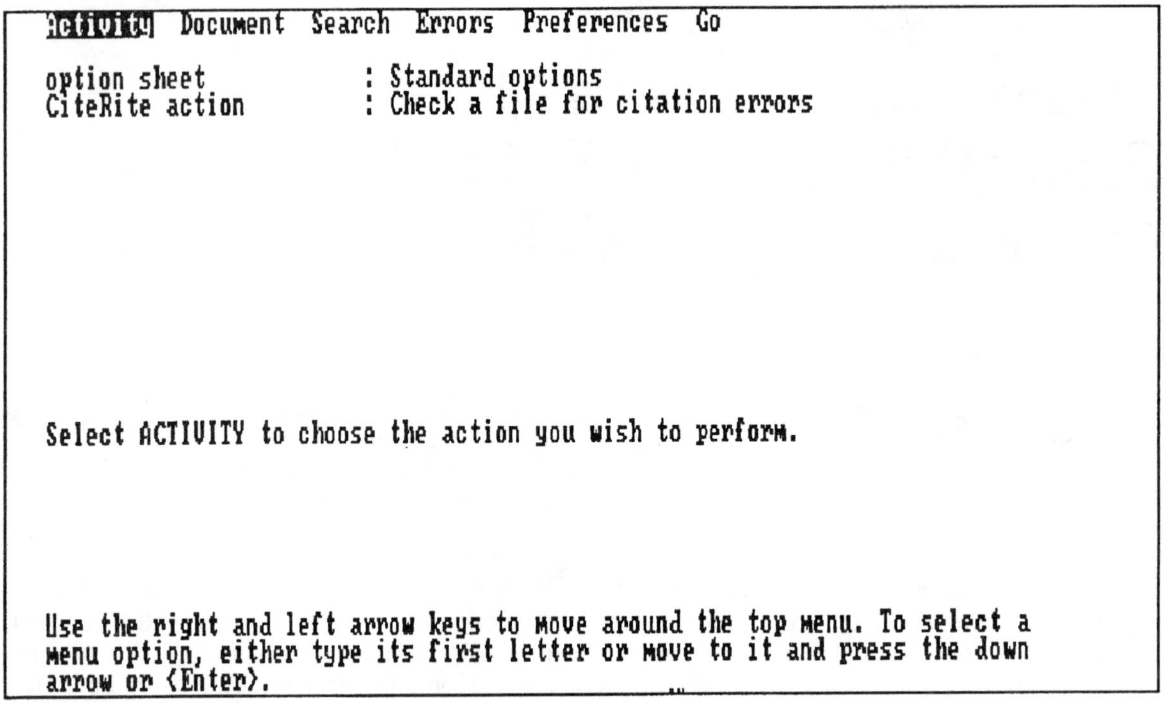

```
 Activity  Document  Search  Errors  Preferences  Go
option sheet          : Standard options
CiteRite action       : Check a file for citation errors




Select ACTIVITY to choose the action you wish to perform.




Use the right and left arrow keys to move around the top menu. To select a
menu option, either type its first letter or move to it and press the down
arrow or <Enter>.
```

change yourself. At the time of this writing, no other company makes a product to compete with CiteRite, so Jurisoft may not have an incentive to make a major structural change in its program. Standing alone, however, it is still a significant improvement over manual checking.

FULL AUTHORITY

I remember the first time I ever saw Full Authority create a table of authorities from a brief. Even though I have watched word processing, database managers, and other software change the way we practice law, this program really amazed me. In a matter of seconds, a table was created for a 95-page brief. It looked professional, the citation form was correct, and the style was customized to meet the requirements of a particular district court. I had not marked the citations in any way in the text—the program simply recognized them for what they were. It even placed citations it did not recognize in a miscellaneous category so I could shift them to the correct spot within the table.

I kept thinking of all the hours spent and

aggravation endured by lawyers and their secretaries through the years to create these tables. I remembered what problems resulted when the inevitable errors occurred: when items were moved, typically requiring substantial portions of the table to be retyped; when occasionally a jump cite would be missed; or when the citation form was not to the liking of a particular (or picky) judge. Talk about an answer to a lawyer's prayers!

The menus on Full Authority are similar but not identical to those of CiteRite, since both are products of Jurisoft. Once Full Authority has completed its work (usually in less than two minutes), you simply print out the table using your word processor. It is true that WordPerfect, Microsoft Word, and some other word processing programs allow you to create a table of authorities, but to do so requires you to mark each citation as it is typed. For example, let's say I want to include the case of *Smith v. Jones*, 123 F.2d 402 (1950) in my table of authority, as well as any short forms of this cite. After typing it, I would block it, hit the [**MARK TEXT**] key, select TABLE OF AUTHORITY, and indicate the level; and I would need to do this with each cite. In addition, if I want 123 F.2d, at 404 to also appear in the list, I must also mark it and designate it a short form. Full Authority, by contrast, recognizes *Smith v. Jones* for what it is, including any subsequent short forms, and includes it in the table of authority all within a matter of seconds, without the need for human help.

CHECKCITE

CheckCite is really a communications program that will search a document or file for cites, call LEXIS via the modem attached to your computer, and then Shepardize and/or AutoCite all those citations. When it has completed the task, it signs off from LEXIS and prepares a report of its findings.

Once the program has searched your document, it may report that there is a questionable reporter. CiteRite will not check a cite that contains a questionable reporter. If there are changes you can make to the document to correct a citation, hit [ESCAPE], and go back to your word processor to correct it. If not, select any other key, and the program will begin to log onto LEXIS. Once it is logged on, you may simply leave the program running. It will automatically log off when completed and save the results in the file you have specified in the document screen.

If you have used CiteRite, Full Authority, or CompareRite, you will find the menus on CheckCite very familiar. One additional menu, though, is Billing. This can be set up to give you a report of the cost of checking the citations after the program has done its magic and long before your monthly bill comes from LEXIS.

In addition to cite checking, CheckCite can also retrieve the actual cases for you using Lexsee. Why would you want to use this capability? One reason would be to see the cases cited in opposing counsel's brief. You could scan their document into your word processor and, utilizing CheckCite, retrieve the actual case, as well as Shepardize and AutoCite each citation within it.

WESTCHECK

One of the advantages of living in a free market economy is that competition makes for better products. West Publishing Company did not sit still when its competitor Mead began marketing CheckCite. Their product WESTCheck permits you to check Shepard's Preview as well as Shepard's and InstaCite on WESTLAW. The advantage of Shepard's Preview, of course, is that it allows you to check citations some weeks or even months before they appear in print. The most recent edition of the WESTCheck software also allows you to use their QuickCite option. QuickCite essentially enables you to search for your cite in very recent slip opinions.

Another advantage is that WESTCheck can be used with a mouse. Once the opening menu appears, you can enter the pull-down menus by either holding down the [ALT] key and hitting [F] or by using the mouse and clicking open the File menu.

To get started you must create a citations list (see Figure 4.7). Select "Extract from document" from the File menu and [ENTER]. You will be asked to name the document, the word processing program under which the document was created, and the client identifier. After initial processing, the program creates a file listing all of the citations it has found. This file will have the same name as your original document, but with VER as the extension.

You can review and make changes to the citations in the list before going on-line by selecting the Browse menu. Then, if you have set the program for automatic function, WESTCheck will sign on to WESTLAW without pause, using the AutoRun command.

The program assumes you wish to check all cites in InstaCite, Shepard's, Shepard's Preview, and now QuickCite. Like CheckCite, you can walk away from the computer once it starts working and do something else. It will automatically log off WESTLAW when it is finished.

Many lawyers find it useful to let these programs run at night when the computer is not otherwise occupied. You can see your results either through your word processor or in the Print command under the File menu. You can also view your results in Browse mode. I personally prefer the report format of WestCheck, which puts all the retrieved information on a particular cite all together. You may recall that CheckCite puts all the AutoCite data first, followed by that of Shepard's. On the other hand, CheckCite works with more word processors. If you are using anything but WordPerfect, you are going to have to convert it to ASCII to use

FIGURE 4.7 WESTCheck New Citations List

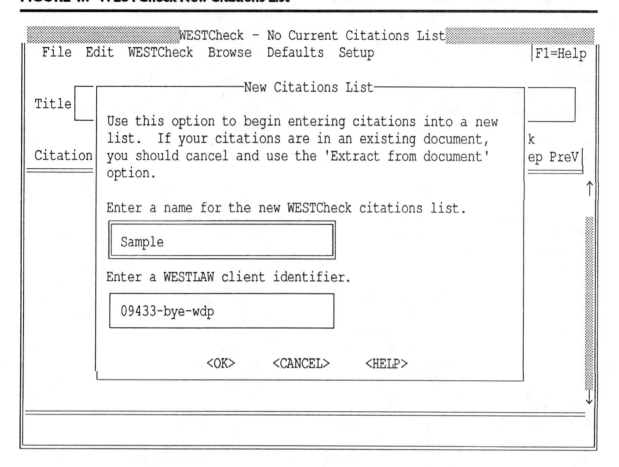

WESTCheck. For a more detailed comparison of the two programs, see Griffith, "Cite Checking Software," in *Law Office Computing*, April/May 1992, 102–15.

CONCLUSION

All of these products greatly enhance your ability to produce a quality product, both in form and content—all while saving you time and effort. Can there be a better argument for their use today?

Catherine Pennington is director of library services at Chadbourne & Parke in New York City. She was formerly the associate law librarian and adjunct professor of law at St. John's University, Jamaica, New York. Cathy received her M.L.S. and J.D. degrees from Brigham Young University and is a member of the State Bar of Texas. An active member of the ABA's Section of Law Practice Management, she is books editor for Law Practice Management *magazine and editor of* Network 2d, *the section's computer and technology newsletter.*

Now Lawyers Can Dictate to Their Computers

Harold L. Burstyn

Ever envy James T. Kirk of Star Trek fame for his ability to talk to the Enterprise's computer? Are you convinced that you'll never learn to type? Harold Burstyn, section editor and patent lawyer, found a new program that lets you dictate directly to the computer. At $5,000, it may seem expensive, but prices drop quickly in the computer world. Fast 486 computers, which cost $5,000 a few years ago, are now selling for less than $2,000.

Keyboard skills mark the clearest division between lawyers who use computers and those who don't. Those of us who learned to type in high school, college, or on the job, can generally master the new machines, if only to peck out an occasional letter or memo. But those who haven't learned typing—even hunt-and-peck typing—waste too much time locating the characters on the keyboard to make the transition. And those of us who use computers every day for, say, legal research, or estate and trust calculations by spreadsheet, return to the trusty dictating machine when we need something in a hurry.

But what if we could dictate, not to a machine whose tapes must be transcribed by the secretary, but directly to the computer? Wouldn't a computer that takes dictation revolutionize the way all of us practice law? That's certainly the conclusion I've come to after several years of trying to persuade lawyers that computers are the way of the future.

Today, I'm happy to report, you can set yourself up with a computer that takes dictation. Though it's neither cheap nor simple, it can be done. With a one-time expenditure of about $7,000 and a couple of weeks of meticulous training, you can equip yourself with a computer that answers your every command. Without ever touching a key, you can dictate all your pleadings, briefs, memos, letters, documents, and even faxes, produce them, and speed them on their way.

What's the secret, and why haven't you heard already about this startling development? There are several reasons.

First, no one outside the legal profession, certainly not the computer people who work on converting speech to text, seems to understand how inextricably we lawyers are tied to words and their embodiment on paper. Since words are, at bottom, speech, no profession needs speech-to-text conversion more than lawyers. But the marketing of speech-to-text systems seems focused on medical doctors for the comprehensive systems and on warehouses (e.g., parts inventory and distribution) for the simple systems.

Second, though many computer companies are rumored to have speech-to-text products under development, the glamor these days lies in multimedia, with its possibilities for electronic entertainment of the masses.

Third, computer people find lawyers difficult to market to: skeptical, hard to sell, generally unwilling to modify their work habits. Lawyers, the computer people say, never invest enough time (or money) to get as much from their computers as the hardware and software can give them.

There's a fourth reason why you haven't heard of the computer that takes dictation. So far as I can tell, there's only one product you can buy today that will revolutionize the way you practice. And most of the pieces one sees in print about what computers can do for lawyers either discuss general computer functions or compare products. No one who's not a paid publicist likes to write about a single product.

Nevertheless, there is only one product I can discuss here: DragonDictate, from Dragon Systems, Inc., of Newton, Massachusetts. Dragon-Dictate converts speech to text at about 40 words per minute. However, it's not the speech that you and I use in conversation, and you have to train DragonDictate carefully for a couple of weeks to recognize your voice. Learning to make each utterance discrete—that is, to separate each word or phrase by a tenth of a second—takes time, but it can be mastered. Dragon Systems claims that training the system can be difficult, but I didn't find it so. I was up to about 93 percent on my third try with the first sentence of Lincoln's Gettysburg Address (my choice!).

Perhaps the reason I did so well was that my trainer was an experienced employee of Dragon, where I dropped in for a demonstration one day. There wasn't time for me to do more than scratch the surface, but I watched my trainer as he first dictated and printed both a letter and a facsimile message and then filled in a spreadsheet entirely with voice commands. Though he has keyboard skills, he claims that DragonDictate's efficiency makes it his choice for getting work done.

What is DragonDictate and what does it cost? DragonDictate is "a discrete utterance, speaker-adaptive speech recognition system." Its primary active vocabulary has 25,000 words, to which you can add another 5,000 words or phrases. Dragon-Dictate's second vocabulary contains 80,000 words, derived from the *Random House Unabridged Dictionary;* 10,000 of them are proper names.

To run DragonDictate, you must have an MS-DOS computer with an Intel 80386 or 80486 processor running at 20 MHz or faster, a hard disk with 10 MB free storage, 8 MB of RAM, and one expansion slot. Such a computer costs about $2,000 at today's prices. For $4,995, Dragon Systems offers a DragonDictate system: a speech recognition board that fits into the expansion slot (ISA, MCA, or EISA), the software (on four 1.2 or 1.44 MB diskettes), a headset microphone that plugs into the board, a manual, and a tutorial. As the software runs in terminate-and-stay-resident mode (TSR), it becomes the front end to any program you use. I saw DragonDictate demonstrated running XyWrite III+, a word processor, and Lotus 1-2-3, a spreadsheet, by means of voice commands alone.

With DragonDictate installed on your machine, you start the training. Each utterance is limited to five seconds, and you space them one-tenth of a second apart. If you have to spell a word, such as a proper name, you use the International Communication Alphabet (the "Alpha, Bravo, Coca" some of us learned in the armed services or as pilots of aircraft). If DragonDictate makes a mistake, you say "oops," and the screen gives you a choice of alternatives. If your word or phrase is one of them, you either press the designated function key or say the numeral. DragonDictate instantly replaces the improper word with the proper one. If you've gone beyond the mistaken word, you say "left one" or "left two" to bring up your alternatives.

CONCLUSION

Although I trained for only a few minutes, I could see that a busy lawyer might become impatient in working the system up to its peak performance. However, the result is certainly worth the effort. Wouldn't every lawyer want to dispense with the cumbersome current process of dictation: of speaking into a hand-held recorder, giving the tape to a secretary to transcribe, and editing the transcript that results? With Dragon-Dictate the lawyer can dictate directly to the machine, edit by voice on the screen, and print out the document with voice commands. It seems to me that DragonDictate, and the comparable products that will surely follow, show us the future of law practice. We use our voices every day to advocate our clients' causes and to direct those who help us. Why not command our computers the same way?

(Since I wrote these words, Dragon Systems has started marketing to the legal profession. The same person who got me started demonstrated DragonDictate at Legal Tech '92 in New York City in February. He reported that one law firm in Toronto had installed 10 systems and was negotiating for another 25. So we may all soon be dictating to our computers.)

Harold L. Burstyn is a member of the New York and Florida state bars and a registered patent attorney. He practices with the Morrison Law Firm in Mount Vernon, New York, and consults on legal automation.

Spreadsheets in Litigation

Kenneth M. Laff

Although computerized electronic spreadsheets revolutionized the business world, they are strangers to the law office. Kenneth Laff, a former trial lawyer who is now a full-time consultant, provides a simple, easy-to-follow explanation of what spreadsheets are and how they work. He then suggests several ways to use them in a litigation practice.

Though spreadsheet software has changed the way companies do business, most lawyers have yet to discover their utility. Their reluctance to use spreadsheets is puzzling. Perhaps they just "don't do numbers"; many lawyers are intimidated by figures. When you combine that intimidation with a natural fear of computers, the barrier can become formidable.

Have you ever had to add or subtract in your practice? If so, you could benefit from a spreadsheet. If there is any calculation or series of calculations that you must make (or have your secretary or paralegal make) repeatedly, you are wasting a significant amount of time and taking an unnecessary risk of error if you do not use a spreadsheet.

In this chapter, I explain what a spreadsheet is and how simple, reliable, and efficient it can be. Then I discuss several ways in which I have used spreadsheets in litigation: to compute damages, analyze settlement proposals, understand (and attack) witnesses whose testimony relies on spreadsheets, assist in antitrust counseling, and manage cases.

WHAT IS A SPREADSHEET?

A spreadsheet consists of columns, generally labeled alphabetically across the top, and rows, generally numbered along the left. It may contain words, numbers, or formulas. Figure 4.8 is a spreadsheet.

The boxes created by the intersections of columns and rows are called *cells*. Cell A1 (the intersection of Column A and Row 1) contains the word *Assets*. Cell B2 contains the number $8,000.

Cell B3 *displays* the number $2,000, but it actually contains the spreadsheet equivalent of the familiar formula "assets minus liabilities equal net worth."

To create a formula in a spreadsheet, one may refer to the location of the cells that are used in the calculation. For example, the actual formula in Cell B3 is B1–B2, where B1 is the cell containing the amount of assets and B2 is the cell containing the amount of liabilities. Once you have entered the formula, the spreadsheet does the calculation for you, looking back to the referenced cells for data. As soon as one changes the data in the referenced cells, the spreadsheet automatically recalculates the cells containing formulas. That instant calculating ability is what makes spreadsheets so valuable.

SELECTING SPREADSHEET SOFTWARE

I have created most of the spreadsheets discussed in this chapter using WordPerfect Corporation's PlanPerfect software. However, most of the features in my examples exist in other popular spreadsheet programs, such as Lotus 1-2-3, Excel, SuperCalc, WINGZ, Quattro Pro, and 20/20.[1] Which spreadsheet program you choose

FIGURE 4.8 A Spreadsheet

	A	B
1	Assets	$10,000
2	Liabilities	$ 8,000
3	Net Worth	$ 2,000

FIGURE 4.9 Spreadsheet Showing Total Interest for the Period

	A	B
1	Principal Amount	$476,284.39
2	Interest Rate	9.25%
3	Beginning Date	3/18/85
4	Ending Date	9/5/86
5	Annual Interest	$44,056.31
6	Per Diem Interest	$120.70
7	Total Number of Days	536
8	Total Interest	$64,696.38

FIGURE 4.10 Spreadsheet Employing Formulas

	A	B
5	Annual Interest	B1*B2
6	Per Diem Interest	B5/365
7	Total Number of Days	B4-B3
8	Total Interest	B6*B7

for your practice depends on a number of factors, as well as how the features of a particular program meet your personal needs.

You should consider whether a particular program runs on your existing hardware platform, operating system, and user environment (including processor type and available main memory), whether another group in your firm already uses a spreadsheet program, whether you require a multiuser product, and whether anyone on your staff is already trained in the program. While Lotus 1-2-3 has had the largest share of the market, PlanPerfect is a program worth considering by lawyers already familiar with the command structure of WordPerfect's word processor, which PlanPerfect uses.

A SIMPLE INTEREST SPREADSHEET

Several years ago an associate at my law firm was reviewing a draft affidavit from an officer of our client, a bank. The affidavit specified, among other things, the interest due on a note. The associate was concerned because he did not want to submit an inaccurate affidavit, and he was unable, with his calculator, to reach the same figure the client had calculated. In fact, though the associate labored long to recheck his calculation, there was a difference of over a thousand dollars.

To solve the mystery, I created a simple spreadsheet. The note at issue was in the amount of $476,284.39, with simple interest at 9.25 percent per year. The note was made on March 18, 1985, and the computation called for interest through September 5, 1986. I set up the spreadsheet to count the number of days at issue, compute the daily interest on the amount of the note, and multiply the two to get the total interest for the period, as shown in Figure 4.9.

The spreadsheet employed several formulas, as shown in Figure 4.10.

To compute the annual interest (Cell B5), I

FIGURE 4.11 Spreadsheet Showing Calendar Arithmetic

	A	B
1	Principal Amount	$476,284.39
2	Interest Rate	9.25%
3	Beginning Date	3/18/85
4	Ending Date	9/5/86
5	Total Interest	B1*B2/365*(B4-B3)

multiplied the principal amount (Cell B1) by the interest rate (Cell B2). To compute per diem interest (Cell B6), I divided the annual interest (Cell B5, the amount just derived) by the number of days in a year (365). To compute the total number of days (Cell B7), I subtracted the beginning date (Cell B3) from the ending date (Cell B4). Finally, to compute the total interest (Cell B8), I multiplied the per diem interest (Cell B6) by the total number of days (Cell B7).

The formula for total number of days illustrates a very useful feature of spreadsheets—calendar arithmetic. When you enter a date in the cell, the spreadsheet program stores the cell, for computational purposes, as the number of days since December 31, 1899, allowing easy calculation of time intervals. Of course, a single formula could perform the entire calculation, as shown in Figure 4.11. However, when one creates a spreadsheet, it is often better to use simple, discrete formulas, so that the operation of each may be separately tested.

My *initial* result was the same as my associate's. However, I had created the spreadsheet in less time than he had needed to perform the calculation, it was easier for me to check the accuracy of my work, I could print the spreadsheet to have a permanent (and readable) record of my calculations, and I could perform instantaneous "what if" analysis to solve the mystery.

VALIDATING YOUR SPREADSHEET FORMULAS

While it is unlikely that your spreadsheet software will create an error, it is important that you test your formulas. Anyone who has received a monthly utility bill for $10,470 can ap-

preciate the scope of error that a human being and a computer can combine to make. To validate a spreadsheet, try simple facts and see how the formulas operate. To validate my simple interest spreadsheet, I used it to calculate 10 percent interest on $1,000 for one year. The answer, $100, conformed to my knowledge of what the answer was, and I was assured that my formulas were correct (or, at least, that they correctly embodied what I believed to be the correct assumptions).

"WHAT IF" ANALYSIS

The next step was to perform "what if" analysis (i.e., to start changing the assumptions built into the spreadsheet to see if we could match the bank officer's results). The first thing we did was to use a 360-day year, which we accomplished by changing the formula for per diem interest (Cell B6) from B5/365 to B5/360. That change of formula moved us in the direction of our client's result, but it did not get us all the way there. We next tried adding a day to the total number of days, which we accomplished by changing the formula for Cell B7 from B4-B3 to B4-B3+1. That change, too, increased the total interest, but it did not raise it as high as our client's result. However, by combining the two changes, we matched the client's total exactly.

The associate called the client and confirmed the two assumptions upon which the bank computed interest. First, the bank used the convention of a 360-day year (12 months of 30 days) to compute per diem interest. Second, the bank counted the first day of the loan. That is, if a customer borrowed money on Monday and paid it back on Tuesday, he or she was charged two days' interest.

FIGURE 4.12 Restructured Spreadsheet with Two Added Formulas

	A	B
1	Principal Amount	
2	Interest Rate	
3	Beginning Date	
4	Ending Date	
5	Charge Interest for First Day? (Yes or No)	
6	Days per Year (360 or 365)	
7	Annual Interest	B1*B2
8	Per Diem Interest	IF(B6=360,B7/360,B7/365)
9	Total Number of Days	IF(B5="YES",B4-B3+1,B4-B3)
10	Total Interest	B8*B9

MODIFYING A SPREADSHEET FOR REPEATED USE

I then proceeded to modify the spreadsheet for use in the future. To do so, I restructured the spreadsheet to handle alternative assumptions regarding the number of days in a year and whether the first day of the loan was to be counted. I also built in protection so that the spreadsheet could be used safely by others.

I restructured the spreadsheet by adding two formulas that allowed for the alternative cases, as shown in Figure 4.12.

The new formulas in Cells B8 and B9 are examples of IF-THEN-ELSE logic. According to the formula for per diem interest (Cell B8), IF the number in Cell B6 is 360, THEN divide the annual interest (Cell B7) by 360 to get the per diem interest; ELSE (otherwise), divide the annual interest by 365. (The parentheses define the boundaries of the IF statement.) The formula for total number of days, Cell B9, applies the same principle, and it shows that spreadsheet formulas can reference words as well as numbers. According to the formula in Cell B9, IF Cell B5 contains the word *yes*, THEN subtract the beginning date (Cell B3) from the ending date (Cell B4) and add one to the result; ELSE, simply subtract the beginning date from the ending date.

To protect the spreadsheet from misuse by others, I took several steps. First, I *locked* all of the cells except B1, B2, B3, B4, B5, and B6 so that no one would be able to alter the text or formulas. Only those cells for which input ought to change from case to case could be modified. Second, I set up the spreadsheet to place the user automatically at the first cell into which data could be entered (Cell B1) when he or she retrieved the spreadsheet. Then each time the user entered data, the spreadsheet automatically moved to the next appropriate cell. This is the MODEL feature of PlanPerfect.[2]

Third, to make printouts of the spreadsheet more useful, I added an explanatory title and a footer that automatically printed the current date. Fourth, I added custom help messages. If the user pressed the program's **[HELP]** key, a message appeared that explained what to do in the cell into which the user was entering data.[3] For example, if a user pressed the **[HELP]** key while in Cell B1 ("amount of principal"), the message "Enter the amount of money on which interest has accrued (e.g., the amount borrowed or the amount of the judgment)" appeared. "Legal help" can be built into a spreadsheet as well. I added Cell C2 containing a formula, IF (B2>.45,"*USURY*"), which displays the warning *USURY* if the interest rate exceeds 45 percent.

My law firm's repeated use of this spreadsheet to calculate interest in "normal" and "bank" cases saved time and increased accuracy.

FIGURE 4.13 Spreadsheet Tracking Medical Expenses

	A	B	C
1	1/5/90	Reed Ambulance	$322.58
2	1/10/90	Rose Hospital	$4,325.00
3	1/12/90	Dr. J. L. Lewis	$893.25
4	11/14/90	Dr. J. L. Lewis	$45.12
5	11/14/90	Osco Pharmacy	$10.00
6			----------
7	**TOTAL**		**$5,595.95**

Another obvious use of spreadsheets would be to compute prejudgment and postjudgment interest. Where necessary, one can create formulas that compound interest or that apply varying statutory interest rates to the appropriate time periods.

WHEN THE OTHER SIDE USES A SPREADSHEET

When your opponent presents a spreadsheet, you must analyze it just as thoroughly as you would any other piece of evidence. Spreadsheets appear more and more frequently in litigation, both as client documents produced during discovery and as bases for expert opinion.

The first step in analyzing a spreadsheet is to get the spreadsheet itself in electronic form, in addition to a printout. Make sure your discovery requests are framed to include electronic media. Then analyze the formulas to see (and attack your opponent on) the assumptions that underlie those formulas. Is a present value calculation based on a 4 percent interest rate? Is a total mysteriously divided by two? Find out why. Spreadsheets can be imposing as evidence (especially if printed out on "official-looking" 82" by 14" green bar paper on a grainy dot-matrix printer), but they crumble quickly if any of their underlying assumptions are discredited.

Don't be afraid to go on the offensive. Run your own "what if" analyses with your opponent's spreadsheet. Witnesses who have created spreadsheets, even experts, are often unaware how dramatically their results will change when one or two of their assumptions are var-

ied. A witness might agree that 7 percent would be a more reasonable rate of interest without any idea of how significantly it would change his or her results.

USING SPREADSHEETS FOR ROUTINE CALCULATIONS

Very simple spreadsheets can speed the routine calculations that often accompany accounting calculations in litigation. Accumulating medical expenses could be tracked through a spreadsheet like the one shown in Figure 4.13.

I created this example with the Table and Math functions of WordPerfect; no separate spreadsheet program was required. Cell C7 contains the "+" code to add up the figures above it.

Many other kinds of litigation accounting can be accomplished more efficiently with a spreadsheet. Tracking of costs and disbursements requires only the same simple totaling of the medical expenses example. A personal injury settlement sheet can easily be automated to allocate client's and counsel's shares of a recovery and subtract disbursements. A spreadsheet can also prepare a case budget and track outside counsel fees.

USING SPREADSHEET GRAPHS TO MAKE YOUR POINT

Spreadsheet programs prepare graphs that can help litigators illustrate the point the spreadsheet is making. For example, if you tracked medi-

FIGURE 4.14 Spreadsheet Showing Medical Expenses Broken Down by Category

	A	B
1	EXPENSE CATEGORY	AMOUNT
2	Hospital	$7,000.00
3	Doctor	$2,000.00
4	Medication	$1,200.00
5	Other	$ 500.00

FIGURE 4.15 Pie Chart Showing Medical Expenses by Category

MEDICAL EXPENSES BY CATEGORY

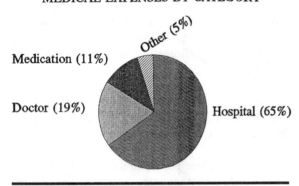

cal expenses with a spreadsheet as shown above, you could total the expenses by category. Suppose medical expenses for a plaintiff were broken down as shown in Figure 4.14. With the spreadsheet's graphing feature, we can create a pie chart that shows where the money was spent, as in Figure 4.15. Suppose you try to prove damages from a predatory pricing conspiracy in your client's Western sales region, by comparing the rate of growth in sales in the Western and Eastern regions. You could track the sales and compute the rates of growth with a spreadsheet like Figure 4.16.

However, the spreadsheet makes a presentation that is less than dramatic. You can illustrate your point far more persuasively by turning the spreadsheet into a graph, as shown in Figure 4.17.

CALENDAR ARITHMETIC

As discussed above, spreadsheets calculate the number of days between two dates—that is, they perform calendar arithmetic. With calendar arithmetic and the database capabilities of spreadsheet

software, one can create a litigation calendar and tickler system.

I designed a spreadsheet similar to the one shown in Figure 4.18 for a multicase litigation with a large staff. Here I've modified it to represent a calendar for one lawyer.

Column A holds the date of the event being tracked; Column B holds the time of day, if any, of that event; Column C holds the day of the week of the event; Column D holds the number of days from the current date (the current date should always be printed as part of a header or footer); Column E holds the case name; Column F holds the party or parties to whom the event pertains; and Column G describes the event.

This litigation calendar spreadsheet requires only two formulas. The formula used throughout Column C calculates the day of the week for the date shown in Column A.[4] The formula used throughout Column D, days until event, calculates the difference between the event date from Column A and the current date.

The litigation calendar makes use of the database features of spreadsheet software. If you add new entries at the bottom of the list, you can then sort the entire calendar chronologically (the rows placed in date and time order). You can extract categories of data, such as all rows relating to a particular case, from the entire list to view and print them separately. Thus it's easy to create individual case as well as comprehensive calendars.

A more complex spreadsheet could calculate the due dates themselves based on the applicable rules of practice and on factual data such as method of service.

OTHER SPREADSHEET USES ABOUND

There are countless other ways, both simple and complex, to use spreadsheets in litigation. Spreadsheets often help settlement analysis, as you compare the total monetary value of your adversary's position to your own, or to your adversary's previous offer. Spreadsheets make it easy to see what will happen to the value of a settlement if there is a change in an assumed variable, such as the interest rate.

Where some of the settlement will not be paid until some time in the future, your spreadsheet will compute the present value of a future payment or stream of payments. Structured settlements in personal injury cases are particu-

FIGURE 4.16 Spreadsheet Tracking Sales and Computing Rates of Growth

	A	B	C	D	E
1		1986	1987	1988	1989
2	SALES				
3	Western Region	$1,000,000	$1,200,000	$1,250,000	$1,200,000
4	Eastern Region	$1,500,000	$1,725,000	$2,001,000	$2,361,180
5	% GROWTH				
6	Western Region		20	4	-4
7	Eastern Region		15	16	18

FIGURE 4.17 Graph of Data Shown in Figure 4.16

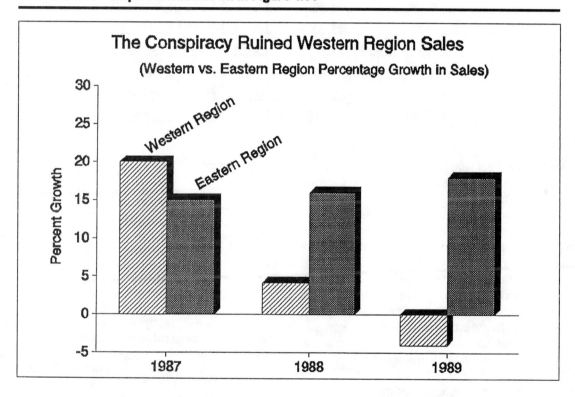

larly amenable to spreadsheet analysis. Suppose you are negotiating the settlement of a personal injury claim for an infant client. It may make sense to include a lump-sum payment at the time college tuition payments are due. It is extremely helpful in your negotiations to have a spreadsheet that can instantly report that a payment of $100,000 in 20 years is worth only $21,454.82 today, assuming a constant 8 percent interest rate. Similarly, it is essential to know that payments of $1,000 per month for 20 years ($240,000) are worth less than half of that today, again assuming an 8 percent interest rate.

A spreadsheet that applies a percentage chance of winning to an expected recovery at trial provides another useful tool in deciding whether to accept an offer of settlement.

With a spreadsheet, you can analyze any economic loss, such as lost income or lost profits, to determine whether to support such a claim, whether to attack the amount of an opponent's demand, or whether to deal with an expert wit-

FIGURE 4.18 Spreadsheet Showing Litigation Calendar for One Lawyer

	A	B	C	D	E	F	G
1				Days			
2	Event		Day of	Until			
3	Date	Time	Week	Event	Case	Party	Description
4	3/9/90		Friday	12	Smith	Defts	Last day to designate non-parties
5	3/13/90		Tuesday	16	Jones	All	Discovery cutoff
6	3/15/90		Thursday	18	ABC Corp.	All	Dispositive motions due
7	3/20/90	9:30am	Tuesday	23	XYZ Corp.	Pltf	Meet with client
8	3/20/90	3:00pm	Tuesday	23	Jones	All	Deposition of Marian Keane
9	4/12/90		Thursday	46	ABC Corp.	Pltf	Responses to 1st interrogatories due
10	4/20/90		Friday	54	Smith	Deft	Report to insurer
11	5/14/90		Monday	78	Smith	All	Discovery cutoff
12	8/8/90		Wednesday	164	ABC Corp.	All	Status conference, Magistrate Harvey
13	9/2/90		Sunday	189	Smith	All	Trial
14	12/3/90		Monday	281	Jones	Pltfs	Trial Notebook due
15	2/1/91		Friday	341	ABC Corp.	Pltfs	Last day to request pretrial conf.

ness. Spreadsheets are extremely helpful in computing support payments and division of property in matrimonial actions.

Very complicated formulas in a spreadsheet may seem daunting, but using them is a piece of cake compared to making the same complicated calculations manually or with a calculator. I once created a spreadsheet that applies the "market structure screen" from the U.S. Department of Justice Antitrust Division Vertical Restraint Guidelines. It took time to create the spreadsheet, but the calculations are so cumbersome that the time invested in the spreadsheet paid for itself the second time I used it.

The list of spreadsheet uses goes on and on, and I hope you will add to it. Whenever a case takes you into the world of numbers, let a spreadsheet be your guide.

ENDNOTES

1. Although most spreadsheet products operate in a similar fashion, the structure of formulas may differ from program to program. For example, the formula in the previous example, B1–B2, would be +B1–B2 in Lotus 1-2-3. The use of a product for the examples in this article is not an endorsement of the program.

2. An entire spreadsheet may be password protected to prevent unauthorized persons from seeing its contents.

3. Pressing the [HELP] key a second time brings up the program's standard help messages.

4. You do not have to type the formula into each cell to use it throughout a column. Spreadsheet software allows the user to copy a formula (or any other type of cell) just as one copies a block of text in a word processor. One cell may be copied to a group of cells, and blocks of cells may also be copied.

Kenneth M. Laff is a management consultant in the Denver office of Ziegler Ross Inc., a national consulting company specializing in law firm automation, litigation support, strategic planning, and placement. Mr. Laff is a member of the Colorado and New York bars and practiced law most recently with Holme Roberts & Owen in Denver, where he was a partner in the litigation department.

Valuation of Claims and Settlement Structures

Joshua Mitteldorf
Alice W. Ballard

Several software packages are now available that make the valuation of settlement structures quick and convenient, even for lawyers who have only passing familiarity with computers. Performing these calculations in-house instead of hiring an economist has several advantages for the litigator, and these advantages are explored and illustrated in the examples below. Perhaps the most important is an extra degree of flexibility afforded in the negotiation process.

Valuing damage claims is a fact of life for most litigators. A plaintiff seeks compensation for losses sustained at different times in the past and those projected in the future. In today's world, the dollar value of a case cannot be separated from the interest computation that helps determine that value. To depend on experts for such computations can be both expensive and inconvenient. Economic experts can take hours or days to provide present value calculations, and they generally do not work with you interactively or provide multiple "what if" scenarios.

Now that computers are present in most law offices, there is no reason lawyers can't do these calculations themselves. Several good software packages are commonly available to bring these calculations within the grasp of computer-literate lawyers. Most enable you to assign a value to simple claims in a few minutes' time and to model complicated structures with a little more effort. Just as the spreadsheet has made possible a type of thinking that you would never attempt with a hand calculator, smart financial programs are now changing the way people think about the valuation of claims. In some cases, the computational tool can add a new dimension to the art of settlement negotiations.

In this chapter we will focus on one such program. Per%Sense is a general purpose financial calculator, with additional screens for loan analysis, financial planning, investment analysis, and current accounts. To show how these kinds

of programs can be used, we will discuss four situations where damages calculations are required. The first three examples are straightforward computations of a type that lawyers routinely refer to experts. The last example will show you how you can be more creative in your approach to structuring a settlement once you have become comfortable with the program's operation.

Please beware that we developed and market Per%Sense, so our views on this particular program may not be without bias. Our purpose, however, is to demonstrate the utility of this type of software, not to market a particular product. At the conclusion of this article we will mention several other good programs that should be considered.

PRESENT VALUE OF LOST EARNINGS

In February 1991, Mr. Abner lost his eyesight in a home accident involving a piece of defective machinery. His medical bills in that year totaled $85,000, with an additional $18,000 in 1992. He is 45 years old now and expects he will never be able to work again. He had been earning $610 per week.

If Mr. Abner's case were referred to you, one of the first questions you would like answered is, "What is the present value of his tangible losses?" Figure 4.19 shows how you would set up Per%Sense to answer this question.

FIGURE 4.19 Computing Present Value of Tangible Losses

| File   Edit   Settings   Windows   Calc   Help/Examples   PRESENT VALUE SCREEN |

Single Payments:			Periodic Payments:					
Date	Amount	Value	From	Through	PerYr	Amount	COLA%	Value
6/15/91	85,000.00	92,650.26	3/ 1/91	6/ 1/12	52	610.00		356,121.51
3/30/92	18,000.00	18,343.23						

	As of	True Rate %	Loan Rate %	Yield %	Value
Present Value	6/20/92	8.5000	8.5302	8.8717	467,115.01

Settings: COLA: Ann 360 1950 12perYr

FIGURE 4.20 Projecting Changes in Salary over 20 Years

| File   Edit   Settings   Windows   Calc   Help/Examples   PRESENT VALUE SCREEN |

Single Payments:			Periodic Payments:					
Date	Amount	Value	From	Through	PerYr	Amount	COLA%	Value
6/15/91	85,000.00	92,181.77	3/ 1/91	6/ 1/12	52	610.00	3.000	454,507.27
3/30/92	18,000.00	18,322.86						

	As of	True Rate %	Loan Rate %	Yield %	Value
Present Value	6/20/92	8.0000	8.0267	8.3287	565,011.90
	6/20/92	8.5000	8.5302	8.8717	549,069.42
	6/20/92	9.0000	9.0338	9.4174	534,095.45

Settings: COLA: Ann 360 1950 12perYr

The screen is organized in three blocks. The upper left block is for single payments. The two medical bills are entered there, together with their approximate dates. The upper right block is for periodic payments. The $610 per week has been entered there. The *From date* was taken from the first missed paycheck. The *Through date* represents Abner's projected retirement date at age 65.

At the bottom of the screen, today's date is entered in the *As of* column, along with the estimated interest rate. The value has been computed and appears in the lower right-hand box. All data in reverse type (white-on-black) is Per%Sense's output. Data in normal type was entered by you.

Whether it is computed in-house or by an expert, this computation is subject to the same uncertainties. What will be the average interest

FIGURE 4.21 Value of Tas-T-Cola's Claim

Datafile: Test Data

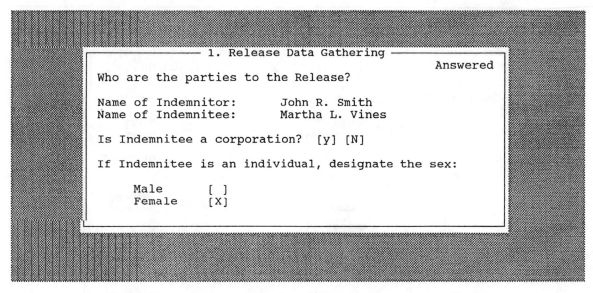

```
┌──────────── 1. Release Data Gathering ──────────┐
│                                        Answered  │
│ Who are the parties to the Release?              │
│                                                  │
│ Name of Indemnitor:     John R. Smith            │
│ Name of Indemnitee:     Martha L. Vines          │
│                                                  │
│ Is Indemnitee a corporation?  [y] [N]            │
│                                                  │
│ If Indemnitee is an individual, designate the sex: │
│                                                  │
│     Male      [ ]                                │
│     Female    [X]                                │
└──────────────────────────────────────────────────┘
```

ARROW KEYS move   PGDN/PGUP next/prev frame   F7 exit

rate over the next 20 years? How would your client's salary have changed over that time if he had been able to work? Figure 4.20 explores these changes.

In the upper right, the column labeled *COLA%* is for cost of living adjustments. The 3 percent figure entered there represents a guess that Abner's salary might have increased at a 3 percent annual rate over the course of his career.

In the bottom block, there are now three lines, repeating the computation for interest rates of 8, 8.5, and 9 percent. The presumed COLA has substantially increased the value of the claim, but it is comforting to note that there is less than 5 percent difference in the present values when the lowest and highest rates are used. (Payments far in the future are most affected by the interest rate, and the contribution of the far future to the present value is relatively small.)

The above analysis is typical of what you might expect from an expert's report. With a program like Per%Sense, you or your paralegal can generate this information in a matter of minutes.

We'll come back to this case at the end of the chapter, but for the present, let's explore another example, illustrating the use of Per%Sense when the interest rate must change with time.

VARIABLE INTEREST RATES

The Tas-T-Cola company claims that but for unfair competition from Zip-E-Cola, it would have earned $6 million in 1985, $8 million in 1986, $10 million in 1987, and $12 million in 1988. The applicable statute dictates that interest on these amounts be computed according to the average T-Bill rate for each year. These rates for the years in question were: 12 percent, 9.5 percent, 7 percent, and 6 percent. In January 1989, what is the value of Tas-T-Cola's claim?

The screen shown in Figure 4.21 is a variant of the Present Value screen and permits use of an interest rate table: a present value can be computed when the interest rate varies over time. This screen is accessed by pressing letter *V* (for Variable Rate) from within the regular *Present Value* screen.

At first glance, the rate table at the bottom left looks just like the data block at the bottom of the regular screen. However, the meaning here is somewhat different: In the regular *Present Value* screen, different lines of this block represent alternative computations of present value. Each line represents a complete summary of all payments above.

In the *X* screen, the different lines specify a

FIGURE 4.22 Actuarial Table

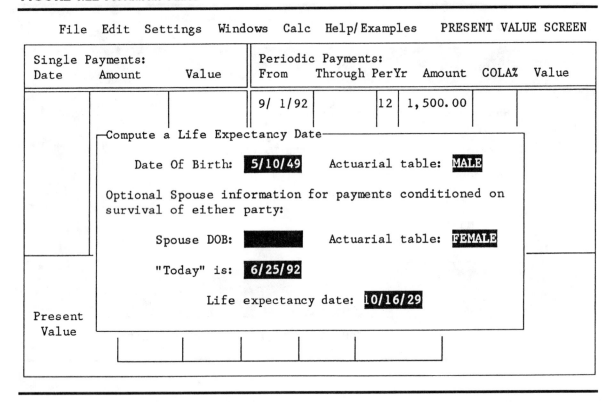

table of rates and the time periods when they are in force. The first line's date is XX, indicating that the rate applies from the beginning of the period in question. Each subsequent line begins with a date at which it goes into effect. A single present value is computed using the entire rate table; the amount appears in the lower right of the screen.[1]

The lost profits were entered as single deposits in the middle of each year in question (July 1). As in the previous example, the numbers that appear white-on-black are output, and the numbers in regular type were entered by you. With compound interest computed at the specified rates, the value of the total claim is now $40,894,439.59.

This screen also offers an option to compute simple interest. The concept of simple interest grew up in the days of low interest rates and pencil calculations. In contemporary financial calculations, the concept of simple interest seems artificial, since it implies two kinds of money, only one of which is entitled to earn interest. Nevertheless, there are some states in which a plaintiff is only entitled to claim simple interest on his past losses. It is clear that the survival of this dinosaur is not due to any *simplification* of the computation process, since in these same

states, the present value of future losses is always computed using compound interest. The use of simple interest *decreases* the amount of the claim if losses were sustained in the *past*, but if simple interest were used on *future* losses, the present value would be *enhanced*. So the selective use of simple interest constitutes a bias against the plaintiff.

The mirror image of damage valuation is settlement valuation. While damage valuation for a case requires just one calculation, settlement valuations need to be updated constantly as negotiations progress. This makes the use of a fast, convenient program much more important. We shall see below how valuation of settlement offers can even suggest paths to a better settlement.

VALUING A SETTLEMENT OFFER

With Per%Sense, the procedure for evaluating structured settlement is no different from that for evaluating a claim: The payments are listed at the top of the screen, today's date is entered at the bottom of the screen, a discount rate is chosen, and the value appears at lower right. Additional complications arise when a payment structure is specified to continue for as long as the recipient is alive.

FIGURE 4.23 Present Value Based on Life Expectancy

File Edit Settings Windows Calc Help/Examples   PRESENT VALUE SCREEN

Single Payments:			Periodic Payments:					
Date	Amount	Value	From	Through	PerYr	Amount	COLA%	Value
			9/ 1/92	10/ 1/29	12	2,000.00		**267,127.25**

	As of	True Rate %	Loan Rate %	Yield %	Value
Present Value	6/25/92	8.5000	**8.5302**	**8.8717**	**267,127.25**

Settings: COLA: Ann 360 1950 12perYr

PAYMENTS THAT CONTINUE FOR LIFE

Often a settlement will be structured as an annuity, with payments that continue for the plaintiff's lifetime. Computing the present value of such payments poses an interesting challenge: The traditional way of estimating such a value is to use a cutoff date; Per%Sense supports this approach, but also offers a more accurate alternative.

For the cutoff method, first find the plaintiff's life expectancy from a table; then assume that payments will continue through that date but not beyond, and compute a present value.

Per%Sense automates this process, with a built-in table of life expectancies. You can press [CTRL-L] and enter the plaintiff's date of birth, select an appropriate actuarial table (basic male and female tables are supplied), and calculate a cutoff date. (See Figure 4.22.)

The present value calculation may then be concluded in a straightforward fashion. In this example, payments of $2,000 per month begin in September 1992 and continue for the life of a 43-year-old annuitant. The life expectancy date is inserted as the *Through date*, terminating the periodic payments. Note that Per%Sense has changed the expected date of death slightly, to the nearest exact payment day. (See Figure 4.23.)

But this is not the most accurate available estimate of the desired present value. We know that there is some probability that the plaintiff may die before the cutoff date and a probability that he may die after the cutoff date. But in the context of a present value computation, these don't quite cancel out. The key point is that, because of the time value of money, the later payments, after the cutoff, are worth less than corresponding payments before the cutoff. Neglecting both probabilities always results in an *overestimate* of the present value.

The correct way to approach the problem is to consider each payment separately, compute its present value, then multiply that value by the probability that the plaintiff will still be alive on the corresponding date. The sum of these products (*pv* x *prob*) is the best estimate of the actuarial present value.

Per%Sense offers this computation. Instead of a cutoff date, we enter an ellipsis. Per%Sense interprets this to mean that payments continue into the indefinite future. Then press [CTRL-A] to perform an actuarial computation. After prompting for a date of birth, the computation shown in Figure 4.24 appears.

Notice the letter *L* on the line where the payments are specified. This indicates that the payments are contingent on the plaintiff continuing to live. (Other contingency options are available, including *Not contingent* and several options that can depend on survival of either a subject or spouse.)

The total present value is $256,478.15 instead of $267,127.25. The cutoff approach has overes-

FIGURE 4.24 Actuarial Computation

File Edit Settings Windows Calc Help/Examples	PRESENT VALUE SCREEN

Single Payments:			Periodic Payments:					
Date	Amount	Value	From	Through	PerYr	Amount	COLA%	Value
			9/ 1/92	10/ 1/29	12	2,000.00		**256,478.15**

	As of	True Rate %	Loan Rate %	Yield %	Value
Present Value	6/25/92	8.5000	**8.5302**	**8.8717**	**256,478.15**

Settings: COLA: Ann 360 1950 12perYr

---

timated the value by approximately 4 percent compared to the actuarial approach. For older plaintiffs, this figure can be 10 percent or more.

What about amounts payable on death (POD)? Again, the traditional approach is simply to compute a life expectancy date, then assume that the amount POD comes due on that date. The correct approach is to consider separately every day in the future. The present value of the POD amount paid on that day is multiplied by the actuarial probability that the plaintiff will die on that day, and the contribution from each day is summed to give an overall present value of the POD amount. Per%Sense supports both the traditional and the actuarial approach. The difference in present value here can be as much as 50 percent.

You may be curious about text on the screen in both the *Actuarial* and *Life Expectancy* calculation windows requesting DOB and actuarial data for a spouse. This data is optional and is used for computing annuities that are payable to either husband or wife. Per%Sense will compute a two-person life-expectancy date or perform a true actuarial calculation.

NEGOTIATING A STRUCTURED SETTLEMENT

We return now to the product liability case of our first example. We will see how Per%Sense can aid in negotiations and creative planning for a structured settlement.

The lawyer for Grinding Gears Tool Co. calls you to offer $480,000 to settle Abner's claim—or so he says. The money is to be spread over 20 years so Abner can't take it all to Atlantic City tomorrow. This works out to $2,000 per month. (See Figure 4.25.)

Using a T-Bill rate of 8.5 percent, you compute the value of the settlement as $228,000. Opposing counsel says his carrier calls it $198,000. You quickly compute that they must be using a 10.5 percent interest rate. (Do this just by blanking the cell for *True Rate* and inserting their $198,000 figure in the *Value* column. Per%Sense automatically finds the blank cell and fills it in. See Figure 4.26.)

A rate of 10.5% is probably what their long-term investments are yielding, but no matter. The important thing to you is that you have learned that they are using a higher interest rate than you are. Money in the far future looks bigger to you than it does to them. This fact will help you to construct a settlement that looks bigger to you than it does to the defendant.

The next day, you bring Abner into your office and explain to him the terms of the offer. He doesn't really understand the interest or the present value, but focuses on the sum of the payments—$480,000 sounds like a lot of money. But he has one concern: In 1998, his daughter will enter college; in 2001, his son will enter college. He feels that $2,000 a month is enough to live on, but it doesn't leave room for two tuition bills.

Private college tuition averages $9,600 today,

FIGURE 4.25 Negotiating a Structured Settlement

File	Edit	Settings	Windows	Calc	Help/Examples	PRESENT VALUE SCREEN

Single Payments: Date Amount Value			Periodic Payments:					
			From	Through	PerYr	Amount	COLA%	Value
			9/ 1/92	8/ 1/12	12	2,000.00		**228,009.02**

	As of	True Rate %	Loan Rate %	Yield %	Value
Present Value	6/25/92	8.5000	**8.5302**	**8.8717**	**228,009.02**

Settings: COLA: Ann 360 1950 12perYr

FIGURE 4.26 Computing the Value of Settlement

File	Edit	Settings	Windows	Calc	Help/Examples	PRESENT VALUE SCREEN

Single Payments: Date Amount Value			Periodic Payments:					
			From	Through	PerYr	Amount	COLA%	Value
			9/ 1/92	8/ 1/12	12	2,000.00		**198,000.00**

	As of	True Rate %	Loan Rate %	Yield %	Value
Present Value	6/25/92	**10.4720**	**10.5178**	**11.0400**	198,000.00

Settings: COLA: Ann 360 1950 12perYr

---

and it has historically been increasing by 4 percent per year. Here's how to set up Per%Sense to adjust this number for inflation. The two lines at the bottom of the screen represent the two separate calculations, for Fall 1998 and Fall 2001. Notice that the 4 percent figure is in the *Yield* column because inflation rates are conventionally quoted as yields (i.e., with one year's worth of compounding already in the figure as quoted. See Figure 4.27.)

At this rate, a tuition bill in 1998 will be $12,234, and $13,762 in 2001. You go back to your settlement screen and see if you can construct a settlement that makes everyone happy. If they are offering $198,000 in their terms, they will probably go to $400,000 eventually (using their interest rate). Abner needs $103,000 up front to pay his medical bills, plus 1/3 of the total settlement for your fee. That means: $133,000 + $103,000 = $236,000 up front. Then the two tuition bills must be covered. How much does that leave for monthly payments? Ask Per%Sense this question by entering the two lines for the tuition payments that you know have just been computed, and the *Value* at the bottom of the screen.

FIGURE 4.27 Adjusting College Projected Costs for Inflation

```
   File   Edit   Settings   Windows   Calc   Help/Examples    PRESENT VALUE SCREEN
```

Single Payments:			Periodic Payments:					
Date	Amount	Value	From	Through	PerYr	Amount	COLA%	Value
6/25/92	9,600.00	**12,234.72**						

	As of	True Rate %	Loan Rate %	Yield %	Value
Present Value	9/ 1/98	**3.9221**	**3.9285**	4.0000	**12,234.72**
	9/ 1/01	**3.9221**	**3.9285**	4.0000	**13,762.40**

Settings: COLA: Ann 360 1950 12perYr

FIGURE 4.28 Setting Up the Monthly Payment Dates

```
   File   Edit   Settings   Windows   Calc   Help/Examples    PRESENT VALUE SCREEN
```

Single Payments:			Periodic Payments:					
Date	Amount	Value	From	Through	PerYr	Amount	COLA%	Value
6/25/92	236,000.00	236,000.00	9/ 1/98	9/ 1/01	1	12,234.72	4.000	**23,227.94**
			9/ 1/01	9/ 1/04	1	13,762.40	4.000	**19,068.13**
			9/ 1/92	8/ 1/12	12	**1,231.70**		**121,703.93**

	As of	True Rate %	Loan Rate %	Yield %	Value
Present Value	6/25/92	10.5000	**10.5461**	**11.0711**	400,000.00
	6/25/92	8.5000	**8.5302**	**8.8717**	**427,045.45**

Settings: COLA: Ann 360 1950 12perYr

Set up the monthly payment dates, but leave the amount blank, to be filled in. (See Figure 4.28.)

In this computation, you've entered the college tuition as one payment per year in September. You've already estimated the cost of tuition in 1998 and 2001; you specify a COLA of 4 percent to keep up with increases during the time the children are in college. The *Single Payment* in the upper left, coinciding with the *As of* date below, is a cash payment at the time of the settlement. It is valued at exactly its dollar amount, since there is no time for interest to accrue. You specify both the rate and the value in the lower block, leaving Per%Sense to compute the third line of the *Periodic Payments* column. The monthly amount turns out to be only $1,232. Can Abner live on that? Probably not, he says. He has said he needs $2,000. But after 1998, he'll be eligible for a pension and will no longer need the income from his settlement. (See Figure 4.29.)

In the above screen, you have entered $2,000 in the *Amount* column in the upper right, and left

FIGURE 4.29 Computing Amount of Monthly Payments

```
    File   Edit   Settings   Windows   Calc   Help/Examples   PRESENT VALUE SCREEN
```

Single Payments:			Periodic Payments:						
Date	Amount	Value	From	Through	PerYr	Amount	COLA%	Value	
6/25/92	236,000.00	236,000.00	9/ 1/98	9/ 1/01	1	12,234.72	4.000	23,227.94	
			9/ 1/01	9/ 1/04	1	13,762.40	4.000	19,068.13	
			9/ 1/92	1/ 1/00	12	1,997.84		121,835.61	

	As of	True Rate %	Loan Rate %	Yield %	Value
Present Value	6/25/92	10.5000	10.5461	11.0711	400,000.00
	6/25/92	8.5000	8.5302	8.8717	416,940.96

```
    Settings:   COLA: Ann 360 1950 12perYr
```

the *Through* date blank. You are asking, "How long can he continue to receive his $2,000 per month, consistent with the total present value of $400,000? Per%Sense decided that payments could continue through January 1, 2000, and adjusted your $2,000 to $1,997.84 to make the value come out exact.

So this is the structure to aim for in your negotiations. From your point of view, with an 8.5 percent effective rate, the value looks $17,000 better. (This is the last line in the bottom block.) If the settlement goes through, you and your client must decide whether your fee is to be 1/3 of the $400,000 or 1/3 of $416,940.

This kind of thinking and exploration is really too cumbersome to undertake while working with an expert long-distance. Having a program like Per%Sense in your office gives you the flexibility to think creatively about settlement structures and to optimize the benefit to your client.

CONCLUSION

Financial planning was once an art, based on good instincts and a bit of guesswork. But as sophisticated software has become accessible to those with average mathematical abilities, business decisions have acquired a quantitative foundation, and companies are more competitive as a result.

This power is available to the legal profession as well, and some litigators are learning to use it to advantage. Inevitably, the type of computation embodied in Per%Sense will become integrated into our thinking and strategizing about settlements; our horizons will widen, creativity will be stimulated, and the result will be better settlements for both plaintiff and defendant.

PROGRAMS TO CONSIDER

There are several programs that will do these kinds of calculations and they can also be computed on a spreadsheet if you know the appropriate formulas. Here are some worth considering:

PI Economist ($250) and Structured Settlement Economist ($175.00) are available from Advocate Software, Box 10967, Oakland, CA 94610, (800) 800-1393.

Determining Damages : Economic Loss ($495) and Determining Damages : Structured Settlements ($395) are available from Shepard's/McGraw-Hill, P.O. Box 35300, Colorado Springs, CO 80935, (800) 525-2474.

Per%Sense ($99.95) and Per%Sense Pro ($350.00) are available from Ones & Zeros, Inc., 708 West Mt. Airy Ave., Philadelphia, PA 19119, (800) 882-2764.

ENDNOTE

1. From this it may appear that the X screen is a more powerful variant of the Present Value Screen.

Why use the regular screen at all? The answer, as we will show in a later example, is that it is sometimes useful to solve for a specific interest rate. This is an "implicit rate," or "internal rate of return (IRR)." This computation cannot be performed on the X screen, because it is structured so as to allow for multiple interest rates.

Joshua Mitteldorf is the designer and programmer of the Per%Sense software package. After receiving his physics BS from Harvard and MS from The University of California at Berkeley, he studied Chinese language in Taiwan, taught emotionally disturbed teenagers, then spent several years as a private piano instructor in the Boston metropolitan area. Returning to the world of academic science, he conducted research in fuel cell technology and wrote a Ph.D. dissertation in theoretical astrophysics at the University of Pennsylvania. Under the name Ones & Zeros Unltd., he continues to provide consulting services and writes software for financial computations, while working for environmental causes, teaching classes in yoga, and playing French horn in a community orchestra.

Alice W. Ballard is a lawyer in Philadelphia, specializing in civil rights and employment-related issues. After receiving her B.A. and J.D. from Harvard, she first practiced poverty law in rural Maine. Since 1976, she has been in private practice with Samuel and Ballard, PC. Equal employment opportunity is the mainstay of her practice, and her recent interests include sexual harassment, age discrimination, and pension rights.

Using Timeslips to Help Manage Your Litigation Practice

Carol L. Schlein

> Keeping time is one of the least favorite parts of a litigation practice. In this article, Carol Schlein will show you how one popular program lightens the burden and can help you keep track of your firm's time and disbursements.

Are you tired of filling out time sheets by hand and trying to add up all of the ".1s" at the end of the day? Are your secretaries threatening to quit because they're going blind reading your scrawl on Daytimer sheets? Or have you just read the title of this chapter and are thinking to yourself, "I'm a plaintiff's personal injury lawyer. What good is a time and billing program to me?" Read on.

If you have a personal computer on your desk (or in your office), Timeslips, or one of the many other time and billing programs, may be the answer. As you will see, programs like Timeslips provide excellent tools for recording your time and expenses and preparing bills based on hourly rates. And, while my focus will be on Timeslips in an hourly-rate litigation practice, such programs can also help a contingency practice, both to keep track of expenses and to manage cases.

OVERVIEW

Timeslips consists of two related programs: TSTIMER and TSREPORT. In TSTIMER, you enter your time and disbursement slips on your computer as your day progresses. In TSREPORT, you or your secretary create your bills and other reports. Timeslips has become more sophisticated since its creation in 1984. It now runs on either MS-DOS–compatible computers or Apple Macintosh computers. It can also be used on a local area network.

KEEPING TRACK OF TIME

The TSTIMER portion of Timeslips is modeled on a traditional time slip for recording time. That's how the program got its name. Typically, we record our time on a paper slip and give it to a data entry person, who in turn records the entries in the computer. The sticking point with this system is usually the lawyer. If you are like me, the thought of having to write out the same description continually is enough to make you long for a job where you don't need to keep track of your time. Some of us dislike the process so much that we put off preparing our time records until the end of the month, which makes everyone unhappy and isn't good for the firm's bottom line.

Timeslips makes the process quick and easy, even for nontypists. When you call up TSTIMER, you get a Time Entry screen that looks like the paper slip I used to use. (See Figure 4.30.) At that point, you can quickly identify client, matter, time, or disbursement information by typing the first few letters or numbers that identify each entry. The program then finds the match for you and automatically enters the full description. If that sounds too formidable, you can select each entry from a table.

The only typing necessary is to describe your services. Although I am not the best typist, I quickly discovered that it's just as easy to type a short description as to write it out in longhand. Moreover, Timeslips allows you to create custom abbreviations. You type an abbreviation such as

FIGURE 4.30 TSTIMER Time and Disbursement Entry Screen

```
Attorney          1        CLS Carol            ◄ Rate 2 :    150.00
Client.Matter    [3    ]   Brown's Drugs
Time Code/$DISB  [1    ]   TIME

   | |. . . . . . . . . . . . . . . . . . . . . . . . . . . . . . . . . . . . . |
   |                                                                           |
   |                                                                           |
   |                                                                           |
   |                                                                           |
Reference  [             ]            Time estimated [0:00:00   ]
Date       [07/23/92] Through [07/23/92]  Time spent       0:06:03

Will be a new slip │BILLABLE   │TIMER: ON │Value:           15.13
1 timer on
♦ Create a Slip ♦

F3   Duplicate field          Tab       Next field     Esc  Quits
F5   Timer on/off             Shift-Tab Previous field
F6   Duplicate rest           PgUp      First field
F10  Accept and assign rates  PgDn      Last field

Description      F9·Abbreviations  ←→↑↓ Home End Ctrl-←→ moves.
Alt-W·Word check  Alt-S·Suggest word  Alt-I·Toggle iteractive
F1·Help                    │07/23/92 05:45:59 pm │♦Timeslips N5.00    ♦
```

tcc followed by a punctuation mark (e.g., space, comma, period), and the program automatically converts the abbreviation into the phrase *telephone conference with client regarding*. If you initially set up abbreviation phrases that begin with a lower-case letter, you have the option of changing the case of the initial letter as you type. Using the example above, if you type *Tcc*, the phrase will be expanded to *Telephone conference with. . . .*

Figure 4.31 shows a sample abbreviation list set up under Abbreviations (from TSREPORT Main Menu, select Settings, then Custom Text, then Abbreviations).

Timeslips offers other shortcuts that help make the program easy to use. For example, when you call it up, the program usually inserts your name and today's date. If you want to change the date of a slip, for example, to record time while out of the office, you simply press the gray plus [+] or minus [-] keys on the number pad of the keyboard to change the date forward or backward a day at a time. If you need to return to today's date, simply press [T] (today's date).

Timeslips is at its best when a lawyer records work as it occurs. You enter time in various ways: tenths of an hour; hours and minutes; start and stop times; or using the clock built into your computer, you can record your time with the timer as you perform a selected task.

The start-and-stop time option is convenient for litigators, who spend long blocks of time on a single activity. For example, you enter the time of day you started the deposition and the time you finished (e.g., 9:00 A.M. to 3:45 P.M. The computer then calculates that you spent 6 hours and 45 minutes.

Timeslips' Timer option lets you turn on a stop-watch as you begin an activity, such as a telephone call with a client. Depending on how you set up your computer, you can pop up the timer over other programs, start the timer, then suspend Timeslips (while the timer continues ticking) and switch to other programs such as your calendar or word processor. You continue to capture the time until you have completed the activity. Depending on the format of your bill and your personal preferences, you can either edit that slip to add additional time and description to it during the course of the day or create a new slip for each activity.

With Timeslips you determine the billing status of each slip as you create it. The default, or

FIGURE 4.31 Timeslips Custom Text—Abbreviations List

```
┌ Abbreviations

   Abbrv      Meaning

   [CTAP ]  │ court appearance on behalf of
   [DS   ]  │ divorce and settlement proceeding
   [MW   ]  │ meeting with
   [PSC  ]  │ prepare summons and complaint
   [SC   ]  │ settlement conference
   [TCC  ]  │ telephone call with client regarding
   [TCF  ]  │ telephone call from
   [TCOC ]  │ telephone to opposing counsel
   [TCT  ]  │ telephone call to
   [[FAX ]  │ Facsimile charge
   [[FF  ]  │ Filing Fee
   [[PHO ]  │ Photocopies at $.20 per page


   more ↓ 1 through 12 of 256 total displayed

──────────────────────────────────────────────────────
   The abbreviation is associated with a meaning.  The meaning will replace
   the abbreviation when entered into the description area of a slip.
└ ←→↑↓ Home/End PgUp/PgDn·Move F5·Delete Esc·Quit
```

preset option, is billable by the lawyer's rate. Timeslips release 5.0 adds the ability to bill at up to six different rates for each lawyer. If your firm bills each client at a separate rate regardless of the timekeeper, you can change the global option in Settings under the Operational Preferences (in release 4.0 and above) to bill by client. You can change an individual slip to be billed by client or activity. Figure 4.32 shows the options available.

These options are like selecting food from a Chinese menu—in release 5, you use the **[F9]** key to see the options. The default options are to make the slip billable and to use the default billing rate determined in Setting/Data-Financial or in the Client's nickname, if you have designated one different from the default. You can also use these options to make a slip a "NO CHARGE," which means the text will print on the bill but the dollar amount normally associated with it will not be included in the total. With the billing options available, you can also override the designated rate or give the slip a flat charge. The Flat Charge option is useful if you have given a client a rate that governs a specific slip's value. For example, you may make an arrangement with a client that a day in court on trial will cost *x* amount of dollars. During the course of the

trial, you typically will have several days in court and much time that is straight hourly time.

Perhaps the most important feature of Timeslips is that it can run as a TSR (or memory-resident) program. This means you can call up Timeslips in the morning, start your clock running on a project, and then switch (via a special "hot-key" combination) to another application, such as your word processing program. If you have to switch to another project, or you need to turn off the clock, simply press the appropriate hot-key combination. Timeslips pops up on top of whatever you are working on. You then turn off the timeslip, switch to another one, or take some other action. This capacity to switch back and forth with no effort gives the program added utility.

Because Timeslips is so versatile, many lawyers choose it even though their firm uses a different time and billing program to prepare bills. At the end of the month, summary reports from Timeslips can be transferred into the firm's program by a data entry clerk. In addition, Timeslips exports its reports to many other time and billing programs. This flexibility gives Timeslips' users the best of both worlds: easy time entry and compatibility with the firm's billing system.

FIGURE 4.32 TSTIMER Billing Options

```
 Attorney        [1    ] CLS Carol          ◄ Rate 2 :    150.00
 Client.Matter   [3    ] Brown's Drugs
 Time Code/$DISB [1    ] TIME
 ┌                                                                ┐
 │ Telephone call from Opposing Counsel to discuss settlement ····│
 │ offer for slip and fall case.│·································· │
 │                                                                │
 │                                                                │
 Reference  [              ]        Time estimated [0:00:00  ]
 Date       [04/09/92] Through [04/09/92] Time spent     [0:18:00  ]

 Slip 7 of 9       │BILLABLE    │TIMER: OFF│ Value:           45.00

 ♦ Set Billing Options ♦                      F10·Done   Esc·Quit

 Billing status [B]illable    Rate source   [Attorney       ]
 Repeat         [N]o          At level      [2]
 Add to flat fee [N]o         Rate value    [150.00    ]


 Billing status Choose the billing status for this slip.
 B·Billable, D·Do not bill, N·No charge, H·Hold, S·Summary
 F1·Help              │07/23/92 05:47:37 pm │♦Timeslips N5.00   ♦
```

RECORDING DISBURSEMENTS

Tracking disbursements in Timeslips is like tracking time. The entry screen is the same. The difference occurs when you enter the activity. Instead of entering the type of matter or activity, you enter a disbursement activity. All disbursement codes start with a $ to distinguish them from time codes. When you enter the $ in the Activity field of the entry screen, the lower right-hand corner of the screen changes from Time Estimated and Time Spent to Quantity and Price.

Timeslips lets you enter disbursements in several ways. You can enter specific amounts, such as messenger charges or filing fees. You can also record unit costs, where the number of units determines the charge to the client. Examples include photocopies, fax transmissions, mileage, and legal research. Timeslips lets you enter the number of copies or fax pages and a unit rate; it then calculates the cost to the client. You can also enter flat costs for situations where the charge is X dollars for the service regardless of the actual use.

For example, if your firm wants to charge for telephone calls but doesn't have a charge-back system, you could bill each call at a minimum cost. Another option is the Markup feature for selected disbursements. In the Client Information screen for each client, you enter the percent you want to mark up. When you set up (or edit) each disbursement activity that you want marked up by that percent for those clients, you select markup *Yes*.

ENTERING PAYMENTS AND MAKING ADJUSTMENTS

During the course of the month, if your practice is well run, you receive payments from clients. You enter these payments in the Transaction screen for that client under the Client Information section. Highlight the client's name, press the **[F9]** key, and you see a screen similar to that shown in Figure 4.33. Entering payments is relatively straightforward. Making write-ups or discounts is a little trickier.

To write up an amount, you must decide if

FIGURE 4.33 Timeslips Transaction Entry Screen

```
┌ Enter transactions for: Brown's Drugs      Cur Bal:     0.00 Funds:      0.00 ┐
│                                                                               │
│   Date        Description                   Amount      Status                │
│                                                                               │
│  [07/19/92] [Payment - thank you        ] [500.00   ]                         │
│  [07/23/92] [10% COURTESY DISCOUNT       ] [-10.00   ]%                        │
│  [ / / ] [                               ] [         ]                         │
│                                                                               │
│                                                                               │
│           1 through   3 of   3                                                │
├── Date        Description ────────────────────────────────────────────────── │
│  [ / / ] [                                ]                                    │
│                                                                               │
├───────────────────────────────────────────────────────────────────────────  │
│  Enter the transaction date. MM/DD/YY                                         │
│  Use T for Today          07/23/92                                            │
│     S for Same as last 07/23/92                                               │
└ ←→↑↓ PgUp/PgDn·Move F2·Delete billed F5·Delete line Esc·Cancel F10·Accept ────┘
```

you are writing up the time, the disbursements, or the total amount of the bill. Depending on your answer, you select either Adjust Time Charges, Adjust Expenses, or Adjust Entire Bill. I recommend that the date of this item coincide with the last day of your billing cycle. If you are adjusting upwards, you enter the *difference* between the calculated amount and the new amount. Since you don't want the client to see the information on the bill, you should be sure that the Show field is set to N (No).

To give the client a courtesy discount, you want to be sure that the client sees it. To do this, you edit the words *Adjust entire bill* to read *COURTESY DISCOUNT* by erasing the old text with your backspace key and typing the new description. In the amount field on the Transaction screen, you enter a minus sign [-] followed by the amount of the *difference* between the original amount and the adjusted amount. For example, if the original bill was $2,000, you can give the client $200 off or you can dr,op the amount owed by 10 percent. To do this, you would enter -$200 in the amount field or -10 percent in the percent field. To be sure that the client sees this on the bill, you change the Show option to Y (Yes).

CUSTOMIZING THE PROGRAM: TIPS & TRICKS

Multiple Lawyer Rates

Releases of Timeslips prior to 5.0 were limited in their ability to attach specific billing rates for the lawyers to specified clients. Release 5.0 adds the ability to set up a rate table, designate which rate is in effect for which clients and use both names and initials on bills.

In setting up earlier versions of Timeslips, you can designate different rates for the same lawyer (e.g., for different clients or in-court and out-of-court work). Because Timeslips only prints the first three letters of the lawyer nickname on bills (if you choose to have initials print), you can set up the nicknames (e.g., three initials) followed by information about the rate to help data entry people select the correct rate. For example, if I had separate rates for in and out of court, I could set up my nicknames as [CLS 200] and [CLS 225 IN COURT]. Timeslips searches for each nickname by separating it from the others around it.

To take advantage of that feature, you could designate your two rates as regular or special by including an *s* as part of your nickname for in court work (e.g. [CLSs 225 IN COURT]). Using this example, the person entering the timeslip would simply type CLSs when the work is done in court. If you didn't add the *s*, your operator would have to type [CLS (space) 22] to distinguish this rate from the other. In fact, this feature can shortcut typing in all of the nickname-based fields in the entry screens.

Another approach is to place the type of work performed (usually, matter type) into the Activity field. In this situation you keep the fist letter of the type of work unique, if possible. This allows you to type a single letter in the Activity field to select the right matter type. Similarly, you can include the single letter as part of the client's nickname so that they are linked as the operator enters the slips. Figure 3.30 is an example of the Time Entry screen with these options included.

Timeslips 5 adds 16 user-defined fields that can be used to sort information. This expands the Controller function, which allows you to group cases by a common characteristic. In versions of Timeslips prior to 5, Controller was the only field you could do this with. The Controller field was intended for the responsible or billing lawyer; that is, the lawyer who reviews the worksheets and bills at the end of the month. If you didn't need that function, you could use Controller to designate type of case, billing cycle, or some other grouping. Timeslips 5 adds the ability to have a number of sorting capabilities. Among the fields you may want to define are originating attorney, referral sources, billing cycle, type of case, and date of origination.

Managing Your Cases

Timeslips has other uses in a litigation practice. You can designate type of law in the Activity field (or custom field, depending on which version you are using). Depending on your practice, you might use this for general categories such as real estate, estates and trusts, or litigation. If you have a specialized practice, you can refine this further by designating types of personal injury cases or, if you are an insurance defense lawyer, by insurance carrier. You can thus sort your clients and matters by type of case as well as generate reports about the firm's caseload. Reports such as Summary by Activity give you a graphic picture of the hours and fees generated by subspecialties within your firm. Ad-

ditionally, you can create user-defined timeslip and client reports to analyze information about the lawyers and their work and the clients and their billings, respectively. These report options let you select which fields of information you want in a report along with specific data and date ranges. Timeslips 5 adds even more reports, including productivity and realization information so that you can see what a lawyer is billing and collecting.

Timeslips has also added a Notes feature. This, too, can record and track information about your cases. It provides you with a screen's worth of notes that print or display as needed.

WHY BILL CONTINGENCY CASES?

Because they operate on contingent fees, many personal injury lawyers don't keep track of their time. This gives them a false sense of earning power; they have no idea how much time they actually spent in return for the percentage or flat fee. While a million-dollar settlement may seem like a windfall, you've actually lost money compared to billing the same case at an hourly rate if your average billing rate is $200 and your firm has spent more than 5,000 hours on the case. Accurate tracking of lawyers' time can locate your financial breakeven point. This information helps you select cases.

Getting Reimbursement for Costs

A typical problem for lawyers handling contingent-fee cases is keeping track of and billing for costs advanced. To avoid playing banker for your clients, you must bill disbursements regularly. Clients are more likely to pay a small bill than a large one. Billing frequently and in smaller dollar amounts is a better way to ensure collection and keep your client satisfied.

It also improves your cash flow. This is particularly important in a firm that relies heavily on contingent fees, since the money collected from cases is less predictable and more erratic than in traditional hourly billing practices.

Preparing Fee Petitions Using Timeslips

Recording your time with Timeslips—even if it does not need to appear on a bill—can assist you if, at the end of a case, the court requires you to prepare a detailed bill for your actual time spent. (Courts are doing this with increasing frequency in many jurisdictions.) Suppose you are preparing a case for trial and need to formulate your strategy and consolidate your notes since the beginning of the case. If you have been recording your time with Timeslips with detailed descriptions, you can create a scratchpad file, import archived slips from the beginning of the case, and print a User Defined Timeslip Report. This report gives you a chronological listing of all your notes with the dates they were entered. Be sure to select *Print Billed Items* from the print menu (options menu in release 5) to include old and new slips. In addition, Timeslips can print any report to a file. This file, in ASCII format, can be brought into your word processor for further editing if necessary.

Evaluating the Profitability of Your Case Load

With a number of reports in Timeslips you can analyze the profitability of the firm's case load, lawyers, and practice areas. From the Timeslip Reports menu (Slip Reports in release 5), you display or print graphic charts of lawyers' hours, dollars brought in, or dollars per hour. A similar chart analyzes all cases or cases by practice area (if you use the Activity field for type of case).

Client history reports as well as billing worksheets include information that compares standard hourly rates to the actual amount billed and collected. This information can be analyzed further by printing it to a file and manipulating it in a spreadsheet program such as Lotus 1-2-3. While other time and billing programs may offer more extensive management reports, few are as flexible and inexpensive.

CONCLUSION

As we move toward graphic-oriented programs, I anticipate that programs such as Timeslips will be modified to take advantage of mice, touch screens, voice input, etc. The computers we use to record this information will soon fit easily in our briefcases with our all-in-one cellular phone/modem/fax. In fact, I wrote and edited this chapter on a four-pound computer! Billing programs such as Timeslips may soon permit us to type in or—better yet—ask, "How were our collections on the Jones case?" and see a report comparing the Jones case to our hourly rates, measuring the amount of money received against the number of hours worked, etc. In the meantime, we have tools available today to enhance the practice of law and serve our clients better.

Carol L. Schlein is a lawyer and president of Law Office Systems, Inc., a consulting firm with offices in New York and New Jersey, that assists law firms with automation selection, implementation, and training. She is a member of the Council for the American Bar Association's Section of Law Practice Management as well as chair of the section's Beginning Computer Interest Group. In addition, she is an active member of and frequent speaker for the New York and New Jersey state bar associations.

Using Computers to Identify Conflicts of Interest

Douglas O. McLemore
Kurt L. Schultz

> Conflict checking is important for all lawyers. The larger a firm gets, and the longer it has been around, the more complex the task becomes. In this chapter, Douglas McLemore and Kurt Schultz of the Chicago firm of Winston & Strawn detail both the implementation of their automated conflict checking system and its integration into other aspects of the firm's business operations.

The last thing any law firm wants is to inadvertently sue one of its own clients or a business owned by a client. Not only is such an act against all ethical canons, it is bad business. Yet, given the complexity of modern life, these and other conflicts of interest are not always readily apparent. A law firm must employ safeguards to identify conflicts before it agrees to represent a new client. This is truer today than ever before.

A conflict of interest occurs whenever a law firm represents an interest opposing that of a present or former client. It can involve seemingly unrelated clients, their lawyers, branch offices located thousands of miles apart, and matters that have long been resolved. Some law firms screen for conflicts in a relatively informal way, by reporting new matters during daily meetings or circulating memos listing new clients. Such methods rely upon lawyers to recall the potentially conflicting names or situations and bring them to the attention of the firm.

A more businesslike approach requires the development of an index of current and previous clients and all other interested parties. To be most effective, the index must be cross-referenced to client files. New clients are checked against the index, and when a match is found, the responsible lawyers sort out whether there is a conflict.

COMPUTERIZED SYSTEMS

For the large law firm, informal conflict-checking methods are insufficient. The sheer number of lawyers, the distance between branch offices, and the multitude of matters in which the firm is involved necessitate a more sophisticated system. This is where the computer excels.

A computerized conflict system is essentially a large database, an automated (and expanded) version of the cross-index described above. It should include the names of all clients, company officers, subsidiaries, parent companies, and any other related individuals or companies.

Winston & Strawn installed a computerized conflict system in April 1989. Today the firm can check a new client for a conflict in minutes. The system generates a one-page printed report on each potential conflict, providing the name of the present or previous client, a description of the matter, the responsible partner, and the location of the office.

Sometimes a conflict check produces dozens of reports; other times, none. It still remains to the lawyers, possibly in concert with their clients, to resolve the nature and level of importance of any conflict.

PROCEDURES FOR ACCEPTING NEW CLIENTS

The computerized conflict system also helps the procedure for accepting new clients. To be profitable, a law firm must control the acceptance of new clients and of new work for existing clients. We needed procedures for this purpose, and we integrated the conflict system into them.

The new procedures ascertain that a new client and/or new work are consistent with the standards established by the firm; that the client has the financial capabilities to pay for legal services; that the lawyers assigned to the matter have the proper level of expertise; and that representation is not contrary to the interests of any existing clients.

Here is how these procedures work at Winston & Strawn, with particular emphasis on conflict management:

1. The partner recommending a new client completes a form that details the nature of the work, participating lawyers, financial information, and conflict of interest information. The last requires a list of all individuals, businesses, and other parties affiliated with the new client. If it is a litigation matter, the names of key and/or expert witnesses could be included in the list.

2. The department head approves the form, verifying that the firm has the expertise to perform the services and approving the individual lawyers assigned to perform them.

3. The names supplied on the client form are checked for conflicts. Reports from a search into the computer data base are attached to the form.

4. Potential conflicts are referred back to the partner responsible for the new client. They are usually resolved by a telephone call to the lawyer responsible for the existing matter. In most instances, no real conflict is found.

5. Genuine conflicts must be resolved. Often a client will sign a waiver, particularly when the matter is not confrontational or adversarial. If questions persist, a firm lawyer experienced in conflict issues may analyze any legal/ethical issues.

6. The final determination about any conflict is made by the managing partner or the executive committee before representation of a new client begins.

7. We also gather information useful to our marketing efforts, such as source of work or industry, in the client acceptance process.

This entire process normally consumes no more than a day or two, so that lawyers may begin the new work without delay. Compliance with these procedures has been excellent, because the accounting system cannot issue a billing number until all forms have been approved.

Once we accept a new client, we input the names of all affiliated parties into the database for future conflict checks. A good conflict system can include a wide variety of information. For example, some law firms input the names of all outside business interests of their own lawyers to guard against potential conflicts.

The computerized system has speeded up and improved the firm's ability to determine if conflicts exist. We have yet to hear of any potential conflict failing to be identified.

COMMERCIAL SOFTWARE

Winston & Strawn uses a program designed by TMC, the same company that developed the

---

Computerized Conflict Checking: How Skadden Does It

Leon Cohen

Skadden, Arps, Slate, Meagher & Flom currently has more than 1,000 lawyers, seven offices in the United States, six offices outside the United States, and more than 15 practice areas. The firm has dealt with over 5,000 companies during the last eight years. Not surprisingly, conflict of interest is a major concern to the firm. Because of our size, our only realistic option for keeping track of conflicts was a computerized system.

Skadden, Arps uses an IBM 4381-14 mainframe computer. This computer has 16 million characters of memory, disk drives that provide access to 27.5 billion characters, tape drives for back-up and archiving, communication controllers that allow any lawyer with a personal computer and the proper

continued on page 154

Computerized Conflict Checking: How Skadden Does It *(continued)*

passwords to communicate with the mainframe, and an optical scanner. We have three major systems running on the 4381: accounting (LAWPACK), docketing, and full-text retrieval (BRS Search). (LAWPACK also runs on Wang & DEC computers; BRS Search also runs on IBM PCs and DEC.)

The data processing department, working with the partners on the conflict of interest committee and the library staff, designed an automated conflict of interest information retrieval system that uses, to the greatest extent possible, data that already exist in our other major systems. We also purchase databases from vendors who compile information from SEC filings and sell it for much less than it would cost any one firm to acquire. As necessary, we also manually enter information from lawyers into the conflict of interest database.

The conflict of interest system uses BRS Search to retrieve data from two databases. One of the databases contains information compiled from our accounting system, our docketing system, and data entered from new matter, partner, associate, and library memos. The other database contains corporate parent, child, and sibling relationships that we create from data we buy from DISCLOSURE and Standard & Poor.

When we designed the conflict of interest system there were five problems that had to be resolved:

1. We had to find out what information about an entity we needed to determine whether that entity *might* cause a conflict.
2. We had to decide where that information would be obtained.
3. We had to select the computer hardware and software that the system would run on.
4. We had to design a database to contain all the necessary information in an easily searchable format.
5. We had to set search procedures that allowed a searcher to locate all relevant information with a minimum of effort.

The first step in designing the system was to determine what information we needed. The conflict of interest committee, the library staff, and the data processing department together created a list of questions, for example: "Are we involved in litigation with an entity?" "What parents or siblings does it have?" and "Who is on its board?" We also determined where we might get this information.

Once we had our requirements for information under control, we designed custom databases that enable the library staff, who perform the searches, to retrieve data with minimal effort. The corporate library retrieves data by:

1. Searching our client/litigation/attorney file. (If the search succeeds, the requester receives the names of the responsible lawyers.)
2. If the company in question is not in this file, the DISCLOSURE file is searched.
3. If there is a parent company, it is searched for in the client/litigation/attorney file.
4. If there are children or siblings with DUNS numbers (a unique number assigned by Dun & Bradstreet to businesses), they may be searched for in the client/litigation/attorney file (automatically, by pressing a function key, at the option of the searcher).
5. If there are children or siblings without DUNS numbers, they may be searched for on the client/litigation/attorney file manually—at the option of the searcher.
6. Searching an S & P database—only if we need information about a person who may be an officer or member of the board of directors.

Today there are programs for micro-, mini- and mainframe computers that can help automate a conflict of interest system. Any firm that has automated their accounting, litigation support, docketing, or word processing can add a conflict of interest system to the same hardware. The most important decisions are what information is needed, who is responsible for gathering and disseminating this information, and who will use this information to decide whether a conflict exists.

Computerized Conflict Checking: The Cravath Approach

Daniel E. Sesti
Gloria Zimmerman

In 1981 Cravath, Swaine & Moore undertook to check conflicts by computer. We began by surveying the legal marketplace for systems that checked for conflicts automatically. We learned that most firms implemented conflict checking from the master name index of their time and billing system. However, we found one firm that indexed all their new business memos with their automated litigation support (ALS) software. We quickly decided to use that approach as well, as it required very little programming. Thus we could focus on those aspects of checking for conflicts especially suited for computerization.

We decided that the best way to assure the system's integrity was for the records department to capture the data present on a new-business memo (e.g., client name, full matter title, client contact, responsible lawyer, a description of the transaction or case being undertaken). That information keyed into an ALS-like text retrieval system allowed us to search all words and phrases.

In fact, the ALS software we selected (IBM's STAIRS) was already installed on our IBM 4300-series mainframe, so we could automate rapidly. The challenge was training the staff to use the computer system in place of the manual one. Today a number of PC-based text retrieval programs provide features similar to IBM's STAIRS.

OUR PROJECT'S SCOPE. Defining the scope of the project was complex. We discovered that some firms were capturing data from only the past ten years and others were going all the way back to the date the firm was founded. A few firms were just going forward from some fixed point in time.

Determining what to capture was a matter of determining how much retrospective information could help support business decisions from a legal as well as an institutional perspective. We decided that, for most matters, going back ten years was enough to determine if a conflict existed. Furthermore, we decided not to keep all possible affiliate names in our database. When we check for a conflict, the library staff provides a current list of affiliate names for us to search in our internal database.

We also decided that we had to train the staff in the new systems and procedures as quickly as possible. To begin, we entered all new matters as quickly as possible, initially going back three years. The staff made the transition to the computerized system and finished inputting three years of historical data faster than we had expected. So we then entered five more years. The whole process took less than two years. Thus, by the time we went live, we had ten years of historical data on line.

IMPLEMENTATION ISSUES. After settling our approach and scope, we turned to implementation. The issues we faced included:

- Controlling the quality of the data. We devised a procedure to assure that, after data entry, all data is proofread and corrected before entering the database. Spell-checking software helped with the proofing.
- Assigning a control person to create the database and monitor the timely input of new information. In addition, this individual had to monitor the entry of historical data.
- Determining who would have access to the database.
- Training Records Department personnel to input data with a system editor and to search with the new software.
- Assigning to the project an MIS analyst who solved problems and coordinated training.
- Determining if the hard-copy output provided by the software would be satisfactory to the partners.

RECENT IMPROVEMENTS. To supplement our system, we keep a historical database of completed

continued on page 156

Computerized Conflict Checking: The Cravath Approach *(continued)*

conflict checks that we search upon each new inquiry. This database allows the present requesting partner to confer with the earlier requesting partner when a company currently under consideration shows up in the historical database. It is particularly helpful to the current requestor to know when the firm refused new business as a result of the earlier conflict check. By filling what could otherwise be a gap in our information, the historical database of past conflict checks further reduces the chance of a conflict of interest arising.

Moreover, the new-business memo database itself has been expanded to encompass most of the records department's document indexing and record-keeping functions. It is now a records management system that also fully supports the process of checking for conflicts. This database holds all the data elements we need to track the life cycle of a client file (the records management function). In addition, the document-level index, cross-referenced to names, enhances conflict checking and helps the lawyer locate precedents. Thus, by choosing ALS software as the technological foundation for our system, we have economically integrated three essential functions of a database (conflict checking, precedent searching, and records management).

---

firm's financial accounting system. The selection did not require either a long study process or the hiring of a consultant. We simply chose a highly regarded package that was compatible with the firm's accounting system. Other systems are available to accomplish the same objective. They must, however, work smoothly with the information already present in the firm's billing system.

Getting our system into operation took about three months, primarily to convert and input all necessary data. The first step was to transfer electronically a list of past and present clients from the firm's docket system. Lawyers verified clients' names and addresses and provided names of additional related parties. These new names then had to be input manually by two data entry clerks employed temporarily.

Today only one employee, a data processing clerk who received one day of training from the software company, operates the system. Two other employees know how to use it, providing backup for vacations, etc. The clerk inputs all

data and conducts all conflict checks. In addition to processing new client forms, the clerk also can respond quickly to informal telephone requests regarding conflicts.

As with any computer system, a conflict system is only as good as the information it contains. Fortunately, the more the firm uses the system, the better the information gets. We're still working to improve related-party information.

CONCLUSION

Conflicts of interest are expected to grow more common as firms consolidate and expand and legal matters become increasingly complex. The trend by many corporate clients of parceling work out to specialists in several law firms, instead of maintaining an exclusive relationship with one firm, further multiplies the opportunities for conflicts. The law firm that fails to develop a strong system to deal with these conflicts is jeopardizing its own future.

---

*As chief administrative officer of Chicago-based Winston & Strawn, **Douglas O. McLemore** helped develop the new client acceptance procedures described in this article. A certified public accountant, he previously was associated with Arthur Andersen & Co. in both accounting and administrative capacities. He is a member of the Association of Legal Administrators.*

***Kurt L. Schultz,** a partner in Winston & Strawn's Chicago office, is a member of the firm's Litigation Practice Committee. He practices in the area of commercial litigation and has been active in the firm's Technology Committee, which chose the firm's new computer system and supervised development of the client acceptance procedures.*

A graduate of the Bernard Baruch School of Business Administration—C.U.N.Y., **Leon Cohen** *(sidebar) has been involved in the programming, design, and installation of data processing systems since 1957. As director of data processing, Mr. Cohen was responsible for installing a computer system at Skadden, Arps, Slate, Meagher & Flom that is used for accounting, financial management, litigation support, expert systems, conflict of interest, and other law firm areas. Mr. Cohen has been a frequent speaker at the annual Law Firm Technology Conference and other seminars.*

Daniel E. Sesti *(sidebar) is currently the MIS Project Manager for Cravath, Swaine & Moore. He is an active member in the East Coast Association of Litigation Support Managers and is closely involved with all database software at the firm.*

Gloria Zimmerman *(sidebar) is director of records administration for Cravath, Swaine & Moore. She is coauthor of* Guide to the Management of Legal Records *(ARMA, 1986). Ms. Zimmerman is an active member of the Association of Records Managers and Administrators (ARMA), serving as chair of ARMA's Legal Services Steering Committee and as co-chair of that committee's Records Retention Subcommittee.*

Hypertext and Hypermedia: Turning Data into Useful Information

Joost Romeu

Litigators are always looking for new and better ways to organize cases and to interrelate various segments of each case as they develop. In this article, Joost Romeu takes us to the cutting edge of such technology with his discussion of hypertext and hypermedia, a new and exciting way to relate the different aspects of a developing case to each other on an ongoing basis.

Litigators are explorers. Preparing a case means finding, organizing, and presenting evidence and related information. The information may be stored on computers, videotape machines, and tape recorders. It may be in closets, books, magazines, and notepads. It may come from other lawyers, expert witnesses, illustrators, or even through the grapevine. By exploring the jumble, you develop links and intuitive hunches. With hypertext, you can map this information in ways that reflect the goals of your investigation while respecting your developing mindset and understanding.

WHAT IS HYPERTEXT?

In 1945, Vannevar Bush, president of Carnegie Institution in Washington, D.C., suggested that someday technology would deliver information free from the linear restrictions that shaped the way we read books and viewed films. Later termed *hypertext*, this idea has affected all forms of information technology.

In the mid 1980s, the first personal computer hypertext program, Guide, was introduced on the Apple Macintosh. Later, Apple introduced HyperCard, a hypertext program of its own. Though similar programs have appeared on the Macintosh and PC, HyperCard is today's predominant hypertext development platform.

HyperCard stores information in files called *stacks*. The stacks are made up of *cards*. (See Figure 4.34.)

Each card has a background and a foreground. The background controls items on the card that repeat throughout the stack; the foreground controls items particular to that card. These items consist primarily of buttons and fields. You establish relationships between the buttons, fields, cards, and stacks through *scripts*. Scripts are short programs written in HyperTalk, a simple, natural-language programming tool. (See Figure 4.35.)

Scripts can also be used to establish links between stacks and other electronic media such as video camcorders, computers, and tape recorders. But you don't need to write HyperTalk scripts to create a stack you can use.

HYPERTEXT AND HYPERMEDIA: AN ELECTRONIC WINDOW

Hypertext and hypermedia are ways of organizing, arranging, recalling, and presenting information. They differ from the typical database in that they provide an extremely flexible approach to information. Imagine you have to consolidate evidence for a case. Your material includes police reports, affidavits, letters and memos, videotape footage, tape recordings, charts, diagrams, and photographs. You expect

FIGURE 4.34

This HyperCard card is a customized version of a commercial stack. Though it appears very similar to a database record, there are links at work in the background that allow the user to easily get and incorporate relevant information much more flexibly than through a typical database.

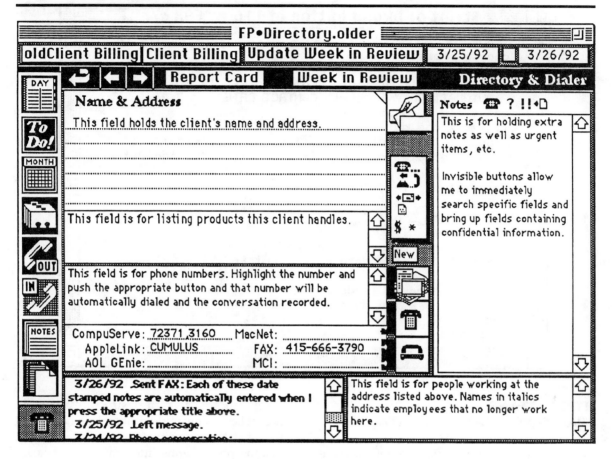

more information to come in, but you don't know what form it will take.

Consolidating this material using a traditional database requires that you predict the form the data will take. You categorize the information you expect to get into fields. One field establishes a common link to all the pieces of evidence. Other fields focus on very specific answers about very specific questions concerning the material at hand. You arrange sets of fields into records. Only after you've made these decisions do you start to enter data into the fields your database provides. Already the database-specific decisions you made may prejudice the information you're about to enter.

A hypertreatment can record information in its native form (e.g., a photograph of a gun, a copy of a memo, a videotaped deposition). You build the database as you establish associations between one piece of information and another.

As you expand your information base, you link this material to material that's been previously incorporated. For example, while considering information relevant to testimony being presented, you may decide to assign a link to a portion of the testimony. That link may tie that information to a videotape segment that more clearly explains the testimony by demonstrating it in context.

Hypertext links don't dissect information. A hypertreatment allows you to maintain information integrity while constructing a synthesis based on relationships you discover. Hypertreatments affect the way you approach information. Rather than applying bits and pieces of information to your game plan, a hypertext approach encourages you to investigate the information and establish your game plan symbiotically. The systematic approach you construct not only helps develop your argument, it also can be used to display your points to a jury.

FIGURE 3.45
This HyperCard script controls the operation of the title FAX on the HyperCard stack pictured above. The scripting language, HyperTalk, is very easy to program and understand.

```
Script of bkgnd button id 116 = "FAX s/r"

on mouseUp
  choose browse tool
  wait 3
  set the scroll of field "LatestNotes" to 1
  --AUTOMATICALLY FILLS IN CONTACT DATE
  get field "ContactDate"
  if it <> the date then
    put it into last line of field "PrevContactDate"
    put the date into last line of field "ContactDate"
  end if
  get rect of field "LatestNotes"
  delete item 4 of it
  delete item 3 of it
  click at it
  if the Commandkey is down then
    type " " & the date & "   .Sent FAX: "
  end if
  if the Optionkey is down then
    type " " & the date & "   .Received FAX: "
  end if
end mouseUp
```

HYPERDATA VS. TRADITIONAL DATABASE DATA

Hypermedia is not a substitute for the traditional database. It's a different approach to information—including information provided by more traditional databases. A hypertext link can establish an immediate relationship between a reference and its underlying document. Given a piece of information, a link can directly access a relevant footnote, photograph, dictionary, or encyclopedia entry. This is hypertext at its simplest.

Hypertext not only maintains the links, it also provides interactive and instant access to the linked material. Rather than relegating relevant information to a field on a record, a hypertext link may take the form of an invisible button, attached to a word in a document. You might only need to point to that *hot* word to cause the computer to instantly return that word's definition or play a recording that, by embodying the point being made in a film sequence, drives that point home.

Sophisticated hypertext structures have no inherent beginning, middle, or end. Dynamic and interactive, these structures can link documents, diagrams, photographs, interactive spreadsheets, charts, and graphs. The linkages can elaborate, explain, summarize, query, or provide alternatives. Like the way our mind works, hypertext structures are not limited by the front-to-back, top-to-bottom nature of the written or recorded information we normally encounter.

These capabilities can be important to the litigator. Evidence is seldom neat, clean, or compartmentalized. To properly investigate information, the litigator needs to see evidence in context, from various perspectives. Predigested or codified information invariably loses some of its flavor. Litigators also need to inspect vast and varied types of information. Letters, photographs, videotape segments, excerpts from legal documents and jurisprudential procedures, contracts, tape recordings, etc., all play a role in the trial analysis.

Evidence is not the only information the lawyer requires. Extensive on-line databases containing legal precedents and trial transcripts, data appearing in magazines and scientific journals, reference books, and encyclopedic information can be accessed by modem via telephone or purchased on large storage media (e.g. optical disks) and linked to the database. All of this needs to be integrated into the final picture.

HYPERTEXT VS. TRADITIONAL INFORMATION HANDLING

Even with the most modern facilities, traditional information handling is a time and labor-intensive activity. Hard-copy lookup and photocopy reproduction is slow, bulky, and wasteful. Taking notes and trying to keep them in order is an art in itself. Today's litigator requires faster and better electronic search, retrieval, update, and cross-referencing facilities. Manual browsing is too slow and prone to error.

Using a database, the litigator can employ powerful text string search strategies, which can be far more effective than manual methods. But hypertext provides more natural and tactile ways of implementing relevant search strategies. Pointing to a button tied to a historical quote could bring up a video tape segment showing that speaker making that utterance.

Getting to the information is only half the battle. To keep track of the investigation, the litigator must bring to bear an arsenal of tools to reference, footnote, and annotate the finds. With hypertext we can use the computer as a real assistant, mapping search strategies, taking relevant notes along the way, and exploring side avenues as they present themselves.

HYPERTEXT AS A DEVELOPING STRUCTURE

Hypertext links can develop as an investigation develops. They do not have to be predetermined. Links can be expanded or changed at any time. (The other side of this coin is that, used irresponsibly, hypertext links can be overwhelming, connecting practically every piece of data to every other and rendering the data structure irrelevant.)

HYPERTEXT AS A COLLABORATIVE EFFORT

Hypertext is exceptionally well suited to a multiperson effort. One person can author the basic data, another can link relevant material. Specialists can be called in to inspect, correct, illustrate, or expand portions of the project. Each participant works on the existing structure, establishing links spotlighting those areas they best understand. Temporary holding areas can be established for parts of the investigation that are not yet complete.

Eventually the litigator goes through the information, picking those parts relevant to the presentation and arranging them into a cogent whole. The presentation can actually be a display consisting of a series of hypertext links to printed material, charts, video presentations, and testimony. If, at the last minute, the litigator decides the presentation needs to go into further detail, the hypertext database can be instructed to pursue an alternative avenue.

HYPERTEXT AS AN INFORMATION PRESERVATIVE

Hypertreatments can help to preserve your real evidence. Real evidence is a form of hard copy. It is unwieldy and fragile. Handled and exchanged, hard copy can be misplaced, lost, and unwittingly destroyed. By transforming this hard copy into electronic form or "soft copy" (for example, digitizing photographs, documents, film segments, and sounds), evidence can easily be recalled, stored, reproduced, compared, inspected, and telecommunicated. Soft information is impervious to wear and tear or loss. The original remains safe and intact.

THE TRANSITION TO HYPERTEXT

Hypertext's (and hypermedia's) transition from drawing table to desktop has not been easy. It has had to wait for technology to introduce high speed, multimedia, personal computers with graphical interfaces. Though hypertext is not a complex concept, hypertext applications require computer users to feel comfortable with their computers as investigative tools.

Hypertext and hypermedia have been possible because of the following technical advancements:

- Computer hardware that can access and process information quickly (virtually instantaneous response speeds are required to provide the interactive response we expect of a hypertext link).
- Computer hardware capable of controlling external electronic equipment.
- An easy-to-use interface that employs icons (on-screen symbols rather than words) and meaningful visual cues (e.g., switches, knobs, and buttons) rather than cryptic codes and typewritten procedures.
- Integrated computer software—text processors, graphics programs, illustration programs, video digitizers, chart generators, and spreadsheets that can talk to each other.
- Users that can accept their computers as flexible, interactive tools that respond as intelligent machine/companions rather than as computational idiot savants.

A HYPERTEXT PLATFORM

Litigators interested in pursuing hypermedia can find hypertext programs, or programs with some hypertext functionality, available for most personal computers. However, I recommend the Apple Macintosh and HyperCard for the following reasons:

- Its graphical interface is a masterpiece that uses subtle visual cues to guide the user through the computer environment.
- It provides an integrated and consistent graphical environment—anything you can see on the Macintosh screen you can cut, copy, or paste into a hypertext program.
- Apple's latest operating system software complements hyperactivities by providing intra-application facilities that allow applications to interactively address each other.

CONCLUSION

Hypertext provides a more natural way of generating, storing, querying, browsing, and linking information. It will significantly impact the way data is dealt with and understood in the future. In redefining data's natural order from linear to nonlinear, it will change the way we view information, the way we view each case as it develops, and, in turn, the way we view the world.

Joost Romeu of CUMULUS (CompuServe # 72371,3160) is a graphic specialist and hypertext programmer specializing in graphics and related services for the legal environment.

Section 5
Toward the Future: Project Management, Risk Analysis, and Expert Systems

Harold L. Burstyn

In the nineteenth century, machine production with interchangeable parts revolutionized manufacturing. Now we seem to be in the midst of an equally breathtaking revolution. This time it is the tasks that require human intellect that are becoming increasingly mechanized. The means of this mechanization is the computer. To those who have hitched their wagons to the replacement of human brainpower by machines, the branch of computer science called artificial intelligence (or AI) is the holy grail. Though skeptics abound, lawyers seeking to improve the value of what they do are adopting new kinds of "intelligent" software by the day.

This section looks to the future as well as the present. For years, business leaders have used project management and risk analysis techniques for decision making; lawyers have shunned such methods like the plague. That will change. As David Cotellesse and Morris Raker demonstrate, lessons learned in the business world have particular application to litigation analysis. As clients become aware of these tools, they will start to demand them at the risk of losing their business. Rather than wait until they have no choice, smart litigators will be the first to raise the issue.

It is a small step from project management and risk analysis to the use of expert systems in a law practice. As Charles Pear explains, an expert system is a program that provides on a computer the thinking of a human expert. You provide the question and it gives you the answer. We begin with a look at several expert systems that one public attorney uses in his criminal practice every day. We continue with a look at more sophisticated systems, both past and future. We close the book by asking whether expert systems might someday replace lawyers. (Not a chance!)

If you are tempted to skip this section as pie in the sky, think again. In the next decade, project management techniques and expert systems will challenge and change how we practice law, perhaps to a greater degree than any other aspect of the computer. The first to master the power of these programs will gain a tremendous advantage over the competition. The last to do so may not be practicing law in the 21st century.

Managing Litigation with Project Management Software*

David P. Cotellesse

What do you mean I have to prepare a budget? This is litigation. Did Congress make George Bush prepare a budget for the Gulf War? Like it or not, litigation is no longer unrestrained warfare and clients want to know what it will cost up front. David Cotellesse, a former trial lawyer in Houston, Texas, shows us how project management software can help you get your case under control and provide a budget for your client.

The afternoon sun was slanting into the room that Thursday as Quigley wrapped up his summation. It was not really a summation, of course; he was describing his strategy for handling the case to his client's general counsel. Nonetheless, he was eloquent and powerful. His logic was impeccable. His preparation and advocacy were impressive. So, there was a little uneasy feeling in the pit of his stomach when the General Counsel, Smith, hesitated. Usually, Smith could be counted on for a hearty endorsement of Quigley's strategic brilliance. Something was different today.

Quigley pressed. "You've come to the right place, Smith. We can help you."

Smith sighed. "That's all well and good, Quigley," he said, "but, how much will it cost us?"

Quigley's response was quick and practiced. "That depends."

"Depends on what?"

"Well, you've got a complicated piece of litigation here," said Quigley. "There is a lot of uncertainty. All the issues won't be clear until we've had some discovery. There are lots of ways this thing could play out. Right now, I can't tell you

how much it will cost. Let's get into it a little and see how things develop. Then I'll be able to give you a 'guesstimate.'" Quigley rested, hoping that, as in the past, this explanation would suffice.

"Quigley," Smith said, in a tone of resignation, "the company has always valued your help. You've pulled our chestnuts out of the fire more than once." He hesitated and then continued, "Things are different since we were bought out by Amalgamated Industries. There is a lot more reporting. My management is under a lot of pressure to do a better job of forecasting its cash needs, especially litigation expense. Amalgamated is putting pressure on management, and management is putting pressure on me. Quigley, I need you to prepare a budget for this case."

"A budget!" Quigley gasped. "You can't budget a case like this. There are just too many uncertainties. Sure, we can make some predictions about the case, but, as you well know, the court and the other side are always full of surprises. How can I give you a budget when neither of us can predict what might happen six months or a year down the road? What happens when old Mordley suddenly adds a dozen witnesses to his deposition list? What happens when Judge Blacklaw lets him get away with it but refuses to extend the discovery cutoff? Smith, you just can't budget for that kind of uncertainty."

"Nevertheless," Smith said, "management insists on a budget. I fought them on this, Quigley.

---

*This chapter first appeared in *Litigation Applications* (vol 3., no. 4 [Winter/Spring 1992]:1), a newsletter published by the Litigation Interest Group of the ABA's Section of Law Practice Management.

I told them everything you told me. I told them it's just not possible—too much uncertainty, I said. Do you know what they said?" Smith laughed mirthlessly. They said, 'Smith, starting right now, you're going to have to submit an annual litigation budget, with quarterly updates. You'll have to start forecasting litigation expenses, including settlements and losses.'"

Smith looked Quigley in the eye. "I need your help on this, Quigley. In fact—and I hate to put it this way after all these years—but unless you can help me, Amalgamated has threatened to bring in their New York lawyers."

Quigley was speechless.

After a pause, Smith continued, "Our company deals with uncertainty all the time, and we still have to budget and forecast. There's nothing else to do about it. I need your help, and not only on this case. I need it on all the cases your firm is handling for us. We've all got to adapt to the 'needs of the 90s,'" Smith pontificated. They agreed to talk again on Monday.

LATER THAT AFTERNOON

"I'll give Davis a call," Quigley said to himself after Smith had left. Davis had been Quigley's partner for 10 years before he left to form his own case management consulting business. "He's always been into computers and all that," Quigley thought as he dialed Davis's number. "Maybe he'll have some ideas." He did, and they agreed to meet the very next morning.

FRIDAY MORNING

"Isn't there some software program or something you can recommend that can handle this problem?" Quigley asked hopefully, as he finished explaining the situation to Davis.

"You don't have a software problem, Quigley," Davis replied. "You have a management problem."

Quigley groaned.

"It's not all that bad," said Davis. "It's just a new way of thinking. It's a shame they didn't teach us a little about management in law school. But, since I've been in business for myself, I've had to learn. I can help you."

"Thank God!" said Quigley. "But, how can we do a budget without computers and spreadsheets and all that?"

"Let's take this one step at a time," said Davis. "First, let's define the problem. What do we mean by *management* anyway?" he asked. "How do you manage your cases?"

Quigley thought for a moment. "To put it simply," he said, "I decide how to try the case and I get ready. I make decisions and I implement them," he said, self-satisfied.

"That's a good start," said Davis. "But, what happens when things change?"

"I deal with change when it comes up."

"That's the rub, isn't it?" chuckled Davis.

"Yes, I guess so," said Quigley. "If we could just make decisions and implement them, management would be simple," he said, "and I could give Smith his budget."

"If there were no change, Quigley," Davis replied, "there would be no need for management. Accommodating change is what management is all about. If we're going to develop a budget for Smith, we need a way to accommodate change. We need a model for making decisions and implementing them in an environment of uncertainty and change. We need a planning process."

"Planning!" roared Quigley. "All of a sudden, you've got me talking about budgets, management, and now planning. I'm just a simple trial lawyer, Davis. I understand strategy and tactics. I know how to pulverize a witness on cross-examination. I know how to dazzle a jury with my charm, wit, and eloquence. I don't have time for planning. Just get me a budget," he commanded, exasperated.

"Quigley, when you prepare to cross-examine a witness, do you try to anticipate the answers? Are you prepared, whichever way the witness goes?" asked Davis.

"Of course," said Quigley impatiently. "Every good trial lawyer does that."

"Naturally," said Davis. "That's called planning. You go through a logical process to prepare yourself for any contingency. There's no reason why you can't use the same process for case management. All we need is to map out a logical planning sequence and follow it. If we do that, we'll be in a position to give Smith his budget and you'll have more control over your case preparation."

Quigley's interest began to perk up. "What do we do first?" he asked. "I have a meeting with Smith on Monday."

Davis's answer was immediate. "Every manager knows that because life is uncertain, a forecast is no better than the assumptions that go into it. We need to develop some planning assumptions. You already have some of them. I remember how you operate. You've already assessed Smith's case, haven't you?"

"Of course," said Quigley. "We've evaluated the law and the facts. We have a pretty good idea what we have to persuade a jury of to win. I don't have the evidence yet, but I know what I need to get—at least until something changes, of course."

"Of course," Davis agreed, "that's the whole idea. If we use your assessment of the case to plan trial preparation, we can use the plan to make a budget forecast. Then, when things change, we can update our assumptions, the plan, and our forecast. If we've done a good job of documenting our assumptions, the plan, and the forecast, it will be easy to explain to Smith what has changed and what the impact will be on the budget forecast. That way, Smith will have what he needs to report to his management. Quigley, that's exactly the way our clients manage and budget their businesses."

Quigley thought for a minute. Then he said, somewhat animatedly, "I'm beginning to like this. If we get Smith involved in this process, he'll not only understand what it takes to try his case, he'll be committed to the plan, won't he?"

"Now you're getting it," said Davis. "The case strategy will reflect management's needs, and you'll get a lot more support. Not only that, but you'll find it easier to focus your preparation."

"Sounds good to me," said Quigley.

"So, I'll prepare a preliminary planning questionnaire for the meeting with Smith on Monday," said Davis. (See Figure 5.1.) "We'll explore the client's situation and needs. We'll go over your theories of recovery and defense and evaluate the controlling facts. We'll see if there are any possible third-party claims. We'll identify the key participants from both parties. That will help estimate the number of depositions. We need to be sure to include experts. Along with discovery, we'll discuss damages and settlement. Then, after we've answered these questions, we'll need to discuss strategy," Davis said.

"Strategy!" said Quigley, "I've already decided on strategy."

Davis laughed. "That's not what I meant," he said. "Have you and Smith agreed on whether this is a bet-the-company case, to be defended at all costs, or something less? Will you need to develop the case a bit to make that decision? Or

FIGURE 5.1 Preliminary Planning Questionnaire

I. CLIENT SITUATION
Background of case
Financial impact
Operating considerations
Reporting needs

II. THEORIES OF RECOVERY
Legal basis
Controlling facts

III. THEORIES OF DEFENSE
Legal basis
Controlling facts

IV. THIRD PARTY CLAIMS
Legal basis
Controlling facts

V. KEY PARTICIPANTS
Plaintiff
Defendant
Third party

VI. DISCOVERY
Documents
Interrogatories
Admissions

VII. DAMAGES

VIII. SETTLEMENT

IX. EXPERTS
Identify
Select
Define scope of work
Define deliverables
Engagement letter

X. LAW FIRM RESOURCES

	Names	Percent Avail.	Rates
Lawyers			
Paralegals			
Clerical			
Support			
Outside Vendors			

is this a case that you already know needs to be settled? One of the most important planning assumptions is how the case needs to be handled."

"I see," said Quigley, "we can't really define our case preparation objectives until the client and I agree on strategy, can we?"

"You're catching on," said Davis. "After you

agree on strategy and case objectives, then you can formulate a plan of action for your lawyers and paralegals. And that, of course, will be the basis for Smith's budget."

"I see where you're coming from," said Quigley. "How long, after we develop the planning assumptions, will it take you to come up with the plan of action?" Quigley asked. "While you're doing the plan, I'll wrap up the pleadings and start discovery."

"Not so fast, there, Quigley," said Davis. "It doesn't work like that. You know me—I'd like nothing better than to plan your whole case. I love creating order out of chaos. But it wouldn't be your plan—it would be mine; and you wouldn't follow it. Before we can give Smith a budget, we need a plan of action that you and Smith agree on," said Davis. "*You* have to do the plan, Quigley."

"But, I don't know how, and I just don't have the time," Quigley said plaintively.

"It sounds to me, Quigley, like you don't have time not to plan—not if you want to keep this case," Davis replied.

"All right, all right!" said Quigley, "But, I'll need some help. I don't even know what goes into a plan detailed enough for budgeting."

"That's not a problem," said Davis. "I can give you a format for a case management plan. (See Figure 5.2.) After our initial planning meeting, where you and Smith agree on the planning assumptions, we'll take a few days and I'll help you develop the elements of your plan of action."

"We'll start with your assessment of the case. That will come straight from the answers to the preliminary planning questionnaire. So will your case strategy and objectives—how you want to develop the case. With that information, you can flesh out an action plan to cover the necessary work in no time."

"How will we do that?" asked Quigley, his confidence suddenly sagging.

"Quigley, we're just going to follow a logical process. First, I'll help you divide the case into logical phases. How do prediscovery planning, document discovery, deposition program, and trial preparation sound for starters?"

"Sounds logical to me," said Quigley.

"Then, we'll identify all the activities, tasks and work product that we think you'll need for each phase of the case, including working with experts, jury research, and litigation support. We'll need to think about things like numbers of

FIGURE 5.2. Case Management Plan

I. ASSESSMENT OF CASE
Use Initial Planning Questionnaire to set up development of Case Management Plan.

II. STRATEGY
What should we recommend the client do:
    Fight
    Settle
    Develop

III. OBJECTIVES
Identify specific objectives that will accomplish client's strategy.
    Controlling fact findings
    Acceptable range of objectives

IV. ACTION PLAN
Major tasks, activities, and work product by phase of the case:
    Pre-discovery planning
    Document discovery
    Deposition program
    Trial preparation
Major milestones
Resource assignments (lawyers, paralegals, experts, etc.)

V. CONTROLS
Time line schedule
Litigation budget forecast
Mechanism for tracking progress
Updating
Management reports
Change controls

depositions and how long they will take, for instance."

"Well," said Quigley, "it sounds all right, but what about the contingencies? That's where I came in. What good will all this do if we can't predict what the judge or old Mordley will do?" Quigley asked, exasperatedly. "You know them. They can gum up the best of plans!"

"That's just the point," said Davis, "you have years of experience with both Mordley and Judge Blacklaw. You already know what they'll do."

"Yeah," said Quigley, "Mordley will wage guerrilla warfare. He'll have us responding to discovery motions every Monday morning, complaining that we're hiding documents. He'll add a dozen witnesses to the deposition program at the last minute. Judge Blacklaw will let him do it, too, and won't give us any slack on the discovery cutoff date. That's what scares me about all this planning and budgeting."

"Quig, old friend," Davis said, all too familiarly for a consultant, "you've just answered your own question. Because of your experience, you already know that you'll need extra time in the plan for discovery motions, for last minute depositions, and to gear up to meet unreasonable deadlines. We can put these things in the plan, and therefore, in the budget forecast. And, remember, just like managers, we're going to define our assumptions and base our forecasts on them. If our assumptions change, we'll change our forecasts and be prepared to explain why.

"But, you've brought up another important topic," said Davis.

"What's that?" asked Quigley, apprehensively.

"Resources," Davis replied. "The lawyers and paralegals who are going to do all this work. We'll need to identify them, their availability, and their billing rates."

"Why do we need to do that?" asked Quigley. "You know our firm—we've always come up with the resources to get the job done."

"I know," said Davis, "but if we're going to forecast expenses for Smith and his management, we need to assign all this work to lawyers and paralegals and capture those costs. You see, we're not doing all this planning in a vacuum. We're going to turn the plan into a project schedule. We're going to assign all the activities and work product to lawyers and paralegals, and they all have billing rates. We'll put all that on a computer, using project management software, and use it to forecast expenses for Smith."

"Davis, now I know you've lost your mind. You know that I don't know anything about computers." Quigley felt he was back to square one.

Davis beamed confidently. "That's where I come in," he said. "After you've developed your plan of action, I'll turn it into a project schedule, using the project management software I have on my computer. But to do that, I need all this information. I need a detailed work plan of all the tasks and activities and your estimate of how long the work will take, the people who will do the work, and their billing rates. I need to know your schedule deadlines and your predictions about the contingencies you can foresee. That's why I said at the beginning of this meeting that you don't have a computer problem; you have a management problem. Once we get a handle on that problem with a sound, logical planning process, putting the information into a computer

schedule model will be easy. Then, we'll use the computer to generate a schedule of work hours and dollars for the budget forecast."

"I think I'm beginning to catch on," said Quigley. "You're right, this is really just a new way of thinking about the problem. I know what I need to do. It's just that I've never learned how to put it into project management terms. That's where you come in, isn't it?" he asked.

"That's right," said Davis. "I can guide you through the planning sequence, and I can provide the computer services that you'll need to actually produce the budget. The plan has to be yours, though. The budget forecast is just a matter of reflecting your plan in terms of work hours and costs. That's the easiest part of the job. The hard part is the planning."

"It doesn't sound so hard," said Quigley. "From what you've just said, we'll have a meeting with Smith on Monday, and over the next few days, we'll knock out a plan. That's right, isn't it?" Quigley asked.

"There's a little more to it than that," Davis replied. We'll need to follow a logical planning sequence. (See Figure 5.3.) Our meeting on Monday with Smith is just the start. After that, I'll help you develop a preliminary case plan. We'll frame it around the major milestones in the case, such as the answer date, serving notices for depositions, a discovery cutoff date, and ultimately a projected trial date. We'll identify the major phases, activities, and sequences. We'll estimate the effort required and the durations of these various activities. Finally, we'll assign resources to each task. Drafting this preliminary plan should take us a few days if we concentrate on it.

"When we've done that, we'll need another meeting to review what we've done. In addition to Smith, we need to invite the associates who will be working with you on the case. The way to be sure that a plan is workable is to get input from the people who have to implement it.

"Then, we'll prepare a final plan. As part of this process, we'll resolve all conflicts," said Davis.

"Conflicts! What conflicts?" asked Quigley, his blood pressure increasing.

Davis calmed him. "Resource conflicts, Quigley, not legal conflicts. We'll want to be sure we haven't assigned our lawyers and paralegals more work than they can actually get done.

"Then we'll need a final meeting with Smith," Davis continued. "At every step of the way, it's important to keep the client on board. That way, when the job is done, everyone will not only know what the plan is, they'll be committed to it.

"After Smith has approved the plan, we can convert it into a computer schedule. We'll use the schedule to generate Smith's budget. And don't worry, Quigley, I'll provide the computer expertise to get this step done."

"You'd better," said Quigley, "I don't know anything about those computers, and I don't want to learn."

MONDAY MORNING

"I like what I'm hearing about this planning process," Smith said after Quigley and Davis had made their presentations. "I need to know more about what this budget is going to look like, though," he said.

Davis fumbled momentarily in his briefcase and retrieved some loose papers. "I brought some samples to show you. These are from a computer model of a case management plan I have on my computer. I developed this model based on my experience here at the firm. The first sample is called a Gantt chart. (See Figure 5.4.) It's a timeline picture of the life of the case. It portrays the milestones, the phases of the case, and the major activities in each phase. Because it is visual, a Gantt chart is a good way to check the logic of your plan.

"The second sample converts the Gantt chart into estimated work hours. (See Figure 5.5.) It shows the hours estimated for each month during the life of the case and the totals at the end. Again, these numbers are the result of the assumptions that go into the plan.

"Then, because we also have the billing rates, we can convert these hours into dollars. That's the third sample. (See Figure 5.6.) This report is the budget forecast you need, Mr. Smith," Davis said.

"You mean your computer can do all that?" Quigley asked, incredulously.

Davis turned serious. "Quigley, this is important. My computer can crunch all the numbers. It can spit them out more ways than either of us cares to look at. It can even draw pictures. But, it can't plan your case. Please don't be overwhelmed by the computer. As I said before, this isn't a computer process; it's a management process. Specifically, the budget is the result of a logical planning sequence—a process that must be accomplished by the lead lawyer. That's you. You can't delegate the planning to a computer. If

FIGURE 5.3. Logical Planning Sequence

INITIAL PLANNING MEETING

Work Product
Planning Questionnaire

Activity
Collect planning data and assumptions

PRELIMINARY PLAN

Activity
Recommend strategy
Develop milestone schedule of major activities, sequences, effort, and durations
Identify resources

PRELIMINARY PLANNING REVIEW MEETING

Work Product
Preliminary case plan, schedule, and budget forecasts

Activity
Review case plan milestone schedule and resource assignments
Revise assumptions, sequences, etc.

FINAL PLAN

Activity
Complete fully-resourced plan based on revised planning criteria
Resolve conflicts
Develop dollar and staffing budgets

FINAL PLANNING REVIEW MEETING

Work Product
Final case plan, schedule, and budget forecasts (See Elements of the Case Management Plan)

Activity
Review final plan, schedule and budget forecasts
Make final revisions
Approve plan, schedule and budgets

PROGRESS REPORTING

Activity
Collect actual staff hours and dollars expended
Update budget and schedule
Prepare management reports

you do, these schedules and forecasts won't be worth the paper they're printed on."

"O.K., O.K.," said Quigley, "I get the message. There's no way I can just buy some software and solve this problem. You've convinced me.

"I'm mildly curious, though. What happens to your computer model when, as I've already

FIGURE 5.4 Gantt Chart

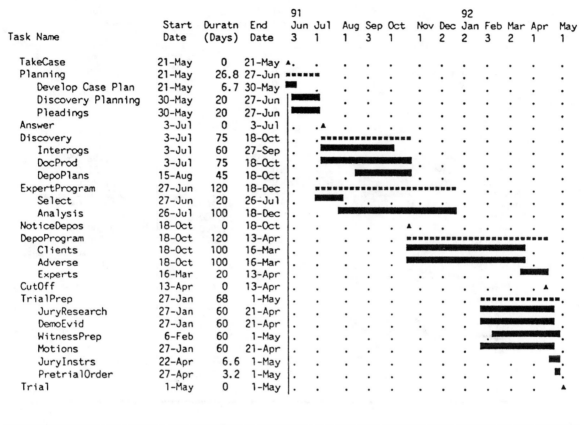

```
Schedule Name : LMI Trial Preparation Schedule
Responsible   :   Litigation Management Incorporated
As-of Date    : 21-May-91          Schedule File : TRIAL


                                   91                        92
                 Start  Duratn  End   Jun Jul  Aug Sep Oct  Nov Dec Jan Feb Mar Apr  May
  Task Name      Date   (Days)  Date   3   1    1   3   1    1   2   2   3   2   1    1

    TakeCase     21-May    0   21-May ▲.   .    .   .   .    .   .   .   .   .   .    .
    Planning     21-May  26.8  27-Jun ■■■■■■    .   .   .    .   .   .   .   .   .    .
      Develop Case Plan
                 21-May   6.7  30-May ■■   .    .   .   .    .   .   .   .   .   .    .
      Discovery Planning
                 30-May   20   27-Jun  ■■■      .   .   .    .   .   .   .   .   .    .
      Pleadings  30-May   20   27-Jun  ■■■      .   .   .    .   .   .   .   .   .    .
    Answer        3-Jul    0    3-Jul .   .▲    .   .   .    .   .   .   .   .   .    .
    Discovery     3-Jul   75   18-Oct . ■■■■■■■■■■■■■■■    .   .   .   .   .   .    .
      Interrogs   3-Jul   60   27-Sep . ■■■■■■■■■■■■    .    .   .   .   .   .   .    .
      DocProd     3-Jul   75   18-Oct . ■■■■■■■■■■■■■■    .   .   .   .   .   .    .
      DepoPlans  15-Aug   45   18-Oct .   .   ■■■■■■■■    .  .   .   .   .   .   .    .
    ExpertProgram
                 27-Jun  120   18-Dec . ■■■■■■■■■■■■■■■■■■    .   .   .   .   .    .
      Select     27-Jun   20   26-Jul . ■■■■     .   .   .    .   .   .   .   .   .    .
      Analysis   26-Jul  100   18-Dec .   ■■■■■■■■■■■■■■■■    .   .   .   .   .    .
    NoticeDepos  18-Oct    0   18-Oct .   .    .   .   ▲    .   .   .   .   .   .    .
    DepoProgram  18-Oct  120   13-Apr .   .    .   .   . ■■■■■■■■■■■■■■■■■■■■   .    .
      Clients    18-Oct  100   16-Mar .   .    .   .   .  ■■■■■■■■■■■■■■■■■   .    .
      Adverse    18-Oct  100   16-Mar .   .    .   .   .  ■■■■■■■■■■■■■■■■■   .    .
      Experts    16-Mar   20   13-Apr .   .    .   .   .    .   .   .   .   . ■■■■   .
    CutOff       13-Apr    0   13-Apr .   .    .   .   .    .   .   .   .   .   ▲    .
    TrialPrep    27-Jan   68    1-May .   .    .   .   .    .   .   ■■■■■■■■■■■■■■■■■■
      JuryResearch
                 27-Jan   60   21-Apr .   .    .   .   .    .   .   ■■■■■■■■■■■■■■   .
      DemoEvid   27-Jan   60   21-Apr .   .    .   .   .    .   .   ■■■■■■■■■■■■■■   .
      WitnessPrep 6-Feb   60    1-May .   .    .   .   .    .   .    .■■■■■■■■■■■■■■
      Motions    27-Jan   60   21-Apr .   .    .   .   .    .   .   ■■■■■■■■■■■■■■   .
      JuryInstrs 22-Apr   6.6   1-May .   .    .   .   .    .   .   .   .   .   ■   .
      PretrialOrder
                 27-Apr   3.2   1-May .   .    .   .   .    .   .   .   .   .   .■   .
    Trial         1-May    0    1-May |   .    .   .   .    .   .   .   .   .   .   ▲
```

```
  ■■■■ Detail Task      ■■■■■ Summary Task     °°°°° Baseline
  ▪▪▗■  (Progress)       ═■■■■ (Progress)       ►►► Conflict
  ▗■──  (Slack)         ■■■── (Slack)          ▪▪■ Resource delay
  Progress shows Percent Achieved on Actual     ▲ Milestone
  ---------------- Scale: 5 days per character ------------------
```

TIME LINE Gantt Chart Report, Strip 1, Page 1

---

predicted, old Mordley turns everything upside down with discovery that's not in our plan?" Quigley asked, new doubts rising. "At that point, your computer model isn't worth much, either, Davis."

"That worries me too, Davis," Smith added. "My officers and directors don't like surprises. How can this process help me keep management informed when unforseen events happen?"

"I'm glad you asked that question," Davis said. "What we have here is only a forecast based

on planning assumptions. We all agree—things will change during the life of the case. When they do, having a plan and a schedule will allow us to correct for them and forecast the cost. The secret is to track progress under the plan as we go. Every month, we'll need to enter the actual work accomplished and the hours spent into the computer schedule. The computer can then generate reports to tell us how we're doing compared to our forecast.

"Then, when old Mordley adds a dozen wit-

FIGURE 5.5 Estimated Work Hours

```
Schedule Name : LMI Trial Preparation Schedule
Responsible   :   Litigation Management Incorporated
As-of Date    : 21-May-91           Schedule File : TRIAL
```

	91	92	Total
TakeCase			0.0*
Planning	435.0		435.0*
Develop Case Plan	59.0		59.0
Discovery Planning	200.0		200.0
Pleadings	176.0		176.0
Answer			0.0*
Discovery	1,850.4		1,850.4*
Interrogs	67.2		67.2
DocProd	804.0		804.0
DepoPlans	979.2		979.2
ExpertProgram	2,752.0		2,752.0*
Select	32.0		32.0
Analysis	2,720.0		2,720.0
Notices			0.0*
DepoProgram	3,400.0	4,200.0	7,600.0*
Clients	1,500.0	1,500.0	3,000.0
Adverse	1,900.0	1,900.0	3,800.0
Experts		800.0	800.0
CutOff			0.0*
TrialPrep		2,860.0	2,860.0*
JuryResearch		336.0	336.0
DemoEvid		480.0	480.0
WitnessPrep		1,176.0	1,176.0
Motions		768.0	768.0
JuryInstrs		50.0	50.0
PretrialOrder		50.0	50.0
Trial			0.0*
Total	8,437.4	7,060.0	15,497.4*

nesses to the deposition program, we'll be ready for him. First, we'll preserve our historical schedule. That will be our permanent baseline for comparison. Then we'll revise the plan and schedule to add the depositions and assign lawyers and paralegals to handle them. We'll use the computer to calculate what the new costs will be. That will be your revised budget, Mr. Smith. Quigley will be able to stay on top of the case, no matter what happens, and you'll have a convenient, understandable way to keep management up to date on the costs," Davis said.

"I like this whole package," said Smith. "The planning process gives me a chance to make sure that the handling of the case supports management's objectives. The budget forecast is precisely what I need. And, the ability to update the forecast and to warn management about cost increases before I get Quigley's bills will be a real benefit to me."

Smith continued. "Quigley, I'm going to tell management that you've done it again. I challenged you to give me a budget, and you've come up with a solution. I'll look forward to meeting with you again next week to review the preliminary case management plan." Smith chuckled, cocked a significant eyebrow toward Quigley, and continued, "You know, Quigley, I'm glad that you'll be continuing on the case. I really wasn't looking forward to working with Amalgamated's New York lawyers."

Quigley's sigh of relief was barely audible.

SOFTWARE INFORMATION

There are many MS-DOS–based project management software packages on the market for less than $600. The program featured in this chapter is TimeLine, version 4, which is available from

FIGURE 5.6 Budget Forecast

```
Schedule Name : LMI Trial Preparation Schedule
Responsible   :  Litigation Management Incorporated
As-of Date    : 21-May-91           Schedule File : TRIAL
```

	91	92	Total
TakeCase			0.00*
Planning	76,012.50		76,012.50*
Develop Case Plan	14,012.50		14,012.50
Discovery Planning	34,000.00		34,000.00
Pleadings	28,000.00		28,000.00
Answer			0.00*
Discovery	203,280.00		203,280.00*
Interrogs	12,000.00		12,000.00
DocProd	75,000.00		75,000.00
DepoPlans	116,280.00		116,280.00
ExpertProgram	424,000.00		424,000.00*
Select	8,000.00		8,000.00
Analysis	416,000.00		416,000.00
Notices			0.00*
DepoProgram	370,000.00	478,800.00	848,800.00*
Clients	155,000.00	155,000.00	310,000.00
Adverse	215,000.00	215,000.00	430,000.00
Experts		108,800.00	108,800.00
CutOff			0.00*
TrialPrep		395,154.17	395,154.17*
JuryResearch		52,800.00	52,800.00
DemoEvid		70,800.00	70,800.00
WitnessPrep		147,600.00	147,600.00
Motions		109,440.00	109,440.00
JuryInstrs		8,552.63	8,552.63
PretrialOrder		5,961.54	5,961.54
Trial			0.00*
Total	1,073,292.50	873,954.17	1,947,246.67*

Symantec. It is a menu-driven program, with a relatively friendly user interface. A quick-pick feature provides a shortcut through some of the menus. TimeLine, version 4, also comes with a graphics package.

One of the most important features to look for in a project management program is ease in laying out the project. TimeLine uses an easy-to-set-up outline format, and displays your outline with a Gantt chart, using time bars to represent scheduled activities. TimeLine also has other layouts. PERT charts let you visualize the relationships and dependencies between the various phases and tasks in the project. Histograms let you study resource assignments visually.

TimeLine, version 4, has a greater inventory of reports than version 3. Schedule layouts can be printed out in Gantt charts, PERT charts, and in a tree chart form. A detail report gives you a description of every task in the schedule. The status report lets you identify tasks that should be completed, are in progress, or are just starting, on a daily, weekly, or monthly basis.

Several crosstab reports let you tabulate tasks, resources, work hours, and dollars several ways—total, as spent, to go, etc. The key to these reports is to keep the schedule updated with actual performance information. With this information, these reports do the hard work of keeping the lawyer and client up to date on hours worked and dollars spent.

TimeLine also has a baseline feature, which lets you track actual performance against scheduled activity. TimeLine gives you the option of displaying the Gantt layout with the baseline. This way, as you to enter actual performance data, you can see at a glance how you are doing.

With the baseline feature, many other cost and schedule tracking reports become available. The cost and schedule status report is particularly useful. This report shows, according to the baseline, how many dollars should have been spent, as of the date of the report; how much work was actually achieved, expressed in dollars (based on percentage completed data); and what the client actually spent to achieve this result. The report also computes cost and schedule variances expressed in dollars. The cost and schedule status report is especially useful for keeping a general counsel informed.

TimeLine has many features that are beyond the scope of this chapter. On the whole, I have found it easy to work with. Its features have enabled me to create a template for scheduling a typical lawsuit. With a well-thought-out case management plan, I can use this template to make case-specific project schedules and budgets.

Exact prices and additional information about TimeLine are available from Symantec Corp., 10201 Torre Ave., Cupertino, CA 95014-2132. The phone number is (408) 253-9600.

David P. Cotellesse practices law in Houston, Texas. From 1987 to 1991, he was president of Litigation Management Incorporated. Before organizing Litigation Management in 1987, he was a partner with Baker & Botts in Houston, where he tried antitrust and commercial cases.

Software to Model the Uncertainties in Litigation

Morris Raker

Morris Raker, a lawyer in Boston, describes how decision tree software, a type of expert system, can assist in analyzing complex cases. With such software, you can employ sophisticated probability theory to assess the strengths and weaknesses of your case and to better evaluate settlement possibilities. Where settlement is not yet possible, it can also help identify which factual or legal inquiries should be pursued first.

Several years ago, I began looking for a more efficient way to respond to the uncertainties inherent in litigation. It soon became clear that the place to look was not in law journals but in business schools where methods for enhancing the quality of management decisions made in the face of uncertain outcomes have long been developed. Consider, for example, a middle manager who must recommend to management whether their company should embark on a particular R&D project and then defend that recommendation. Like a trial lawyer with a new case, this manager is faced with a number of uncertainties. Unlike the lawyer, however, the manager must often make an ultimate recommendation, and the company must decide whether to commit substantial funds to a project, at a time when the outcomes of most of the major issues remain highly uncertain. How much will the project cost? How long will it take to complete? Will it be successful from a technological standpoint? Even if it is a technological success, will it be a commercial success? Are competitors working on a comparable product? If so, will they beat the company to market? And so on.

To make a recommendation, the manager must make a detailed, quantitative analysis of all of these factors. One technique for doing so is Bayesian decision analysis, which uses decision trees to structure complex problems. It has been used for years in the business community. Bayesian methodology can also be applied with great success to legal problems, including litigation.

Lawyers usually refer to uncertainties as issues. Litigators first identify the issues in a case and then proceed, through discovery, legal research, and the use of expert witnesses, to reduce the factual and legal uncertainties. This process leads to an adjudication that provides an ultimate resolution of the factual and legal issues.

Decision analysis in litigation can determine a fair settlement value and what (if any) factual inquiries and legal analyses might productively be undertaken prior to settlement. It can also help identify the issues on which to focus discovery and trial preparation in the event that settlement cannot be reached.

BREAKING DOWN THE ISSUES

In civil litigation there are usually two principal uncertainties:

1. Will the defendant be held liable?
2. If so, what will be the amount of the judgment?

Both of these issues usually depend on the outcome of subsidiary issues. Thus the issue of liability will often depend on the outcome of a factual inquiry undertaken through discovery, the nature and complexity of the issues to be resolved by the jury, the credibility of potential witnesses, the possibility of an effective counterclaim, unresolved issues of statutory interpretation, and the instructions given by the judge to the jury.

The size of the judgment may be affected by many of the same issues. The value of the judg-

Evaluating Personal Injury Cases

Joseph L. Kashi

Several software and database programs can help personal injury lawyers better evaluate the settlement and verdict value of their cases.

Jury Verdict Research (JVR) distributes an excellent statistical database for use with PCs. The database provides statistical information regarding the likelihood of proving liability for many types of injuries, and the settlement and verdict value of each case. By taking into account the probability of success and other statistical adjustment factors, this program allows you to evaluate each case on your office computer.

Compared to manual case evaluation methods, the JVR software has several major advantages:

- It is immediately available in your office.
- You can try different "what if" hypotheses to test the effect of the individual factors in your case.
- The database is upgraded about every six months.
- It is inexpensive compared to JVR's fee to do a custom analysis of your case.
- I have found the software package to be far easier to use and more comprehensive than JVR's printed manuals.

A similar database oriented toward defense lawyers is available to members of the Defense Research Institute.

One word of caution: JVR's case valuation analyses are extremely sensitive to the assumptions that you make and to your ability to objectively evaluate such factors as the strength of a particular witness's testimony. They should be used with great caution and accepted as a rough guide only. Some experienced trial judges have commented that the results tend to be on the high side, perhaps because plaintiffs' lawyers tend to report mostly the cases of which they are proud. JVR's customer service, in Horsham, Pennsylvania, can be reached at (215) 784-0860.

Shepard's/McGraw-Hill, in Colorado Springs, publishes Determining Economic Loss in Personal Injury Cases. Version 2 may be useful to any personal injury plaintiff or defense firm. It's like having an economist friend who'll give you a quick rule of thumb about the value of the economic losses in your case. The occupational wage rate database is quite comprehensive. Economic loss evaluation is a necessary part of any case evaluation.

Future medical and economic losses often must be reduced to net present value or the present value of a complex structured settlement must be evaluated. In these cases, you'll also need an amortization calculation program. TIMESLIPS Corporation publishes PercentEdge. I found this program to be useful but not as comprehensive as I desired. You'll find it helpful in determining the value of mortgages or simple settlement payment terms, but more complex calculations may require a legal-specific present value calculation program. Several are available and usually advertised in *Law Practice Management, Law Office Computing,* and *The Lawyer's PC.* Since these programs often tend to have idiosyncratic interfaces, I suggest that you get a few demonstration disks and evaluate them before deciding on which program to purchase.

ment from the plaintiff's perspective and its cost to the defendant will also be affected by the defendant's financial capacity, the amount of time that will elapse before payment, and the future costs of litigation, including legal fees and internal costs.

Once counsel has done the legal and factual analysis needed to file a complaint or answer, decision analysis can help to develop a meaningful and insightful course of action. This does not mean that the results of the analysis would not change if various uncertainties were resolved. The value of the case is likely to change, possibly up and possibly down, as legal or factual uncertainty is reduced. However, even an increase in value does not necessarily result in a net benefit to the client. The cost of resolving uncertainty is often greater than the resulting enhancement in value. Sophisticated clients are fast becoming aware of this.

A HYPOTHETICAL

Assume you are a senior litigator in Manhattan law firm. One of your important clients is Churn Securities, Inc., a Wall Street broker-dealer. During the 1980s, Churn invested heavily for its own account in the shares of companies believed to be takeover candidates. Churn's investments included a large position in the common stock of Target Chemical Company, a West Coast manufacturer of agricultural chemicals.

In June 1986, Target was acquired in an LBO by Raider & Greed, a partnership that purchased several companies through LBOs. Churn had acquired 4 percent of Target's common stock during the preceding three months. These shares were tendered at the time of the LBO for a cash payment of $53 per share. Churn thus received $8 million for its 4 percent position, $2.3 million more than it had paid for the shares.

Initially, Target appeared able to cope with the increased burden of debt service from the LBO. However, serious cash flow difficulties arose early in 1988 after one of its principal products, an insecticide sprayed on fruit trees, was identified as causing cancer in humans. The resulting sharp reduction in income forced Target to file a Chapter 11 reorganization petition in June 1988.

Early the next year, Churn was served in an adversary proceeding brought by the debtor. The complaint filed with the bankruptcy court alleged that the LBO constituted a fraudulent conveyance. It demanded that Churn and the other former stockholders return to Target all the cash they received in the LBO in exchange for their shares.

The bankruptcy proceeding is in California. You referred Churn to a local bankruptcy expert, Philip Preference. Now, nine months and $50,000 in legal fees later, Churn's president, Sigmund Trade, seeks your help.

Initially incredulous that his public market transactions could be deemed fraudulent, Trade has become increasingly concerned with the possibility of an adverse judgment and the probability of enormous legal fees, whether he wins or loses. Pointing out that the securities business is itself under pressure, he expresses frustration that

Preference recently told him that it is far too early in the case to assess either the extent of Churn's ultimate exposure or the basis on which settlement might be pursued.

Arguing that it doesn't make sense to spend $500,000 in legal fees to avoid the possibility of overpaying $100,000 in a settlement, Trade has asked you to meet with Preference, who will be in New York the following week on a discovery matter, and then develop a decision-tree analysis of the case.

USING DECISION ANALYSIS

You arrange to have two meetings with Preference, one just after he arrives in New York and one the next day. At the first meeting, Preference goes over the case with you in reasonable detail, explaining both the strengths and weaknesses of the plaintiff's position. The principal factual issues in the case, you learn, are whether Target was rendered insolvent by the LBO and, if so, whether the stock received by Target constituted fair value for the cash paid out. The first of these factual issues may depend on whether, as claimed by the plaintiff, Target's balance sheet at the date of the LBO overstated the value of the company's assets and substantially understated its liabilities.

There are also some interesting legal issues. Preference informs you that the application of fraudulent conveyance laws to LBOs has not met with universal approval from courts and commentators and, moreover, that there appears to be no case in which the concept has been applied to payments received by public shareholders, as distinguished from insiders.

Furthermore, it turns out that the suit seeks from Churn not only the $8 million received for the shares held in its own account, but also another $3.5 million it had received on account of shares of Target held in street name by Churn's customers. Since Churn acted only as a conduit in the transmission of these funds to the actual shareholders, Preference has considered filing a motion for summary judgment on this aspect of the complaint.

At the conclusion of the first session, you explain that the next day's meeting will involve the assignment of certain numeric values to each point in the case analysis. These will include the size of any adverse judgment, the amount of interest on the judgment, the likely size of future legal fees, and other costs of going forward with the litigation, including the fees of expert wit-

FIGURE 5.7 A Chance Tree

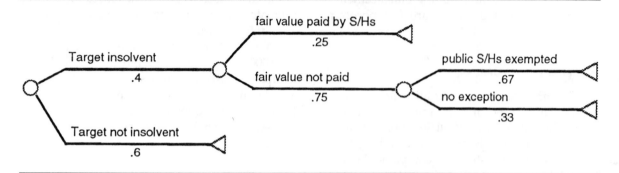

nesses. You ask Preference to estimate each of these amounts prior to the next meeting.

In addition, you want to assign probabilities to the various possible outcomes of the principal legal and factual issues. So you ask him to make a list, for each of the issues, of the reasons why a judge or jury might rule against Churn, and another list of the reasons supporting a favorable ruling. Finally, you ask Preference to come up with his best estimate of the amount at which Churn could settle the case at this time.

The costs to Churn of continuing to litigate entail not only out-of-pocket fees to lawyers and other experts, but also the considerable transaction costs associated with having to conduct business under the cloud of uncertainty. At the very least, it is costly for a business to have its managers spending their time and efforts on litigating past issues, rather than attending to current matters and planning for the future. Furthermore, a potential liability of some $15 million, right out of the firm's capital, could act as a continuing constraint on Churn's ability to make investments freely or to otherwise carry on its business activities.

You question Trade, and he confirms that this is, indeed, a material issue. He estimates that it will cost Churn at least $50,000 annually in lost productivity of executives and support personnel forced to deal with extensive discovery requests and other matters concerning the litigation. Moreover, in order to minimize the risk that loss of the litigation could result in capital impairment, Trade has decided that he must treat the amount at risk as borrowed funds to be repaid on demand, rather than as a portion of the firm's equity capital. In response to your request that he try to quantify the effect of this treatment, Trade explains that he expects to earn at least 20 percent per year on the firm's capital, while, in

contrast, his conservative investment of the $15 million at risk cannot be counted on to earn over 9 percent. Even taking tax savings into account, he concludes that this is likely to cost Churn $1.2 million in lost income for each year that the case drags on.[1]

DEVELOPING A CHANCE TREE

In advance of the second meeting with bankruptcy counsel, you develop a chance tree that depicts the principal legal and factual issues discussed at the first meeting. (See Figure 5.7.)

A chance tree models only uncertainties, while a decision tree also shows at least one set of decision options. Most litigation can be modeled first as a chance tree to depict the issues in the case.

I find that the development of the basic chance tree forces me to think about the case both rigorously and creatively. The resulting tree is an excellent communications tool that both identifies the issues and puts them into perspective. For example, the lawyers working on different aspects of the case can see precisely how their respective part fits into the whole. This can mean avoiding misunderstandings and the possibility that days of research might be wasted on the wrong issue.

These trees also provide a graphic means of communicating to clients what their cases are really about. To the extent that this communication is a sobering experience, I believe it is better for it to occur early in the case rather than just before trial as so often happens. In much the same way, a chance tree can focus settlement negotiations on the issues and their likely outcomes, which is often a productive means of reaching a mutually acceptable figure.

Ultimately, the chance tree can be modified

into a decision tree when decision options, such as settlement and the hiring of an expert should be considered.

Theoretically, all of this is possible without using a computer. Trees can be drawn by hand, and the arithmetic, even present value computations, can be done with a hand-held calculator. As a practical matter, however, lawyers usually find the process far too frustrating and time-consuming.

Drawing and calculating by hand even a medium-sized tree is tedious. The task becomes extraordinarily time-consuming when a large tree is involved. Furthermore, certain of the analytical strengths of decision analysis, such as the ability to appraise the potential value of additional discovery or legal research, or to use sensitivity analysis to determine whether reducing existing uncertainty is desirable before accepting a settlement offer, require additional manipulations or calculations of the tree. For these types of analyses, decision analysis software is virtually indispensable.

Frustrated in my inability to locate software offering all the features I wanted, including first-rate graphics and ease of use, I developed my own. Called DATA, it has been available in a Macintosh version since August 1988. If all goes well, our company, TreeAge Software, Inc., will bring a PC version to market soon.

We are not the only game in town. Texas Instruments markets decision analysis software called Arborist, which runs on IBM PCs and compatible machines. The Strategic Decision Group, a consulting firm with strong ties to Stanford, offers industrial-strength software called Professional Supertree, which runs on virtually any platform.

READING A CHANCE TREE

Reading a decision or chance tree is quite easy. Chronologically, it flows from left to right in the same order that the represented decisions (if any) are to be made and the uncertain events resolved. Any squares are *decision nodes*. They indicate a decision is to be made among the alternatives represented by the branches that emanate from the node.

It would be easy to make the right decision if we knew in advance what the outcome would be. Normally, however, uncertainty intervenes. But even though we don't know precisely what will happen, we can with reasonable accuracy identify the range of possible outcomes and their relative probabilities.

Circles, called *chance nodes,* represent this uncertainty in the tree. The branches emanating from a chance node represent all of the possible outcomes of that particular uncertainty. Each branch represents an outcome exclusive of the others. Since the outcomes represented at a given chance node are collectively exhaustive and mutually exclusive, the sum of their individual probabilities must be one.

Litigation usually involves multiple uncertainties. This complexity makes it very difficult to assess directly the probability of winning or losing. However, if the case is broken into its component issues, an experienced lawyer can develop the probable outcome of an ultimate issue simply by estimating the probabilities associated with each of the underlying issues.

For example, based on the law and the pleadings, for this LBO to be treated as a fraudulent conveyance, the plaintiff will have to establish that Target was insolvent (liabilities exceeded assets) at the time of the transaction and that Target received from its shareholders less than fair value for the amounts paid to them.

Assume there is a 40 percent probability that Target will be found to have been insolvent and a 75 percent probability that the shareholders will be found to have paid less than fair value. The probability that the plaintiff will be successful on both issues is the product of the two separate probabilities, or 30 percent. In this case there is a third issue—whether the court will apply the fraudulent conveyance law to require the former public shareholders to return what they had been paid for their stock, notwithstanding the absence of any proof that they were guilty of actual fraud. If that probability is 33 percent, the likelihood that the plaintiff will win falls to 10 percent.

Each branch of the tree, beginning at the root node at the far left and ending at one of the triangular terminal nodes, represents one of several possible scenarios. If a reasonably complex litigation is broken down into a number of issues, the resulting tree may have hundreds or even thousands of scenarios.

MODIFYING THE CHANCE TREE

At your second meeting, Preference suggests some modifications to the initial tree structure.

First, he wants the tree to reflect his belief that Churn is less likely to be held liable for the

FIGURE 5.8 Tree Including a Decision Node

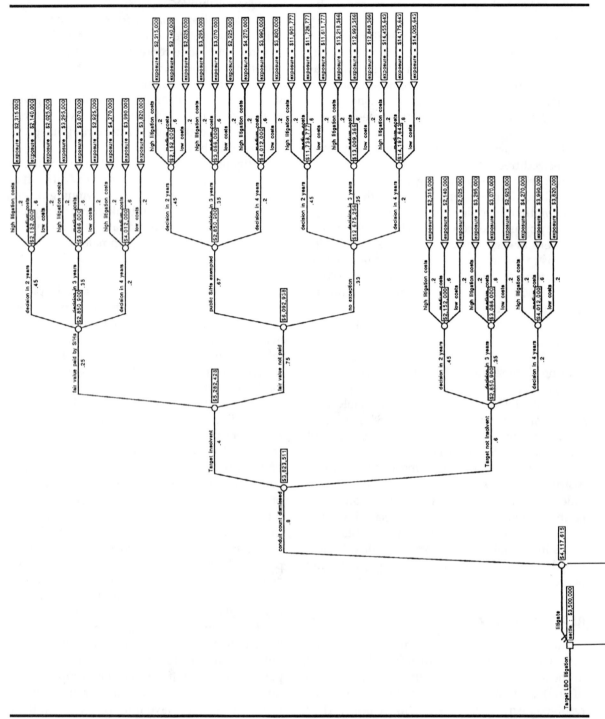

$3.5 million it received as a conduit than for the funds received for its own account. Once you point out Trade's estimate of the enormous costs imposed on Churn simply on account of continuing uncertainty on this issue, Preference agrees that he should promptly file a motion to dismiss the count related to the conduit funds.

The motion will be filed in 10 days and probably decided within 120 days. A favorable ruling would free up sufficient capital to cut Trade's cost estimate by $380,000 per year.

Preference also wants to modify the tree to deal with his uncertainty concerning when the case will finally be decided. This modification

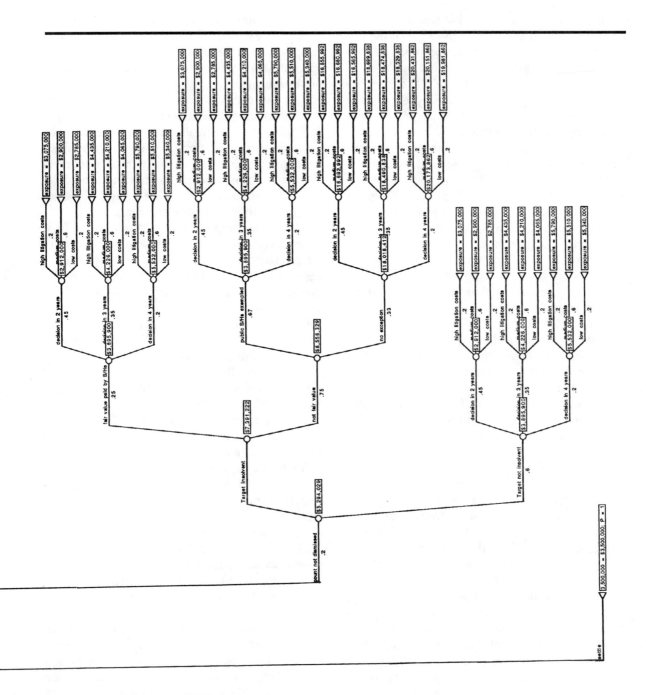

will affect a number of other issues, including the amount of legal fees, expert witness fees, interest on any award, and costs of the type estimated by Trade on an annual basis.

The tree in Figure 5.8 reflects these modifications. It also includes a decision node for purposes of analyzing settlement, based on Preference's expectation that the plaintiff would now accept an offer of $3.5 million. Figure 5.8 also illustrates the extensive information provided by the software when the tree is *rolled back* or calculated.

When the software rolls back the tree, it calculates the value (which may be a net cost) of each scenario. These values, known as *payoffs*, are shown in the small boxes to the right of the terminal nodes at the end of each branch. The software also calculates the probability that a given scenario will, in fact, be the one that occurs. As mentioned above, this probability equals the product of each of the individual probabilities that comprise the scenario.

The expected value of litigating takes into account all of the possible scenarios. It is the weighted average of all the payoffs, with the weighting based on the probability that a given payoff will occur. In this case, the expected value of litigating is $4,117,615, shown in the box to the right of the Litigate node.

You will note that a value is displayed at every chance node. These figures are the expected values of the subtrees rooted at the various chance nodes.

This information, which would be extremely tedious to derive without a computer, is very valuable in analyzing the case. For example, it tells you the value of being at a given node, assuming that all uncertainty were eliminated to the left of that node. The difference between that value and the expected value shown at the prior chance node is the most that one should spend to resolve the intervening uncertainty.

The payoff is calculated at each triangular terminal node from a formula that incorporates the various cost and revenue (if any) factors in that scenario. In the fraudulent transfer case you are doing for Churn Securities, the payoff formula incorporates the estimated present value of future legal fees, expert witness fees, Churn's internal costs (both for personnel and lost investment income), and any judgment, plus interest at the legal rate. Note that expenses already incurred—sunk costs—are irrelevant to the analysis, except to the extent that your assessment of the issues and their associated probabilities reflects the knowledge gained by incurring those expenses.

Depending on whether the case takes two, three, or four more years, and on whether costs turn out to be high, medium, or low, legal fees may range from a low of $250,000 to a high of $700,000, and expert witness fees may range from $35,000 to $90,000. The payoffs displayed in Figure 5.8 are based on these projections. Trade's estimates of internal costs also enter the calculations: $1,250,000 per year, falling to $870,00 if the motion for partial summary judgment is granted.

Interest on any judgment is calculated at 8 percent per year over the appropriate period, and the payment is discounted to present value at 10 percent for two, three, or four years, depending on the scenario.

At the decision node, the software recommends settlement, because the cost of settling at $3,500,000 is substantially less than the expected value (cost) of litigating. However, the analysis depends on estimates. Is refinement of the current estimates required before committing to a settlement figure? Such a refinement would, of course, require additional expense and time.

Here the computer really comes in handy. It permits you to do a sensitivity analysis on any of the estimated values, whether they are probabilities or the values used to calculate the payoffs. For example, assume that Preference is particularly uncomfortable with his assessment of the probability that Target will be found to have been insolvent at the time of the LBO. There has been minimal discovery to date, and he is concerned that this issue will depend on whether the plaintiff's experts can develop a convincing case that Target's financial statements had significantly overvalued assets and understated liabilities.

In other words, based on what he now knows about this matter, Preference is satisfied with his estimate of a 40 percent probability that the plaintiff will prevail on the issue of insolvency. However, he is concerned that discovery might change this estimate drastically.

In response to your questioning, he states that discovery is not likely to resolve the issue completely. In his opinion, discovery could possibly increase the likelihood of a finding of insolvency to as high as 70 percent or decrease it to as low as 20 percent.

The question, then, is whether the settlement recommendation is sensitive within this range. If the cost of settling remains less than the expected value of litigating without regard to whether the probability of the insolvency finding is 20 percent, 70 percent, or anywhere in between, it makes no sense to spend the money and time needed to resolve the uncertainty.

This analysis appears graphically in Figure 5.9. The horizontal line at the graph's bottom represents settlement for $3.5 million. The sloping line represents the expected value of litigating as the probability on the insolvency issue moves from 20 percent to 70 percent. If the lines had crossed, it would mean that the decision is sensitive within

FIGURE 5.9 Sensitivity Analysis on Issues of Insolvency

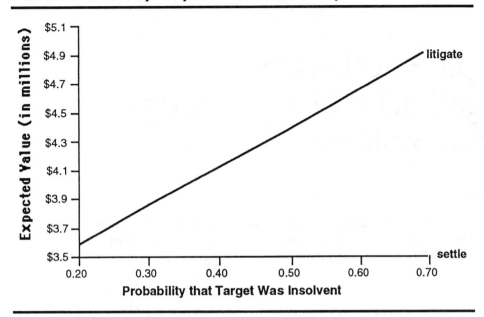

the probable range. Since in this case they don't intersect, Preference's uncertainty on this issue is irrelevant to the question at hand.

CONCLUSION

This has been a brief introduction to the use of decision analysis software to analyze litigation. The software provides additional analytical tools. Though not described, they are directly relevant to the issues that customarily arise in litigation, particularly in the area of dealing with a client's aversion to risk.

If, like most lawyers, you have no background in decision analysis, you should consider a one- or two-day seminar. Programs specifically for lawyers are offered by two California-based companies, the Center for Litigation Risk Analysis, 3000 Sand Hill Rd., Menlo Park, CA 94025, (415) 854-1104; and the Beron Group, 430 Cowper St., Palo Alto, CA 94103, (415) 327-3351. Each of-fers public seminars at a variety of locations and private seminars by special arrangement.

ENDNOTE

1. This example was taken from a period of relatively high interest rates. Different times may call for the use of different rates. Depending on the spread, the net cost to Churn may differ from the amount calculated above, but the methodology described remains the same.

The same applies to certain of the legal issues considered in the case. These were novel when the article was written but have now been decided in the context of the Kaiser Steel LBO and resulting bankruptcy. Thus, the issues are largely unchanged, but one's probability assessments are likely to be different as a result of intervening events. This is the same thing that happens during the course of a case where, from time to time, discovery, legal research, various rulings by the court, and other events will call for reassessment of the probabilities and values previously entered into the tree.

Morris Raker advises companies and trial counsel in applying decision analysis both to reach better settlements and to reduce the transaction costs of litigation. He has lectured on this subject at Harvard, MIT, Stanford, Boston University, and Tufts. He is also CEO of TreeAge Software, Inc., which developed the software described in this article.

Joseph L. Kashi (sidebar) is a sole practitioner living in Soldotna, Alaska. He received his B.S. and M.S. degrees from MIT in 1973 and his J.D. from Georgetown University Law Center in 1976. His practice consists primarily of contract and personal injury litigation.

Simple Solutions to Litigation Problems Through Expert Systems

J. Ronald Sutcliffe

Ron Sutcliffe, an Alaska prosecutor, uses a simple but sophisticated expert system to assist in analyzing Alaska's complex Fish and Game statutory provisions. He shows how anyone can put such a system to use in his or her practice.

Alaska's sports enthusiasts often joke that you shouldn't go fishing or hunting unless your companions include a judge, a district attorney, and a game warden. This way, at least, you're likely to avoid an inadvertent violation.

Alaska's Fish and Game statutes and regulations are complex. They reflect the enormity of Alaska's wildlife resources and prescribe everything, from where you can hunt or fish to prohibited methods of taking salmon and how large or small your fishing hook must be. Penalties range from small fines with no possible jail time to mandatory minimum fines of tens of thousands of dollars and nonsuspendable jail time. Administrative regulations provide for suspension of sport and commercial licenses and for forfeiture of assets, no small matter when a valuable commercial fishing vessel or aircraft is a potential target for seizure. Sentencing often befuddles even experienced judges.

TIRED OF FISH AND GAMES? TRY SORTING IT OUT WITH AI

When I was first appointed assistant district attorney in a rural area of Alaska, I attempted to sort out Fish and Game penalties using a paper matrix listing the fines and jail time for many common violations. This approach soon proved unworkable because there were so many possible violations and penalties. Since I had previously used Paperback Software's VP-Expert, I turned to this inexpensive artificial intelligence program to sort out the Fish and Game code's complex web of regulations.

Using VP-Expert

VP-Expert is a so-called expert system generator, in effect an application of artificial intelligence techniques. It allows you to build what VP-Expert calls a *knowledge base system* (or KBS). Once completed, anyone can use the KBS to assess certain factual issues and be guided toward an appropriate conclusion.

The program, from Paperback Software, includes several practice expert systems to help get you started. The one I received consults with the user and tells him or her which industrial solvent would be appropriate to clean a given surface. Paperback Software also offers a wine-selector expert system, written by a prominent oenophile.

Getting started with VP-Expert is easy. The manual details in a logical sequence the steps to construct your knowledge base. To build the KBS, you create in an IF-THEN format a series of rules leading to a solution to a particular problem. In the case of the Fish and Game code, I focused on determining the penalty for an infraction of the regulations, given the offender's previous record (if any) of Fish and Game convictions.

The Fish and Game Knowledge Base System

In designing the Fish and Game KBS, I initially divided the statutory provisions into four groups of violations: commercial fisheries, sport

FIGURE 5.10 Spreadsheet for Induction of Rules regarding Commercial Fishing

CATEGORY	STATUTE	TYPE	PRIORS	MAXIMUM PENALTY
COMM-FISH	AS 16.05.475	VIOLATION	NONE	$3000
COMM-FISH	AS 16.05.475	MISDEMEANOR	2	1 YEAR, $15000

fisheries, trapping, and hunting. The commercial fisheries subsection alone required over 75 rules.

There are two methods of creating the initial KBS: induce or edit. The induce feature allows you to create a spreadsheet from which VP-Expert then writes the rules for you. Figure 5.10 shows an example of a spreadsheet from which rules regarding commercial fishing could be induced. From the induction of this spreadsheet, VP-Expert would write the following rules:

```
RULE 1
IF   Category= Comm-Fish AND
     Statute=AS 16.05.475 AND
     Type=Violation AND
     Priors=None
THEN Penalty=$3000
RULE 2
IF   Category= Comm-fish AND
     Statute=AS 16.05.475 AND
     Type=Misdemeanor AND
     Priors=2
THEN Penalty=1 YEAR, $15000
```

The alternative to induction is to write your own rules using the editor function of VP-Expert. To set up the Fish and Game KBS, I initially used the edit feature to write the rules. The editor uses the [ALT], [CTRL], and [SHIFT] keys to change options at the bottom of the screen. The options allow you to choose among standard word-processing features, including global replacement and copy functions. The copy function is particularly useful when creating rules that are identical except for one variable. Once you've written the rule, you may add a DISPLAY line that includes other information. In the commercial fish KBS, I included a DISPLAY listing asset forfeiture and license suspension:

```
RULE 2
IF   Category= Comm-fish AND
     Statute=AS 16.05.475 AND
     Type=Misdemeanor AND
     Priors=2
THEN Penalty=1 YEAR, $15000
DISPLAY "The penalty appears in
```

AS16.05.723 and in addition to the above jail and $ fines the court SHALL forfeit seized fish or their value. The court MAY revoke the license or right to limited entry permit for up to one year under AS16.05.710.";

Following rule creation, you must write the questions that lead the user down the decision paths toward the desired solution. In the commercial fisheries KBS, the initial question sets the offense category (i.e., commercial fish, hunting, sport fish or trapping). The *code*—the word processing document you create—is shown below.

```
ASK category: "Which category of
     offense is applicable?"
CHOICES category: Commercial-
     fish, hunting, sport-fish,
     trapping;
```

For the next question, namely, which statute the offender violated, the KBS code you write is similar to the initial question. (In the actual KBS there are dozens of statutes to choose from.)

```
ASK statute: "Which statute has
     the offender violated?"
CHOICES statute: AS16.05.440,
     AS16.05.470, AS16.05.510
```

The commercial fish KBS then goes on to ask whether the prosecution is for a violation or misdemeanor, asks about the offender's record, and then displays the maximum penalty and any asset or license forfeiture that is appropriate.

After creating the KBS, you must test its accuracy. This process involves executing the KBS to see if syntax or other incorrect statements exist in the code. If improper wording or punctuation appears in the KBS, then VP-Expert will tell you which line contains the offending language. After correcting any basic errors in the KBS, you determine whether the suggested solution is accurate. I usually resort to the statutes during the testing process to doublecheck the accuracy of the KBS.

FIGURE 5.11 Screens from the Commercial Fish KBS

```
WHICH CATEGORY OF OFFENSE DOES THE CRIME FALL UNDER?

Comm-Fish        Sport-fish      Hunting       Trapping

WHICH STATUTE IS THE OFFENDER CHARGED UNDER?

AS16.05.440         AS16.05.475        AS16.05.480

AS16.05.490         AS16.05.510        AS16.05.520

AS16.05.632         AS16.05.665        AS16.05.675

AS16.05.680         AS16.05.685        AS16.05.690a

AS16.05.690b        AS16.05.800        AS16.05.835

AS16.05.840         AS16.05.850        AS16.05.880

AS16.05.895


HAS THE DEFENDANT BEEN CHARGED WITH A MISDEMEANOR OR VIOLATION?

Misdemeanor         Violation

IS THIS THE DEFENDANT'S FIRST, SECOND OR MORE CONVICTION?

(Note: Choose Second for anything after the first conviction)

First               Second
```

Executing the KBS requires you to return to the opening screen and choose CONSULT from the main menu, just as if you are consulting an expert. After the system loads, press GO and the questioning begins. You select choices by moving the cursor and pressing [ENTER]. Figure 5.11 illustrates screens from the commercial fish KBS.

If the user of the KBS selected Comm-Fish, AS16.05.475, a prosecution as a strict liability violation, and a first offense, the KBS would display the result shown below:

```
THE PENALTY IS $3000 and in
addition the court SHALL forfeit
any seized fish or their value.
```

Once you've got the KBS up and running, Paperback Software will sell you a runtime version of the program for a fraction of the original program's cost. This version doesn't allow the development of knowledge base systems but does allow you to use the KBS. You may distribute your expert system for popular use without every user buying a complete copy of the program.

ROBERT'S RULES OF ORDER, REORDERED

Any municipal lawyer will tell you that there is nothing more terrifying than to be seated next to the mayor, in the middle of a council or assembly meeting, with a huge sneering audience, and have an elected official ask you a question on some arcane rule of order. It's always something like, "Gee, Mr. Attorney, can we rescind this vote? We did last year. You know, the one we reconsidered five times and then tabled for the work session, but then we forgot to do the work session?"

The above scenario, having happened to me one time too many, caused me to bring *Robert's Rules* to order with VP-Expert. This project was even more complex than the Fish and Game code. The enormity of the task at first overwhelmed me—to the point that I was unable even to structure an outline of how to proceed.

Eventually, I treated each rule as a separate module. Once each rule was coded, it was an easy task to incorporate the separate modules into one large expert system that brought smiles to even the most hardened parliamentarians.

My initial choice for the first module was

reconsideration of votes. This is a common question, easily and often raised and not always clearcut. It usually arises in a context something like, "Mr. Attorney, last week we voted to give a foreign country our airport; we'd like to reconsider that vote." There are many political interactions and forces that encourage elected officials to reconsider a vote. On the other hand, there's a checklist of reasons why they can't reconsider, all printed plainly in *Robert's Rules*. However, finding these prohibitions in *Robert's* is quite another question.

VP-Expert takes care of all of these contingencies. When I wrote this application, I envisioned attending council meetings, portable computer in tow, ready to be the parliamentarian of the universe. Having basked in my thoughts of eminence for a while, I realized that the council wouldn't need a parliamentarian if they had the complete VP-Expert knowledge base. In the interest of job security, this VP-Expert application has lain fallow in my desk for several years, but here's how it works with the reconsideration issue.

Upon consulting "Bob's KBS," as I named it, a screen appears asking which rule you have a question about. You need only position the cursor over the rule and press [ENTER], or click if you're using a mouse. Some of the other motions listed are motions to table, to rescind, to enter on the minutes, to suspend the rules, to withdraw, to adjourn (one of my favorites), and to postpone.

Once you have selected the rule for discussion, VP-Expert asks what problem you are having with it. A number of choices present themselves, including whether the motion is debatable or amendable. However, the most common question regarding reconsideration is "Can we reconsider?" There are literally dozens of subrules that determine the answer to this question. For instance, the vote can't be reconsidered unless the motion to reconsider is made at the same or next meeting and then only if made by someone who voted on the prevailing side last time.

To answer the simple question, "Can we reconsider?" VP-Expert (and any lawyer without

VP-Expert) must go through a number of steps. The second screen asks the user whether the motion has been previously reconsidered and, if so, whether it has been amended. A click on the NO answer brings up more interrogatories, asking the types of previous votes. Finally, VP-Expert asks if someone from the prevailing side is making the motion and if the present meeting is the same meeting or the first meeting since the vote to be reconsidered. If the answer to any of the last three questions is NO, VP-Expert states that you cannot reconsider.

Admittedly, there are lawyers who can process these questions faster than my 10-MHz laptop, but the point is that many small towns and clubs relying on *Robert's Rules of Order* can't afford to have a lawyer present at every meeting. While I'd be the last to suggest replacing your parliamentarian with an expert system, VP-Expert—used properly (and cautiously)—may benefit many organizations. It illustrates the power of commercially developed expert legal systems. As a lawyer, I always want my expert system at hand for those particularly bizarre questions about things like suspending the rules. The adjournment rules I've got down, but these others. . . .

CONCLUSION

VP-Expert presents a unique, inexpensive opportunity for persons with expertise in small corners of the law to spread that knowledge around via broadly disseminated, interactive computer databases. Large firms could easily adapt VP-Expert for analyses of policy or litigation procedures. Arcane questions about civil or criminal procedure, or the interaction between the bankruptcy code and article 9 of the UCC, are other obvious areas in which an expert system would be very useful.

By committing their knowledge to a systematic KBS, practitioners would spend less time training or assisting paralegals, avoid malpractice more easily, and generally do a better job. The uses for VP-Expert and other expert systems are only beginning to be tapped.

J. Ronald Sutcliffe works as an assistant district attorney for the state of Alaska. His government office in Juneau overlooks the Gastineau Channel and features an aging model 50Z IBM PS/2 and pictures of large fish he has caught.

Artificial Intelligence in Action

Charles E. Pear, Jr.

How can artificial intelligence techniques be used in a litigation practice? Charles Pear, former practitioner and now law professor, will show you how these techniques can be used today. You will be amazed at how expert systems can be used to solve complicated litigation problems and even more so about programs looming on the horizon.

Throughout the 1980s, lawyers invested heavily in information processing technology to improve their practices. Unlike the accounting firms, however, they largely ignored the computer's ability to harness firm expertise through knowledge-based software systems.[1] Instead, lawyers focused on automating peripheral tasks, such as accounting, word processing, and docket control, previously performed manually.[2]

Recently, however, a few lawyers have realized that expert systems designed for the legal profession offer the potential to expand the services they offer while cutting costs, increasing productivity, raising quality, and, most important, increasing income. In the private sector, for instance, a lawyer at a Canadian law firm can bill $1 million annually with the assistance of three clerks and a computerized expert system for managing foreclosure litigation.[3] With an expert system to help create loan documentation, a medium-sized American law firm won a major share of a legal market previously the almost exclusive province of large law firms.[4]

Public sector lawyers also find that, through imaginative use of expert systems, work that previously required the attention of experienced litigators can be delegated to paralegals and junior lawyers. For example, Brooklyn police arrest hundreds of felony suspects daily, each of whom must be arraigned and charged within a day. In the past, each request required that a lawyer from the District Attorney's office interview the arresting officer to learn the facts and determine what charges to file. In 1989, however, the District Attorney's office developed CACE, an expert system that permits a paralegal, rather than a lawyer, to interview the arresting officer. Based on the facts presented, CACE recommends the appropriate charges for each suspect and prints a copy of the applicable provisions of the New York Penal Code.[5]

The Brooklyn DA with the CACE system and the Canadian and American law firms are reaping the rewards of modern computer technology by harnessing their own legal knowledge through expert systems, a branch of artificial intelligence. With quick access to scarce and valuable knowledge through this technology, these lawyers enjoy benefits that translate directly into dollars. In addition, the two law firms have also gained a competitive advantage over other firms in their region—an edge that will be difficult to overcome.

This article explores how these techniques work. It starts with an overview of artificial intelligence and expert systems. It then describes three imaginative systems designed for litigation:

- The Hearsay Rule Advisor predicts whether hearsay evidence will be admissible under an exception to the hearsay rule and supplies relevant case authorities.
- The System for Asbestos Litigation (SAL) calculates the likely dollar value of an asbestos case for settlement purposes.
- EPSILON (ExPert System in the Law Of Negligence) forecasts the damages awarded by a trial court in an automobile accident case claiming soft tissue injuries to the plaintiff's back or neck.

ARTIFICIAL INTELLIGENCE AND EXPERT SYSTEMS

Artificial intelligence or *AI* may be the most intriguing idea to have emerged from modern computer technology. It has sparked debate on the nature of intelligence, whether computers really can be intelligent, and whether they should be intelligent.[6] But trial practitioners care little about such academic tempests. To a litigator, artificial intelligence is important only if it is useful; anything beyond that is filed away under "artificial irrelevance." This chapter focuses, then, on AI programs that are useful in litigation from a practical perspective.

For our purposes, artificial intelligence refers to a program that makes a computer more useful by emulating human problem-solving methods.[7] Although artificial intelligence has many subfields, the branch most often used in the legal context is the expert system.

What Is an Expert System?

Although there is no generally accepted definition of *expert system*, for our purposes an expert system is a program that provides on a computer the expertise of a human expert. Like its human counterpart, an expert system gives advice. It formulates this advice by collecting information on the details of the problem at hand and then applying its own store of knowledge to the facts gathered.

An expert system's knowledge often takes the form of a series of IF-THEN rules. For example:

```
IF it is raining
THEN take your umbrella to work.
```

A collection of such rules on a particular subject area is called a *knowledge base*. These rules codify the accumulated knowledge and reasoning skills of the human expert, which can then be made available to nonexperts.

Of course, the same result occurs when an expert writes a book. With a book, however, the reader must learn and understand the basic concepts and then apply them to the problem at hand. By contrast, using an expert system is like a consultation with the expert: The user asks the expert a question; the expert then determines what issues are relevant and asks the user for information. The expert then analyzes the problem for the user and provides an answer to the user's ultimate question. An expert system can do this very

quickly, usually in less time than the user would spend searching the index of a book. Using an expert system, a practicing lawyer or a paralegal can analyze legal problems as well as or better than the leading human legal experts in the field and can do so more consistently and often faster than the system's human counterpart.[8]

Limits of Expert Systems

Although expert systems appear intelligent and can be very impressive in actual use, there are limits to their capabilities. They generally do not learn from experience. They do not truly *understand* their rules, so they do not know how and when to break them. They sometimes have difficulty recognizing "hard" cases. Perhaps most important, they do not know when they have exceeded the limits of their expertise. For this reason, expert systems are most profitably employed by lawyers who are either knowledgeable in the subject domain or sufficiently experienced to recognize when the system, like a newly admitted lawyer, has exceeded its expertise. As one commentator has observed:[9]

> No matter how much expertise has been programmed into an expert system, the person using the system must have substantial knowledge in the area of law in order to use it properly; practice support systems have not reduced practicing law to "something done with the push of a button"....

Classes of Expert Systems for Lawyers

There are many kinds of expert systems. Although they all use the same underlying principles, they have different goals and produce different results. Expert systems for lawyers include the following:

- *Document assembly systems* produce legal documents such as pleadings, settlement agreements, contracts, wills, and loan documents. Given a particular set of facts, these systems require only minutes to draft legal documents that take hours or days to produce by hand or with a simple word processor.
- *Diagnostic systems* analyze statutory or case law in the context of a given fact situation, diagnose the legal consequences of certain acts, or forecast the likely effect of changes in legislation. The Latent Damage System, for example, is a diagnostic

legal expert system. Given a fact pattern involving latent damage, the system determines the date after which an action is time barred.[10]

- *Planning systems* analyze alternate courses of action to determine which one will produce an optimal result. For example, TAXADVISOR helps lawyers conduct estate and tax planning for clients with large estates. Given a factual scenario, the system suggests how the client might best order his or her affairs, including what insurance to buy, and whether to establish a trust, make inter-vivos gifts, and so on.[11]

- *Monitoring systems* monitor legal databases for new rulings affecting the lawyer or his or her clients. For example, LRS helps lawyers monitor new caselaw and statutes affecting the law of negotiable instruments.[12]

- *Retrieval systems* provide intelligent search tools to help lawyers use legal databases effectively. FLEXICON, for example, is an intelligent search system designed to locate relevant case law and statutes without using traditional key word search techniques. Instead, the system automatically analyzes every case for key concepts. It does this by examining the cases and statutes cited by the judge as well as the text of the opinion. It uses this analysis to build a conceptual profile of the case and then adds the case to a concept-oriented index of all cases in the database.[13]

- *Case management systems* organize case information, estimate case value, and suggest tactics and strategies for settlement and trial.

- *Procedural guides* assist lawyers in meeting the procedural requirements of statutory and case law.[14] For example, Power Sale[15] is a commercially available mortgage foreclosure system. It helps the lawyer take an action through the foreclosure process, making sure that all procedural requirements and deadlines are met. It also generates all pleadings, correspondence, client status reports, service instructions, and other documentation needed to manage a foreclosure litigation practice.

- *Intelligent checklists* assist lawyers in auditing or reviewing compliance with legal regulations.[16]

THE HEARSAY RULE ADVISOR

The Hearsay Rule Advisor predicts whether a particular hearsay statement will be admissible at trial under an exception to the hearsay rule. The system was developed by Marilyn T. MacCrimmon, a leading Canadian authority on the law of evidence and a professor at the University of British Columbia, and by Susan J. Blackman, an LL.M. candidate at the same university. They have successfully implemented a prototype, and their test results indicate that the system correctly predicts hearsay exception rulings consistent with the decided case law.[17] Efforts are now underway to locate funds to expand and refine the system so that trial judges and counsel may use it in the courtroom during actual trial proceedings.

The Hearsay Rule Advisor contains a database of cases that address when and under what circumstances a particular hearsay statement will be admissible. The system is designed to base its conclusion on an analysis of the cases in its database. Upon reaching a conclusion, the system lists the grounds that support its findings and those that may work against it. The system also offers a list of citations to cases that support its conclusion. The user can select any case on the list, and the system provides a summary of the facts and holding of that case.

Trial counsel can use this system to explore in advance of trial how a particular hearsay statement can be admitted or excluded. As well, counsel can use the list of case authorities to marshal arguments for or against admission. Because the system provides objective information, it can also predict the arguments of opposing counsel. This gives trial counsel an opportunity to evaluate the strengths and weaknesses of his or her opponent's likely arguments in advance of trial.

How It Works

To the user, the Hearsay Rule Advisor operates like any other expert system. First, it gathers relevant facts by asking the user various questions about the nature of the hearsay statement and the surrounding circumstances. The following screen shots depict part of a dialogue between a user and the system in a hypothetical case involving the dying declaration exception to the hearsay rule. Judy is the name of the person who made the hearsay statement (the *declarant*). Note that the user's responses to the system's

FIGURE 5.12 Dialogue with Hearsay Rule Advisor

```
Are you able to produce Judy in court to testify?
     yes
     no
HRA >no

Why is she unavailable
     1.dead
     2.other
HRA >1

What type of proceedings are you involved in?
     1.civil
     2.criminal
HRA >2

Was the death of Judy the subject of the charge?
     yes
     no
HRA >yes

Was the statement made after the injuries occurred?
     yes
     no
HRA >yes

Does the statement identify the person who caused Judy's death?
     yes
     no
HRA >yes

Does the statement reflect facts (as opposed to being opinion)?
     yes
     no
HRA >yes

Into which category would you place the injuries:
     1.  multiple wounds with heavy external bleeding, death in minutes to
     hours - short time.
     2.  one or few wound(s) with little external bleeding, death in hours to
     days - slower death
     3.  all other injuries - e.g.. drowning, poisoning, wounds from a fist
     fight, complications for an illegal operation. Little or no external
     evidence of injuries, rapid or slow death.
HRA >1

Did Judy indicate she believed she was dying?
     1.  she stated positively that she was dying. e.g.. I am dying, I shall go,
     (to spouse) You are about to lose your wife.
     2.  she said she was dying but qualified that belief so as to indicate it
     was not absolute - e.g., I think I am dying, Remove me or I shall die of
     cold.
     3.  other words or actions - e.g., asking for a priest, making a will,
     providing for children.
     4.  no indication she believed she was dying.
HRA >1

Did a doctor tell her that she was dying?
     yes
     no
HRA >no

Did people around her believe she was dying (do not include the doctor)?
     1.yes
     2.no
     3.information-unavailable
HRA >1
```

FIGURE 5.13 Conclusion

```
I have concluded that the facts of your case match evidence that is almost
always admissible under the dying declaration exception to the hearsay rule.
This is because the following factors are present in your case-
* The declarant's death was the subject of the charge.
* The declarant was actually dying at the time the statement was made.
* The statement concerns the cause of the declarant's death.
* The declarant would have been competent to testify in court.
* The statement concerns facts.

and because the declarant had a settled, hopeless expectation of death which is
shown by-
* Multiple injuries, heavy bleeding, rapid death.
* The declarant stated positively s/he was dying.
* Bystanders believed the declarant was dying.


The following factors may work against you:
 * No doctor told the declarant s/he was dying.

Would you like to see the cases that support my decision?
    yes
    no
HRA >
```

FIGURE 5.14 Supporting Cases and Their Citations

Dying Declaration

```
Debortoli v. The King
  [1926] SCR 492

Nembhard v. The Queen
  [1982] 1 All ER 183 (JC PC)

R. v. Bernadotti
  (1869) 11 Cox CC 316 (Manchester Assizes)

R. v. Davidson
  (1898) 30 NSR 349 (NS CA)

R. v. Giovanzzi
  (1919) 16 OWN 291 (Ont. Div. Ct., App. Div.)

R. v. McIntosh
  [1937] 4 DLR 478 (BC CA)

R. v. Mulligan
  (1973) 23 CRNS 1 (Ont. SC)
```

Enter Command (F1 for help)

questions appear immediately following the "HRA >" prompt. (See Figure 5.12.)

Based on the facts gathered in the interview, the system reaches a conclusion on whether the statement will be admissible under the hearsay rule. When it reveals its conclusion it also offers to display the supporting cases. For example, based on the facts shown above (and other facts),

the Hearsay Rule Advisor concluded as shown in Figure 5.13.

If the user asks to see the supporting cases, the system displays a list of the cases and their citations as shown in Figure 5.14.

The system can display a summary of the facts and holding of each case on the list. A case summary is shown in Figure 5.15.

FIGURE 5.15 Case Summary

Debortoli v. The King

> The deceased was injured on 27 November 1925 and was admitted to hospital suffering from a "severe wound". She made a declaration on January 8, 1926, and signed it. The declaration stated that the wound was inflicted by the accused with a knife. At the time of this statement she did not have a settled hopeless expectation of death. On January 15, one day before she died, a police detective asked her if her previous statement was true. The previous statement was read to her, and when it was over she made a mark, as she was too weak to sign it.
>
> The Appeal was dismissed, and the declaration was held to be admissible. The fact that the declaration of January 15 was identical to the one that she made one week earlier when she did not know that she was going to die is a factor that affects only the weight of the statement or its credibility, but does not affect its admissibility.
>
> HELD: The declaration was admissible.

Enter Command (F1 for help)

The Hearsay Rule Advisor is remarkable because it captures the expertise of a legal expert, a professor of the law of evidence, and places it within reach of the average lawyer in an easily manageable form. It is even more remarkable that the system can justify its analysis by citing and giving summaries of the actual cases most likely to govern a given fact pattern.

What distinguishes the Hearsay Rule Advisor from other legal expert systems is its structure and the manner in which it reaches its conclusion. It does so in a series of steps. First, the knowledge of the expert was plumbed to develop a list of those factors the expert deemed relevant to admissibility under the decided case law. These factors became the questions to which the program requests answers in its dialogue with the user.

Second, each reported case (except test cases purposely omitted) was examined for each factor and a profile of the case was created. A case profile consisted of a list of the factors and the corresponding answers for the particular case.

Third, a table listing each of the factors for all of the cases was created. Each case's profile was entered into the table. Figure 5.16 shows part of a sample table.

Fourth, the entire table was entered into a database. Fifth, a summary of each case was entered into the system. Sixth, the case summaries were cross-indexed with the table of cases.

The Hearsay Rule Advisor uses an expert system to apply the information in the database to the facts at hand. It does so by gathering facts from the user to develop a profile of the user's case. This profile is compared to the profiles of the cases in the database. The system finds cases where evidence similar to the user's was admissible and those where it was not. This comparison permits the program to calculate the likelihood of admissibility.

As new cases are decided, their profiles can be added to the database. Shifts in the standards for admissibility reflected in the case law will likewise be reflected in the database of cases and in the system's analysis of those cases. This technique enhances the maintainability of the system and thereby provides a partial solution to the perennial problem of keeping the system's expertise up to date.

THE SYSTEM FOR ASBESTOS LITIGATION ("SAL")

With over 21 million exposures to asbestos, the prospect of over 200,000 related deaths, and the avalanche of lawsuits stemming from those exposures, the Rand Corporation undertook to develop an expert system to evaluate for settlement purposes an asbestos injury claim. The re-

FIGURE 5.16 Sample Table

NO.[1]	INJ.[2]	DEC-BEL[3]	DEC-TOLD[4]	A-D[5]	BY-BEL[6]	SHE[7]	VERDICT[8]
6	1	1	N		U	Y	GUILTY
27	1	1	N		O	Y	GUILTY
22	1	N	N		O	Y	GUILTY
31	1	N	N		O	Y	GUILTY
18	2	3	Y	A	DR	Y	U
19	1	2	Y	A	DR	Y	GUILTY
9	2	2	N		DR&O	Y	U
13	1	1	N		U	Y	GUILTY
15	1	1	Y	A	DR&O	Y	GUILTY
25	1	N	Y	A	DR	Y	GUILTY
3	2	1	Y		DR	Y	GUILTY
1	2?	2	Y	A	U	Y	U
24	2	1	N		U	Y	NOT G
8	3	3	Y	A	DR	Y	GUILTY
20	3	1	Y	A	DR&O	Y	U
26	3	1	Y	A	DR	Y	GUILTY
40	1	1	N		O	Y	GUILTY
30	2	1	N		DR&O	Y	NOT G
41	3	1	N		Y	Y	NOT G
43	2	1	N		U	Y	GUILTY
45	1	1	N		O	Y	GUILTY
47	2	1	Y		DR&O	Y	GUILTY
10	3	1	Y	A	DR&O	Y	U
48	2	1	Y		DR&O	Y	GUILTY
54	3	1	Y	A	DR	Y	GUILTY
51	3	1	N		U	Y	GUILTY
57	2	1	N		U	Y	GUILTY
46	2	1	N		DR&O	Y	GUILTY
56	1	1	Y	A	DR	Y	GUILTY
55	3	1	Y?		U	Y	NOT G

U means unknown

1. The case number.
2. Type of injuries: 1 - multiple injuries, heavy bleeding, rapid death; 2 - one injury, little bleeding, slower death; 3 - other, e.g., complications from an illegal operation, poison, drowning.
3. Declarant's belief that she was dying: 1 -she stated positively she was dying; 2 - she said she was dying but qualified it; 3 - she otherwise indicated she believed she was dying; N - no indication she believed she was dying.
4. A doctor told the declarant she was dying: Y - yes; N - no.
5. The declarant acknowledged the doctor telling her she was dying: A - agreed; D - denied.
6. Bystanders believed the declarant was dying: DR - doctor believed; O - others believed.
7. Court concluded settled, hopeless expectation of death: Y - yes; N - no.
8. The verdict in the case.

sult was the System For Asbestos Litigation (SAL), an expert system that calculates the dollar value of an asbestos claim, developed under the direction of Dr. Donald A. Waterman. A prototype that demonstrated the viability of the system was successfully implemented.[18]

SAL's Features

SAL was designed to help lawyers and insurance adjusters evaluate claims from asbestos exposure. The system considered only a single disease, asbestosis, and a single class of claimants, insulators, to promote equitable early settlements. The system was based on the expertise of lawyers handling such claims in Cleveland, Ohio, and it incorporated knowledge about the medical issues of asbestosis. In all, SAL included rules addressing the following issues in varying degrees of depth:

- *Losses suffered:* SAL considered the medical damages suffered by the plaintiff by reason of the asbestos exposure, based on

FIGURE 5.17 SAL Rules

```
IF      (the plaintiff is not working
        or the plaintiff is working part time
        or the plaintiff's job-status is reduced
        or (the plaintiff is retired
                and the plaintiff's age is less than 65))
        and ((the plaintiff's pulmonary function test does not
                show "serious restrictive disease"
                and the plaintiff is not diagnosed with
                an obstructive lung disease)
            or the plaintiff's pulmonary-function-test does
                show "severe restrictive disease")
        and the plaintiff's activities are restricted,

Conclude that the plaintiff is partially disabled by
        asbestosis is TRUE.
```

symptoms and medical laboratory tests, the primary focus of SAL's analysis. SAL also took into account special damages such as medical expenses and general damages for loss of physical capacity and so on.

- *Liability:* SAL assessed the plaintiff's history of exposure to asbestos but made no attempt to address liability issues on a broader scale.
- *Plaintiff's responsibility:* SAL also considered whether the plaintiff must be allocated some part of the responsibility for his injury as a result of, e.g., smoking, knowledge of the risk, etc.
- *Case characteristics:* To a limited degree SAL adjusted for personal characteristics of the plaintiff such as age.

SAL was written so that lawyers who used it could understand its rules, since lawyer acceptance of SAL's results hinged on whether SAL adequately explained how it reached the settlement figure and what rules it considered in doing so. To meet that concern, SAL incorporated an "explanation facility" that allowed it to explain its reasoning and results. As a result, SAL rules are very readable, as Figure 5.17 reveals.

SAL's Future

The System for Asbestos Litigation showed great promise in helping resolve large numbers of asbestos cases. It reached the stage of a fully operational research prototype. Regrettably, the untimely death of Dr. Waterman, the driving force behind SAL, led the Rand Corporation to abandon the project.

THE EPSILON PROGRAM

EPSILON (ExPert System in the Law Of Negligence) is a set of expert systems and databases that each address issues in tort cases. The systems are part of the FLAIR (Faculty of Law Artificial Intelligence Research) project under the direction of Professor J. C. Smith, a leading authority in tort law and jurisprudence in the common law world and executive director of the IBM Center for Law and Computers, a nonprofit research center located at the University of British Columbia's law school.

The EPSILON program has several components that perform a variety of functions, ranging from evaluation of the plaintiff's cause of action to forecasting the damages awarded by a trial court hearing an automobile accident case claiming soft tissue injuries to the plaintiff's neck or back.

Some components of the EPSILON system are actually in use by judges and trial lawyers in ongoing litigation. Studies now under way will gauge the effectiveness of the systems in speeding the resolution of tort claims short of trial.

The Nervous Shock Advisor

The initial work on the EPSILON system began in 1986 with the Nervous Shock Advisor (NSA). This expert system determines whether a plaintiff has a cause of action for nervous shock, also known as *emotional distress* and *post-traumatic stress disorder*.

In arriving at its conclusions, the system considers whether the plaintiff personally suffered any injuries, the relationship of the plaintiff to other victims, the proximity of the plaintiff to other victims at the time of the injury, and so on.

FIGURE 5.18 Whiplash Database Help Screen

```
┌─────────────────────────────────────────────────────────────────┐
│  ABOUT THE WHIPLASH DATABASE                                      │
│ ─────────────────────────────────────────────────────────────    │
│                                                                   │
│      The Whiplash Database contains hundreds of reported and      │
│      unreported soft-tissue injury cases decided in British       │
│      Columbia courts since 1985.  The Database is continually     │
│      updated and reflects the most recent trends in this area     │
│      of the law.                                                  │
│                                                                   │
│      The four main divisions under which you may conduct your     │
│      search of the Database are:                                  │
│                                                                   │
│          Non-pecuniary damages (pain and suffering awards)        │
│          Past and future income loss                              │
│          Symptoms (specific medical conditions)                   │
│          Specific damages issues (e.g., thin skull, mitigation)   │
│                                                                   │
│      Cases relevant to your inquiry may be retrieved from the     │
│      Database by specifying various search parameters under each  │
│      of these divisions.  More information on Database searches    │
│      and case retrieval is available from the Help System at the  │
│      Database Menu.                                               │
│                                                                   │
│                                                      HELP INDEX   │
│ ─────────────────────────────────────────────────────────────    │
│  ESC: exit; ENTER: select highlighted topic; F1: Index           │
└─────────────────────────────────────────────────────────────────┘
```

Based on the information provided, the Nervous Shock Advisor determines whether the plaintiff has a cause of action and provides the basis for its determination.

The Nervous Shock Advisor then offers to furnish the cases upon which it relied in reaching its decision. If the user asks to see the cases, a list is displayed on the computer screen. The user can review a summary of each case, including excerpts from the actual decision.

The system next offers a list of cases relating to the symptoms of the plaintiff (as determined in the dialogue between the computer and the user). After that, the system suggests what arguments may be most effective in defending against nervous shock claims and offers to display a list of cases where the defense was successful. Finally, the system can display the full text of the leading case on a particular topic to familiarize the user with the legal principles involved.

The Whiplash Database

Starting in 1988 the FLAIR team produced the Whiplash Database containing current British Columbia judgments awarding damages for whiplash cases (case involving soft tissue injury to the neck or back). Note that in British Colum-

bia nearly every whiplash case is decided by a judge and without a jury; in perhaps half of these cases, the judge issues a written decision. The database contains summaries of all written and oral judgments entered, both reported and unreported, since January 1985.

The Whiplash Database provides users with quick, up-to-date, and easy to understand information about the damages awarded for pain and suffering in whiplash cases. The system also provides summaries of closely matched cases in support of specific whiplash claims. Users search the database from a menu-driven, multiwindow interface that includes hypertext links to help screens. Figure 5.18 shows a sample help screen.

The system allows the user to retrieve cases by specifying general search parameters such as age, gender, and occupation of the plaintiff; recovery period and severity of injury; identity of the judge; medical conditions common to soft-tissue injury; legal issues relevant to the calculation of whiplash damages; and various types of pretrial and future-income loss indicators. Figure 5.19 shows the initial entry point where a user sets search criteria for a pain and suffering case.

By positioning the cursor anywhere the word *ALL* appears, the user produces either a menu or a hypertext help screen. For example, notice

FIGURE 5.19 Initial Entry Screen

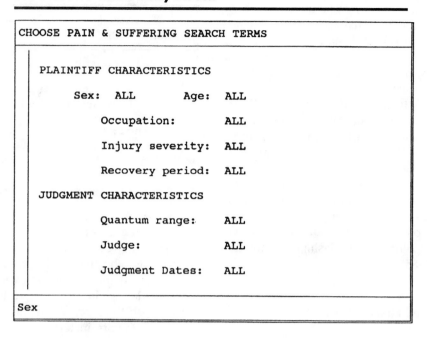

```
┌─────────────────────────────────────────────────┐
│ CHOOSE PAIN & SUFFERING SEARCH TERMS             │
│  ┌                                               │
│  │   PLAINTIFF CHARACTERISTICS                   │
│  │                                               │
│  │        Sex:  ALL         Age:   ALL           │
│  │                                               │
│  │             Occupation:         ALL           │
│  │                                               │
│  │             Injury severity:    ALL           │
│  │                                               │
│  │             Recovery period:    ALL           │
│  │                                               │
│  │   JUDGMENT CHARACTERISTICS                    │
│  │                                               │
│  │             Quantum range:      ALL           │
│  │                                               │
│  │             Judge:              ALL           │
│  │                                               │
│  │             Judgment Dates:     ALL           │
│  │                                               │
│ ─────────────────────────────────────────────── │
│ Sex                                              │
└─────────────────────────────────────────────────┘
```

FIGURE 5.20 Menu Listing All Judges

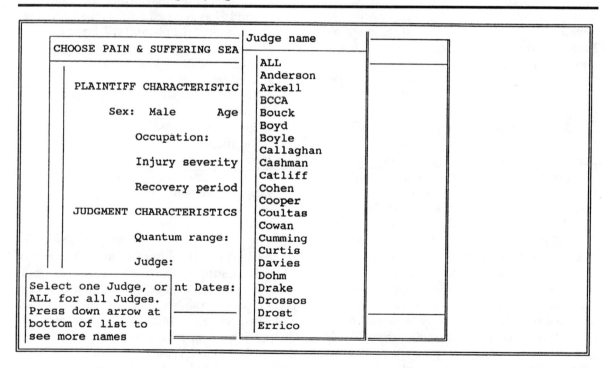

```
                              ┌ Judge name ─────┐
┌─ CHOOSE PAIN & SUFFERING SEA │                 │ ┌─────┐
│ ┌───────────────────────────│ ALL             │ │     │
│ │                            │ Anderson        │ │     │
│ │   PLAINTIFF CHARACTERISTIC │ Arkell          │ │     │
│ │                            │ BCCA            │ │     │
│ │      Sex:  Male      Age   │ Bouck           │ │     │
│ │                            │ Boyd            │ │     │
│ │             Occupation:    │ Boyle           │ │     │
│ │                            │ Callaghan       │ │     │
│ │             Injury severity│ Cashman         │ │     │
│ │                            │ Catliff         │ │     │
│ │             Recovery period│ Cohen           │ │     │
│ │                            │ Cooper          │ │     │
│ │   JUDGMENT CHARACTERISTICS │ Coultas         │ │     │
│ │                            │ Cowan           │ │     │
│ │             Quantum range: │ Cumming         │ │     │
│ │                            │ Curtis          │ │     │
│ │             Judge:         │ Davies          │ │     │
│ ┌──────────────────────────┐│ Dohm            │ │     │
│ │ Select one Judge, or     ││nt Dates:  Drake  │ │     │
│ │ ALL for all Judges.      ││ Drossos         │ │     │
│ │ Press down arrow at      ││─── Drost        │ │     │
│ │ bottom of list to        ││ Errico          │ │     │
│ │ see more names           ││                 │ │     │
│ └──────────────────────────┘└─────────────────┘ └─────┘
```

the entry for *Judge*. By placing the cursor on this item and pressing a key, the user displays a menu listing all judges, as shown in Figure 5.20.

With this feature the litigants can search the awards of the trial judge assigned to their case. Note that *BCCA* in the list of judges refers not to a trial judge but to the British Columbia Court of Appeals. This restriction can limit the search to those cases reviewed on appeal.

Once the user finalizes the search criteria and retrieves the cases, the system offers to provides a report. These reports summarize the cases and display the number of cases retrieved, their average pain and suffering award, the inflation adjusted average, and the range of awards involved. A sample report is shown in Figure 5.21.

The user can then request a more detailed report. Several levels of detail are available. Figure 5.22 is the simplest of these reports. If the user requests, more detail can be furnished on any particular case.

The FLAIR team placed a copy of the Whiplash Database in the Vancouver Judges' Library for ongoing consultation by the judiciary. In response to requests from lawyers who learned of the system by word of mouth, it provided a duplicate of the database at the Vancouver Barristers' Library. In 1992, a number of copies were licensed for use by automobile insurance adjusters. The Whiplash Database now contains over 1,200 British Columbia whiplash judgments dating back to 1985.

The Whiplash Expert System

The FLAIR team is now integrating several expert system components with the Whiplash Database to form the Whiplash Expert System. This system produces a complete medical characterization of the plaintiff's soft tissue injury case and then, based on the reported case law, performs a legal evaluation of the medical evidence.

A medical doctor with expertise in soft-tissue injuries to the neck or back will help to develop the medical element of the system. Using the doctor's medical knowledge, the medical expert system component asks the user a series of questions relating to the plaintiff's symptoms. From the user's responses, the system develops search criteria and searches the Whiplash Database for cases involving similar symptoms.

Judges and leading trial lawyers practicing in the subject area will help in the development of the legal element. Based on the cases found in response to the medical evaluation of the case, the system's legal component arrives at a single and specific dollar value likely to be awarded to the victim at trial. By contrast, the original Whiplash Database provided only a range of the dollar value of the victim's injuries based on a statistical analysis of the reported cases.

The Whiplash Expert System component of EPSILON is nearing the final stages of a workable prototype. The FLAIR team hopes to test the system in actual settlement conferences and various alternative dispute resolution environments in the near term.

FIGURE 5.21 Sample Report

```
SEARCH RESULTS

  Total records:  8 / 643

    Mean quantum:  $ 8,312
    Inflation-adjusted:  $ 8,989

    Range:  $ 4,000 - $ 20,000
```

The Loss-of-Future-Earnings System

The FLAIR team has begun work on a new expert system component of EPSILON to evaluate a plaintiff's claim for lost future earnings. Two economists who frequently serve as expert witnesses at trial are the domain experts.

Calculating damages for future earnings is complex, so the system must take into account a number of factors, including:

1. The average annual income the plaintiff would have earned but for the injury, less the amount the plaintiff will be able to earn.
2. The period of the loss.
3. Contingencies.
4. The discount rate (for inflation and interest).
5. Expenses incurred in earning income.
6. Taxation.
7. Fringe benefits and pensions.
8. Postretirement income.
9. Spare-time activity.

FLAIR's loss of future earnings expert system estimates a plaintiff's prospective loss of income based on all relevant factors. The user of the system supplies basic information, such as the plaintiff's gender, age, education level, occupation, prior earnings, projected period of loss, and prospective earnings. The system then produces a printed report that contains, among other things, the amount claimable as lost future earnings and the details of how that amount was calculated.

CONCLUSION

Although many of the tools described in this chapter were developed by academic or research

FIGURE 5.22 The Simplest Report

```
SCREEN PREVIEW:      Records 1 - 8 / 8

Thu Apr 19 15:52          EPSILON WHIPLASH DATABASE              PAGE#  01
                            NON-PECUNIARY DAMAGES
            * = whiplash not primary injury or other injuries included

QUANTUM   SEVERITY   DISABILITY        CASE           JUDGMENT   BCD CITATION
                      PERIOD                           DATE

   4,000  mild       1 month    Viel v. Taylor      Jan 25/88 [1988] 3333-01
   4,000  not spec.  1 month    Sharp v. Hirji      Feb 23/89 not yet avail.
   6,000  moderate   6 months   Howard v. Meixner   Jan 29/85 [1985] 3399-07
   7,000  not spec.  3 months   Preston v. Pickwell Sep 14/88 [1988] 3398-32
   7,000  mild       3-4 mos.   Dhillon v. Pilkey   Nov 25/88 [1989] 3398-02
   7,500  moderate   3-4 mos.   Williams v. Genovese Jan 20/87 [1987] 3398-20
                                   (1)
  11,000  moderate   5 months   Mikulic v. Schnepf  Oct 10/85 [1985] 3399-32
  20,000  moderate   > 3 mos.   Drake v. Stevenot   Jan 04/89 [1989] 3399-32




F10/PgDn: Next page   PgUp: Prev page   ESC: Output Menu
```

institutions, corporate and private sector lawyers have begun developing and using similar tools in their daily practice. For example, Fulbright and Jaworski, a large Houston law firm, has an expert system to help with case management. Although it began as a docket system, the system now provides expert advice on matters such as venue motions. Among other things, it contains information on the characteristics and prejudices of judges and juries in various Texas counties. Using the system, a litigator can determine what venue is most likely to prove favorable for hearing the case at hand.[19]

Litigation is fiercely competitive. Litigators are continually searching for techniques and tools that may give them an edge. Though the tools discussed here can provide significant competitive advantages, they are costly and time-consuming to develop. Lawyers who use them do so to obtain a competitive edge; hence, they may be unwilling to provide the kind of detail contained in this chapter. Even so, awareness of and interest in such tools is rising dramatically, as evidenced by the explosive growth of the ABA's Document Assembly Interest Group. This group expanded from a handful of lawyers in 1987 to several thousand in 1991.[20]

In addition to the direct competitive benefits, expert systems may also offer indirect benefits of great consequence to private law firms. It is no longer uncommon for a lawyer to move from one firm to another or to strike out on his or her own. Such lawyers take their form files with them and set up shop elsewhere, none the worse for the move. As firms begin to develop their own expert systems, however, a lawyer who leaves the firm will be unable to take with him or her a copy of the firm's proprietary software.

This limitation may have two important effects. First, a lawyer whose practice relies heavily on such tools may be reluctant to attempt practice without them or to join another firm that lacks comparable tools. Second, firms that have these tools may find that they are more attractive to law students and to lawyers considering a move. This attractiveness may stabilize those firms whose practice is highly automated in ways that cannot be readily duplicated.

Expert systems and intelligent databases offer lawyers an opportunity to practice law more efficiently and effectively than ever before. Until recently, the legal profession has largely ignored this technology. Firms that have begun to explore it report astonishing results. Many other firms, especially those seeking world-class status, are now embracing this technology and devoting significant resources to developing it. The great law firms of tomorrow will be those that employ this technology today as a strategic tool for ensuring their long term growth and prosperity.

ENDNOTES

1. The major accounting firms developed and use large expert systems as strategic tools for gaining a competitive advantage in their work. Keyes, Jessica, "AI in the Big Six," *AI Expert*, May 1990.

2. Richard E. Susskind, "Lawyers Fail to Plead the Full Case for Computers' Potential,"*Financial Times (London)*, February 19, 1990.

3. Mark D. Tamminga, "A Case Study in Legal Automation." In Proceedings, ABA National Institute on Computers as Your Expert Partner, American Bar Association, 1990.

4. Charles E. Pear, Jr., "Expert Systems and the Race For Clients." In *Technological Evolution of the Legal Profession: Computers as Your Expert Partner* (American Bar Association, 1988).

5. Steven S. Weiner, "CACE: Computer-Assisted Case Evaluation in the Brooklyn District Lawyer's Office." In *Proceedings of the Second International Conference on Artificial Intelligence and Law*, The Association for Computing Machinery, Inc., 1989. See also Damond Benningfield, "Artificial Intelligence: The Mechanical Paralegal." In *Texas Lawyer*, October 30, 1989, sec. 3, p. 12.

6. See Richard E. Susskind, *Expert Systems in Law—A Jurisprudential Inquiry*, London: Clarendon Press, 1987.

7. See Donald A. Waterman, *A Guide to Expert Systems* (Reading, Mass.: Addison Wesley, 1986), p. 3.

8. Susskind, in *Expert Systems* states: "Expert systems are computer programs that have been constructed (with the assistance of a human expert) in such a way that they are capable of functioning at the standard of (and sometimes even at a higher standard than) a human expert" (p. 9).

9. Marjorie A. Miller, "Using Practice Support Systems," *Legal Economics*, May/June 1988.

10. See Richard E. Susskind, "The Latent Damage System: A Jurisprudential Analysis." In *Proceedings of the Second International Conference on Artificial Intelligence and Law*, The Association for Computing Machinery, Inc., 1989.

11. R. Michaelsen, "A Knowledge-based System for Individual Income and Transfer Tax Planning." Ph.D. thesis, University of Illinois, Champaign-Urbana, 1982.

12. Carole D. Hafner, "Representation of Knowledge in a Legal Information Retrieval System." In R. Oddy, S. Robertson, C. van Rijsbergen, and P. Williams (eds.), *Information Retrieval Research* (London: Butterworths & Co., 1981).

13. J. C. Smith and D. Gelbart, "Beyond Boolean Search: FLEXICON, A Legal Text-Based Intelligent System. In *Proceedings, The Third International Conference on Artificial Intelligence and Law*, The Association for Computing Machinery, Inc., 1991.

14. Richard E. Susskind, "Artificial Intelligence: What It Is and How It Will Affect Lawyers." In *Program Book*, 7th Annual PC Strategies for Lawyers, American Bar Association, 1992.

15. Simlaw Systems Ltd. (in Canada: 144 Front St. West, Suite 700, Toronto, Ont. M5J 2L7; (416) 971-8454; fax (416) 971-8456). Or Expertext Inc., 25 East Washington, Suite 600, Chicago, IL 60602; phone: (312) 444-1030 or (800) 387-2625; fax (312) 444-1033).

16. Richard E. Susskind, "Artificial Intelligence: What It Is and How It Will Affect Lawyers."

17. To test the system, a randomly chosen 20 percent of the cases were omitted from the system's database and not used for its design. Upon completion of the working prototype, the facts of the omitted cases were fed into the system and its predictions compared to the court's actual holdings. These tests showed that the system fares well in predicting the outcomes of the test cases. See Marilyn T. MacCrimmon, "Expert Systems in Case-based Law: The Hearsay Rule Advisor." In *Proceedings of the Second International Conference on Artificial Intelligence and Law*, The Association for Computing Machinery, Inc., 1989.

18. J. Paul, D.A. Waterman, M. Peterson, and J.R. Kipps, "SAL: An Expert System for Evaluating Asbestos Claims." In Proceedings, First Australian Artificial Intelligence Congress, 1986.

19. Benningfield, Damond, "Artificial Intelligence."

20. The author is vice-chair of this interest group. Readers interested in joining should contact either the author at the University of British Columbia or, preferably, the staff of the ABA's Section of Law Practice Management at their Chicago offices.

Charles E. Pear, Jr. is the co-chair of the ABA Section of Law Practice Management's Hypermedia Interest Group. He is presently a visiting professor (law and computers) on the Faculty of Law at the University of British Columbia.

Expert Systems: A Replacement for Lawyers?

Thomas H. Gonser

If expert systems are so smart, will we soon put ourselves out of a job? Tom Gonser, one of the pioneers in legal computing and a past administrative leader of the ABA, takes a look at this important issue. He also discusses one of the first legal expert systems, which he developed for Boise Cascade in the 1970s.

For the past decade, lawyers have kept track of their time, billed their clients, kept their accounts, and prepared their documents with computers. Recently, some lawyers have taken the next step—using computers for legal research, for automated litigation support, and even for the production of certain repetitive types of legal documents. Most of these tasks involve looking backward—that is, searching some type of database, finding relevant information, and presenting it to us in whatever form we've specified.

In the coming decade, many lawyers will use computers to look forward—to help analyze legal problems and deliver legal services. Systems available today can draft wills, prepare and file tax returns, and even evaluate litigation issues. Systems available tomorrow may help us practice law.

Do these capabilities mean computers will eventually make legal judgments? Will lawyering skills be replaced by the analytical skills of computers? Should we start looking for new careers? Of course not. Computers can help lawyers improve the quality of the legal services they provide but they will not replace us. Nonetheless, with the present confusion about what a computer can and cannot do, someone is sure to make the argument that computers will replace lawyers. The pace of computer innovation is simply faster than our capacity to understand it.

In this article, I discuss both the potential and the limits of technology in our future legal practice. As I will demonstrate, some of the most promising new computer uses in delivering legal services hardly threaten to replace lawyers, since only lawyers have the skills to use them properly. These innovative technologies will simply become another tool for lawyers to deliver quality legal services efficiently.

USING COMPUTERS TO LOOK FORWARD

Two categories of forward-looking computer applications are proving invaluable to the legal profession. The first is commonly called an *expert system*. This term is the same as *practice system* or *forms generator*. Such a program uses data and predetermined choices to create the documents for a particular transaction. Whole files full of related documents can be generated almost instantly.

A second, and quite different, category of legal software uses computer models. In effect, a computer program emulates the way a lawyer analyzes an issue. While it may sound a bit intimidating, the use of computer models doesn't replace a lawyer's skill; it relies on it. Let's look at each of these two categories of software and see just how Orwellian they really are.

EXPERT SYSTEMS

Anyone who has created a form on a word processor and then filled in the blanks has created the most basic type of expert system. The form can be used again and again, and only the blanks need be considered. But computers have the potential to automate the production of virtually any type of document, transaction, or legal service. Not surprisingly, they can do so in far

Decision Support

Joseph L. Kashi

Once reserved to those with powerful computers and unlimited budgets, computerized decision-making programs are now available to all litigators. With Criterium from Sygenex, (15446 Bel-Red Rd., Suite 450, Redmond, WA 98052, 206-881-5500), a lawyer can easily apply systematic criteria for decision making. The program dissects any issue into discrete, readily understood elements, ranks them, and weighs alternative courses. Because you can reuse and revise the decision tree, you can significantly improve your decision-making process.

Another useful decision support program is BestChoice3, from Sterling Castle (702 Washington St., Suite 174, Marina Del Rey, CA 90292-5598, 800-323-6406).

more sophisticated ways than by merely filling in the blanks of a form.

Perhaps one of the earliest and most easily understood examples is the will-preparation software developed many years ago by Professor James Sprowl, then of the American Bar Foundation and the faculty of Chicago-Kent Law School. Sprowl's program used a high-level language he developed specifically to support expert systems. Unlike a typical form, with blanks to complete, Sprowl's system incorporated a series of questions, the answers to which were later used in the program both to supply the information needed to complete a will and to assist the lawyer in making choices about optional provisions. Not only were options identified, but also the legal consequences of their inclusion or omission.

With the answers provided by the lawyer, the program created a document that incorporated all relevant data and all decisions made by the lawyer with respect to the options presented. The resulting document was both first draft and finished product ready for signature. Instead of making two trips to the lawyer's office, the client could have a finished product in a single visit.

As computers have become more friendly, less costly, and more powerful, more and more of these expert systems have come to market. Any area of law that relies on documentation with a lot of repetition is appropriate for expert system software, regardless of the size or scope of the transaction. Thus any type of pleading, contract, application, or other transaction of a recurring nature can be created by an efficient, accurate expert system.

For those lawyers who take advantage of this potential, the payoff is the delivery of a higher volume of consistently accurate legal services at potentially lower costs to the consumer. This in turn has obvious competitive implications for the delivery of many types of legal services and raises legitimate issues of how legal services might be more appropriately priced in the future.[1]

Because of substantial development costs, larger firms and corporate law departments may be better positioned to develop their own expert systems in-house. Both can use such programs to institutionalize their judgment, their biases, and even their culture. They can also assure that standards of quality are met and monitored throughout the institution by developing their own systems. In contrast, smaller firms and sole practitioners may have to rely on expert systems that have been developed by others. Although this may be likened to relying on a form book, it can be a fundamentally different prospect. While one can read a form and quickly determine whether a particular phrase or clause fits your particular need, you can't ordinarily read a software program to see whether all options have been presented, or even whether the computer has selected the most appropriate ones.

USING COMPUTER MODELS TO EVALUATE LAWSUITS

Having identified expert systems as one category in the process of delivering technological legal services, let's look at a second approach:

using computer models to evaluate lawsuits. While this category has not yet attracted an agreed-upon definition, I call it *computer-assisted legal analysis,* or *CALA.*

There are two essential premises of CALA: (1) a checklist of considerations that a lawyer uses (or should use) in making certain kinds of legal assessments can be identified, and (2) in most cases, a lawyer can express quantitatively an opinion about the impact of such considerations.

As corporate lawyers know, the strategic value of a lawsuit is more than a function of pure economic exposure. Though potential damages are a key issue, one must consider other factors as well, such as the impact the case can have on future cases, potential adverse publicity, the cost of key corporate executives' time spent on the litigation, and the costs of the litigation itself.

COMPUTER ASSISTED LEGAL ANALYSIS AT BOISE CASCADE

In the late 1970s, the legal department of Boise Cascade Corporation developed an experimental computer program, INVALUE, that analyzed the potential economic effects of each lawsuit then pending against it.

INVALUE asked the lawyer/user three types of questions:

1. What is the prospect of winning on the issue of liability and the current estimate of damages should the plaintiff prevail?
2. What is the lawyer's estimate of all costs and expenses that would be incurred should the matter go to trial?
3. What subjective factors are likely to influence settlement decisions? (The lawyer was asked to estimate the impact of such factors on a scale of 1 to 10.)

Since every question requested a numerical answer, expressed in dollars, units of time, percentages, or on a scale of 1 to 10, the program used simple arithmetic to compute a case's value.

INVALUE's purpose was to help the legal department estimate a dollar value representing the total economic impact on the company if the matter were pursued through trial. This estimate provided a more realistic basis for assessing the potential litigation cost to the company than the more traditional "what's it worth" settlement value.

Such a structured system to evaluate all cases in which the client company was a defendant offered numerous benefits:

- In an environment where several lawyers had responsibility for evaluating new lawsuits, it assured a greater consistency in case evaluation.
- The company could establish priorities for its caseload based on the investment value calculated for each lawsuit, thereby ensuring that those cases with the highest value could be attended to commensurately with their potential economic impact.
- By comparing the relationship of all cost factors to the INVALUE computation, an early settlement strategy could be facilitated. For instance, if the cost component of pursuing a case through trial were 90 percent of the computed investment value, an early settlement might be indicated. Conversely, if the total costs were a relatively low percentage, trial might be a preferred option.
- INVALUE provided a new method for communicating with the client. A business executive often has an unrealistic opinion about the value of a lawsuit that challenges his or her particular area of responsibility. However, when confronted with the more objective information that a particular case has an estimated economic impact of $50,000, an earlier, more realistic assessment might be made.

Though INVALUE provided a new way to evaluate the economic impact of a lawsuit on a defendant company, it could not provide the more traditional settlement value of a claim or case. In later years, however, I designed a subsequent version of the program called COMPROWISE to provide this information as well as the corporate cost factors given by INVALUE. The initial provider of the American Bar Association's ABA/net service made COMPROWISE available for experimental use by other lawyers. It is currently being fine-tuned for potential use in law firms. To date, neither INVALUE nor COMPROWISE has been released as a commercial package, although INVALUE has been licensed to third parties, and later versions of COMPROWISE are currently being tested.

UNANSWERED QUESTIONS

As more and more expert systems and computer modeling programs come on the market, we must begin to address a host of new issues that necessarily arise when one lawyer considers using an expert system developed by another. Some of them are:

- Who will be the primary developers of such systems? Will they be practicing lawyers? Law professors? Market vendors?
- Might the creation and marketing of such systems to lawyers constitute the unauthorized practice of law?
- To what extent may a lawyer rely on such systems in delivering legal services? What will be the required standard of care?
- What will the authors of expert systems that malfunction be liable for?
- What role, if any, should bar associations—in particular the ABA—play in evaluating expert systems?
- Will the availability of expert systems invite an entire new generation of do-it-yourself programs for consumers of legal services? What measures would be required to protect the public?

By raising these questions, I do not mean to downplay the potential benefit of expert systems to lawyers and consumers alike. However, until these matters receive the conscious attention of the legal profession, the potential for expert systems will not be fully realized.

CONCLUSION

In developing and using sophisticated programs at Boise Cascade and at the ABA to perform computer assisted legal analysis, we have arrived at certain tentative conclusions:

- Litigation evaluation models lead to a more consistent, structured process for case assessment. For some cases, they provide an early indication of settlement strategy.
- While there is value in an off-the-shelf CALA model, such models can be of even greater value to the lawyer if they are customized. To customize, one adjusts certain values in the program to reflect the value judgments of the lawyer or firm.
- One must remember that the results from a CALA model are only one measure of the value of a claim or lawsuit. They cannot be viewed as scientifically precise. And they most certainly do not replace a lawyer's professional judgment. They are rather another yardstick to complement a lawyer's informed assessment.

From this brief review of the role of current technology in actively assisting professionals in the delivery of legal services, it should be apparent that lawyers need not feel threatened with extinction at the hands of a keyboard and screen. Rather, the proper role of an expert system is to assist lawyers in improving their speed and accuracy in the art of lawyering. The CALA model offers a new tool in the early valuation of claims, perhaps leading to more efficient and more objectively based settlement strategies. However, these new productivity tools will also force us to face squarely a host of difficult and troubling new questions that must be addressed before these tools can be fully integrated into our professional practices.

ENDNOTES

1. How to bill for more efficiently produced work product is treated extensively in *Beyond the Billable Hour: An Anthology of Alternative Billing Methods* and *Win-Win Billing Strategies: Alternatives That Satisfy Your Clients and You*, both edited by Richard Read and published by the ABA's Section of Law Practice Management.

Thomas H. Gonser resides in Friday Harbor, Washington. His firm, T.H. Gonser & Associates, offers consulting services to the legal profession. Mr. Gonser is a former executive vice president of the American Bar Association.

Joseph L. Kashi (side bar) is a sole practitioner living in Soldotna, Alaska. He received his B.S. and M.S. degrees form MIT in 1979 and his J.D. from Georgetown University Law Center in 1976. His practice consists primarily of contract and personal injury litigation.

Appendix
Setting Up an Automated Litigation Office: Practical Considerations for Litigators

Joseph L. Kashi

Throughout this book we have looked at software that can make litigators more productive in their practices. Whether you use outlining software, document assembly techniques, or any of the other available productivity tools, you will see a positive impact on your practice. Lawyers, and especially litigators, have much to gain from using computers in their practice.

So how does one get started? How does a litigator go about setting up his or her office? This appendix takes a first step toward answering those questions, focusing on some of the basic issues to consider. We begin with Arthur Miltz sharing his perspectives on setting up a small IBM-compatible litigation office. As a counterpoint, Ron Crittenden discusses programs to use in a Macintosh-based office. Miltz and Joe Kashi then share their thoughts on peripheral devices and networking issues. The book closes with a few ideas on how to get more help.

This section does not provide a comprehensive look at automation issues, nor does it intend to do so. Setting up an automated office could be the subject of an entire book, and that is not our primary focus. Moreover, computer software and hardware change by the minute, and no book could stay current for more than a short time. We suggest that you view these chapters as a starting point. From the basic issues identified here, you can move forward to focus on your own office's needs and problems. We hope these ancillary chapters will help you get started.

Setting Up an Automated Litigation Office: One Firm's Approach

Arthur Ian Miltz

> Computerizing a litigation practice is a formidable task. While no book can tell you everything you need to know, Arthur Miltz offers some practical tips based on his firm's experience.

In this chapter I'm going to discuss how to set up an automated office for a small litigation firm. I'll give you an overview of the basic types of programs you'll probably need, and I'll talk about other options you may consider. I'll also talk about the software choices I made and the reasons for those choices. Hopefully, my experiences may help you as you move toward automation. Keep in mind that we use IBM and IBM-compatible equipment, and that is what I'll be talking about.

BEGINNING

The first step in setting up an automated litigation office is to choose the software you will use. Although practices and needs vary, most of us should consider several types of programs. They include programs for word processing, for databases, for calendar control and docketing, and for accounting and spreadsheets. (Contact information for the products mentioned in this chapter can be found in the accompanying sidebar.)

WORD PROCESSING

Word processing is the backbone of any law office computer system, so give considerable thought to choosing your word processing software. Is most of what you do correspondence? How much of it is briefs? How badly do you need the capability for automated footnoting on each page? How much of your work is pleadings or lengthy agreements? How much of your work is repetitive, with only a small part of a document changed from case to case?

How comfortable is your typing staff likely to be with computers? Talk to them—it's important, and a big help, to have their input into all of this. They probably have a much better idea than you about the real answers to the types of questions I've suggested. For that matter, what kind of staff situation do you have? Do you have high turnover? Are you likely to have an ongoing need for new people to learn the word processor you choose?

Consider compatibility and program updating. Most word processing programs are not compatible with one another. If you need to exchange word processing files with clients or colleagues, find out what programs they use and include that information in your decision-making process.

Word processing programs, like most others, are periodically updated. The more popular programs that have a large base of users are likely to be updated more often. However, each upgrade can be expensive and will require time to learn to use its new features. Whatever programs you choose, make sure you really need the new features being offered before you decide to purchase an upgraded version.

Other Word Processing Features

Many word processors include spelling checkers. Some also have a thesaurus, where you are offered a choice of synonyms (and perhaps antonyms as well). This can be especially useful if you do any substantial brief writing or other narrative-style writing. Word processors may also have a redlining feature—the ability to compare different versions of a document and indicate the changes between them. If your work involves a lot of drafting, this is a valuable feature to consider. (There are also separate programs you can buy that just do the redlining.)

Explore the capability of your word processor (together with whatever printer you choose) to print envelopes and large mailing labels. Some make this hard; others make it very easy. This is especially important if you choose a laser printer.

The range of available features goes on and on. I could not possibly discuss anywhere near all of them, and you really will not have enough time to analyze them all in deciding what you need. That is why you should start with an analysis of your own needs, rather than with an analysis of the features of any particular program. Once you have done so, you can begin to look into word processing programs and decide which you want. The same types of questions should be asked in connection with each type of program you consider.

Leading Word Processing Programs

There are a number of word processing programs on the market. The leader, by far, is WordPerfect. Microsoft Word and Word for Windows are gaining ground and are always favorably reviewed. You may also want to consider AmiPro by Lotus, WordStar, or MultiMate.

Our Word Processing Choice

For many years we used a simple word processing program called Volkswriter (Volkswriter Deluxe Plus, to be precise). Although my fondness for Volkswriter was partly nostalgia, since I "grew up" in computers with it, there are many good things to recommend it.

Unfortunately, the company recently went out of business and the program is no longer available. But many of the reasons I liked it are things to look for in any word processing program you may consider. It was relatively inexpensive and did everything we needed—not everything some of the other, more powerful programs could do, but everything *we* needed. Above all, it was easy to learn and use. Any reasonably intelligent and motivated secretary, paralegal, law clerk, or lawyer could learn to be productive on it in only a few hours. Sophistication would take longer, but at least they were up and running.

It wasn't state of the art, nor industry-standard, but it was right for us. In the sidebar to this chapter, I have listed several good, currently available, and widely used commercial word processing programs that are popular with lawyers. Keep these considerations in mind and choose the one that is right for you.

DESKTOP PUBLISHING

Desktop publishing relates closely to word processing, but focuses on presentation rather than content. Desktop publishing software allows you to produce forms, newsletters, and even letterhead using a variety of type styles, sizes, and layouts. I know one firm that no longer uses an outside printing company for its letterhead—the letterhead is printed on the first page of every letter along with the letter itself.

A detailed description of desktop publishing software is beyond the scope of this article. You should know, however, that many word processors, such as WordPerfect and Microsoft Word, incorporate desktop publishing features. You may find that your word processor has all the desktop publishing power that you will ever need.

Leading Programs

There are several popular desktop publishing programs worth considering. Two of the leaders are Ventura Publisher and Aldus PageMaker.

DATABASE PROGRAMS

A database program is an extremely valuable tool, and should be part of every law office. Briefly, a database program manages and sorts large amounts of data in various ways and provides you with reports, either on your computer screen or printed out on paper. You can think of it as a collection of file cards. You put various items of information on each card and store it in the computer. Then, when you want to find something, or want a list of the cards in a certain order, the computer sorts them for you very rapidly without missing anything. The speed and accuracy with which computers perform such tasks is one of the main reasons they have become such valuable tools.

Litigation-Specific Databases

There are a number of litigation databases marketed for lawyers that you may want to consider. They keep comprehensive information about each of your cases. For example, personal injury litigation databases may contain complete identifying information about the parties and counsel, a description of the event, statute of limitations data, identification of the attorney working on the file, full listings of medical expenses, lost earnings and other "specials," data about legal costs, information about the status of discovery and experts, and much other relevant, important data.

These programs are useful to have once all the data is in them, but they also require a lot of staff time to input the initial data and to keep it current and up to date. You must decide whether the time and expense of maintaining such a program is worth its benefits. If you have such a program and don't keep it up to date it becomes worse than useless—it becomes dangerous. Databases of this type may require a "dedicated" operator, whose full-time job is maintaining and updating the information in the database.

Leading Programs

There are a number of programs to consider in this category. Several of the leaders are PINS, LawBase, PLEAS, Legal Edge, CaseMaster III, and Mitratech. Prices vary and each has different strengths and weaknesses. Before buying, consider whether a particular program fits your needs.

Our Database Choice

I decided against using the more comprehensive litigation database programs because I didn't feel they were worth the time and effort required to input the information. Instead, I chose a simple, shareware database program called PC-File+. PC-File+ has been updated; the current version is PC-File 6.5.

PC-File does things very quickly and it is very user friendly. You don't have to learn arcane commands and instructions. If you take the time to read the instructions on the screen at each stage, using it is very simple. In fact, in our office the database is maintained by a paralegal who had no computer experience before she came to us. We showed her how to access the program and a little bit about how it works, she read part of the manual, and she does very well with it.

The Initial Databases We Established

Initially, we established databases of open and closed files, and various name and address databases for clients, other attorneys, experts, etc. The fields in each record in the open and closed files databases are identical. This makes for easy transfer from one to the other when a case is closed. A copy of each record and its fields is shown in Figure A.1.

Obviously, several of the latter entries are only filled in when the file is closed and the record is transferred to the closed files database. Several of the closing entries call for monetary figures. PC-File+ also has limited computational ability, so we can use it to do some analysis for us.

In the sections that follow, I'm going to describe our various databases in detail. This is not because I think any of you will ever need exactly what we need, but because they provide a good case study for you of just how a database may be used.

Our Files Database

When a file is opened, we enter it in the open files database. We enter the client's name, the file number, a code to indicate where expense money comes from, the initials of the attorney working on the case, the forwarding attorney, the statute of limitations month and year, the month and year the file was opened and a simple code for the type of case it is.

The statute of limitations entry contains a date until suit is started, at which time an "s" is entered in that field. If a file is forwarded, an "f" is placed there.

At least once a month the open files database is sorted, first by attorney working on the case, then by statute of limitations, and finally alphabetically. This means that the database is broken down first by attorney. Within each attorney's

FIGURE A.1 Each Record and Its Fields

```
===============================================================================
           Name [Williams, John ]
            No_ [4936    ]
            Exp [B  ]
             Wk [Aim    ]
           Fwdr [Branch    ]
        Fwd_To [          ]
            SOL [S      ]
   Date_Opened [1989/10 ]
   Type_Of_Case [MM        ]
   Date_Closed [1990/05 ]                      ===================
     Total Fee [212,501.24  ]                  : D Delete        :
   Disbursments [12,496.28   ]                  : M Modify        :
       Net_Fee [141,667.49  ]                  : F Find (cont.) :
      FWD_Fee [70,833.75   ]                  : S new Search    :
            Box [49   ]                         : E End of file   :
                                                : B Beginning "   :
                                                : N Next record   :
                                                : P Prior record :
                                                : R get by Rcd#   :
                                                : + browse down   :
                                                : - browse up     :
                                                : Q Quit finding :
                                                ===================
```

FIGURE A.2 Fields and Layout of Lists

```
                               PNDPLUS
March 7, 1992      at  1:16 p.m.
Name            No_   Fwdr      Wk     Date_Ope Type_Of_Case Page 1 SOL
============== ====== ========== ====== ======== ============= =========
Schnell, Hans  4962           Aim    1991\10  SF            1992\12


Marks, Scott   4990   Willis    Aim    1991/11  MM            1993/01


Elton, Thomas  4845   Stewart   Aim    1991/01  Auto          S


Gallas, Sylvia 4857   Higgs     Aim    1991/04  Auto          S


Garcia, Jose   4959           Aim    1991/09  PL            S
```

```
_____
TOTALS:
Printed     5 of the        5 records.
PRIMARY SORT FIELD: SOL
SELECTION CRITERIA:
All records
```

section, his or her files are then arranged with the file having the earliest statute of limitations date (but not yet in suit) first, the next second, and so on. If more than one case has the same month and year of upcoming statute of limitations, they will be arranged alphabetically.

After the database is sorted, we print a list (a "report" in database terminology) for each attorney, containing his or her own workload, showing first the cases with statutes of limitations coming up, and then the rest of the files. A sample of the fields and layout of these lists is shown in Figure A.2.

We have arranged the report so that only certain of the categories are printed on each attorney's list. It is not necessary to print all the fields in a record in any report—you can select only those you need for the purpose of the report, and you can change the selections from report to report.

We have also arranged the list format to provide a number of blank lines surrounding each case entry, so that the attorney can make notes on the list itself as the cases are worked on.

At the end of each month the lists go back to the paralegal who maintains the database, with changes noted. She updates the database, re-sorts and prints new lists.

After the monthly attorney lists are done, we then sort the entire open files database alphabetically and print a comprehensive alphabetical list of open files, showing the file number, the attorney working on the case and a few other categories of information. A sample of this report form is shown in Figure A.3.

Finally, we periodically sort the entire open files database by file number and print a list by number, also showing client name and attorney working on the case. This report format is the same as Figure A.3, except that the list is sorted on number, rather than name. Obviously, the lists could be sorted in many other ways and an endless variety of reports printed—we select what we need, as each of you will do.

Client and Attorney Databases

When a file is opened and entered in the open files database, the client information (and information about the forwarding attorney if we don't already have it) are also entered in their appropriate databases. These are used primarily for periodic mailings to clients, forwarders, etc.

FIGURE A.3 Sample of Report Form

```
                   FILELIST
March 7, 1992                   Page 1

Name                No_    Exp Wk
================    ======  === ======
Elton, Thomas       4845    c   Aim
Gallas, Sylvia      4857    c   Aim
Garcia, Jose        4959    t   Aim
Marks, Scott        4990    t   Aim
Schnell, Hans       4962    b   Aim


_____

TOTALS:

Printed 5 of the 5 records.

PRIMARY SORT FILED: Name

SELECTION CRITERIA:
All records
```

Our database program also has some limited word processing functions, so that if we wanted to we could type a form letter into the database program itself and then have it print the form letter addressed to each person, or selected people. In addition, our database program will print mailing labels to go with the form letters.

Transcripts Database

We also have a database of transcripts, which includes information provided by several other firms as well, so that if any of us needs information about a particular witness we can see who has any such testimony, in what kind of a case it was given, etc. A sample of the fields in those records is shown in Figure A.4. We include the name, court and number of the case, and whether it is a deposition or trial transcript. We also show identifying information about the attorney who has the transcript and we note a brief description of the area addressed by the witness in that particular transcript.

Other Programs to Consider

There are a number of excellent general-purpose database programs on the market and each has strengths and weaknesses. Among those to consider are Q&A, dBase IV, PC-File, Alpha Four, RBase, and Paradox. Many of these programs are discussed in detail in *Winning with Computers, Part One.*

FIGURE A.4 Sample of the Fields in Records

```
Record number 183
===================================================================================
       name Wilson, James P., M.D.
       case Harris v. Newmark, et al
         ct Superior, Law, Bergen
         No L-194498-90 MM
        dep S
      trans
       date 1991\10\04
       atty Brian Scofield                    =====================
      phone 908-555-1515                      : D Delete           :
     mptype Gyn                               : M Modify           :
                                              : S new Search       :
                                              : E End of file      :
                                              : B Beginning "      :
                                              : N Next record      :
                                              : P Prior record     :
                                              : R get by Rcd#      :
                                              : + browse down      :
                                              : - browse up        :
                                              : Q Quit finding     :
                                              =====================
```

Calendar and Diary Programs

Every lawyer needs a diary or calendar program of some sort. There are stand-alone programs, which provide only the calendar or diary functions, and there are comprehensive programs designed for lawyers that include calendars and diaries together with many other capabilities.

A full range of cost and complexity are available. As always, you must first evaluate your needs. Is your firm large enough to need a comprehensive office calendar? Do your lawyers have individual computers so that they need individual calendar programs? Will diary books serve you better? There are some tasks that it does not pay to computerize, depending on the size of the firm and the volume and type of work.

Leading Programs

There are dozens of good calendar and diary programs on the market, and I will not try to mention all of them. Among the docketing programs to consider are DiaryMaster II, Abacus, Docket/CM, and dDiary. There are too many good calendar programs to list. Try several and choose one that fits your needs.

Our Diary Choice

Since our staff makes extensive use of computers, and since we do not need a comprehensive office calendar, we chose to get a very simple

diary program, which is used mainly by our paralegals and law clerks to keep track of follow-ups. This has worked very well for us. Lawyers with PCs in their offices can have a simple personal diary on their computer if they prefer, or they can still keep a handwritten diary.

We chose a diary program named dDIARY, which is a stand-alone program that is part of a system of related programs for lawyers called the dLEGAL SYSTEM. dDIARY is simple. Anyone who merely follows the screen instructions can learn to use it in less than an hour. The manual is only a few pages long, and it is really not even necessary to read it at all. This simplicity was in keeping with our overall philosophy of getting the simplest program that met our needs, and which is as easy as possible to learn and use. A sample report from dDIARY is shown in Figure A.5.

OTHER PROGRAMS AND CAPABILITIES—A POTPOURRI

There are a variety of other programs and equipment that should be considered as you make your initial choices about automation. You may not choose to invest in them at the beginning, but you should at least be aware of them. Although I won't try to discuss any of them in detail, I will touch on several briefly, so that you will have a starting point if you want to explore any of them further.

FIGURE A.5 Sample Report from dDIARY

```
Report for >>> DBL Date of Report :06/15/92
Page No. 1
                      Report of Selected  dDIARY Events

Event       Time    Class       Description                           Person
Date                Category
---------------------------------------------------------------------------

Thursday            MELNICK     requested disposition of summons # 248978   DBL
06/11/92            4645        for David Nelson

Friday              FELD        requested medical records & bill from       DBL
06/12/92            4602        Dr. Jones

Friday              BLOOM       client should send $100.00 for medical report   DBL
06/12/92            4734        from Dr. Wilson

Saturday            O'BRIAN     requested medical records and bill from     DBL
06/13/92            4759        Central Hospital.call Jane

Sunday              MELLON      should get medical authorization returned by    DBL
06/14/92            4629        client
```

Main Menu Programs

These are programs that come up automatically whenever the computer is started, and to that the computer returns automatically whenever you exit a program that you were working in. They display, by name and/or number, the identity of all the programs you use. To start a program you simply select it or enter its number. Everything else is automatic.

We use such a program, and it has made it much easier for us to become comfortable with the computers. There are many such programs available—some commercial and some shareware. They are all quite similar and it doesn't matter much which one you choose.

Figure A.6 shows the screen from our main menu program, which is named the "Program Director."

Leading Programs

There are several programs that offer shell capabilities. Windows allows you to switch between programs by clicking a mouse on different program icons. WordPerfect Office allows you to hot-key between most programs. Also consider Program Director and Direct Access.

Spreadsheets

Electronic spreadsheets revolutionized computer use in the business world. Basically, they put accounting and financial spreadsheets on the computer, and whenever a single number in the spreadsheet is changed, the program automatically recalculates everything else based on the change. Forecasting thus became relatively simple and much of the tedium of repeat calculations was eliminated. Today, spreadsheets have gone far beyond financial uses and can be used in a number of ways in a litigation practice.

Leading Programs

The three leading programs are Lotus 1-2-3, Quattro Pro, and Excel. All come in both DOS and Windows versions. You might also want to try a good shareware alternative called AS-EASY-AS.

RAM-Resident and TSR Programs

One category of programs are known variously as pop-ups, RAM-resident, or TSR (terminate and stay resident). Their primary advantage is they can reside, invisibly, in your computer's RAM memory until you summon them with a special keystroke combination. What makes them different from other programs is that they can pop up in the middle of another program you are working with and then disappear when you are finished, leaving the original program unaffected. Their primary strength lies in speed of access and the fact that you don't have to exit and store your original program to use them.

FIGURE A.6 Screen from Main Menu Program

```
                    THE PROGRAM DIRECTOR MENU
                    ------------------------

     1   VOLKSWRITER DELUXE PLUS##     9   PC-FILE PLUS##############

     2   VOLKSWRITER DELUXE########    10  FIRST PUBLISHER##########

     3   INSTALL LIGHTNING########     11  Xtree######################

     4   DE-INSTALL LIGHTNING#####     12  Total Word################

     5   WORDFINDER################     13  Calendar##################

     6   TYPEWRITER PROGRAM########     14  Not In Use################

     7   OKIDATA U93 CONTROL PGRM#     15  Not In Use################

     8   DIARY#####################     16  Not In Use################

                    ^Selection Number:]_



^F1]Help ^F2]Instructions ^F4]DOS Commands ^F5]Modify Menu ^F6]Setup ^F7]Exit
```

Examples of useful TSR or pop-up programs include an on-screen calculator (just like a hand-held one except that it is on the computer screen), a notepad (if you want to jot something down while you are working in another program and would rather do it in the computer than on paper), a names and addresses file, or computer time slips for timekeeping.

Let's say you are working in your word processor and want an address. If you have such a program and it is RAM-resident or TSR, you can call it up on top of your word processor, get the address (and sometimes even paste the address information into your word processor letter) and then immediately go back to your word processor without taking the time to exit or load either of the programs (which are much more time-consuming tasks).

Or, for example, suppose you are working in your database or word processor and need a calculator, or have a sudden idea you don't want to forget. You can similarly call up the calculator, do the calculation and return to the database, or call up the notepad, make the entry you want, and return to your word processor.

Leading Programs

There are too many ram-resident and TSR programs to list here. One of the first to become popular was Sidekick, which has evolved to Sidekick Plus. Others include InfoSelect and Memory Mate.

Accounting Programs

There are various programs that will do your accounting and bookkeeping (subject, of course, to your inputting all of the data). They will keep your payroll, print your checks, keep your trust and business account records, etc.

Whether or not it pays to implement such a program really depends on the size of your firm and the volume of accounting and bookkeeping work you have. We considered whether or not to computerize this aspect of our practice and decided against it when we compared the amount of manual time we spend per week on such tasks without automation to what would be involved in setting up and maintaining such a program. As always, your decision must be based on your own analysis of your own situation.

Leading Programs

One of the most popular is Quicken. Others include DacEasy, Peachtree, and One-Write-Plus.

CLOSING THOUGHTS

By now, you have your programs and your computers and printers and you're ready to start to use and benefit from them. There are, however, some other things to keep in mind, and a few things to think about as you proceed.

Consultants

When we decided to computerize we hired a consultant. Considering that we knew nothing about any of this, and had no one to guide us, we really had no alternative at the time. The consultant was a good security blanket, and may not be a bad choice for anyone for some initial setup help and guidance. But unless your firm is large enough to afford continuing professional computer support on an ongoing basis, you quickly reach a point where you must start learning to solve problems yourself.

Storing Data and Making Backups

Anytime the power is turned off, whatever you were working on that is not stored on a disk is gone forever. Period. There is no way to ever get it back. Believe me, the power will fail at some time, or someone will turn off a machine without remembering to check that all data was stored, or a hard disk will crash (lose its data) and you won't be able to get data from it.

With these things in mind, there are two rules:

1. Store Often While You Work.

In a word processing program you should store every few paragraphs. In other programs you should store every few entries. It takes a little longer, but it's better to develop good habits and never go through the trauma of losing your work. Some programs remind you to store every several minutes, and store for you if you are gone and don't respond to the reminder.

2. You Are Only as Good as Your Last Backup.

If your disk fails, your data will be lost unless you have backup copies. Backups should be made of all data at least once a day, preferably on two separate copies, which are kept in two separate places for safekeeping. Backups can be made through your operating system (DOS), but that is slow. There are programs, both commercial and shareware, that will facilitate faster, easier backups. Backups can be either on floppy disks or on tape. From the day you start to use your computers, back up all your data every day. Don't learn the hard way!

Data Storage and Archiving Files

Hard disks will fill up, and you do need to periodically delete files or transfer them to floppy disks for storage. If you have a lot to retain in storage, there are also programs that let you compress (archive) the files on the floppy disks, so that you can get more on them and thus need fewer of them.

If you use floppy disks for storage, be sure you label them comprehensively—you'll never remember what's on which one. They all look alike and the task of putting each one in the computer disk drive to see what's on it is frustrating and time-consuming.

Upgrading—A Word of Warning

As I was doing the final revisions on this article, I happened to see a letter to the editor of a lawyers' computer newsletter, saying that the writer had purchased new equipment that was not compatible with his old computers. Now, having already bought the new equipment, he was asking (apparently for the first time) about converting the vast amounts of data and information he already had stored on disks using his old system so that he could use them on the new equipment. He was surprised to find out that conversion wasn't automatic, if at all possible.

I was amazed. From time to time we will all upgrade some or all of our systems. We may upgrade hardware or software, or both. We may modify existing systems, add new components or units, or replace what we have. However, *before* you ever decide to buy new computer equipment that is not fully compatible with what you've had, whether it is to replace other equipment or in addition to what you have, you should have all the information about converting your old data, forms, etc., to the new format.

HOW MUCH DO YOU NEED TO KNOW?

For your system to be effective and productive you need to have at least one person in the office who understands the basics of how the equipment and programs operate. (This is differ-

Software for Your Law Office

WORD PROCESSORS

WordPerfect
1555 North Technology Way
Orem, UT 84057
(800) 451-5151

Microsoft Word
One Microsoft Way
Redmond, WA 98052-6399
(800) 426-9400

Ami Pro
5600 Glenridge Drive
Atlanta, GA 30342
(800) 831-9679

WordStar
201 Alameda del Prado
Novato, CA 94949
(800) 227-5609

MultiMate
Borland International
1800 Green Hills Road
Scotts Valley, CA 95067
(800) 331-0877

DESKTOP PUBLISHERS

Ventura Publisher
15175 Innovation Drive
San Diego, CA 92128
(800) 822-8221

Aldus PageMaker
411 First Avenue S.
Seattle, WA 98104
(800) 685-3608

LITIGATION-SPECIFIC DATABASES

PINS
8-E Music Fair Road
Owings Mills, MD 21117
(410) 363-1976

LawBase
Apogee
6825 East Tennessee Avenue
Denver, CO 80224
(800) 527-6433

PLEAS
Lawyers Software Publishing Company
1095 Klish Way
P.O. Box 2765
Del Mar, CA 92014
(800) 247-5327

LegalEdge
1150 First Avenue
King of Prussia, PA 19406
(215) 337-5835

Case Master III
Software Technology, Inc.
1621 Cushman Drive
Lincoln, NE 68512
(800) 487-7111

Mitratech
9763 West Pico Boulevard
Los Angeles, CA 90035
(800) 852-4188

GENERAL PURPOSE DATABASES

PC-File
ButtonWare, Inc.
325 118th Avenue, S.E.
Bellevue, WA 98005
(800) 528-8866

Q&A
Symantec
10201 Torre Avenue
Cupertino, CA 95014
(800) 441-7234

dBase IV
Borland International
1800 Green Hills Road
Scotts Valley, CA 95067
(800) 331-0877

Alpha Four
One North Avenue
Burlington, MA 01803
(800) 852-5750

R:Base
Microrim
15395 30th Place, S.E.
Bellevue, WA 98007
(800) 248-2001

Paradox
Borland Internatonal
1800 Green Valley Road
Scotts Valley, CA 95067
(800) 331-0877

CALENDARS AND DIARIES
Diarymaster II
Litigation Technologies, Inc.
651 West Mount Pleasant Avenue
Livingston, NJ 07039
(800) 362-5381

Abacus
6725 Mesa Ridge Road
San Diego, CA 92121
(800) 726-3339

Docket/CM
Juris, Inc.
151 Athens Way
Nashville, TN 37228
(615) 242-2870

dDiary
2500 Highland Road
Hermitage, PA 16148
(800) 544-4437

MAIN MENU PROGRAMS
Microsoft Windows
One Microsoft Way
Redmond, WA 98052-6399
(800) 426-9400

WordPerfect Office
1555 North Technology Way
Orem, UT 84057
(800) 451-5151

Direct Access
Fifth Generation Systems
10049 North Reiger Road
Baton Rouge, LA 70809
(800) 677-1848

SPREADSHEETS
Lotus 1-2-3
55 Cambridge Parkway
Cambridge, MA 02142
(800) 872-3387

Quattro Pro
Borland International
1800 Green Hills Road
Scotts Valley, CA 95067
(800) 331-0877

Microsoft Excel
One Microsoft Way
Redmond, WA 98052-6399
(800) 426-9400

AS-EASY-AS (shareware)
Trius, Inc.
231 Sutton St.
P.O. Box 249
North Andover, MA 01845-1639
(800) 468-7487

RAM RESIDENT AND TSRs
Sidekick Plus
Borland International
1800 Green Hills Road
Scotts Valley, CA 95067
(800) 331-0877

Info Select
Micro Logic
P.O. Box 70
Hackensack, NJ 07602
(800) 342-5930

MemoryMate
Broderbund Software
P.O. Box 6125
Novato, CA 94948-6125
(800) 521-6263

ACCOUNTING
Quicken
Intuit
P.O. Box 3014
Menlo Park, CA 94026
(800) 624-8742

DacEasy
17950 Preston Road
Dallas, TX 75252
(800) 322-3279

Peachtree
1505 Pavillion Place
Norcross, GA 30093
(800) 247-3224

One-Write Plus
Meca Software
55 Walls Drive
Fairfield, CT 06430
(800) 288-6322

ent from learning the programs themselves.) Inevitably, problems will arise. Most of them are minor if at least one of you understands the operating system and has an overview of how things work. If no one does, you will have no choice but to call in outside help for every problem. That is not only expensive, but it is also time-consuming. Remember that until help arrives, you do not work.

KEEP SHAREWARE IN MIND

A few times in this article I've talked about shareware. Keep shareware in mind when you think you may want a new program. Very often you can find what you need in shareware for much less money than any commercial program will cost. Not every shareware program is good, but a lot of them are very good, and you will be better off for considering this source of software as your needs grow and expand.

Arthur Ian Miltz practices law in Livingston, New Jersey, in the medical malpractice, product liability, and other personal injury areas. A certified civil trial attorney, Mr. Miltz is a member of the New Jersey and New York bars. Mr. Miltz is active in the American Bar Association's Section of Law Practice Management, where he serves as vice chair of the section's Beginning Computer Users Interest Group and Litigation Interest Group. He is also chair of the Computer Applications Committee of the Essex County, New Jersey, Bar Association, chair of the Product Liability Committee of ATLA-New Jersey, and the author of the Discovery volume of Matthew Bender & Co.'s Art of Advocacy series, as well as numerous book chapters and articles.

Practicing Law with a Macintosh Computer

Ronald L. Crittenden

Ron Crittenden practices law with a Macintosh computer. He provides a counterpoint look at setting up a law office using software for the Macintosh computer. Although he can't discuss every package on the market, and the market changes by the day, he will give you a starting point for your own investigation and selection of software.

In the personal computer world, the Macintosh is like a Porsche with an automatic transmission: a fast, elegant performer, yet easy to drive. Lawyers using the Macintosh get there quicker—and have more fun on the way. Because of its ease of use, the Macintosh's *graphical user interface* or *GUI* has become the preferred user environment for all personal computers. The Microsoft Windows operating environment for IBM-compatible computers has become very popular, and there are a number of other products that claim to make IBM PCs and compatibles work like a Macintosh. They only partly succeed.

That is because the GUI is only one part of the whole. Windows is a software "shell" operating on top of DOS; both DOS and Windows are required to run Windows. Windows manipulates DOS and therefore retains some of its limitations. Countless articles on the subject note the lack of many features available on the Macintosh, as well as the many problems encountered by Windows users. Some of these persistent problems have included slow speed, software bugs that cause crashes, and the amount of room Windows takes up both in memory and on the hard disk.

Another problem is consistency. During the heady growth of the DOS environment, developers approached their products in many different ways. There were few development standards among the clones, IBM compatibles, networks, and peripheral products. Windows, as just one component of the computer system, is vulnerable to the inherent weakness of any other part.

The Macintosh, on the other hand, is an integrated system of hardware and software formed by one vision and one company, Apple Computer, Inc. Because Apple is the sole source of both the basic computer hardware and the operating system, it has much more control over the development of peripheral products than IBM had over DOS or IBM compatibles. Apple has published guidelines for developers of software and peripheral products and has created a strong expectation among its users that the guidelines will be followed. This expectation, whether the software is or is not labeled "Mac-like," acts as a powerful incentive for developers to adhere to the guidelines.

The Macintosh guidelines promote uniformity of interface and operation among Macintosh software applications. This uniformity, as well as the integrated nature of the hardware and the operating system, give the Macintosh user the extraordinary ability to exchange data between programs. A graph created by a spreadsheet can be moved effortlessly into a brief in a word processor. A piece of text from a word processing document is easily enlarged and turned into an overhead slide for courtroom use. An accident or crime scene is diagrammed and then moved into another software program to create overlays and/or animated sequences to demonstrate a progression of events to the jury. While these may sound difficult, in practice they are easily within the grasp of the average Macintosh user.

WHAT MAKES IT A MAC?

Apple introduced the Macintosh in 1984. It is not character based (as are IBM-compatible DOS-based machines), but rather graphics based, meaning that screen dots or pixels are the smallest unit that can be manipulated. The Macintosh can display word processing documents almost exactly as they print on paper and stores them in the computer in "folders" you can see pictured on the screen. Folders can contain documents, graphics, other types of files, or other folders. You name files in English, using up to 32 characters, as opposed to DOS, which is limited to eight characters plus a three-character extension. You see all of your programs, folders, and other files pictured in "windows" on the screen or neatly organized in lists.

Macintosh also popularized a much easier way of navigation: the mouse. It is equipped with a button, and you use it as an all-purpose device to point to and generally manipulate objects on the screen. You can open and close files, edit and move text or graphics, and perform almost all other commands with a few clicks of the mouse. A variety of menus, buttons, and other on-screen controls complete the interface.

The advantage of these machines over other computers has become apparent to many users. You need not memorize commands. Just point and click, click and drag. Name files in English. Sounds can be added. There is built-in networking, what some people refer to as "plug and play." You can open more than one program at a time, and cut and paste information between programs. The Macintosh removed many of the obstacles imposed by other computers to learning and using software. It is more elegant. Even fun.

Desk accessories—software utilities and aids such as calculators, miniature word processors, and quick reference guides—are available at all times, regardless of what software is running. Desk accessories enhance the usefulness of the Macintosh even more. Desk accessories available for the Mac now number in the hundreds.

Every Macintosh has built-in file sharing, plug-and-play networking, a microphone and speaker for sounds, and the ability to use as many programs simultaneously as memory will allow. Hard disks are available that hold billions of characters. New devices such as CD-ROM drives, voice navigation software, high-speed modems, miniature portables, multimedia products, color scanners, and printers continue to provide new capabilities.

CONNECTIVITY AND NETWORKING

Few computers these days exist in a homogeneous environment. Law offices have differing preferences and needs, and have usually made a mix of purchases over time. Consequently, they often have a need for different kinds of computers to communicate. The Macintosh offers numerous options.

DOS to Macintosh

All current Macintosh computers are equipped with a floppy drive that will read and write DOS-formatted disks by using special software. Two inexpensive programs offer nearly transparent file exchange capabilities: Access PC and DOS Mounter. With either, you simply insert the disk into the Macintosh, and the disk and file appear on the screen. An MS-DOS document can then be opened by a Macintosh word processing, spreadsheet, or graphics program as appropriate.

A Macintosh can even run DOS programs with the addition of a hardware product, the Mac 286/386 series by Orange Micro, or a software product called Soft PC. Another software product, RunPC, allows a Macintosh to communicate with and operate a PC. Run PC can be operated over a network, allowing access to DOS programs from any Macintosh computer on the network. MacLinkPlus/PC offers document translation capabilities for a wide range of Mac and PC programs.

Macintosh to Others

A host of other products exist that allow a Macintosh to communicate with IBM mainframes, IBM 36 or AS400 computers, Digital Equipment computers, UNIX workstations, and many more.

Networking and E-mail

Every Macintosh is equipped with built-in networking hardware. Connecting one Macintosh to another and sharing files is literally a matter of plugging in the appropriate cables and making a few software selections. This capability is called LocalTalk.

Ethernet networking is also available for the Mac. The newest and most advanced models, the Quadras, have built-in Ethernet. Other Macintoshes require installation of an internal Ethernet card. Add an Ethernet hub, and the network speed is quadrupled. Other network products include FaxGate, which allows users to send a fax by choosing to fax instead of print, and NetModem, which allows users on a network to share a modem.

There are a number of network server products for the Macintosh, including AppleShare and DataClub. Novell's NetWare fully supports the Macintosh. Another product, NetMounter, provides a low-cost alternative for connecting Macs to Novell networks.

E-mail programs abound for the Macintosh. QuickMail, WordPerfect Office, and Microsoft Mail are three. Some of these packages are also available in versions for other computers and operating systems, and can operate with their sibling versions on a mixed network.

Remote Network Access

For firms with separate offices, or the desire to directly link with a client, TeleBridge acts as a bridge between two remote networks. It appears to users as one continuous network.

Apple ships a remarkable product called Remote Access with every PowerBook, Apple's laptop version of the Macintosh, and the product is also available separately. This software allows a computer equipped with a modem to access the office computer or network (or any other suitably equipped computer) and use it just as though you were at the office. After set-up, you click on a special icon with the mouse, type in your password, and the connection is automatically made. You can check your E-mail, copy a file to your remote computer, leave a message for your secretary, review your work, or print on the network printer. With Remote Access, you are only a click away.

OFFICE, CASE, AND DATA MANAGEMENT

Without a computer, life is ruled by little pieces of paper. Names. Call backs. Reminders. Time slips. Case lists. To-do lists. Calendars. With the computer, it all goes in one place— and, more importantly, it can be *found* in one place. This alone is one of the greatest benefits of a computer.

Contacts, Names, and Addresses

There are many programs available to keep track of names and addresses for the Macintosh. TouchBase allows you to enter names and addresses into separate fields and find a person or group of people very quickly and easily. You can define five other fields according to your needs and sort on any of these fields. You can very easily import, export, add, delete, and sort some or all records. A "notes" area allows you to enter up to 15 pages of single-spaced notes, and you can include an automatic date and time stamp with a click of the mouse. With a modem, TouchBase will also dial your phone with a mouse click.

You can print envelopes, labels, phone books, lists, etc.—with a selection of envelope styles, label sizes, and return address styles—in whatever typeface you choose. It even automatically prints bar codes. The database can be accessed by more than one person simultaneously over a network. It can automatically place information in its companion calendar program, DateBook, at the touch of a button, and vice versa. If you want a phone number or address on your calendar, and a record of your calendar appointment in the notes section of the contacts database, you press the TouchBase icon while setting up the appointment, and the information is copied both ways.

There are a number of other good choices for contact databases, including Address Book Plus and Dynodex, that operate much like TouchBase. Some prefer a card approach without specific fields. QuickDex and Intouch offer simplicity and speed, acting as a catch-all location for names, phone numbers, and notes that can be instantly retrieved. Because of their speed, they are particularly good for large networks where many different users require access to a of very large number of names.

Calendar

If there is a profession that needs a calendar, the law is it. Judges are increasingly cranky about lawyers missing court dates, as are malpractice insurance carriers. Luckily, there is a selection of good, network-capable calendars available for the Macintosh that work well in the law office. DateBook, as mentioned above, allows you to set appointments by date, times, group, category, summary, and longer description or notes. To-do lists carry from day to day until checked, and alarms can be set minutes, hours, days, weeks, or months before an event, and they can also be set to recur at specific intervals, on specific days of the week, or on specific dates. The calendar can be viewed and changed by your secretary or others (with the appropriate passwords) on a network. DateBook also offers the advantage of data sharing with TouchBase.

For offices needing to track the activities of more than one attorney on a central calendar, Now Up-to-Date offers many similar features. Other good programs include WordPerfect Office, which also offers an E-mail feature, and Meeting Maker. Both are capable of scheduling meetings and checking other calendars for conflicts. Law Office Manager (which I'll discuss in greater detail below) has some legal-specific features in the calendar portion of its case management program.

Timekeeping

Timeslips III is a very flexible timekeeping and billing program. On the Mac, you always have access to Timeslips a mouse click away. And because you can keep as many programs open on a Mac as memory will allow, it is there instantly. You can name a client on the fly, start a timer while you talk (or enter the elapsed time), and enter notes about the session by typing or using codes. Even lawyers who do not charge by the hour use this program to monitor efficiency, time on a case, or to support a request for fees.

Most important, the program can automatically assemble the slips to prepare a bill. You can charge by client, activity, or lawyer, and easily adjust billings, rates, times, or notes. Lawyers who start using Timeslips III are amazed at how quickly the bills can be produced, and, if necessary, altered. Quarterly bills become monthly. Timekeeping features appear in some case management programs as well.

Timeslips Accounting Link directly imports data into five general ledger programs available on the Macintosh: Accountant, Inc., ACCPAC, atOnce!, Great Plains, and Multiledger. In addition to these, numerous other general accounting packages are available.

Case Management

Staying on top of cases is a challenge for a busy lawyer or firm. A case management program (which is a specific kind of database) handles the process. The key is to find one that keeps track of the information that is important to your practice. There are several available for the Macintosh, from comprehensive single-user programs to a very ambitious program for large firms.

Small- to medium-sized firms may have an interest in Law Office Manager. This case management program organizes the work into Clients (with personal, employer, contact, and notes screens), Matters (with subcategories of opposing, witnesses, documents, and notes), Jobs (with date, description, priority, warnings, and whose job it is), and a document management area (that tracks whether it is sent or received, how, when, to whom, from whom, if certified, and content summary). Additional features include automatic city and state entry when a zip code is entered, automatic conflict checking, custom report configuration, a custom label generator, and a form writer in which forms can be created and stored that can place the desired fields (name, address, etc.) in the appropriate places. The calendar is capable of being configured for tickler dates according to your state's requirements.

Other programs include LexaFile, a comprehensive office, case, and task manager for the single attorney; Office Wiz, which offers timekeeping as well as office management; and MacLaw, a very comprehensive law office management program for a larger law firm.

For complex litigation, some lawyers use project management software. These allow more control over jobs and resources and can be helpful in planning the work, displaying the time lines, and creating milestones. Programs available on the Macintosh include FastTrack, MacProject II, MacSchedule Plus, MetaDesign, Micro Planner, and Microsoft Project.

Databases

Many Macintosh users design their own databases for expert witnesses, case management, chronologies, etc. These users often use flat-file database managers, which are less complex than relational databases. One of the most popular, powerful, and easy to use is FileMaker Pro. Also available in the flat file category are Panorama and Q&A, which is new to the Mac but widely accepted by DOS users.

For users who need a relational database (in which several databases are combined to act as one, such as clients, cases, bills, etc.) or a high degree of complex customization, 4th Dimension and Double Helix are unique to the Macintosh and are supported by a network of developers that provides custom programming for specialized needs. Database programs that will serve more than one kind of computer include Oracle, Sybase, Omnis Seven, and FoxBASE+. The latter can read dBASE-compatible files.

WORKING WITH THE MACINTOSH

Most of an lawyer's work involves expressing concepts through documents—creating, modifying, sending, receiving, and responding to them. Here are some of the ways a Macintosh aids this work.

Outlining Software

Outlining software offers lawyers the ability to brainstorm, create documents, track to-do items, and make presentations. The two major outlining programs for the Macintosh are MORE and ACTA. Of the two, MORE has more features.

The main benefit of an outlining program is the ability to create an outline by typing the topics as they occur to you, then moving them with the mouse to the desired order. To move a topic over or under another one, you simply select it with the mouse, and then, holding the mouse button down, drag it to its new location. A topic can also be moved to the left or right. If you want to look at part of the outline, you can remove all the other topics by command. If you want to look at only one topic, you can expand all points below it to show while the others remain hidden.

In MORE, you can look at your outline in regular outline form, or, by one click, change your view to either a bullet chart or a tree chart. All or part of the document can be printed in any of these three views.

You can also create presentations that turn the outline into slides or pieces of the outline that will display a set number of topics. Color can be added and graphics (selected from an included library or from other sources, such as public domain clip art) can be pasted in for emphasis. A slide can be made to appear for the audience while speaker notes appear on your monitor.

MORE offers all of the usual word processing tools: tabs; text alignment; line spacing; and font or typeface choice, including size, style (bold, underlining, shadow, etc.), and color. MORE also has a graph creation module. Numbers placed in a spreadsheet-like screen can then be displayed as a graph. There are a variety of graph types to choose from, and creating a graph is fast and easy.

Word Processing

All major word processing software is available on the Macintosh, including WordPerfect, the most widely used word processing software in law offices. But many lawyers who use a Macintosh favor Microsoft Word: its outlining is superior, it can automatically generate a table of contents from the outline, and it has better merge capabilities.

Several Macintosh word processors, such as MacWrite II and WriteNow, stress ease of use. Others, such as Nisus, offer features of special interest to lawyers. One feature allows you to index all occurrences of a word by entering it in the PowerSearch function.

Another category of word processing software is called *groupware*. Instant Update and Mark Up allow many people to collaborate on a document. The former creates an instant composite over a network, while the latter retains the original document and each collaborator's comments.

There is also a growing number of integrated software packages that typically offer a combination of word processing, graphics, spreadsheet, database, and communications capabilities in one program. Each module of the program, however, functions separately to some degree, so that you would open a word processing document, for example, in the word processing module. The programs have varying degrees of integration of use. For instance, some will allow you to use the graphics tools while working on a word processing document. None of the modules offer the features of their full-fledged counterpart programs, but for many users, they will provide nearly all the functionality needed. These integrated programs are good choices for PowerBook users and others short on computer memory or disk space. Most can convert files to and from other program formats. Some of the integrated programs available are ClarisWorks, Microsoft Works, and BeagleWorks.

Redlining Software

While word processing programs offer redlining capability, none offer the features and speed of a dedicated redlining program, such as DocuComp II. With this program, a subsequent draft of a document can be easily and quickly compared to an older version by a couple of clicks of the mouse. You can view the comparison in a split screen window with the newer file above the older. The program shows additions underlined and deletions by strike-through (or other user-defined ways, including color). Moved text is displayed in bold. You can print out a composite file that combines the two and lists the number of changes.

Spreadsheets

Good for manipulating rows of numbers, they also make good presentation tools with their graphing capabilities. Lotus 1-2-3 and Resolve are available on the Macintosh, but the most popular spreadsheet program for the Mac has been Microsoft's Excel. On the Macintosh, these programs will automatically produce a variety of graphs in color and in three dimensions. (The charts and graphs in *USA Today* are produced on a Macintosh.) Good graphs make great presentation tools, both in and out of court. Graphs can make sense of a row of numbers and show relationships that might otherwise be unclear.

Forms Software

Lawyers are big consumers of forms. But forms take up space and cost money. Most forms can be duplicated on the Macintosh and will be accepted by the court or agency.

Forms software falls into two categories: premade and create-your-own. Some forms in the former category are produced by the MacForms Company, which offers MacForms Consolidated Federal Bankruptcy, MacForms California Judicial Council Forms, and MacForms Arizona Family Law Forms. Federal tax preparation forms are available from the makers of MacinTax.

Software to create your own forms is available in such programs as Informed Designer, Fast Forms, and SmartForm Designer. Drawing tools let you create lines and boxes and specify fields or places where the data will be typed. FileMaker Pro, the database program, has good form-generation capabilities that can be used for this purpose. Electronic forms offer many advantages: they are easily customizable when the official form changes, they can be personalized if appropriate, and they take up no space and have no further cost.

Another use of form-generation software for all offices that use Microsoft Word is a program by MacForms that creates Formal Letterhead and Personalized Pleading Paper. With this program, you can create your letterhead and your own pleading paper on demand. Hundreds of typefaces are available for the Macintosh, and the text can be sized and rotated to read vertically along the margin.

Document Databases

The Macintosh filing convention of using 32-character names in English makes document handling much easier on the Mac than it is on a DOS-based machine; nevertheless, some firms with large document production need document management software. MarcoPolo is one program for the Macintosh that provides document management capabilities. It allows users to index and archive documents after they are created in a group document center by coding key words, author, date, etc. Documents can be searched for these codes or by content. Up to 16 documents can then be displayed at once, showing the highlighted location of the word being searched in each page. The program can be used with scanners and optical character recognition software, as discussed below.

Clause-It, by Masterite Software, is a document database program that stores documents, generally by user-defined type, such as Lease of Real Estate, Sale of Personal Property, etc. Each clause of each document is further separately identified by clause type and the concept or topic for that clause. A lawyer can attach rules to a clause that define when the clause should or should not be used. To create a new document, one can modify an existing document or create an outline by choosing from the separate clauses in the database that are appropriate.

Graphics

Most of us are used to thinking that the practice of law deals with words only. But, increasingly, firms are finding that graphics can be very powerful communication aids—for example, by showing the interlocking ownership in seemingly unrelated companies, describing the organizational structure of a company, showing the setup of a trust and how the proceeds would be distributed upon the death of the testator, making diagrams of accidents, and creating simple maps with legends. Firm brochures, settlement briefs, and many other kinds of documents can be enhanced by the use of graphics.

Draw and Paint Programs

Computer graphics can be generally grouped into three categories: (1) "draw" or "object" graphics, which appear as graphic elements (lines, circles, etc.) on screen but which are actually composed of computer instructions; (2) "paint" graphics, which consist of a compilation of pixels (bitmaps); and (3) scanned images. Many artists, graphic display houses, and animators now rely heavily on computer assistance. In preparing demonstrative evidence, settlement brochures, and marketing presentations, the Macintosh-equipped lawyer is in an excellent position to exchange data and work closely with professionals in the graphic field.

Most of the legal applications for graphics will call for draw programs. Programs include MacDraw Pro and MacDraft. Two well-known PostScript drawing programs—an advanced type—are Adobe Illustrator and Aldus Freehand. Combined drawing and painting programs include Canvas and SuperPaint.

Paint programs for the Macintosh include MacPaint; Painter; Studio/1, 8, and 32; PixelPaint Professional, and UltraPaint. For manipulating scanned images, particularly useful for cropping and retouching photographic or other half-tone images, there is Color It!, ColorStudio, Digital Darkroom, ImageStudio, and Photoshop.

An extensive library of Macintosh software also exists to do *computer-assisted drafting* or *CAD*, which allows for rendering, modeling, video image handling, and animation.

Clip Art (Ready-Made Graphics)

Creating a graphic can be as simple as selecting one from a commercial clip art program (disks filled with pictures of common objects). Some clip art products have specific purposes, such as MediClip, which consists solely of pictures of

body parts. In a personal injury case involving a broken femur, say, you can take a picture from the MediClip database, put it into a graphics program, add arrows and text to illustrate the broken bone, and then place the modified picture into a word processing document.

One very high-end program for the Macintosh, A.D.A.M., takes this several steps further. The human body has been drawn in a very powerful graphics program that allows the user to display a part of the body layer by layer in three dimensions. Originally designed for medical instruction, it has found use in personal injury and medical malpractice cases. A user can actually display a cut or surgery, show where the incision was made, display the layers, and show, for example, the precise location where a nerve was cut. The body part can be shown in three dimensions and even slowly rotated to show all sides.

Page Layout Programs

As lawyers grasp the capabilities of computers, they will make increasing use of graphics, and documents prepared by lawyers will contain the graphic elements currently found in commercially produced publications. Many firms now use page layout programs to produce firm brochures. More and more firms are sending out newsletters and even news updates when there are changes in the law.

Page layout programs differ from word processing programs chiefly in their superior control over placement of text, graphics, and style elements, although the higher-end word processors now have a number of these features. You can use page layout programs to create nearly anything a publisher or advertising agency creates. If it requires special printing or paper, you send the computer output by modem or on disk to a commercial printer. All commercial graphic service bureaus and printers can process Macintosh output. QuarkXPress, FrameMaker, and PageMaker are three of the most sophisticated page layout programs. For users with simpler needs, Personal Press or Publish It! Easy could be good choices.

Printing

The Macintosh started the desktop publishing revolution because of its graphic and page layout capabilities. Not the least of its success was due to LaserWriter printers. Users are able to expand, contract, rotate, stretch, and other-

225

wise manipulate text and objects. They can then print the output on a laser printer with near-printer quality sharpness and clarity. Hundreds of typefaces, or fonts, are available to distinguish and customize your documents. Lawyers who use Macintoshes report favorable comments by judges and clients who have viewed their output.

Legal Research and On-Line Services

A Macintosh with a modem can access legal on-line databases such as WESTLAW and LEXIS. Software has been written by both specifically for the Macintosh. Generally, you can copy and save what appears on the screen rather than go through separate downloading procedures.

Other on-line services exist but are not as well known. For medical information, Grateful Med is available. Definitions and abstracts of articles can be quickly accessed. Many courts and some state agencies are now providing on-line access. These allow you to check pleadings and motions that have been filed.

Also available are general services like CompuServe, Prodigy, and one designed specifically for the Macintosh called America On Line, which is particularly easy and Macintosh-like to operate. The cost is $10 per hour in prime time and $5 per hour after 6:00 P.M. Each of these offers Macintosh software to access the service, and all can be used to get stock market quotes, track one's stock portfolio, access breaking news, make a plane reservation, or find information and discussion boards on a very wide range of professional, occupational, and recreational topics. CompuServe, for example, has a special forum for lawyers, paralegals, and court reporters, with extensive data libraries on both substantive topics and law office automation. These services can also be a good source of free software or *shareware*, and many allow for access to information and advice from fellow users.

Scanners and Optical Character Recognition

Scanners offer law firms the ability to place data from paper copies into a computer. Many scanners are available on the Macintosh. Some offer color and sheet feeders. While most are flatbed scanners, some are hand held and are used by passing them over the page. Makers of these products include Abaton, Apple, Caere, Fujitsu, Hewlett Packard, Microtek, and Umax.

If many documents are scanned and stored, an image management scheme must be employed. Optix Document Image Management System can index and archive millions of documents in its database. It can then display multiple "thumbnail" pictures on the screen or show full-size pages. These are not capable of being searched for content. Optix does not support OCR.

When a document is scanned, it is just a picture, not yet readable by the computer as words. To convert the picture into words, the scanned document file must be run through *optical character recognition* or *OCR* software. The ability of OCR to quickly and accurately read the image varies greatly and depends upon the typefaces used, the condition of the original, and the quality of the scanner. Three of the most sophisticated OCR programs on the Macintosh are Accu-Text, Omnipage, and WordScan.

Text Search and Retrieval Software

Word processing programs have a Find feature that allows you to search your open document for a word or phrase. Full-text search and retrieval programs go much further. They search over a number of unopened documents for the words and display the "hits" in a list; then they take you to the highlighted area in the actual text. Some of these programs are capable of very fast searches, thousands of pages per second, because they index each word in them before commencing the search. (See also MarcoPolo, as discussed in the database section above.) Most support Boolean searches: A and B, A not B, A or B, etc., and can locate words within a user-defined distance (e.g., five lines) of one another: "Smith within five lines of Jones."

One such program, Sonar Professional, also has phonetic search for sound-alikes, as well as associated word searches for pairs that often occur close together. Another program is On Location, which is adept at locating documents stored on a hard drive, based on words in the document. GOfer is an inexpensive search utility in a desk accessory format. It does not index files, so its searches are slower than programs that index the files to be searched. However, it is handier than some of the more sophisticated programs for occasional searches.

One law firm using the Macintosh credits a very high-end product for text search and retrieval with winning a case worth millions of dollars. It hinged upon finding one document out of hundreds of thousands in a very short time. The firm did so, by using M.A.R.S., a hardware and software product that is used to scan, code, and OCR all documents related to a case. Three databases result: the scanned image of the document (which is good for signatures, drawings, etc.); the text database, resulting from passing the image through OCR software that allows full text search and retrieval; and the coded material, which allows a search by coded information, e.g., author, recipient, subject, date, distribution, etc.

M.A.R.S. is an extensive combination of hardware and software. It has been used for many important cases involving millions of documents as a way of searching and coping with them. The work of scanning, coding, and the like is often done by a *service bureau*, which is a company that offers services regarding various aspects of computer operations that a law firm or other client may not know how to handle for itself. Some large corporate offices use M.A.R.S. for everyday paper handling. All documents received are scanned in and available over the network to any user with access. This eliminates problems attendant to storing, locating, and accessing the documents. It is likely that this use will grow dramatically in the future. Costs of computer storage continue to decrease, and the abilities of scanners and OCR correspondingly increase.

The Macintosh in Litigation

Some of the programs described above are useful in litigation as well as for other purposes, including graphics and graph production, case management, databases, scanning, and full text retrieval. But a number of Macintosh programs are specifically designed for the litigation lawyer.

Cudgel and TrialMaker act as document, witness, and exhibit databases to prepare the trial notebook. TrialMaker, based upon the popular database program FileMaker Pro, allows the user to enter information about witnesses, documents, exhibits, issues, things to do, settlement discussions, citations, and to summarize data from depositions. These can then be sorted by chronology, issues, etc., and be printed in list form to generate comprehensive reports for a trial notebook. In addition, Cudgel, based upon the database program Double Helix, incorporates a docket-handling system that, according to the publisher, displays docket, calendar, and assignment status across multiple cases. Each offers a preformatted set of reports that can be used as the basis for a trial notebook, and they can be customized for specialized litigation requirements. However, these programs do not offer text retrieval.

Ready For Trial is a Macintosh program developed in response to the special problems of analyzing and organizing transcripts, particularly depositions. Unlike most of its DOS counterparts, which are distributed by specially franchised court reporters, Ready For Trial uses generic text files (known as ASCII, for American Standard for Computer Information Interchange) available from virtually every court reporter.

Ready For Trial permits the organization and analysis of testimony by issue, exhibit, or date when the events testified to occurred. It takes advantage of the Macintosh interface to enable the lawyer to "slice" a transcript into pieces. Each piece can be characterized by any number of issues. References by a witness to an exhibit can be noted or the date when the events occurred. The pieces are then stored in the program's database. The pieces of testimony from any combination of witnesses can be retrieved by issue, exhibit, or date.

The second part of the program deals with its powerful text search and retrieval capability. Words can be found very quickly across a large number of depositions, and sophisticated Boolean searches can be made, similar to the programs made solely for this purpose discussed above.

CONCLUSION

In this brief overview, I have touched upon some of the products of interest to lawyers available on the Macintosh. As I hope to have shown, full productivity, networking, connectivity, tracking, working, and litigation support software exist for the Macintosh. The Mac is more accessible and easier to operate than any other computer. More types of hardware options exist on a Macintosh, as does much easier remote connectivity to one's home base. There is no more painless computer for the beginning or experienced user.

So, you have a choice. First, you can decide *not* to use them, but be forewarned that others are. Second, you can try to learn how they work on a DOS- or Windows-based computer, which will be a test of your ability to wade through and understand voluminous manuals and setup procedures, and which offers a less desirable working environment. Or, finally, you can start using a Macintosh and take advantage of the real GUI, integrated system, not to mention the consistency from program to program that results in the best ease of learning and use available. It fits one lawyer's summation concerning computers for the law office: a good computer is one that's *used*.

If you are tempted to wait until computers get even easier, my advice is: don't. The concepts and procedures used today will continue for the foreseeable future, and most lawyers are computerizing. Remember, the first step is the biggest. Make it the best.

Ronald L. Crittenden is a lawyer and full-time computer consultant, primarily to the legal profession. He formed Crittenden Consulting, a network of consulting lawyers and technical professionals. Mr. Crittenden is a graduate of the University of Michigan Law School. He is a member of the State of Michigan Bar and resides in Ann Arbor, Michigan, with his wife, Corey, and their dog, Chou-Chou.

Peripherals: Keyboards, Video Displays, Modems, Printers, and More

Arthur Ian Miltz
Joseph L. Kashi

Peripherals allow you to communicate with your computer. Arthur Miltz and Joe Kashi provide you with a basic understanding of how they work and what you need to know before you buy.

A peripheral device is any piece of equipment that attaches to the central processing unit of a computer. These include the devices you work with the most: the keyboard, the video monitor and your printer. Without the right peripheral devices, a computer would be useless—deaf, dumb, and blind.

In this chapter, we will talk about the peripheral devices you are likely to need for your law office. These include input devices such as keyboards and optical scanners, output devices such as video monitors and printers, and data storage devices including optical storage equipment and tape backup units. In addition, we will talk about other important devices that can protect your hardware from external damage.

INPUT DEVICES

Input devices allow you to transmit information and instructions to the computer.

Keyboards

Keyboards come in various configurations. The basic letter and number keys are in the same places as on a typewriter. Other special keys come in different places on different keyboards, and some may not be on all keyboards. You can use these to move the cursor (the small blinking indicator on the screen that tells you where you are)

to issue special commands to the computer, or for numerous other special functions.

Keyboard preferences vary. Your reaction to the layout, touch and feel of the keyboard is important and can make the difference between happiness and frustration. Try out several keyboards before making your selection.

Mice and Trackballs

A mouse provides an alternative to the keyboard for moving the cursor and activating computer functions. You move the mouse back and forth on a small pad on your desk, which in turn rolls a ball built into the bottom of the mouse case on the pad. The cursor moves when you roll the ball. When the cursor is where you want it on the screen, you push a button on the mouse to activate a desired function. A mouse can also be used to point or draw on the screen and to activate commands. Depending upon its design, a mouse may either connect through a regular serial port, through a special mouse port, or through a special bus expansion card. All work well.

Mice are useful in working with programs that are designed to work with a mouse. Programs using a graphical interface, like Windows and programs designed for Windows, almost always work better using a mouse. Mice are not useful, and often not even usable, with programs that do not recognize mouse input commands.

Trackballs are upside-down mice. The unit sits on your desk or clips to the side of your portable computer. Instead of moving the unit, you roll the ball with your fingers, and you push the buttons when the cursor gets to where you want it. Trackballs work like mice, except that they require less space.

New variations of the mouse are reaching the market daily. There are pen devices that move the cursor as you move the pen, touch devices that move the cursor as you move your finger, and other alternatives. You will have to decide for yourself which you prefer.

Scanners and Optical Character Readers

A scanner is a device that will read documents or images and convert them into a computer-usable file. Text can be converted directly into one of several word processing formats using optical character recognition (OCR) software. Graphic images can be converted into one of the common graphics editor program formats such as EPS, GEM, or PIC. Scanners are the most convenient means of inserting a graphic image, such as a plat or a survey, into a form, which can then be pasted (inserted) into a word processing document or transformed into an exhibit.

Because of the need to convert forms and documents into computer-usable form, lawyers are among the largest users of scanning hardware and optical character recognition (OCR) software. Software from several vendors can convert hard copy documentary evidence into searchable text. This software can be used with the vendors' own hardware or with scanners from other suppliers.

If you are considering scanning and OCR equipment, keep in mind that even the best of it is less than perfect. Scanning is somewhat slow, and the accuracy of your final result depends a lot on the quality of the document you have to scan in to begin with. With a poor quality original, you may only get a 50% accurate word conversion.

OUTPUT DEVICES

Video Displays (Monitors)

The video display (monitor) is your window into the computer. The typical monitor, whether monochrome or color, will display a screen of 25 lines (about 38 percent of an actual 11-inch-long page) and 80 characters in width (the full width of an 8 1/2-inch-wide page.) Most come in 12- or 14-inch diagonal sizes. Larger sizes are easier to read but cost much more. If you spend most of your time using a graphical environment like Windows or OS/2, then you should seriously consider getting a 16-inch or larger monitor. Smaller monitors are hard to read in the high-resolution video modes commonly used for graphical interfaces.

The video system consists of the monitor and a matching video adapter. Many computers come with the adapter built into the system board of the computer. Some monitors are multi-sync or multi-scan, which means that they can work with a variety of different types of video adapters, including the older EGA and CGA color cards. Many, however, only work with one kind, so, for example, you will need a VGA or Super VGA adapter if you buy a VGA-only monitor. Remember that a Super VGA video card will work with a VGA-only monitor. You simply won't get the greater than regular VGA resolutions.

Monitors vary significantly in resolution, contrast, brilliance, and quality. Before you buy, take a look at several, both color and monochrome.

Monochrome Monitors

Monochrome monitors use different combinations of background and foreground colors. Their normal resolution displays 720 dpi (dots per inch) horizontally and 348 dpi vertically. (The higher these numbers the better the resolution.) They can form sharp, easily read characters and are also capable of displaying some monochrome-only graphics. They are not suitable for more modern graphical user interfaces like Windows or OS/2.

Older IBM-compatible monitors displayed amber or green on black, without any shades of gray. They required a special adapter (Hercules or compatible) to run Windows or to display business graphics, and could not be used to run many games and most graphics programs. Modern monochrome monitors are capable of high-resolution graphics and can display many shades of gray. Given the small difference in price between monochrome and color monitors, there is little reason to forgo color unless you really prefer monochrome.

Full-page monochrome monitors capable of displaying an entire $8\frac{1}{2}$ by 11-inch page are also available. They are usually found in desktop publishing environments and cost much more than most other monitors. They also require special adapters and software drivers. They will not always provide full-screen output with every program.

Color Monitors

Color video displays are available in various resolutions and color display levels, each of which has its own set of adapter cards and monitors. Advanced high-resolution color monitors also include powerful graphics capabilities.

There are several different color and resolution standards available for IBM-compatible computers, and they vary in both price and capabilities. In ascending order, they include CGA (Color Graphics Adapter), which offers a limited number of colors and basic resolution; EGA (Enhanced Graphics Adapter), which offers more colors (16) and better resolution; and VGA (Video Graphics Array), which provides up to 256 colors and an even higher text resolution. CGA (also called RGB) and EGA are obsolete. VGA color is the standard today and is adequate for business usage.

There are also higher resolution graphics cards and monitors available. Generally, these offer better linear resolution along with greater color choices. For a time, Super VGA was considered the high end. Now even higher performance standards such as the 8514A or IBM XGA are available. These VGA-compatible adapter cards usually include hardware to markedly increase screen speed and offer very high resolution and up to 32,768 colors and many shades of gray. With the parallel move toward OS/2 and Windows-based programs and their reliance upon sophisticated graphics, high-resolution systems such as these become increasingly attractive. If you have the choice and the money, consider purchasing a 14-inch or larger monitor and a high-resolution video card that includes a graphics coprocessor or Windows accelerator hardware.

Many programs are now being written to take advantage of color monitors to display information in ways that can be more quickly and easily assimilated. This is particularly true with graphic interfaces like Microsoft Windows and certain database programs. Make sure you view the programs you intend to use on both a color and monochrome monitor before you buy.

Printers

One of the supposed benefits of the microcomputer revolution was that we would be moving toward the paperless office. Sadly, the paperless office still exists only on paper, and it seems we are actually using more paper than ever. Computers and printers simply make it easier to put things on paper.

There are four types of printers in common use: daisy wheel printers, dot-matrix printers, laser printers, and ink jet printers.

Daisy Wheel Printers

Daisy wheel printers use a moving wheel of characters to strike the paper through an inked ribbon and make the image. They are limited to the characters on the wheel. They operate much like a typewriter. Although they produce high quality output, they are very slow and quite noisy. With the advent of higher quality dot-matrix printers and lower cost laser printers, daisy wheel printers are seldom a good office choice.

Dot-Matrix Printers

Dot-matrix printers use tiny pins to strike the paper in different positions through an inked ribbon to form letters and other characters as well as graphic images. Most use 9 or 24 pins, and those with more pins produce better images, but cost a little more and require more maintenance. Better images are obtained when such a printer is used in the letter-quality mode than in the draft mode, but the printing speed decreases considerably.

High quality dot-matrix printers are often fast and can produce a good image. The drawback is that they are noisy and usually slower than a laser printer. Dot-matrix printers are particularly useful for database reports, billing, checks and other routine output because they are inexpensive and can print on continuous form paper, without human intervention.

Both dot-matrix and daisy wheel printers are good for printing checks, summonses, and other documents that need a carbon copy.

Laser Printers

The fastest, highest quality, and often most expensive letter-quality printers are laser printers. Laser printers produce excellent output, are

FIGURE A.7 Options Available on Hewlett-Packard LaserJet Printers

PRINTER	SPEED	FEATURES
HP IIIP	4 ppm	Small, one paper bin plus manual feed; good on an attorney's desk
HP III	8 ppm	One paper bin plus manual feed
HP IIID	8 ppm	Larger, two paper bins plus manual feed or envelope tray, prints on both sides of paper ("duplex").
HP III SI	18 ppm	Same as III D, plus optional network adapter, a few more fonts, more economical toner system, and slightly higher resolution output.
HP 4	8 ppm	Improved graphic resolution (600 x 600 dpi), 45 built-in fonts, and improved processing and memory speed over the LaserJet Series III.

quiet, and can generate between four and eighteen pages per minute. Laser printers can produce an almost unlimited range of graphic images, and they can create newsletters or briefs that look as though they have been typeset. They will allow you to print a wide range of sizes and styles of fonts, so long as your word processing or desktop publishing program can support them. Your briefs will look as if they have been professionally printed rather than typed.

Without getting into technical details, the operation of a laser printer resembles that of a photocopier. It produces entire pages at a time, rather than a line at a time. Laser printers use replaceable cartridges of toner to produce the image on the paper. Each cartridge is good for about 4,000 pages.

The Hewlett Packard LaserJet (HP) was the first affordable desktop laser printer. Since then, HP has steadily improved its laser printers, and the LaserJet Series III became the standard for quality, reasonable cost, and reliability. Almost every software package of consequence supports the HP LaserJet.

Many other manufacturers, including IBM, sell laser printers that emulate the HP LaserJet. Some of these, particularly the newer IBM, Compaq, and Epson models, are considered to be good buys. Because these models tend to change quickly and prices vary dramatically, you should check reliable magazines, such as *PC Magazine* or *InfoWorld*, before you buy. As a word of caution, we note that over the years some vendors' HP-compatible models have turned out to be unreliable or lower in quality. HP and to a lesser extent IBM have provided consistently reliable operation and quality at a reasonable price.

Hewlett-Packard also markets the low-cost personal LaserJet IIIP that prints only four pages per minute, half the speed of the LaserJet III. Its main advantage is that it is less expensive. It is a good choice for anyone not needing the full speed of a regular laser printer. If you're doing a lot of graphics, the HP IIIP may be just what you need. It's nearly as fast in this task as the regular Series III while providing a darker, more consistent image. The HP III and HP IIIP accept many of the same memory boards, accessories, and font cartridges. These are generally not very expensive. Often, installed extra memory and a font cartridge will provide all the extra capability that you might need. A 4-MB HP-compatible memory board, the maximum extra memory that these printers will accept, wholesales for less than $200.00 and may be a good investment.

At the high end, HP markets the LaserJet III SI. It was a breakthrough in a number of ways, and is strongly recommended for heavy applications. It is fast at 18 pages per minute, comes with an optional network adapter, has the highest resolution of all, and supports very large paper bins. Most important, it may be the least expensive to use. Over the long lifetime of the machine, the cost per page of the printer and supplies can be lower than less expensive printers. Consider whether your use will justify the additional purchase price.

Just as this book went to press, Hewlett-Packard announced the release of the HP LaserJet 4. Although priced slightly lower than the LaserJet Series III, it provides a wide variety of enhanced features, including a resolution of 600 by 600 dots per inch, 45 scalable typefaces built-in, a new high-speed RISC processor, and 2 MB of internal memory. It is rated at eight pages per minute and is specially adapted for printing graphics, either through DOS, Windows, or the Macintosh. It is a strong contender for the new standard for law offices.

If you use desktop publishing or produce graphics, you should consider getting a printer that supports the PostScript page description language or that accepts optional PostScript cartridges. PostScript is a standard computer language for describing and printing material where high quality, flexibility, and heavy graphics usage are paramount. PostScript formerly was quite expensive because it required special printers that recognized its commands. The expense, and PostScript's generally slow output speed, limited its general use. Recently, however, manufacturers like Pacific Data Products began marketing PostScript accelerator boards and cartridges (such as Pacific Page) that can convert an ordinary HP Series III printer into a fairly quick PostScript printer.

Ink Jet Printers

Ink jet printers can provide high-quality output similar in appearance to that of a laser printer. Ink jet printers typically are slower, but less expensive than laser printers. They produce 1 to 3 pages per minute and spray tiny droplets of ink on the paper instead of using photocopier technology like laser printers. Their output is surprisingly similar in quality to a laser printer. Both allow you to use different fonts and type sizes. An ink jet printer is often a good choice for home offices with low printing demands or for a printer connected to the attorney's own computer. The HP Deskjet series provides one popular, reliable, and affordable choice. The Deskjet 500C can provide either black and white or color output. As of this writing, however, color output is limited to those programs like Windows and Quattro Pro for which HP provides the necessary software drivers.

Portable ink jet printers are also available. The Canon Bubblejet BJ-10 and Citizen PN48 weigh as little as four pounds, can run from a battery pack, and are a great choice for the "laptop lawyer." We know one lawyer who uses one to produce orders on the spot in the courtroom. Portable ink jet printers also are an excellent backup if your regular printer fails.

COMMUNICATIONS DEVICES

Modems

Modems allow one computer to communicate with another. If you use a PC to access public information services like LEXIS, WESTLAW, and ABA/net, or to access bulletin boards or another PC, you will need a modem. The term *modem* stands for MOdulator/DEModulator. Modems translate the digital signals computers use into the analog signals telephones use, and then translate them back to digital at the other end.

Along with a modem, you will also need a software program to implement your communications. There are several good communications programs available, including several highly regarded shareware programs. Most modems and communications software are Hayes compatible, which means that they support the standard set of commands used in modems manufactured by Hayes.

Internal modems can be installed inside your computer in an expansion slot on your system board. They connect to the telephone via a standard telephone wire and jack. The software then dials your numbers and attends to the other communications tasks that are necessary. External modems can connect with your computer's serial port via a cable, and they plug into the wall outlet for power. Like internal modems, they connect to the telephone line and work with your chosen software. External modems are more expensive and use a serial port on the computer, but are more flexible because they can be moved between several computers.

Modems are rated by their speed of data transmission, measured in baud (bits per second). You divide by 10 to get the maximum number of characters, or bytes, transmitted per second, so that a 2400-baud modem transmits 240 characters per second. As a reference point, this is about four times the speed of the fastest daisy-wheel printers.

Most modems in use today transmit at 2400 or 9600 baud. Faster modems are available at additional cost. Although prices are now dropping, a 2400- or a 9600-baud modem usually provides the best balance between speed and economy. There is downward compatibility, so that faster modems can talk to slower modems. Consider spending a little more and purchasing a modem that includes error correction and data compression software. If you have a comparably equipped modem on the other end, your data transmissions will proceed much faster. (If not, these features don't function.) Such modems meet the V.42 bis standard for 2400-baud modems and the V.32 bis standard for 9600-baud modems.

To connect the home and the office, you can install one modem in your home computer and one in your office and then access one computer from the other to check appointments, work from home, send files, etc. Communications software is needed for this type of operation, but it is neither expensive nor difficult to use. Among the software useful for this type of remote office access are PC Anywhere IV, Carbon Copy, Procomm Plus, PCTools Version 7.1, and Closeup.

Fax Boards

You can also use communications facilities to fax materials via your computer rather than by conventional fax machine. This requires adding another circuit board to your computer. Generally, you can fax things in this way if they are prepared on your computer (for example, by your word processor). You can also receive fax messages via your computer. Unless you have a scanner, you will still need to send regular printed or signed material via a regular fax machine; thus, a fax modem is generally no more than a convenient adjunct to a fax machine.

STORAGE DEVICES

The most common storage devices are hard and floppy disk drives. These are discussed in Arthur Miltz's "An Introduction to Computers for Beginners" in Section 1. However, there are a number of other kinds of storage devices which we will discuss here.

Compact Disks

Compact disks (using the same optical/laser technology as musical compact disks) can also be used for computer storage. They are known as *CD-ROM* (for *compact disk-read only memory*) and can store several hundred megabytes of digital information. The reference to read-only memory means that they can only have data put on them

once by the publisher, and they cannot be erased and reused. In this respect they are more like records (or musical compact disks themselves) than recording tape.

Because of their great storage capacity, CD-ROM disks can be used for permanent storage or for distributing data intended to be kept permanently and used repeatedly. They are used by legal publishers. A CD-ROM drive is becoming standard equipment for many lawyers who regularly access such legal materials. (Compact disks need their own special disk drives and the appropriate software to conduct searches. The disks themselves are removable and interchangeable.)

WORM Drives and Erasable Optical Disks

WORM (*write once read many*) drives are another type of storage device that can be written to only once and cannot be reused. They are similar to CD-ROM disks, but an attorney can store his or her own information on them, without being dependent on a publisher. For example, massive databases of document summaries can be placed on a WORM disk and instantly searched. Likewise, images or animations can be stored and instantly retrieved.

One recent innovation is to combine document summary databases with video images of the documents themselves. You can then search by the document index and also retrieve the full image of the document. This is ideal in litigation in which the parties and their attorneys are in different locations, since the WORM disks can be copied, moved, and searched much more easily than their paper counterparts.

Erasable optical disk drives are becoming more available and less expensive. This is clearly an area to watch in the future, since these removable disks offer almost unlimited storage at a very low incremental cost. After IBM introduced a $3\frac{1}{2}$-inch, 128-MB rewritable optical disk, many other manufacturers, such as Sony, jumped on the 128-MB bandwagon. This is likely to become a standard format in the near future, and prices will probably drop fast.

Tape Backups

Magnetic tape, similar to a standard-size audiotape recording cassette, is often used in what are known as tape backup devices for hard disks. They are useful if you have large amounts of data to back up since they can run automatically, even at night or at other times when no one needs to use the equipment, and you can back up the entire hard disk onto a single cassette. In contrast, if you back up a hard disk onto floppy disks, someone must sit there and change disks until it is done, and you must keep track of a large number of floppy backup disks.

Tape backup systems can be installed in the place of a floppy disk drive, or they can be external. The external ones can also be portable, so that you can move a single tape backup device from computer to computer, changing the tape and connecting it to different computers. Tape backup units are especially necessary for local area networks. Since a good tape unit may not cost much more that $300.00, they are an economical and convenient means of protecting your valuable data. Whenever you run a tape backup, make sure that you verify the backup's accuracy afterwards.

Large digital audio tape (DAT) units, using the same optical technology as compact disks, can store over a gigabyte of information, and are recommended for large network backup units or for large litigation support databases.

CONNECTING PERIPHERALS TO YOUR COMPUTER

All peripheral devices must be connected to the computer mechanically and/or electronically. Most peripheral devices are attached to the central processor through adapter cards that are physically plugged into special sockets on the main system board. These connecting sockets, also called *expansion slots,* and their associated circuitry, comprise the Input/Output (I/O) bus.

Because several manufacturers have begun to differentiate their I/O buses, you can no longer assume that any peripheral adapter card will physically fit or electronically work with any IBM-compatible computer. You must be sure that components are properly matched to the I/O bus because their adapter cards will work only with the I/O bus for which they are designed.

PORTS AND CABLES

Peripheral devices are connected to the computer ports via cables, which come in different configurations suitable both to the device and to the kind of port being used. Keep in mind that cables are not interchangeable. You must make sure that you have the correct cable for the use to which you intend to put it.

A *port* is the doorway to the computer—the external connection via an opening in the case from the computer to the external peripheral equipment. Common types of ports include those for the keyboard and the monitor (each of which has a specialized connector) and more general types such as parallel and serial ports, game controller ports, and ports for connecting external storage devices.

Serial and Parallel Ports

Serial and parallel ports are the most common and the most important ports. Whether a port is parallel or serial tells you how, and how fast, it can transfer data. Serial ports use one wire to transfer data and can handle only one bit of information at a time. Parallel ports use eight wires and can handle eight bits at a time.

Most printers are used with parallel ports, since the faster data transfer lets the printers work faster. Serial ports are used for most communications devices, and for some mice. Parallel and serial ports are not interchangeable.

On IBM and IBM-compatible computers, DOS names serial ports with the prefix "COM" (i.e., COM1:, COM2:) and names parallel ports with the prefix "LPT" (i.e., LPT1:, LPT2:, LPT3:). Only a few parallel and serial ports are available to each computer.

External Storage Device Ports

Ports for connecting external disk drives, scanners, and other external storage devices also have specialized connectors not usually compatible with other types of equipment. The SCSI (Small Computer Systems Interface, pronounced *scuzzy*) port is an industry-standard adapter that lets up to seven SCSI devices, i.e., hard disks, scanners, tape drives, or CD-ROM devices, be daisy-chained together. There are many partially incompatible types of SCSI. Before you buy an SCSI adapter card, make sure that it supports all of the specific peripherals you want to install. If possible, wait until the SCSI-2 standard is established and more widely accepted among peripheral manufacturers.

What Ports You Need

With any computer, you will surely need at least one parallel port for your printer, and a combination of serial ports to let you connect a modem and possibly a mouse. If you are using a bus mouse with its own adapter card, then you will probably not need a second internal serial port. Likewise, installing an internal modem eliminates the need for the serial port otherwise dedicated to an external modem. Whether you want any other ports depends on how you configure your system. Additional ports can be included at the outset or added later as needed. Adding them is generally easy and inexpensive, but sometimes there can be conflicts between devices and network cards that have to be resolved.

PROTECTIVE EQUIPMENT

Once you invest in computer hardware and software, you should also consider various protective devices, including the following.

Surge Protectors

Computers are sensitive to variations in current. Electrical currents occasionally surge, and this can damage the computer. Simple surge suppressors guard against this by keeping current surges from reaching the computers. They plug into the wall outlet on one end and have a strip of outlets, usually with a separate on-off switch and an on-off light, on the other end. They may also have a manual reset switch in the event that a surge causes the circuit to open.

One added benefit of a surge protector is that it can be used as an on-off switch for the entire system. The on-off switches on the computer and on the peripheral equipment are often the first things to break. With a surge suppressor that has its own on-off switch, you can plug everything into it and leave all the other switches turned on, using the surge suppressor as the main switch for the entire system. This will have no adverse affect on any of the equipment and will prolong the life of the individual switches. If the switch on the surge suppressor should break, it is far easier and cheaper to replace the suppressor than it would be to fix any of the other switches. You should also make sure that every surge protector meets UL's 1449 standard.

Better surge protectors, such as the Tripp-Lite Isobar, actually guarantee repair of any equipment damaged if the surge protector fails. You must decide if this is a wise investment for your purposes. Electrical utility tariffs typically exclude damages caused by a power surge.

Uninterruptible Power Supplies

If the current fails, or the voltage fluctuates too much, everything in RAM not already stored on a disk will be lost. This means that at least part of what you're working on at the moment will be lost. Uninterruptible power supplies provide a battery (or, occasionally, a generator) power backup together with a warning mechanism, giving you time to store your data after the power fails. The usual battery system warning period is about 10 minutes. An uninterruptible power supply is desirable for most stand-alone PC applications, but is a MUST with file servers.

Static Mats

Static electricity, generated as you walk across the carpet to your desk, can damage data on your hard or floppy disks. Static mats draw off the static electricity from your body before it can do any damage. They may be floor mats under your chair, or desk mats under your keyboard. They draw off the current when you touch them before you touch the equipment. They are inexpensive, easy to install and require no attention thereafter.

Vertical Stands

We often see desktop computers sitting horizontally on desks. To save space, however, the case and its contents can just as well stand on its side on the desk or the floor. If the cables to the peripherals are not long enough, extension cables of every type are readily available.

Computers can be used in any position except upside down or at an angle. If you have furniture or walls on both sides of a case that is standing vertically, that's fine. If you don't, to guard against its falling over and damaging something, vertical stands are available. These are merely bases that sit on the floor and hold the computer case firmly upright. They are inexpensive and easy to use. Make sure that any floor-mounted computer has good ventilation and won't be jarred inadvertently.

CONCLUSION

Even the most powerful computer is useless without the proper choice of peripherals. Wise choice of the video, data storage, and input devices are crucial to making your investment as productive and as pleasant to use as possible.

Arthur Ian Miltz practices law in Livingston, New Jersey, in the medical malpractice, product liability, and other personal injury areas. A certified civil trial attorney, Mr. Miltz is a member of the New Jersey and New York bars. Mr. Miltz is active in the American Bar Association's Section of Law Practice Management, where he serves as vice chair of the section's Beginning Computer Users Interest Group and Litigation Interest Group. He is also chair of the Computer Applications Committee of the Essex County, New Jersey, Bar Association, chair of the Product Liability Committee of ATLA-New Jersey, and the author of the Discovery *volume of Matthew Bender & Co.'s* Art of Advocacy *series, as well as numerous book chapters and articles.*

Joseph L. Kashi is a sole practitioner living in Soldotna, Alaska. He received his B.S. and M.S. degrees from MIT in 1973 and his J.D. from Georgetown University Law Center in 1976. His practice consists primarily of contract and personal injury litigation.

A Network for Your Law Office

Joseph L. Kashi

Networking, or tying together two or more PCs, printers, and other devices in a law office, is one of the most difficult, yet important, issues in automating a litigation practice. Joe Kashi explains how a network system works and what options are open for your law office.

A computer network, also called a *LAN* or *local area network*, provides a means of connecting two or more personal computers so that they can share programs, data, and expensive components like laser printers. It provides the electronic glue binding together the members of the firm, enabling attorneys and support staff to combine their efforts and work cooperatively on a case. Almost every law office, even a sole practitioner with one or two support staff members, can benefit from a PC network. You will find that you can edit documents, check your calendar or office-wide databases and conflict files, search the firm's brief bank, send messages to your partner, and check the status of a client's billing—without leaving your desk. Without a network, data transfer between individual users is limited to the proverbial "sneaker net"—copying each file on to a floppy disk and hand-carrying it between computers. Networking your law office is one of the best strategies for improving your work product and profitability.

This article provides an introduction to the concepts and terminology underlying the use of networks.[1] Even if you are not a computer "techie," you will find that your ability to use your computer system and to make good purchasing decisions will improve if you have a basic understanding of how it works. Here are the basic concepts.

NETWORK COMPONENTS

Although network design varies from system to system, most have the following general components:

1. *The File Server:* Most networks are built around a central computer that stores office-wide programs and data and sends whatever information is needed to individual computers or other peripheral devices such as a printer. Centrally located data is the great advantage. Each network user has access to central data; your system administrator can backup the network files every night, ensuring that important files are not lost if the system malfunctions.

   At the same time, "your eggs are all in one basket." If the file server breaks down, the entire network is down, and the PCs can only work as single-user systems. For this reason, most good network designs provide some measure of redundancy, such as parallel "duplexed" storage on the file server and regular backup of a user's data to his or her local PC hard disk.

2. *Network Operating System:* This is the software program that controls communications between the file server and each peripheral station and that processes requests for data and files.

3. *Network Hardware*: This is the hardware that allows your computer to communicate between the file server and other pieces of equipment including computers and printers. Included within this category are network adapter cards, which attach to individual computers or printers, amplifiers to boost long cable runs, and the network cabling that physically connects each computer.

238

Network Operating Systems

In order to properly communicate with each other, DOS computers require specialized network software that controls the flow of data through the network. The Novell NetWare 2.2 and 3.11 operating systems are the industry standard, with about a 57 percent market share. Other common network operating systems, such as ArtiSoft's LANtastc and Performance Technology's PowerLAN are compatible with a more generic standard, IBM's NETBIOS. Most networked business programs can operate with either Novell or NETBIOS-compatible network operating systems, but this should be carefully confirmed beforehand. Microsoft OS/2 LAN Manager 2.1 is coming on strong.

Here are some of the prominent network operating systems:

Novell NetWare

The Novell Corporation of Utah offers a number of systems for different size networks. Smaller firms should consider NetWare 2.2. Although NetWare 2.2 includes the option to install it on a nondedicated server, use it only on a fully dedicated file server. The nondedicated file server option is not reliable under day-to-day usage. Even Novell's own technicians strongly recommend against using its nondedicated mode. Medium to large size firms should consider NetWare 3.11 and higher.

Almost all network hardware manufacturers and software publishers support NetWare. Its performance and reliability are the standards of the industry. NetWare should be installed by an experienced technician; it's too complex for a home-brew installation.

OS/2 LAN Manager

Microsoft, which publishes MS-DOS and Windows, also publishes OS/2 LAN Manager, which is newer and in some ways more advanced than Novell. IBM sells a variant of this product, LAN Server. While LAN Manager is technically excellent, the market has not broadly accepted it as of 1992, and even IBM is now supporting Novell. However, if you are a large firm or are considering a transition to IBM's advanced OS/2 operating system, investigate LAN Manager. LAN Manager requires an OS/2 file server, but will service DOS, OS/2, and Windows workstations.

LANtastic

Small law offices should give serious consideration to LANtastic. This product is economical, easy to install and operate, and performs quite well. LANtastic is a good choice for the small office and has received many favorable reviews. It is slower than Novell, but the Ethernet versions can run on cabling that can also be used with Novell should the firm outgrow LANtastic. LANtastic's own Ethernet and 10BaseT cards include a Novell-compatible mode.

Other Common Network Systems

Banyan's VINES, a UNIX-based network operating system, is particularly useful for very large networks that have many different file servers and remote locations. Some new versions of UNIX will support DOS program operation.

PowerLAN, a newer network system by Performance Technology, offers LANtastic-like ease and performance comparable to Novell NetWare 2.2. PowerLAN has received an "Editor's Choice" award from PC Magazine and is available from Performance Technology, telephone (512) 349-2000. It is my personal choice for a small law office network. This fast operating system has highly optimized communications drivers that can squeeze maximum performance from inexpensive and reliable ARCNET cards. PowerLAN also offers a reliable, fast, dedicated server mode.

Novell now markets a simple DOS-based network, NetWare Lite, that lists for $99 per station. Although this easy to use operating system coexists with the same wide variety of hardware and software as its bigger siblings, NetWare Lite is light on performance. I have personally tested most of the common network operating systems, and NetWare Lite is the slowest except for LANtastic's low-end software. In fact, reinstalling PowerLAN on the same hardware more than doubled network speed compared to Lite. If you have severe budget constraints, will not use more than five stations on your network, and intend to install the network yourself, then NetWare Lite is probably the way to go. Otherwise, install Advanced NetWare or PowerLAN.

NETWORK TOPOLOGY AND CABLING

After you have chosen a network operating system, decide on the specific hardware your network will use. Although the basic hardware types do not change quickly, specific network cards do. Choose your network carefully based upon what is available when you are ready to purchase. Whatever you choose, make sure that your specific operating system and network hardware operate together and have adequate file transfer speed and expansion capacity for any likely future needs.

In most situations, at least one of the following network hardware designs will be offered:

1. Ethernet, including 10Base-T.
2. Token Ring.
3. ARCNET and its variants.

All of these designs can do an efficient job under the right circumstances. However, if you do not understand some of the basic differences between them, you can spend much more on your network than necessary. Here is a brief description of each system:

Ethernet

Ethernet has been around for more than a decade and is the most common networking topology. Many larger computer systems such as those manufactured by Digital Equipment, Sun Microsystems, and others use Ethernet as their primary means of communications between terminals. Ethernet, like other network systems, transmits data between computers in small packets. A large program like WordPerfect may require the transmission of 300 packets to start.

The first Ethernet systems connected could network components by coaxial cable, which came in two types, either "Thick" or "Thin." Thick cable could be strung for a substantial distance, and each branch could hold up to several hundred PCs or workstations. Thin cable was used for fewer connections and more limited distances but was less expensive and easier to install.

More recent versions of Ethernet use what is called the 10Base-T standard to allow you to use telephone type cable, which is often referred to as "twisted pair." One primary advantage is that many offices already have spare telephone wire installed. You might thus avoid the cost of stringing extra cable. Unfortunately, some phone systems are not properly wired to allow immediate use of their cable as network connections. Preexisting cabling usually is of inadequate quality for data communications, so you likely will have to spend the money to rewire with data grade cable.

How Ethernet Works

When a computer in the network wants to send or receive a data "packet" on the network, it first checks to see if the network is free. If not, it waits a random amount of time before retrying. If the network is free and two computers try to gain simultaneous access, both will back off and wait a random amount of time before trying again. Ultimately, all computers can gain access to the network because communications proceed at high rates of speed. Under heavy continual load, Ethernet may suffer so many simultaneous access attempts that its load-carrying capability degrades substantially.

Ethernet has a published data transfer rate of approximately 10 megabits per second. This maximum top speed, called the *bandwidth*, is the maximum theoretical speed for the network as a whole, and does not represent the likely top speed between the file server and a single workstation. Single station speed can be much slower because of interference between stations attempting to communicate simultaneously.

Token Ring

Token Ring networks were introduced by IBM and are more efficient and faster than the Ethernet standard because of higher transmission speed and lower interference between stations. The bandwidth for a high-end Token Ring network is now 16 megabits per second, which translates into a single station speed as high as 575 KB per second.

How Token Ring Works

Token Ring architecture requires that each terminal be hooked with the cabling passing from one terminal to the next in a ring. The host computer, or file server, continually passes a series of *tokens*, actually a frame that is capable of holding a message or piece of data. Each token travels from machine to machine throughout the network.

When a terminal or computer wants to send a message, it waits for an empty token and then fills it with its message or request. As the token moves on through the network, the recipient machine watches, grabs the appropriate message, and resets the token to empty status. In this fashion, the system avoids communications interference. You could envision this system as operating like a string of boxcars, with messages and information being loaded and unloaded on a continual basis.

Traditionally, Token Ring has required special cable and connectors for hookup. Token Ring hardware is not cheap: Token Ring cards begin around $350.00 and the wiring costs can raise the per station price considerably. Recently we have seen the emergence of "twisted pair" telephone wire Token Ring cards. However, the office may not be wired properly for this particular network or the quality of the wiring may be poor. Check this carefully before committing.

ARCNET

ARCNET was the first common local area network topology. ARCNET is a form of Token Ring architecture and works somewhat in the same fashion, although the cards for each system cannot be interchanged. It is inexpensive and reliable.

How ARCNET Works

ARCNET generally uses what is called a star topology, with up to 255 computers connected through a series of active and passive hubs. It uses a collision avoidance system similar to Token Ring to eliminate interference between stations. As a result, stations can transmit whenever the network is free—which can result in excellent performance.

This network design has lost some popularity recently because its published specifications list it at a relatively low bandwidth of 2.5 megabits per second. This figure is deceivingly low; in some cases the ARCNET architecture will actually outperform Ethernet.[2] A new ARCNET variant, called Thomas-Conrad Networking System (TCNS) is one of the fastest networking systems available. I have verified multiple station speeds of 1600 KB per second with several stations simultaneously loading the network at that speed.

TCNS can use the same cabling as regular ARCNET and the same network software drivers. As a result, changing from ARCNET to super-fast TCNS is virtually trouble-free. You will probably want to reconfigure your network for best performance, using the very efficient software drivers included with TCNS. Expect to pay about $700 per TCNS station. Considering the simplicity, reliability, and performance of TCNS, this is a bargain.

If you need great speed for only a portion of your ARCNET network for such heavy uses as

litigation support or optical imaging, then you could install one TCNS card in the file server for these uses and simply use the existing ARCNET hardware for less demanding tasks. TCNS offers the blinding speed of fiber-optic systems at a lower cost and without expensive, hard to install fiber optics.

Multiuser Operating Systems as a LAN Substitute

There are a number of other multiuser operating systems that are capable of allowing users to simultaneously execute MS-DOS programs on the same computer. Typically, these operating systems are designed to run on 386 computers because of that chip's inherent multiuser design. These multiuser operating systems include Concurrent DOS 386, V/M 386, and PC-MOS/386.

Consider one of these systems if you only need to give occasional computer access to more than one person. If you do, bear two things in mind. First, if everyone is using a single computer, the performance available to each individual user can be substantially degraded. Second, there is no redundancy. If the single computer becomes inoperative, no one will be able to do any work until the unit is replaced or repaired.

UNIX is an industrial-strength, tried and tested operating system that has many adherents in more technical realms. UNIX systems can support several simultaneous users and form the basis of many larger law firms' minicomputer-based automation systems. UNIX does have some significant drawbacks despite its technical benefits and good performance. It is more difficult to learn than DOS, is not as well standardized (with the resultant lack of general business programs), and will probably require more technical support than most lawyers or end users can provide.

NETWORK APPLICATIONS

Your consultants, vendors, or knowledgeable friends should help you select and implement software that makes special use of a network. These include:

- Document management/searching software (such as PC DOCS and SoftSolution) to help you track and index the documents created on the network.
- Electronic mail software (such as cc:Mail,

Microsoft Mail, and DaVinci Mail) to send documents, telephone messages and other messages, and scheduling information around the network.

- Scheduling software (such as the Network Scheduler).
- Menu systems to make it easier to handle log-in scripts (such as Sabre Menu).

WordPerfect Office and Futurus Team are examples of two programs that combine several of these functions. One comprehensive source of network programs is Valueware, Novato, California (800) 634-8684.

CONCLUDING TIPS FOR INSTALLING A NETWORK

If you plan to install a local area network, start by determining what your needs are, what software you will use, who will have priority for what equipment, and how you will gradually phase in the equipment in order to gain experience without being overwhelmed. Here are some thoughts.

I. Take Your Time!

A phased transition will give you some time to train your in-house office automation person. In a small firm, that person will probably be you. In addition, it is wise to start slowly so that you can evaluate and refine your purchases as you go along. Any computer system, particularly a network used by many people, gains from consistent use. Don't expect instant nirvana. If a computer system is regularly used and new data is entered as it arises, there will soon come a time when everything is on the computer network and works well. Then, you'll wonder how you ever lived without it. This does not occur overnight, and trying to enter all of your old data, form files, form books, etc., in a crash project to computerize everything *now* invites confusion, burnout, and a generally bad experience.

2. Switch to Network Programs

When installing a network, replace your existing software with network versions designed to allow more than one user at a time to access various files. Otherwise, there is a good chance that your data files will become overwritten accidentally and the data corrupted. Fortunately,

many common business and legal applications now provide either built-in network support or are published in network versions at a somewhat higher cost. Allowing more than one person to use a single-user software package is usually a violation of the copyright and licensing agreement.

3. Build In Redundancy

A carefully designed LAN should have some amount of built-in redundancy. One way to accomplish this is to equip the desktop units with hard disks, enabling them to operate on a stand-alone basis. In the event of a major failure of the central LAN file server, the LAN is not totally out of action; you simply cannot get to the data stored on the file server.

Many offices use batch files to copy critical data from the network to the desktop hard disks every night to minimize problems if the system crashes. In addition, by loading your network programs from each local hard disk, accessing only data from the central file server, you will substantially increase your network's apparent performance while reducing its overall load. Often, this trick alone can eliminate the need to install more expensive, faster hardware.

4. Use the Correct Cabling

Make sure that the cabling physically connecting the computers is of excellent quality, properly matched to the network cards, and in compliance with local electrical and building codes. Bad or broken cables and connection points are by far the most frequent cause of network problems after the initial installation is up and running.

5. Make Sure You Have Adequate Power Protection

Every network file server should be protected against momentary power failure by an uninterruptable power supply (UPS). This is a large battery that will power your file server and monitor for a relatively short time so that you can avoid data loss during unexpected power interruptions. Because of the way in which the network operates, file servers are more susceptible to power fluctuations than regular desktop computers, and network data files often suffer greater damage from unexpected power outages than regular desktop computers. Remember, though, that unless your workstations also have a backup UPS, you may still find the program dying in the middle of a critical application and causing file damage. This is particularly common with time and billing programs and other databases. Luckily, small UPSs suitable for individual workstations now cost around $250 or so.

6. Retain a Good Consultant or Know Your Vendor

Don't even think about installing any network without locating a knowledgeable consultant or vendor who will do the work for you or at least provide the technical support and assistance you will undoubtedly need. And *do* check references. You don't want to use a vendor who hasn't set up a system like yours before or who failed to provide good support to another firm. Experience with law firms is particularly important, since the needs of lawyers are often different than other professions and businesses.

7. Make Regular Backups

Have a regular procedure established for daily, incremental backups of data that has changed, with complete backups of the file servers performed weekly.

CONCLUSION

Non-networked PCs are like sole practitioners. Each unit has to do everything, without assistance from others. Networking every PC offers the ability to share tasks and to communicate. With a network, each lawyer and staff member builds upon the work of those around them. A good network is a pleasure to use and will help you get more use out of your computer.

ENDNOTE

1. Although computers made by Apple, DEC, Wang, and other manufacturers can be networked using proprietary solutions, this article concentrates on networking IBM-compatible computers.

Joseph L. Kashi is a sole practitioner living in Soldotna, Alaska. He received his B.S. and M.S. degrees from MIT in 1973 and his J.D. from Georgetown University Law Center in 1976. His practice consists primarily of contract and personal injury litigation.

Where to Get Help: Eight Ideas

The Editors

Feeling a bit lost? Here are some ideas on how to get help.

Computers aren't easy to master, especially for those of us who grew up before the computer era. But it's not as bad as you think. You took a big first step when you bought this book, and a second when you began reading it. Now you are ready to get serious, but you could use some help. Here are some ideas to help get you started.

1. FIND A FRIEND

For every beginner there is a computer guru waiting to help. Look around; find someone who has already computerized. Make friends. Take them to lunch. You'll find them ready to answer questions, offer tips, and even look at your equipment. It can be a big help and the start of a rewarding friendship.

2. JOIN THE LITIGATION INTEREST GROUP

The Litigation Interest Group is made up of 2,000 attorneys, legal assistants, and consultants from several countries who share a common interest in how computers can help improve their litigation practices. The group is sponsored by the Section of Law Practice Management, and its members range from beginners to advanced computer users. It publishes a quarterly newsletter on litigation and computer-related topics called *Litigation Applications*.

The Section of Law Practice Management sponsors a number of other interest groups that focus on computers and technology. Consider joining the Beginning Computer Users Interest Group, the Document Assembly Interest Group, and one or more of the other business-law–related groups. Many of these groups also have newsletters that will interest you.

3. JOIN A LOCAL COMPUTER USERS GROUP

Join a local computer club or users group. Not only will you learn, you will have access to people in your community who can give you help when you most need it. Computer people are friendly folks and very willing to help.

In many areas, you will find a lawyers' user group where you can interact with other lawyers who use the same kinds of equipment and programs you use and have the same kinds of questions and problems you have. You'll find that someone has already had most of your problems (and you'll soon find that you have had some of theirs). You'll also find that they've solved most of the problems and that they're happy to help you do the same. Many user groups also publish excellent newsletters that are worth the cost of membership, even if you don't go to the meetings.

The best ways to find out about user groups in your area are to ask around. Your local bar association may have established one or may be about to do so. In addition, most retailers or consultants can point you in the right direction. If all else fails, follow the ads and articles in professional publications, computer magazines, and the local press.

4. BUY THE LATEST VERSION OF *ACCESS*

The ABA's Section of Law Practice Management publishes an excellent book by Rees Morrison called *Access 1991–1992: A Resource Guide to Legal Automation. Access* is a pocket-sized wealth of information for lawyers with questions about computers. In it you will find tips on how to get started, who to contact for help, and how to learn to use computer software.

5. SUBSCRIBE TO A FEW GOOD COMPUTER MAGAZINES AND NEWSLETTERS

One easy way to keep up with new developments is to subscribe to a few computer magazines or newsletters. Two good magazines for beginners are *PC Novice* and *PC Today*, both published by the same company at P.O. Box 85380, Lincoln, NE 68501-9815. For more advanced reading, try *PC Magazine, PC Week,* or *PC World.* You can find them at most bookstores with a large magazine selection. *MacWorld* is a good magazine covering the Apple Macintosh market.

There are a few magazines that address issues relating to law office technology. The ABA's Section of Law Practice Management publishes several Interest Group newsletters that cover a broad range of technology issues. The Section's magazine, *Law Practice Management,* often publishes articles on technology issues and features a column, "Technology Update," by G. Burgess Allison in each issue. Also, try *Law Office Computing,* from James Publishing Group, 3520 Cadillac Ave., Suite E, Costa Mesa, CA 92626. It covers a wide range of computer/technology topics.

There are a few private newsletters that you should also consider. Try *The Lawyer's PC,* a well-written and practical newsletter published by Shepard's/McGraw Hill. Contact the publisher at P.O. Box 1235, Colorado Springs, CO 80901. Another good newsletter is *Computer Counsel,* written and published by Richard Robbins, 641 W. Lake St., Suite 403, Chicago, IL 60606.

6. TAKE BASIC COMPUTER COURSES

Computer seminars are regularly given by retail computer stores, community colleges, adult education groups, and private educational organizations. Legal groups are increasingly sponsoring programs as well. If your computer has been sitting on your desk and you don't know where to start, one of these courses will help get you going.

7. TAKE ADVANTAGE OF TELEPHONE SUPPORT

If you have a problem, don't try to reinvent the wheel. Pick up the phone. Call the manufacturer or distributor of your hardware or software (the numbers are all in your manuals). Make sure you are at the keyboard when you call, so that you can try what they tell you and tell them how it works as you are doing it.

These people are often your best source of support and information. Don't hesitate to use them, and don't spend endless hours trying to solve a problem you don't really understand. Call at the beginning. You'll be amazed at how simple and easy most problems really are to solve.

8. JOIN COMPUSERVE

CompuServe is a powerful, long-established computer network service. It offers a range of products from electronic mail, to airline information, to on-line shopping. One product that should interest you is the online forum service. Through CompuServe you can access a wide range of forums about computer software, hardware, and automation strategies. For example, most of the hardware, and software vendors participate in vendor forums. If you have a question about your product, it is easier to go online with it than to try to get through by telephone. Although response time isn't instantaneous, you will often get a response in a matter of hours and the help is usually very good. Also, other users browse the forums and will give you their solutions and experiences as well.

There is also a legal forum called *Lawsig.* Through it you can reach hundreds, if not thousands, of lawyers to discuss any topic that comes to mind. As you become accustomed to electronic communication, you will wonder how you ever did without.

THE BOTTOM LINE

The bottom line is—just do it. It's a bit like jumping into a cold swimming pool on a hot day. There is no right time and there is no sense standing and looking. Take the plunge and you will be glad you did. Good luck!

Index

ABA/net
  distribution of experimental computer modeling
    program by, 203
  E-mail using, 117
  gateway to LEXIS and DIALOG systems, 119-20
Abacus diary program, 212
Accounting programs, 214, 217, 222
Acta outlining program, 44, 223
Active Memory, 19
A.D.A.M. anatomy rendering program, 225
Address Book Plus contact database, 221
Addresses, Macintosh with HyperCard to store, 15
Adoption issues, software for, 94
America On Line, 226
Ami Pro (Lotus), 28
  outlining feature of, 44
Application program
  data shared with another, 29
  decision-making, 202
  development, 8
  future, 163-204
  network, 241-42
  as type of software, 7
  Windows versus non-Windows, 27-28
ARCNET network, data transfer process of, 241
Aresty, Neil E., 117-20
Art of Negotiating, The, 45
Artificial intelligence (AI), 163, 188-200
  expert systems and, 189-90
AS-EASY-AS database shareware program, 213
Attorney's Briefcase, Inc., 93
Attorney's Computer Network package, 92-93
AutoDomestic (AutoLaw Corp), 92
Automated litigation support (ALS) software, 155-
  56

Ballard, Alice W., 135-44
Bayesian decision analysis, 175
Beginning Computer Users Interest Group, 244
BestChoice3 (Sterling Castle) decision-making
    program, 202
Billing
  CADA systems and, 82
  hourly vs. value, 67-68
  maximized with document assembly program,
    103-6
Billing software, 4
  case management with, 150
  for contingency cases, 150-51

outlining program as, 58-60, 63
  for recording time and expenses, 145-51
  for team of lawyers, 120, 149-50
Bit defined, 7
Blankity BLANK document assembly program, 77
Blue Sky Advantage document assembly program,
    83-84
Book
  opinions in this, xviii
  organization of, xiv, xvii-xviii
  reasons to read this, xi-xii
Boolean searches, 69
Borgese, Anthony, 86
BOT Financial Corporation, CADA used by, 85
Brainstorming tools, trial law, 42-46
Brief
  tracking versions of a draft, 119-20
  writing and assembling, 121-24
BRS Search full-text retrieval program, 154
Budgeting a case, 37, 173
Burstyn, Harold L., 114, 116, 125-26, 163
Byte defined, 7

CACE expert system, 188
CADA. See Document assembly program
Calculator system in office automation program,
    109, 115, 214
Calculator (Windows) electronic calculator, 31
Calendar
  arithmetic, spreadsheet to calculate, 132
  outlining program to record events as, 39, 60
Calendar programs, 4
  in Futurus Team office automation software,
    110-12
  in GrandView outlining software, 55
  leading, 212, 217
  Macintosh, 221-22
  Windows, 31
Callister, Duncan & Nebeker, CADA used by, 85
Campney, Murphy & Co., CADA used by, 85-86
CAPS (CAPSOFT Development Corp.) document
    assembly program, 77-80, 83-85
Capstone Group, CADA used by, 83
Cardfile (Windows) electronic Rolodex, 31
Case load, determining profitability of, 151
Case management software, 4
  billing program that doubles as, 150
  document assembly program as, 97
  as expert system, 190

for the Macintosh, 221-22
outlining program as, 55-64
Case reports created with outlining program, 59
CaseMaster III database program, 209
cc:Mail E-mail program, 241
CD-ROMs
family law software on, 95
Macintosh, 220
storage capacity of, 234
Central processing unit (CPU), 5
Chance tree
chance nodes on, 179, 182
decision nodes on, 179-81
developing, 178-79
modifying, 179-83
reading, 179
CheckCite cite search program, 123
Checklist
intelligent, 190
of requirements, document assembly program to
create, 98
Child support calculation program, 93-94
Chrysler Corporation, CADA used by, 84
Cite verification software, 120-24
CiteRite (JuriSoft, Inc.) cite checking program, 120-
22
Claims valuation, 135-44
Clause-It (Masterite Software) document assembly
program, 83, 224
Clayton Utz, CADA used by, 86
Clients, procedures for controlling acceptance of
new, 152-53
Clip art programs, 225
Clipboard
Macintosh, 18
Windows, 27
Clock (Windows) digital or analog clock display,
31
Coca-Cola Company, CADA used by, 83
Cohen, Leon, 153-54, 157
CompareRite (JuriSoft, Inc.), 119-20, 123
Competitors, use of CADA by, 81, 83-86
COMPROWISE, 203
CompuServe on-line service, 226, 245
Computer
benefits of using, xiii, 3-4
defined, 4-5
dictating directly to, 125-26
finding help in starting with, 244-45
introduction to using, 1-31
publications, 245
users group, 244
Computer-aided document assembly (CADA). See
Document assembly program
Computer-assisted drafting (CAD), 225
Computer-assisted legal analysis (CALA), 203-4
Computer models to evaluate lawsuits, 202-4
Conflicts of interest

databases to track, 112
identifying, 152-57
management of, 153
Consultants
for network, 243
for office automation, 215
Contingency cases, billing, 150-51
Conveyancing documents, document assembly
program to create, 99-101
Corporate counsel, use of CADA systems by, 82
Correspondence, document assembly program to
automate, 97
Cost reimbursement, 150
Cotellesse, David, 163, 165-74
Cravath, Swaine & Moore, 155-56
Criminal appeal case study, 117-20
Criterium (Sygenex) decision-making program,
202
Crittenden, Ron, 205, 219-28
Cudgel database, 227
Custom Legal Software, 94
Custom software, 8
Cut and paste operations, 18, 27, 71, 115

DacEasy accounting program, 214
Data storage. See Floppy disk and Hard disk
Database program
document, 224
freeform, 198
leading, 209, 211, 216-17
for the Macintosh, 19-21, 222-23
in office automation program, 109, 112-13
purpose of, 19-20, 208-9
research, 94-95
Databases, law firm
attorney, 211
client, 211
conflicts of interest, 112
contact, 221
files, 209-11
hyperdatabases versus traditional, 159-61
initial setup of, 209
litigation-specific, 209
transcripts, 211-12
witnesses, experts, and clients, 112
DaVinci Mail E-mail program, 242
Davis, Polk & Wardwell, CADA used by, 84-85
DaynaFile drive for Macintosh, 11-12
dDIARY diary program, 212-13
Decision analysis, 177-78
Decision tree software, 175-83
Deposition
digests, traditional, 47-48
outlining program to prepare and take, 37-38,
48-54, 60
Desktop publishing
leading programs for, 208, 216
with the Macintosh, 12-13

word processors that incorporate, 208
Determining Damages (Shepard's/McGraw-Hill), 143
Determining Economic Loss in Personal Injury Cases (Shepard's McGraw-Hill), 176
Device drivers, 8
Diagnostic systems as expert systems, 189-90
Diagrams, purpose of, 24-25
Diary program, 4, 212, 217
DiaryMaster II diary program, 212
Dilworth, Paxson, Kalish & Kaufman, CADA used by, 85
Direct Access main menu program, 213
Disbursements, billing program for recording, 148
DISCLOSURE database, 154
Discovery ZX text retrieval format, 118-19
Disk drives, 6. See also individual types
Disk operating system (DOS), 7-8
  Macintosh compatibility with, 11-12
Display. See Monitor
Div/Texas (The Electric Lawyer), 93
Divorce documents, document assembly program to draft, 92-93
Divorce Pleadings System (Attorney's Computer Network, Inc.), 92
DivorceTax (Research Press), 94
dLEGAL SYSTEM, 212
Docket/CM diary program, 212
DocuComp II, 224
Document Assembly Interest Group, 244
Document assembly program, xiii, 4, 65-106
  assembly process using, 68-69
  benefits of, 105-6
  case studies for using, 86-87, 98-106
  costs of, 105
  demand for lawyers familiar with, 83
  as expert system, 189
  in family law practice, 92-93
  integrated into daily law practice, 81-83
  jargon of, 74-75
  in litigation practice, 67-80, 96-106
  managerial aspects of using, 106
  merge features used for mailing lists, 75
  merge features used for pleadings, 71-73
  shells or engines, 74-77
  software vendor list for, 88-91
Dorsey and Whitney, CADA used by, 84
DOS prompt, 8
Dragnet, form file management with, 69
DragonDictate (Dragon Systems, Inc.), 125-26
DUNS numbers, 154
Dynamic Data Exchange (DDE), 27, 29
Dynodex contact database, 221

Eagleson, Robert, 86
Eidelman, James A., 42, 65, 88-95
Electronic mail (E-mail)
  on Macintosh, 220-21
  for networks, 241-42
  in office automation program, 109, 114, 116
Erasable optical disks, 234
Ethernet networking
  10Base-T standard for, 240
  data transfer process, 240
  on Macintosh, 221
Excel (Microsoft) database program, 213, 224
Exhibits, tracking, 22
Expert system
  artificial intelligence and, 189-90
  benefits to law practice of, 188
  classes of, 189-90
  decision tree software as, 175
  defined, 163, 189
  evaluating, 204
  limits of, 189
  litigation problems solved using, 184-87
ExPert System in the Law Of Negligence (EPSILON), 188, 195-99
Expert witness testimony, graphics used with, 14
ExperText document assembly program, 77, 83, 93, 102

Fair Witness outlining program, 13, 18
Family law practice, document assembly software for, 92-93
Fast Forms form program, 224
Fax
  boards, 234
  on Macintosh, 221
  printed with database, 20
  sent or received in background mode, 114-15
Fee petitions, preparing, 150-51
Field defined, 72
File management feature in office automation program, 109
File Manager (Windows), 29
File server, 238, 243
File transfer
  of documents by British solicitors and barristers, 114
FileMaker Pro database program, 20, 222, 224
Files, importing and exporting, 54
Financial analysis program, 93-95
Find and replace operations
  in hypertext program, 161
  in outlining program, 52, 60, 64
First Draft document assembly shell, 85
FLEXICON search program, 190
FlexPractice document assembly program, 68-69, 77, 84, 92
Floppy disk
  backups to, 215
  capacities and sizes, 6
  defined, 6

as permanent data storage unit, 5
Flow charts, purpose and example of, 24-25
Fonts
    for the Macintosh, 12
    for Windows, 29
Form files, software to manage, 69
Forms
    document assembly program to manage stan-
        dard, 96-97
    expert systems to generate, 201-2
    on the Macintosh, 224
    outlining program to create outlines used as
        deposition, 38-40
    precedent, 86
4th Dimension, 21
FrameMaker page layout program, 225
Framework, 43-44
Full Authority (JuriSoft, Inc.), 120, 122-23
Futurus Team office automation program, 109-16
Fuzzy search feature, 69

Gantt chart
    displayed with baseline, 173
    generating, 171
General Counsel document assembly shell, 85
Gigabyte defined, 7
GOfer, 22-23, 69
GrandView (Symantec Corp.)
    case management with, 55-64
    features not included in, 60-61
    outlining and idea processing with, 38, 40-41, 43,
        47-54
Graphical user interface (GUI)
    of Macintosh, 10-11, 17, 219, 228
    of Windows 3.1, 1, 10, 29-30, 219
Graphics on the Macintosh, 13-14, 24-25, 224-26
Graphs
    purpose of, 24
    spreadsheet to create, 131-32
Grateful Med on-line service, 226
Groupware, 223
Guide hypertext program, 158

Hard disk
    advantages over floppy disk of, 6
    capacity of, 7
    defined, 6
    formatting, 7
    as permanent data storage unit, 5
Hardware
    components, 5-7
    defined, 4
    network, 238
Hearsay Rule Advisor, 188, 190-93
Hellmann, Mark, 1, 10-16
Help, places to find, 244-45
Hewlett Packard LaserJet series printers, 232

Holme, Roberts & Owen, CADA used by, 83-84
HyperCard, 14-15, 158-62
Hypermedia, 158-62
HyperTalk scripts, 158
Hypertext features, 41, 50, 93, 158-62

IBM compatible computers
    defined, 7
    key distinctions between Apple Macintosh and,
        8
    program categories for, 27-28
Idea Fisher, 44
Idea Generator, 44
Idea processor. See Outlining program
Informed Designer form program, 224
InfoSelect TSR program, 214
Input devices, 229-30
Instant Recall (Cronlogic) office automation
    program, 116
Instant Update groupware, 223
Interest rates, calculating variable, 137-38
INVALUE (Boise Cascade Corp.), 203-4

Jumpstart document assembly program, 77
Jury instructions, automating, 97
Jury Verdict Research statistical database, 176

Kashi, Joe, 38, 41, 69-70, 109-16, 176, 183, 202, 204-
    5, 229-43
Keyboard
    as hardware component, 7
    as input device, 229
Kilobyte defined, 7
Klein, Marc S., 47-54
Knowledge base system (KBS), 184-87

Lackner Computer Group adoption software, 94
Laff, Kenneth M., 127-34
LAN Manager (Microsoft), 239
LANtastic networking program, 239
Latent Damage System, 189-90
Law Office Manager, 222
LawBase database program, 209
LAWPACK accounting program, 154
LawProcess document engine, 77-78
LawText (RHR Marketing), 93
Legal argument, preparing for, 39
Legal Edge database program, 209
Legal profession, pressure to computerize, xi-xiii
Legal Software Systems domestic law forms, 93
LexaFile case management program, 222
LEXIS
    CheckCite to dial, 123
    Macintosh access to, 226
    Shepard's service of, 120
Linklaters & Paines, CADA used by, 85
Links between hypertext files, 159-61

Litigation calendar, 132
Litigation Interest Group, 244
Litigation practice
    computer-aided document assembly for, 67-80,
        96-106
    Macintosh in, 219-28
    management, project management software for,
        165-74
    office automation program to organize, 109-16
    office automation, setting up, 205-45
    outlining program used in, 37-39
    productivity tools for, 107-62
    spreadsheet program used in, 127-34
    support software for, 4
Litigation, software to model uncertainties in, 175-
    83
LIX document transfer program, 114
LocalTalk, 220
Long, Aldridge and Norman, CADA used by, 83
Loss-of-Future-Earnings System, 198
Lotus 1-2-3 database program, 213, 224
Lotus Agenda office automation program, 43, 116
Lotus Symphony Outliner Add-In, 44

McCarthy Tétrault, CADA used by, 86
MacForms Company, 224
MacinTax tax preparation program, 224
Macintosh (Apple), 10-31
    commands for, uniformity of, 10-11
    communicating with other machines on, 220
    desk accessories for, 220
    graphics with, 13-14, 24-25
    introduction in 1984 of, 220
    key distinctions between IBM compatible and, 8
    law practice using, 219-28
Motorola 68000 series chips in, 5
MS-DOS compatibility of, 11-12
    multitasking with, 22
    networking, 220-21
    operating system, 10
    outlining with, 13
    software vendor list for, 25-26
    text retrieval with, 16, 21-23
    word processing with, 12-13
MacLaw office management program, 222
McLemore, Douglas O., 152-57
MacLinkPlus, 12
Macros
    clause selection with point-and-shoot, 73, 76
    document assembly with, 75
    in office automation program, 115
    in outlining program, 54, 57, 59-60
MacWrite II, 223
Magellan, 69
Mailing labels, 20
Mailing lists, 75
Main menu programs, 213, 217
Mallesons Stephen Jaques, CADA used by, 86
MarcoPolo document database, 224, 226

Mark Up groupware, 223
M.A.R.S. hardware and software, 227
MaxThink (MaxThink, Inc.) outlining program, 38,
    40-41, 44-45
MediClip clip art program, 225
Megabyte defined, 7
Memoranda
    electronic index for, 20
    template in outlining program, 57-59
Memory Mate TSR program, 214
Memory-resident software. See Terminate and stay
    resident (TSR) program
Menu
    computer set up to display, 8
    for network log-in scripts, 242
Merge files, primary and secondary, 72-73
Michigan Friend of the Court, 94
Microprocessors
    Apple and Intel, 5
    for Windows operation, 30
Microsoft Mail E-mail program, 221, 242
Microsoft Word, 208
    document assembly IF statements of, 77
    outlining feature of, 44
Microsoft Word for the Mac, 44
Microsoft Word for Windows, 28-29, 44, 208
Milbank, Tweed, Hadley & McCloy, CADA used
    by, 85
Miltz, Arthur Ian, 1, 3-9, 205, 207-18, 229-37
Minnesota Family Law Database (Digital Legal
    Research), 95
Mintz, Levin, Cohn, Ferris, Glovsky & Popeo,
    CADA used by, 83
Mitratech database program, 209
Mitteldorf, Joshua, 135-44
Modem
    criminal appeal team's use of, 117-20
    external versus internal, 233
    for Macintosh, 221, 226
    speeds, 233-34
Monitor
    adapters for, 230
    color, 231
    as hardware component, 7
    monochrome, 230-31
Monitoring system as expert system, 190
MORE (Symantec Corp.) outlining program, 13,
    18-19, 40, 43, 223
Morgan, Lewis & Bockius, CADA used by, 85
Morrison, Rees, 245
Morrison & Foerster, CADA used by, 85
Motherboard, 5
Motions
    automating standard, 97
    maintaining lists of, 20
Motorola Inc., CADA used by, 83
Mouse
    as input device, 229-30
Macintosh's use of, 220

recommended for using Windows, 30
Multitasking
defined, 8
LIX document transfer program and, 114
Macintosh for, 22
with OS/2, 8
with Windows, 29-30

Negotiation software, 45-46
Negotiator Pro, 45
NetModem, 221
NetWare Lite (Novell), 239
Network, 238-43
applications, 241-42
components, 238
installation tips, 242-43
Macintosh, 220-21
in office automation program, 109
operating systems for, 239
topology and cabling, 239-41
with Windows, 30
Network Scheduler program, 242
NeXT computer GUI, 10
Nierenberg, Gerard I., 44-45
Notebook computers
battery life of, 30
case management with, 55-60
criminal appeal team's use of, 117-20
locating cursor on LCD displays of, 30
Notepad options
in billing program, 150
in office automation program, 109, 112-13, 214
Notepad (Windows) text editor, 31
Novell NetWare, 239

Object Linking and Embedding (OLE), 29
Object Vision (Borland International), 14
Office automation
beginning, 207
with the Macintosh, 221-22
program to organize litigation practice, 109-16
Office Wiz office management program, 222
On Location text search and retrieval program, 226
On Target (Symantec Corp.), 44
One-Write-Plus accounting program, 214
Operating systems, 7-8
multiuser, 241
network, 238-39
Optical character reader, 230
Optical character recognition, 7, 226
Optix Document Image Management System, 226
Order of trial, outlining program to prepare, 38-39
OS/2 operating system
legal software for, 10
multitasking with, 8
Outlining program, xvii, 4, 33-64
applications that include, 43-44
assignment categories in, 55-57, 61-62, 64
examples of uses for, 40, 43

features desirable in, 40-41
headlines, 48-51, 55, 61
in litigation, 37-39, 42-46
Macintosh, 13, 18-19, 223
mental process of using, 35-37
to organize ideas, 35-41
printing with, 54
product comparisons for, 43-44
table of contents produced with, 50, 52
thinking with, 42-43
to-do lists created with, 55-56, 59, 61-63
word processing program versus, 42
Output devices, 230-33
OverDrive document assembly program, 77
Owl Software child-support and divorce inventory
program, 93

PageMaker (Aldus) desktop publishing program,
12, 208, 225
Paintbrush (Windows) drawing program, 28
Panorama database program, 20, 222-23
Paragraph numbering, automatic, 73
Partridge, Mark V. B., 55-64
Paul, Hastings, Janofsky & Walker, CADA used
by, 84
PC DOCS document management program, 241
PC-File+ and PC-File 6.5 database programs, 209
PC-Index, form file management with, 69
PC-Outline (Brown Bag Software, shareware), 38,
40-41
Peachtree accounting program, 214
Pear, Charles E., Jr., 74-75, 80-87, 96-106, 163, 188-
200
Pennington, Catherine, 121-24
Per%Sense, 135-44
PercentEdge (TIMESLIPS Corporation), 176
Peripherals, 229-37
connecting, 235-36
defined, 7
Persistent network connections, 30
Personal information manager (PIM) programs,
19-20, 43
Personal injury cases, evaluating, 176
PERT charts, 173
PI Economist (Advocate Software), 143
PINS database program, 209
Planning systems as expert systems, 190
Planning with outlining program, 39
PlanPerfect (WordPerfect Corp.), 127-28, 130
Pleadings
document assembly program to draft, 71-73, 92,
96-97
maintaining lists of, 20
outlining program to prepare, 37-39
in United Kingdom courts, 114
PLEAS database program, 209
Ports, computer, 235-36
Power Sale mortgage foreclosure system, 190
PowerLAN (Performance Technology), 239

Present value
    of annuity payments, 139-40
    of tangible losses, calculating, 135-37
Pretrial order, outlining program to prepare, 38
Print Manager (Windows), 29
Printer
    daisy wheel, 231
    dot-matrix, 231
    as hardware component, 7
    ink jet, 233
    laser, 231-33
Printing
    on the Macintosh, 225-26
    outlines, 54
Procedural guides as expert systems, 190
Prodigy on-line service, 226
Productivity tools for litigators, 107-62
Program. See Application program and Software
Program Director main menu program, 213
Project for Windows and OS/2 (Microsoft), 44
Project management software, 44, 46
    Macintosh, 222
    managing litigation with, 165-74
Property issues, software for, 94, 134
Public domain software, 8

Q&A database program, 222-23
QuarkXPress page layout program, 225
Quattro Pro database program, 213
Quicken accounting program, 214
QuickMail E-mail program, 221

Raker, Morris, 163, 175-83
Random access memory (RAM)
    defined, 5
    loading time and date and programs into, 8-9
Read-only memory (ROM) instructions, 8
Ready For Trial!, 22, 227
READY! (Symantec Corp.), 41, 43
Real evidence preserved by using soft copies, 161
Record defined, 72
Redlining program, 224
Research databases, family law, 94-95
Research files, outlining programs to manage, 61, 64
Resolve spreadsheet program, 224
Retrieval systems
    as expert systems, 190
    for the Macintosh, 226-27
Robert's Rules of Order, automating, 186-87
Rolodex
    Cardfile electronic, 31
    in office automation program, 109, 112
Romeu, Joost, 158-62
Rouse Company, The, CADA used by, 83

Sabre Menu menu system, 242
Samna IV document assembly IF statements, 77
Scanner, 7, 226, 230

Schechter, Roger, 1, 27-31
Schedule of trial preparation, 172-73
Scheduling feature
    of groups in Futurus Team software, 111
    for networks, 242
    in office automation program, 109
Schlein, Carol L., 145-51
Schlender, Greg H., 71-80
Schmulker & St. Clair, CADA used by, 84
Schuler, Dennis P., xi-xii, 67-70
Schultz, Kurt L., 152-57
Scrivener document assembly program, 77, 85
Sensitivity analysis, 182-83
Separation agreements, document assembly
    program to draft, 92, 97
Separation Agreements, The (Attorney's Computer
    Network, Inc.), 92
Sesti, Daniel E., 155-57
Settlement(s)
    offer, valuing, 138-40
    outlining program for negotiating, 38
    spreadsheet program for analysis of, 132-33
    structures, 135-44
Shapray, Howard, 17-26
Shareware, 8, 218
    database program, 213
    outlining program, 38
Shepard's Preview, 123
Shepardization analysis, automating, 120
Sherrets Smith & Gardner, CADA used by, 85
SideKick Plus TSR program, 214
Siemer, Deanne, xiii-xiv
Simlaw System, Ltd., Canadian pleadings and
    agreements, 93
Skadden, Arps, Slate, Meagher & Flom, 153-54
SmartForm Designer form program, 224
Smith, Cullen, 35-41
Smith, Moskatel, Schlender & Smith, 83
SoftSolution document management program, 241
Software
    application. See Application program
    defined, 4-5
    purpose of, 7
    system, 7-8
Sonar Professional, 16, 22, 226
Spell checking, 52, 54, 208
Spouse support
    calculation program, 93-94
    spreadsheet to compute, 134
Spreadsheet
    analyzing an opponent's, 131
    defined, 127
    formulas, validating, 129
    graphs, 131-32
    leading programs for, 213, 217
    in litigation, 127-34
    for the Macintosh, 224
    reusing, 130-31
    for routine calculations, 131

simple interest, 128-29
for "what-if" analysis, 129
STAIRS (IBM), 155
Standard & Poor database, 154
Standard documents, document assembly program to manage, 96-97
Static mats, 236
Statutes of limitations, tracking, 4
Stop-watch, electronic, 146
Storage devices, 234-35
StreamLine (TechnoLogics, Inc.) outlining program, 40
Structured Settlement Economist (Advocate Software), 143
Submissions, maintaining lists of, 20
SuperCite (SuperLex, Inc.) to Shepardize cases and statutes, 120
Support Arrearage Program (Howarth Ltd.), 94
Surge protectors, 236
Sutcliffe, J. Ronald, 184-87
Switcher, 18
System board, 5
System for Asbestos Litigation (SAL), 188, 193-95
System unit, 5

Table of authorities, automating creation of, 120, 122-23
Tables, graphics program to create, 24
Tape backups, 215, 234-35
TAXADVISOR planning system, 190
Taxes, software for, 94, 224
Taxrammer (Howarth Ltd.), 94
Terabyte defined, 7
Terminal (Windows) communications program, 28
Terminate and stay resident (TSR) programs
cite checking, 121
document assembly, 69
E-mail, 114, 116
leading, 213-14, 217
outlining, 38, 41
speech recognition program, 126
time recording program, 147
Testimony, summarizing, 48
Text retrieval
with Macintosh, 16, 21-23
software for shared files, 118-19
ThinkTank (Symantec) outlining program, 43
ThoughtPattern, 19-20
Time, computer software for tracking, 4, 145-51, 222
TimeLine (Symantec Corp.), 44, 172-74
TimeSlips billing program, 120, 145-51, 222
To-do lists
office automation program to create, 111
outlining program to create, 55-56, 59, 61-63
Token Ring networks, data transfer process of, 240-41
TouchBase contact database program, 221
Trackball as input device, 229-30

Tredennick, John C., Jr., xvii-xviii, 1, 33
Trial lawyers. See also Litigation practice brainstorming tools for, 42-46
Trial notebook, outlining program on Macintosh to build, 18-19
TrialMaker database and template, 20-21, 227
TrueType fonts, 29

Uninterruptible power supplies (UPSs), 236, 242-43
UNIX, weaknesses of, 8, 241
Up-to-Date calendar program, 222

Valuation of claims. See Claims valuation
Vendors, addresses and phone numbers of
accounting software, 217
calendar and diary software, 217
case management software, 90
database software, 216-17
desktop publishing software, 216
document assembly software, 88-90
financial management software, 143-44
form system software, 90-91
idea generator software, 46
Macintosh software, 24-25
main menu software, 217
negotiation software, 46
network, 243
outlining program, 45
project management software, 46
spreadsheet software, 217
TSR, 217
word processing merge/macro utilities software, 90
word processor software, 216
Ventura Publisher, 208
Vertical stands for CPUs, 236
Video adapters, 230-31
VINES (Banyon), 239
Vinson & Elkins, CADA used by, 84
Visual Basic for Windows (Microsoft), 14
Volkswriter Deluxe Plus, 208
VP-Expert (Paperback Software), 184-87

WESTCheck (West Publishing Company), 123-24
WESTLAW
checking cites with, 123
Macintosh access to, 226
Whiplash Expert System, 198
Williams, Robert G., 94
Windows 3.0 (Microsoft)
features of, 28-29
introduction in 1990 of, 27
speed of, 30
Windows 3.1 (Microsoft), 27-31
Advanced Power Management specification of, 30
advantages over DOS of, 27
desktop accessories of, 30-31

features new in, 30
GUI of, 1, 10, 29-30, 219
hardware and software requirements for, 30-31
interface, 28
Mouse Trails used with notebook computers for, 30
multitasking with, 29-30
popularity of, 10
standard and 386 enhanced modes of, 30
Windows NT, 8, 31
Winston & Strawn, 152-53, 156-57
Witness, outlining program to prepare direct or cross-examination for, 39
Word processing
document revisions using, 4
features, 208
leading programs for, 208, 216
with Macintosh, 12-13, 223-24
outline processing versus, 42
outlining features within, 43-44
selecting, 207
with Windows, 28-29
WordPerfect 5.1 (WordPerfect Corp.)
calculations performed with Table and Math

functions of, 131
lawyer's uses of, 42, 71-73
as leading word processor, 208
programming language of, 77
WordPerfect for Windows (WordPerfect Corp.), 28-29
WordPerfect Office (WordPerfect Corp.), 116, 213, 221-22
WordStar (WordStar) document assembly IF statements, 77
WorkForm document assembly program, 77, 84-87
Write once ready many (WORM) drives, 234
Write (Windows) word processor, 28
WriteNow word processor, 223
WYSIWYG capability
of Macintosh, 12
of Windows word processors, 28-29

Xenix, 8

Zimmerman, Gloria, 155-57
ZyIndex for Windows, 16, 52
ZyIndex, form file management with, 69

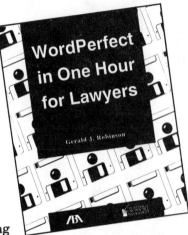

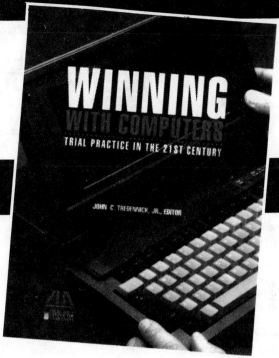

Selected Books from THE SECTION OF LAW PRACTICE MANAGEMENT

Access 1991-1992. Has been thorughly revised to reflect the many new changes in the legal automation world since the 1989-1990 edition. Many new publications, user groups, vendors, seminars and conferences are listed. All entries have been reviewed and—where necessary—updated.

Action Steps to Marketing Success. This book will show you how to turn your marketing ideas into action. You'll learn how to run an ongoing, coordinated, results-oriented marketing program. Numerous forms and sample letters included.

Basics for Buying Your Personal Computer. Will help you ask the right questions and evaluate the right issues. Facts and advice on components, servicing, networking, features to consider.

Basics for Writing Your Law Firm Brochure. Gives advice for planning and creating a brochure. Includes samples of brochures produced by other law firms.

Beyond the Billable Hour. A collection of articles on the subject of alternative billing methods, including value billing. Contributors include small, medium, and large firm practitioners, consultants, and general counsel.

Designing Your Law Office: A Guide to Law Office Layout and Design. Guides you through the entire process. You'll learn how to avoid needless disruption, chaos, and cost overruns. Includes checklists, timetables, diagrams, and drawings.

Fast Forms with Macros: Document Assembly with Word-Perfect 5.0/5.1 (and 4.2). This product, which includes a booklet and diskettes, gives step-by-step instructions that will help you develop your own customized, automated substantive systems — using WordPerfect 5.0 and macros as the basic building blocks.

Flying Solo. A collection of 48 articles discussing major aspects of starting, managing, and maintaining a successful solo practice.

From Yellow Pads to Computers. 35 chapters with real-life computer applications that focus on practical solutions. Especially for the attorney who's been too busy or afraid to use a computer.

How to Start and Build a Law Practice, 3rd Ed. Jay Foonberg's classic guide has been updated and expanded. Included are more than 10 new chapters on marketing, financing, automation, practicing from home, ethics and professional responsibility.

Identifying Profits (or Losses) in the Law Firm. The latest book in the Financial Management Monograph Series. Designed to help firms identify profits (or lack thereof) by their source.

Improving Accounts Receivable Collection: A Practical System. This book will give you the basics for developing an *easy-to-manage, formal* billing and collection system that can cut *months* off the collection process.

Keeping Happier Clients. This book is your guide to better client relations. It describes a whole approach to building strong relationships with clients. Includes questionnaires and tips for follow-up.

LOCATE. Includes listings of law office computer software vendors with indexes listing applications and package names.

Managing Partner 101: A Primer on Firm Leadership. Advice from the corner office that will help any new or aspiring manager. Described as an "indispensable, no-nonsense handbook."

Marketing Your Practice. A complete guide for planning, developing, and implementing a law firm marketing plan. Includes checklists, questionnaires, samples of brochures and newsletters, direct mail pieces.

Practical Systems: Tips for Organizing Your Law Office. It will help you get control of your in-box by outlining systems for managing daily work.

The Quality Pursuit: Assuring Standards in the Practice of Law. This multi-author work provides perspectives on a wide range of issues related to quality assurance and high performance standards, including dealing with the problem partner, partner peer review, training programs.

Winning with Computers. This book addresses virtually every aspect of the use of computers in litigation. You'll get an overview of products available and tips on how to put them to good use. For the beginning and advanced computer user.

Withdrawal, Retirement and Disputes: What You and Your Firm Need to Know. Suggests how you can deal with, or even avoid, the snafus that accompany partner departures. Also discusses how your firm can institutionalize fair and workable policies related to withdrawal, disability, and retirement.

Writing Your Law Firm Newsletter. Get rules and guidance for writing a newsletter, including tips on graphics, timetables, cost-benefit analysis. With sample newsletters created by other firms.

Your New Lawyer. A complete legal employer's guide to recruitment, development, and management of new lawyers.

Order Form

Quantity	Title	LPM Price	Regular Price	Total
_____	Access 1991–1992 (5110297)	$29.95	$34.95	_____
_____	Action Steps to Marketing Success (5110300)	29.95	34.95	_____
_____	Basics for Buying Your Personal Computer (511-0221)	14.95	24.95	_____
_____	Basics for Writing Your Law Firm Brochure (511-0223)	14.95	19.95	_____
_____	Beyond the Billable Hour (511-0260)	69.95	79.95	_____
_____	Designing Your Law Office (511-0263)	59.95	69.95	_____
_____	Fast Forms with Macros (511-0269)	99.00	109.00	_____
_____	Flying Solo (511-0084)...	39.93	44.95	_____
_____	From Yellow Pads to Computers, 2nd ed. (511-0289)...............	64.95	69.95	_____
_____	How to Start & Build a Law Practice, 3rd. ed. (5110293)	32.95	39.95	_____
_____	Identifying Profits (511-0259)...................................	14.95	19.95	_____
_____	Improving Accounts Receivable Collection (511-0273)...	39.95	49.95	_____
_____	Keeping Happier Clients (5110299)	19.95	29.95	_____
_____	LOCATE 1991–92 (5110295)	59.95	69.95	_____
_____	Managing Partner 101 (511-0272)	19.95	29.95	_____
_____	Marketing Your Practice (511-0215)	44.95	54.95	_____
_____	Practical Systems (5110296)	24.95	34.95	_____
_____	The Quality Pursuit (511-0268)	74.95	84.95	_____
_____	Winning with Computers (5110294)	89.95	99.95	_____
_____	Withdrawal, Retirement (511-0211)	29.95	39.95	_____
_____	Writing Your Law Firm Newsletter (511-0216)	14.95	19.95	_____
_____	Your New Lawyer (511-0075)	39.95	49.95	_____

Handling Charge $3.95

Total $ _____

☐ Check enclosed   ☐ Visa   ☐ Mastercard   ☐ Bill me

Account Number _____ Exp. Date _____

Signature _____

Name _____

Firm _____

Address _____

City _____ State _____ ZIP _____

IMPORTANT: A phone call will speed your order if we must contact you: (_____) _____

Return to: American Bar Association, Order Fulfillment 511, 750 N. Lake Shore Drive, Chicago, IL 60611

If you need overnight delivery, call 312/988-5555

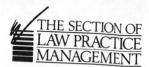
**THE SECTION OF
LAW PRACTICE
MANAGEMENT**

CUSTOMER COMMENT FORM

Title of Book:_____

We've tried to make this publication as useful, accurate, and readable as possible. Please take 5 minutes to tell us if we succeeded. Your comments and suggestions will help us improve our publications. Thank you!

1. How did you acquire this publication:

☐ by mail order   ☐ at a meeting/convention   ☐ as a gift

☐ by phone order   ☐ at a bookstore   ☐ don't know

☐ other: (describe) _____

_____

Please rate this publication as follows:

	Excellent	Good	Fair	Poor	Not Applicable
Readability: Was the book easy to read and understand?	☐	☐	☐	☐	☐
Examples/Cases: Were they helpful, practical? Were there enough?	☐	☐	☐	☐	☐
Content: Did the book meet your expectations? Did it cover the subject adequately?	☐	☐	☐	☐	☐
Organization and clarity: Was the sequence of text logical? Was it easy to find what you wanted to know?	☐	☐	☐	☐	☐
Illustrations/forms/checklists: Were they clear and useful? Were there enough?	☐	☐	☐	☐	☐
Physical attractiveness: What did you think of the appearance of the publication (typesetting, printing, etc.)?	☐	☐	☐	☐	☐

Would you recommend this book to another attorney/administrator? ☐ Yes ☐ No

How could this publication be improved? What else would you like to see in it?

_____

_____

_____

Do you have other comments or suggestions? _____

_____

_____

Name _____

/Company _____

ss _____

te/Zip _____

_____ Area of specialization: _____

We appreciate your time and help.

Fold

Fold

Firm
Addre
City/Sta
Phone
Firm Size: